RUMOR, REPRESSION, AND RACIAL POLITICS

SINCE 1970: HISTORIES OF CONTEMPORARY AMERICA

RUMOR, REPRESSION, AND RACIAL POLITICS

How the Harassment of Black Elected Officials
Shaped Post–Civil Rights America

GEORGE DEREK MUSGROVE

The University of Georgia Press
Athens & London

© 2012 by the University of Georgia Press
Athens, Georgia 30602
www.ugapress.org
All rights reserved
Designed by Walton Harris
Set in 10/13 Minion Pro

Printed digitally in the United States of America

Library of Congress Cataloging-in-Publication Data

Musgrove, George Derek, 1975–
Rumor, repression, and racial politics : how the
harassment of Black elected officials shaped post–civil
rights America / George Derek Musgrove.
    p.   cm. — (Since 1970 : histories of
contemporary America)
Includes bibliographical references and index.
ISBN-13: 978-0-8203-3459-2 (hardback)
ISBN-10: 0-8203-3459-6 (cloth)
ISBN-13: 978-0-8203-4121-7 (paperback)
1. African American politicians — History — 20th
century. 2. Harassment — Political aspects —
United States — History — 20th century. 3. Race —
Political aspects — United States — History — 20th
century. 4. Governmental investigations — United
States — History — 20th century. 5. Prosecution —
Political aspects — United States — History — 20th
century. I. Title.
E185.615.M84 2012
323.1196'073 — dc23   2011027437

British Library Cataloging-in-Publication Data available

To George Walker Musgrove

CONTENTS

ABBREVIATIONS

AALDF	African American Legal Defense Fund
ABEAO-LDF	Alabama Black Elected and Appointed Officials Legal Defense Fund
ABLC	Alabama Black Legislative Caucus
ACORN	Association of Community Organizations for Reform Now
ADC	Alabama Democratic Conference
AME	African Methodist Episcopal
ANSC	Alabama New South Coalition
ATF	Bureau of Alcohol, Tobacco, and Firearms
CBC	Congressional Black Caucus
CIA	Central Intelligence Agency
CME	Christian Methodist Episcopal
COAHR	Committee on Appeal for Human Rights
COINTELPRO	counterintelligence program
CORE	Congress of Racial Equality
COS	Conservative Opportunity Society
CPUSA	Communist Party of the United States
CRA	Civil Rights Act
CRP	Committee to Reelect the President
CSBL	Center for the Study of Black Leadership
CSHAA	Center for the Study of the Harassment of African Americans
CSMEO	Committee on the Status of Minority Elected Officials
CSU	Colorado State University
DIA	Defense Intelligence Agency

DOJ	Department of Justice
ECCO	East Central Committee for Opportunity
EEOC	Equal Employment Opportunity Commission
FBI	Federal Bureau of Investigation
FDIC	Federal Deposit Insurance Corporation
FEC	Federal Election Commission
FEPC	Fair Employment Practices Commission
GAO	General Accounting Office
IGRS	Intelligence Gathering Retrieval Service
IRS	Internal Revenue Service
ISD	Inspectional Services Division
MSC	Mississippi Sovereignty Commission
NAACP	National Association for the Advancement of Colored People
NAHRW	National Association of Human Rights Workers
NATO	North Atlantic Treaty Organization
NBC-LEO	National Black Caucus of Local Elected Officials
NBCSL	National Black Caucus of State Legislators
NBLR	National Black Leadership Roundtable
NCBM	National Conference of Black Mayors
NCC	National Council of Churches
NCLC	National Caucus of Labor Committees
NICCR	National Interreligious Commission on Civil Rights
NLPC	National Legal and Policy Center
NOI	Nation of Islam
NSA	National Security Agency
OCE	Office of Congressional Ethics
OPR	Office of Professional Responsibility
RICO	Racketeer Influenced and Corrupt Organizations Act
RNC	Republican National Committee
RNCC	Republican National Congressional Committee
SCLC	Southern Christian Leadership Conference
SNCC	Student Nonviolent Coordinating Committee
SSS	Special Services Staff
UAI	Urban Affairs Institute
VERA	Voter Education and Research Action Inc.
VRA	Voting Rights Act

ACKNOWLEDGMENTS

FOR ALL BUT THE MOST ORGANIZED, books are all-consuming affairs, and I am not particularly well organized. As such, my family, friends, and colleagues have lived with this project much as I have. For their support I owe a tremendous debt of gratitude. I hope the completion of this project, and my momentary return to normal, will serve as a down payment on that debt.

First and foremost I must thank my parents Margaret and George Gilbert Musgrove, who set the example by earning their doctorates and, through their work, contributing to the New Left insurgency of the 1960s and 1970s. My father's campus organizing earned him a brief period of FBI surveillance, a fact of which I am terribly proud. My mother has written two brilliant children's books, setting a standard of academic achievement for her youngest child. I must also thank a third parent of sorts, Freeman Hrabowski. From the time that I first began playing with his son Eric in 1980 to the time he offered me a scholarship to attend the University of Maryland, Baltimore County, on down to the present, "Doc" has worked both to convince me that I am capable of great things and to create the circumstances that would allow me to achieve the same. Without the examples, advice, and love of such family I would never have become an academic.

I could not have completed this book, indeed might never have tried to write it, without the support and inspiration of Clarence Mitchell III and Mary Sawyer. Mitchell first introduced me to the topic of harassment in 1988 when, at the age of thirteen, I watched my then-next-door neighbor leave his family for prison after his conviction in the *Wedtech* trial. In 1999 I sat down with him to discuss his family's role in the civil rights movement in Baltimore, and he insisted that I explore the topic of harassment instead. This book is the product of his advocacy. The first person that Mitchell suggested I speak with was Mary Sawyer. In 1977 and 1987 Sawyer wrote two of the major reports on harassment, and she has since kept the most detailed files on antiharassment activism. She graciously gave me those files, and they have served as the foundation of my research.

From my discussions with Mitchell and Sawyer, I compiled a list of black elected officials who had alleged that they were the targets of harassment or had engaged in antiharassment activism. They were kind enough to grant me interviews, share their files, and point me in the direction of other sources. The first group that I interviewed were the many activists and elected officials from Alabama who had made that state into ground zero for the antiharassment fight in the late 1980s. They are Mayor Richard Arrington of Birmingham, Council to the Mayor Donald Watkins, City Councilman Spiver Gordon (D-Eutaw), State Senator Hank Sanders (D-Selma), State Representative John Rogers (D-Birmingham), Representative E. B. McClain (D-Bessemer), State Representative John Hilliard (D-Birmingham), and *Greene County Democrat* editor John Zippert. On my trip to Alabama I was fed, housed, and carefully looked after by Allen, Gaye, and Tiffany Porter, and I am forever grateful for their hospitality.

In 2001–2, I secured a Congressional Black Caucus Foundation Congressional Fellowship in the office of Representative Alcee Hastings (D-Fla.). Representative Hastings was kind enough to sit for several interviews and to encourage his colleagues in the Congressional Black Caucus to support my research. Subsequently, I was able to interview representatives Sanford Bishop (D-Ga.), Corrine Brown (D-Fla.), William Lacy Clay Jr. (D-Mo.), Eva Clayton (D-N.C.), James Clyburn (D-S.C.), John Conyers (D-Mich.), Elijah Cummings (D-Md.), Earl Hilliard (D-Ala.), Carrie Meek (D-Fla.), Gregory Meeks (D-N.Y.), Donald Payne (D-N.J.), Bobby Rush (D-Ill.), Robert Scott (D-Va.), Bennie Thompson (D-Miss.), Edolphus Towns (D-N.Y.), Diane Watson (D-Calif.), and Albert Wynn (D-Md.); former representatives William L. Clay Sr. (D-Mo.), Mervyn Dymally (D-Calif.), and Walter Fauntroy (D-D.C.); former chief of staff to representative Walter Fauntroy, Johnny Barnes; and former chief of staff to representative Walter Tucker, Marcus Mason. I am grateful to all of these members and their staff for taking time out of their busy schedules to speak with me.

Adding context to many of these interviews were the recently deceased historian Manning Marable and the political scientist Ronald Walters. Both had written about harassment as early as the 1970s and were kind enough to share their work and recollections with me. They will be sorely missed as a new generation of historians and political scientists struggle to understand what Marable called the "new racial terrain" of the late twentieth and early twenty-first centuries. The Reverend Kenyon Burke, former Colorado lieutenant governor

George Brown (D), and former two-time Louisiana congressional candidate Faye Williams, all of whom played critical roles in antiharassment activism during the 1970s, 1980s, and 1990s, also provided crucial insights during extended interviews.

Throughout the research and writing process, a wonderful group of historians and friends helped me to refine my thoughts and provided much-needed encouragement. As a graduate student at New York University, I had the good fortune to work with Lisa Duggan, Adam Greene, Walter Johnson, Robin D. G. Kelley, and Jeffrey Sammons. They and Van Gosse of Franklin and Marshall University offered insightful comments on my work, saving it from untold theoretical and methodological mistakes. In 2003–4 Trinity College saved me from adjunct work and poverty by granting me the Anne E. Plato Fellowship. Once on campus, I found a dynamic and supportive community, foremost among them Jack Chatfield, Johanna Fernandez, Cheryl Greenberg, Susan Pennybacker, and Jerry Watts. At a crucial stage in the early drafting process, Tanarra Schneider offered invaluable organizational advice, turning a jumble of confused stories about state repression into a proper narrative. In 2007–8, the Center for Africanamerican Urban Studies and the Economy at Carnegie Mellon University provided critical support with a Postdoctoral Fellowship. It also gave me the opportunity to meet and learn from Lisa Hazirjian, Ben Houston, and Joe Trotter. As the manuscript took its final shape, I benefited from the company and brilliant insights of Chris Myers Asch, Prudence Cumberbatch, Peniel Joseph, Sandra Jowers-Barber, Natasha Lightfoot-Swain, Brian Purnell, and Rhonda Williams. My good friend Hasan Jeffries offered an endless stream of professional advice and critical insight. I expect our grandmothers, who were close friends, would be pleased. I must also thank Devin Fergus, a brilliant historian of the post–civil rights era United States, who was kind enough to forward my work to Derek Krissoff, senior acquisitions editor for University of Georgia Press. Derek and the Since 1970: Histories of Contemporary America series editors Renee Romano and Claire Potter were fabulously supportive, reading the manuscript multiple times, providing incisive comments, and answering my endless stream of questions.

Last but certainly not least, I want to thank my wife Michelle Walker Musgrove for her love, undying support, and willingness to listen to me prattle on about harassment for more than five years. With baby on her hip and car keys in her hand, she left the house every weekend for several months so that I had the time and space to finish the manuscript. I am blessed to have her in my life.

RUMOR, REPRESSION, AND RACIAL POLITICS

There is a sense of history, not hysteria. We remember what
happened in the last century.

— Jesse Jackson

When the contexts of the folk texts are juxtaposed to the historical
circumstances of the incidents in question, it becomes apparent that
only a narrow stream of information distinguishes the folk explanation
from the official one. The powers that be are not, after all, unblemished
innocents. . . . In seeking to fill the gaps between what is known about
these events and what remains a mystery, the folk will rely on their sense
of black history to construct motifs consistent with past experience but
applicable to the issues at hand.

— Patricia Turner, *I Heard It through the Grapevine:
Rumor in African American Culture*

INTRODUCTION

"A Sense of History, Not Hysteria"

ON JUNE 19, 1991, CNN aired a special report on the "harassment of black
elected officials." The segment, hosted by reporter Ken Bode, featured some
of the highest-ranking black elected officials and civil rights leaders in the nation. One after the other, they alleged, in the words of National Association
for the Advancement of Colored People (NAACP) executive director Benjamin
Hooks, that the Department of Justice (DOJ) under Presidents Ronald Reagan
and George H. W. Bush had engaged in "selective prosecution of black elected
officials and black leaders" and that some variant of this state "harassment"
stretched back to the late 1960s. They produced some remarkable information
to back up their allegations. Birmingham, Alabama, mayor Richard Arrington
(D) shared his five-hundred-plus-page Federal Bureau of Investigation (FBI)
dossier, which dated back to 1972 when he was first elected to the city council
and boasted a string of official corruption investigations, eleven since 1984, several of which had been leaked to the press, and all of which had been dropped
for lack of evidence. Representative Floyd Flake (D-Tenn.), who just months
before had seen seventeen counts of tax evasion, fraud, and conspiracy against
him and his wife dropped or dismissed for lack of evidence, noted that in the
previous five years, fully 50 percent of the sitting members of the Congressional

Black Caucus (CBC) had been investigated or indicted. Not one had been convicted. And former Maryland state senator Clarence Mitchell III (D-Baltimore), now chair of the Center for the Study of the Harassment of African Americans (CSHAA), added that he had spoken to scores of black elected officials at all levels of government who had shared similar stories of state and news media "harassment."

The several representatives of the DOJ who appeared on the show rejected these allegations and the evidence that underpinned them. Assistant Attorney General Robert Mueller provided the official response, stating, "Race plays no role whatsoever in any decision that we make either to investigate an individual or to prosecute." Frank Donaldson, U.S. attorney for the Northern District of Alabama, was less diplomatic, calling Mayor Arrington's allegations of selective prosecution "simply, outrageously, false." Representative Robert Barr (R-Ga.), former U.S. attorney for the Northern District of Georgia, went even further, arguing that black elected officials' claims were not only false but "the reddest of red herrings." The allegation, Barr continued, "forms a smoke screen around the true evidence of corruption on the part of many public officials . . . and diverts attention of the people from what is really going on, and that is that people are taking power and abusing power." When asked about a recent *Washington Post* study that concluded that black elected officials were five times more likely than their white counterparts to be investigated by the DOJ in the mid-1980s, Barr stuck to his position, dismissing the figure as "meaningless."[1]

The exchange ended in stalemate. At the end of the show, Bode summarized the unbridgeable gulf between his guests: "Neither side seems to have convinced the other. Black leaders say it's racial or political. The Justice Department says it's neither." Unable or unwilling to look behind the two sides' claims, Bode simply reported the allegations.

This 1991 CNN special was just one of many confrontations, stretched across the post–civil rights period, in which black elected officials alleged state and news media repression and government representatives dismissed their claims as conspiracy theory. *Rumor, Repression, and Racial Politics* explores these confrontations, the reasons behind black elected officials' claims, and the evidence that underpinned them. It argues that black elected officials' allegations of harassment reveal a significant pattern of state repression in the years between 1965 and 1974 and disproportionate investigation from 1974 to 1992 and that black elected officials' defense efforts had a pronounced impact on African Americans' understanding of their relationship to the news media and the state during the post–civil rights period.

Exchanges between black elected officials and government representatives like the one aired on CNN in June 1991 were the peculiar product of the post–civil rights era. The period's defining characteristic is the end of legalized segregation and the mass re-enfranchisement of African Americans. With passage of the Civil Rights Act (CRA) of 1964 and the Voting Rights Act (VRA) of 1965, the legal structure of white supremacy crumbled in the South. By the end of the decade, a majority of African Americans were registered to vote.[2] Shifting to accommodate the new political landscape, black activists focused their energies on securing political power, and they were stunningly successful. In the thirty-five years following passage of the VRA, the number of black elected officials increased eighteenfold, from 280 in 1965 to 9,040 at the turn of the century. Subsequently, in the years after 1965, the vanguard of black political leadership shifted from civil rights leaders and preachers to elected officials.[3]

These African Americans experienced stiff white resistance to their entry into electoral politics. For nearly a century, white Americans had denied African Americans access to the levers of political power or relegated them to junior positions within white-dominated political organizations. When, in the years after passage of the VRA, African Americans sought self-determination in those areas where they constituted a substantial minority or a majority of the population, they threatened to displace the white elected officials and political organizations that ruled over their communities. Some white power brokers acquiesced, incorporating or co-opting black elected officials. Others ignored them. Many, however, fought back, often using the state agencies at their disposal to prevent blacks from getting elected or assuming office once elected and to challenge their legitimacy once in office. This struggle was particularly intense in the late 1960s and early 1970s, and again in the mid-1980s, when significant black voter mobilizations accelerated the pace of racial transition.

These white power brokers and elected officials were often assisted by police and intelligence agencies that viewed independent black political activity as inherently subversive. During the second Red Scare of the immediate post–World War II period, municipal, state, and federal governments had created an immense surveillance and counterintelligence apparatus that, by the mid-1960s, they were using against the civil rights and Black Power movements (indeed, against the entire New Left). As part of the political leadership of this insurgent community, black elected officials were also targeted for federal surveillance and counterintelligence. Simultaneously, some white political organizations, both in big cities and in the rural South, used state and local law enforcement and tax-collecting agencies to attack black activists and institutions that threatened to undermine their power.

These intelligence, tax, and law enforcement operations were enabled, and often encouraged, by elected officials in both major political parties. On the state and local level, white Democrats were some of the prime movers. African Americans were most numerous in the Democratic South and Democratic big cities, and their quest for self-determination disproportionately threatened Democratic political machines. In 1968, however, with the election of Richard M. Nixon to the presidency, the Republican-controlled White House became the driving force behind state surveillance and counterintelligence of black elected officials. With his calls for "law and order" and an end to "forced busing," Nixon worked to generate a racial realignment of the American electorate, thereby drawing the criticism of the vast majority of black leadership. Simultaneously, he used the federal tax and intelligence apparatus to attack his political enemies. As a result, black elected officials became some of the primary targets of state surveillance, counterintelligence, and "dirty tricks."

The death of FBI director J. Edgar Hoover, the Watergate scandal, and the subsequent imposition of restrictions on domestic spying by Congress and the states between 1972 and the early 1980s served to reduce intelligence-community harassment of political dissidents — black elected officials among them. For many, the late 1970s provided a much-needed respite from the political battles of the civil rights–Black Power era. But for other black elected officials, the late 1970s were far from placid. Following Watergate, a newfound concern with ethics in government and a dramatic increase in investigative journalism led to increased public scrutiny of all elected officials. For African Americans, the new emphasis on ethics was particularly damaging. When African Americans took over cities, legislative districts, and other jurisdictions previously occupied by white political machines, their vanquished opposition and disgruntled white citizens fed allegations of mismanagement and corruption to the local press and law enforcement. The (almost uniformly white) press corps often printed these accusations, or their own, in the hopes of reproducing the scoops of *Washington Post* reporters Bob Woodward and Carl Bernstein. Few did. They did, however, succeed in instigating scores of government investigations of black elected officials. Though these investigations seldom ended in convictions, they disrupted careers, eroded public confidence in the targeted officials, and reinforced the racial distrust and animosity already existent in U.S. politics.

These investigations were by no means directed solely at black elected officials. White elected officials felt the sting of the new adversary journalism as well. But such nuance was lost on many of the black elected officials who found themselves struggling for political survival in the wake of these scandals. What they saw was a majority-white press seemingly working hand in hand with a majority-white ethics or law enforcement apparatus to investigate their offices. As with the previous wave of surveillance and counterintelligence, the impetus for these investigations of black elected officials was not limited to any one political party or ideological disposition. In 1981, however, this nonpartisan state and news media scrutiny of black elected officials was transformed into a decidedly partisan endeavor.

In the first sixty years of the twentieth century, one party or the other was able to dominate Congress and the White House with relative consistency, thereby establishing a governing consensus. In the years between the turn of the century and 1932, Republicans were ascendant. For the next three plus decades, the New Deal coalition fashioned by Franklin Delano Roosevelt dominated U.S. politics. No longer after 1968. With the advent of the two-party South and the rise of the New Left and the New Right in the Democratic and the Republican parties respectively, the New Deal coalition faltered and Republicans trumpeted their ascendance. Rather than establish a new governing consensus, however, the realignment of the mid-1960s generated a rough parity. Republicans dominated the executive branch, while Democrats held doggedly to the Congress. When Democrats finally did secure the White House (in a noncrisis election) in 1992, Republicans secured control of the House of Representatives (for the first time in forty years) in 1994. More than the House of Representatives and the White House, the Senate has felt the impact of the political stalemate. In the thirty years between 1980 and 2010, control of the chamber has changed hands five times.

The political stalemate of the post–civil rights period led to the rise of what political scientists Benjamin Ginsberg and Martin Shefter call "politics by other means." Amid deceasing voter turnout on both sides of the partisan divide, they write, "contending forces are increasingly relying on such institutional weapons of political struggle as legislative investigations, media revelations, and judicial proceedings to weaken their political rivals and gain power for themselves."[4] Although the authors do not discuss race as part of their analysis, race colored nearly every aspect of this new form of political contestation. By the 1980s, increased black voting and office-holding within the Democratic Party and massive white defections to the Republican Party had made race synonymous with party identification in certain parts of the country, and the most racially conservative elements of the U.S. electorate had gathered under the GOP banner. Subsequently, when Republicans in the Reagan and Bush administrations used the "institutional weapons of political warfare" against their Democratic opponents, the targets of those attacks were disproportionately African American. One of the manifestations of this shift was the racially disproportionate investigation of alleged "official corruption" by the DOJ under Reagan and Bush between 1981 and 1992. In these years, black elected officials were five times more likely than their white counterparts to be investigated by the DOJ. Only in 1993, when newly elected President Bill Clinton ordered his attorney general to replace all sitting U.S. attorneys named by his Republican predecessors, was this racial disparity in investigations all but eliminated.

Black elected officials did not suffer this disproportionate state scrutiny in the years between 1965 and 1992 silently; rather they complained loud and long about what they argued was racial repression. As early as 1967, legislator-elect Julian Bond (D-Atlanta) referred to efforts to deny him his duly elected seat in the Georgia House of Representatives as a second Redemption. Several months later, Representative Adam Clayton Powell Jr. (D-N.Y.) referred to a similar effort in the House of Representatives against him as the application of a "double standard" and a "national conspiracy."[5] Their allegations laid the groundwork for what I call "harassment ideology" — a body of beliefs that explained black elected officials' relationship to the white-dominated state and news media in the post–civil rights period as being primarily one of repression — and set the terms for discussions of state and news media disproportionate investigation of black elected officials through 1995.

In the mid-1970s, fast on the heels of congressional investigations that revealed massive targeting of the black freedom movement by nearly all facets of government, these individual allegations of repression morphed into a widely accepted ideology. In 1975, Colorado lieutenant governor George Brown (D) called for an investigation of what he believed was a pattern of "harassment" of black elected officials. Two years later, and with the help of much of the black political establishment, Mary Sawyer, a former Berkeley, California, civil servant, published a three-hundred-page study of black elected officials' allegations of repression. Hers was the first and only major study of such harassment ever published. Sawyer concluded that harassment was a "response to the new threat posed to the status quo by the real and potential acquisition of political power on the part of blacks." She called on black elected officials to create a legal defense and advocacy organization to combat harassment. Sawyer would reiterate these conclusions in a follow-up study ten years later.[6]

Responding to Sawyer's call, black elected officials produced reports documenting harassment; held press conferences and symposia to alert the public to their findings; and repeatedly attempted to conduct legislative investigations of the government agencies they accused of repression. For a brief period, these black elected officials' allegations captured the black popular imagination. In the late 1970s and again in the late 1980s and early 1990s, somewhere between one-third and one-half of African Americans believed that black leadership was being singled out for repression by government authorities.[7]

My purpose in telling this story is threefold. First, I seek to bring to light an issue that has often made its way into the literature on post-civil-rights-era U.S. politics but has not been examined in any detail. The House of Representatives' official history of African Americans in Congress, for instance, notes that black members of Congress "seemed disproportionately targeted" and that black elected officials "believed they were the targets" of state repression. Political scientists Tyson King-Meadows and Thomas F. Schaller reject such ambiguous language in their study of black state legislators, asserting instead that black elected officials were the targets of "a special initiative conducted by the U.S. Department of Justice and the FBI" designed to "discredit black leaders." Conservative intellectual Dinesh D'Souza, in his polemic *The End of Racism*, dismisses such claims as "racial paranoia" or "a reflexive tendency [on the part of African Americans] to blame racism for every failure, even those that are intensely personal." By reporting black elected officials' allegations of harassment without seeking to determine their veracity, adopting them uncritically, or dismissing them as conspiracy theory, these historians, political scientists, and pundits have transposed a contentious and inconclusive debate into the literature.[8] *Rumor, Repression, and Racial Politics* treats harassment ideology not as a conspiracy theory to be debunked or as an irrefutable truth, but as a flawed but nonetheless revealing attempt to make sense of what was happening to black elected officials in the post–civil rights period. Additionally, it places black elected officials' claims of harassment in the varied historical contexts in which they were made, allowing for a clearer understanding of why they were made in the first place and how closely they hewed to reality.

Second, I aim to illuminate the role of rumor or conspiracy theory—both the system of thought and the label—in the racial politics of the post–civil rights era. Conspiracy theory, in its classic formulation, is the belief that a small group of powerful actors ("they") are secretly plotting to shape events in a manner disadvantageous to the multitude ("us"). This definition was most famously associated with the thought of the anticommunist Right by Richard Hofstadter in his 1964 essay "The Paranoid Style in American Politics."[9] At the very moment Hofstadter was writing, however, a metamorphosis was taking place in American political thought that complicated this definition. Following the multiple assassinations, attempted assassinations, and political scandals of the 1960s and 1970s, a pervasive sense of paranoia became a common element of U.S. political thought. This new conspiracism was both far more indeterminate and far more widespread than that chronicled by Hofstadter. Rather than a fixation on a clearly identifiable minority pursuing specific plans, the new conspiracism was more a willingness to entertain conspiratorial explanations for political events coupled with a deep suspicion of government that made such explanations appear plausible. And the new conspiracism was no longer the property of an isolated minority but of the majority. Discussing this development in his study of conspiracy culture in the contemporary United States, Peter Knight states that during the post–civil rights period "a kind of world-weary paranoia has become the norm."[10]

The spread of the new conspiracism coincided with the end of legally sanctioned segregation and disfranchisement. As African Americans experienced resistance to desegregation and the persistence of inequality in an ostensibly postracist era, they developed ways of explaining their predicament that incorporated elements of the new conspiracism. For black elected officials the new conspiracism played an important role, "fill[ing] the gap between what is known" — that black elected officials are disproportionately targeted for surveillance, counterintelligence, and investigation by the authorities — and "what remains a mystery," exactly who or what is behind the disparity and why. To bridge this gap, Patricia Turner notes in her study of rumor in the African American community, African Americans relied on "their sense of black history to construct motifs consistent with past experience but applicable to the issues at hand."[11] The specific histories to which black elected officials turned were the violent overthrow of the Reconstruction governments in the post–Civil War South — before the 1960s, the only time that black elected officials had achieved anything more than token representation in U.S. politics — and the FBI's surveillance and counterintelligence campaigns against the civil rights and Black Power movements in the mid-twentieth century, which, in the mid-1970s, were being revealed to them by a series of government investigations. Both of these episodes taught African Americans that white elected officials and news agencies would resort to repression when blacks made a concerted bid for political power. Jesse Jackson put the matter best in a 1990 speech concerning disproportionate federal investigation of black members of Congress: African Americans' embrace of harassment ideology, Jackson stated, was rooted in "a sense of history, not hysteria."[12]

To say that harassment ideology is rooted in a sense of black history is not to suggest that it is necessarily a proper means of interpreting events. Conspiracism, to return to Knight, is "neither innately radical nor innately harmful." Harassment ideology was helpful to African Americans in the post–civil rights period in that it encouraged a critical perspective that viewed the intelligence and criminal justice systems as tools of racial oppression, which often they were. It also served as a powerful organizing tool for black elected officials seeking to defend themselves from government investigators. Casting themselves as the symbols of a black community under siege from government and news media antagonists, black elected officials were able to generate significant popular support for their defense efforts.[13] These positive developments were counterbalanced, however, by a host of negative factors. African Americans employ of harassment ideology allowed black elected officials and their supporters to avoid the hard questions about what was actually happening to black elected officials and who was at fault. Additionally, African Americans' embrace of harassment ideology allowed black elected officials to sidestep issues of ethical responsibility and in certain cases dodge prosecution for crimes that the evidence suggests some had, in fact, committed. And perhaps most importantly, black elected officials' employ of harassment ideology left them open to allegations that they were "conspiracy theorists."

At the same time that conspiracism became a popular mode of thought, the term "conspiracy theory" was entering into public discourse as a pejorative. To call something a conspiracy theory in the post–civil rights period was to dismiss the idea as paranoid or delusional and unworthy of further inquiry. The contradictory developments of a spreading conspiracism and the popular use of the term "conspiracy theory" to dismiss certain ideas as beyond the pale led to an interesting popular use of the term. Advocates of a certain idea that could be classed as conspiracism used the term figuratively, even self-effacingly ("It is only a conspiracy theory if it is not true"; "Just because I am paranoid does not mean there are not people out to get me"), while critics of those ideas used the term as a *label* that marked the idea as unworthy of serious consideration. For black elected officials who had assembled a significant amount of compelling information to make their case for a pattern of state and news media repression, this process took the form of dismissing their claims *and* the evidence underpinning them as "conspiracy theory" or "black paranoia." In the process the baby was thrown out with the proverbial bathwater, and authorities never had to answer for the disproportionately high number of investigations of black elected officials uncovered by this research. Indeed, criticisms of black elected officials' allegations often devolved into patronizing discussions of African Americans' peculiar susceptibility to conspiratorial thought.[14]

Last, this study contributes to existing debates on African Americans' relationship to the state in the post–civil rights period. In recent years, several scholars have proclaimed the achievement of a color-blind or postracial state in light of the civil rights reforms of the mid-1960s and generational change, proclamations that became louder and more insistent following the election of Barack Obama to the presidency in 2008.[15] I argue that those very reforms created the political context for the white backlash and the Republican ascendance, and once in power, Republicans disproportionately investigated black elected officials in their pursuit of a party realignment. As such, I discuss the post–civil rights period not as a time of steadily receding racial inequalities and animosities, but as a new racial terrain on which historical actors continue to employ repression and the politics of race in their struggles for power.

This study takes as its starting point black elected officials' allegations of harassment. As such, it draws from a series of reports and news releases created by antiharassment activists: the National Association of Human Rights Workers, Committee on the Status of Minority Elected Officials; the Alabama Black Elected and Appointed Officials Legal Defense Fund; the Black Belt Defense Committee; and the Center for the Study of the Harassment of African

Americans. It also explores the activities of the Lyndon LaRouche–affiliated Schiller Institute, which intermittently propagandized around the issue of harassment between 1995 and 2010. Additionally, it draws from over forty interviews with black elected officials and antiharassment activists. In an effort to ascertain the scope and form of this alleged repression, I conducted an in-depth case study focusing on the most geographically diverse group of black elected officials in the United States: black members of Congress. The case study explores the number of congressional ethics investigations; municipal, state, or federal criminal investigations, indictments, and convictions; Internal Revenue Service (IRS) audits; surveillance and counterintelligence; and ejection from office experienced by the African Americans to serve in Congress during the twentieth and twenty-first centuries. It is based on twenty-five interviews of sitting and former African American members of Congress, news reports of government investigators' allegations against the accused, trial transcripts, and news reports of black congresspeople's allegations of harassment.

Though *Rumor, Repression, and Racial Politics* revolves around instances in which the state or the news media allege wrongdoing by black elected officials, I do not go to pains to determine the guilt or innocence of the accused lawmakers. There are two reasons for this approach. First, there is no data set that measures the rates of corruption or investigation among different groups of elected officials with any degree of specificity. What existing data does measure is the rate of prosecution — a uniquely unhelpful measure since black elected officials' claim is that they were being *selected disproportionately* for investigation during the 1980s and early 1990s. Second, questions of guilt or innocence are, to a degree at least, beside the point. Black elected officials' claims of harassment focus on the behavior of government investigators. This behavior can be examined using existing data, namely, municipal, state, and congressional reports on government lawlessness, trial transcripts, FBI dossiers, and DOJ reports on official corruption prosecutions. Following Ginsberg and Shefter's lead, I view this data as "a *consequence* of investigators' efforts to uncover facts that will embarrass an [official] politically as much as . . . a *source* of that [officials]'s difficulties."[16] This approach may disappoint readers who seek to know whether a specific individual is guilty or innocent. For that I can only offer my apologies.

The news media are also a critical element of this study as they provide the forum in which many of the struggles discussed above take place. Both government investigators and black elected officials sought to harness the news media for their own purposes, the one leaking accusations of wrongdoing against black elected officials to friendly reporters and the other working to expose alleged government repression to the public. That said, the news media are by no means portrayed here as a neutral party that the two sides work to employ. Rather, they are understood as an institution that responds to and creates popular political currents, namely, the rise of adversary journalism in the mid-1970s and the rise of scandal journalism — the news media's devotion of significant resources and time to political scandals — in the late 1980s. As such, I draw heavily from newspaper — and, albeit less frequently, TV — coverage of government investigations of elected officials and related political scandals.

Rumor, Repression, and Racial Politics is divided into six chapters, arranged chronologically. The chapters alternate between discussions of harassment ideology and state repression or disproportionate investigation of black elected officials. Chapter 1 explores the refusal of the Georgia House of Representatives and the U.S. House of Representatives to seat duly elected black representatives Julian Bond (D-Atlanta) in 1966 and Adam Clayton Powell Jr. (D-N.Y.) in 1967, respectively. Bond's and Powell's characterization of their expulsions set the terms for discussions of disproportionate state scrutiny of black elected officials for the following thirty years. Chapter 2 focuses on the larger pattern of political repression of black elected officials in the decade following passage of the VRA. It explores why so many black elected officials were targeted for surveillance, counterintelligence, and dirty tricks between 1965 and 1975. Chapter 3 explores black elected officials' discovery of "harassment" in the wake of Watergate and the congressional investigations of the intelligence community. This section forms the heart of the book. Here, in the midst of the public revelations of government lawlessness and the dramatic increase in news media and government concern with ethics in government, black elected officials tried to figure out what was happening to their ranks and why. Through this process, they created harassment ideology, which would prove to have a significant impact on black political thought through the end of the century. Chapter 4 analyzes Republican efforts to use the federal law enforcement apparatus as a tool of "political warfare" between 1981 and 1992. Republican attacks on the Democratic Party had a disproportionate impact on black elected officials both because blacks emerged as the base constituency of the Democratic Party in the 1980s and because the "Reagan revolution" was rooted in constituencies and policy positions that were distinctly hostile to African Americans. Although the pattern of over-policing and disproportionate investigation discussed in chapter 4 was evident across the country, nowhere was it more blatant and systematic than in Alabama. Chapter 5 explores the pattern of disproportionate investigation of black elected officials in that state. Just as importantly, it explores Alabama black elected officials' remarkably successful efforts to protect their ranks and how those efforts played a critical role in the national struggle against disproportionate investigation. Focusing on the Center for the Study of the Harassment of African Americans, a national antiharassment organization created in 1990, chapter 6 charts the rise and fall of antiharassment organizing between 1987 and 1995. Antiharassment organizing peaked during this period in response to the DOJ's disproportionate investigation of black elected officials under the Reagan and Bush administrations. When this pattern of disproportionate federal investigation declined following the election of Democrat Bill Clinton in 1992, antiharassment activism declined in turn. By mid-decade, black elected officials had all but ceased antiharassment activism. The book's conclusion briefly explores the ways in which "politics by other means" and scandal journalism, which black elected officials identified as harassment in the 1980s and early 1990s, have become the norm in contemporary U.S. politics.

Black elected officials' allegations of harassment give us insight into the larger workings of rumor, repression, and racial politics in the United States in the post–civil rights era. To a significant degree, black elected officials act in this story as a metaphorical "miner's canary," a hypersensitive barometer of the toxicity of modern U.S. politics.[17] The repression and disproportionately high rates of government investigation experienced by black elected officials in the post–civil rights period alert us to the devastating consequences of the white backlash, the surveillance state, the rise of adversary journalism, the increasing use of "politics by other means," and scandal journalism on U.S. democracy. Just as important, black elected officials and their constituents' employ of conspiracism to describe the disproportionate scrutiny of black elected officials — and their detractors use of the label "conspiracy theory" to dismiss their concerns — illustrates the deep mistrust that continues to plague a society marred by pronounced racial inequality and distrust. As both major parties increased their use of political warfare in the 1990s and the early millennium, and partisans on both sides increased their use of conspiracism to define the motives of the opposition, black elected officials' experiences in the years between 1965 and 1995 appear, in hindsight, to be a frightening portent of our present political environment.

Beginning some sad time in 1966, the hope for racial harmony that had flickered in the aura of goodwill that produced the 1964 Civil Rights Act had begun to fade.

—Representative Andy Jacobs (D-Ind.), *The Powell Affair: Freedom minus One*

The inevitable counterrevolution that succeeds every period of progress is taking place.

—Martin Luther King Jr., *Where Do We Go from Here: Chaos or Community?*

CHAPTER ONE

The White Backlash and the Roots of Harassment Ideology, 1965–1968

IN 1967, MARTIN LUTHER KING JR. published his last book-length work, *Where Do We Go from Here: Chaos or Community?* In it, King surveyed the changing racial landscape and the nature of black-white relations at the dawn of the post–civil rights period. After a decade of near constant protest, the civil rights movement had secured federal legislation to end legal discrimination in employment, public accommodations, and voting. The changes were nothing short of revolutionary, and King had good reason to be elated at the progress the movement had made. Despite this progress, King felt a deep sense of foreboding. Fast on the heels of the great legislative triumphs of the mid-1960s came a white backlash that threatened to arrest the development of civil rights reform. A critical mass of whites had always opposed the movement. But in 1966–67, King noticed that even among supportive whites "widespread sympathy with the Negro revolution [was] abruptly submerged in indifference in some quarters or banished by outright hostility in others." King was alarmed not only by the growth of the backlash but also by its ability to alienate many in the black community from the ideas of nonviolence and integration at the very moment when desegregation was taking place. The growth of the backlash, in other words, saw a corresponding growth in the appeal of Black Power among African Americans.[1]

Focusing on two events with which King was intimately involved when he developed this analysis, this chapter explores the effects of the white backlash on U.S. electoral politics and African Americans' evolving understanding of their relationship to the news media and the state in the late 1960s.[2] The first occurred in King's home city of Atlanta, the capital of the New South and the epicenter of the southern civil rights movement. There, on January 10, 1966, the Georgia House of Representatives denied Representative-elect Julian Bond (D-Atlanta) his seat in the state legislature. Bond, who, prior to his election, served as communications director for the Student Nonviolent Coordinating Committee (SNCC), was refused entry to the Georgia legislature by a vote of his white, would-be colleagues under tremendous pressure from white voters and the local white press. His offense was endorsing a SNCC statement opposing the war in Vietnam. King, a resident of Bond's district, led a protest march to the state capitol building and joined a court challenge to the house's action. After a year of legal wrangling capped by a U.S. Supreme Court ruling declaring the Georgia house's action unconstitutional, Bond was seated on January 10, 1967, in a victory for the residents of his district, the civil rights movement, and black America. Yet the young legislator-elect's victory proved bittersweet.

Only hours after Bond was seated, the U.S. House of Representatives denied Adam Clayton Powell Jr. (D-N.Y.), arguably the most powerful black elected official in the nation and an early advocate of Black Power, his seat in Congress. Like Bond, Powell was denied his seat by a vote of his white would-be colleagues under tremendous pressure from white voters and the white press. His offense was openly engaging in the graft that a significant number of his colleagues accepted as a congressional prerogative. King worked behind the scenes to head off the vote, writing House Speaker John McCormack (D-Mass.) that African Americans would "interpret it as an attempt to take reprisals against a Negro who [had] risen to a position of political power." When Congress excluded Powell anyway, King joined other black leaders in condemning the House's action. Powell's case, too, ended up before the Supreme Court. He would not be seated until January 10, 1969.[3]

The Bond and Powell exclusions were both symbol and product of two critical developments in late-1960s U.S. racial politics, developments that would come both to precipitate state repression of black elected officials and to influence discussions of "harassment" throughout the post–civil rights period. First, they demonstrated the increased incorporation of blacks into U.S. electoral politics, a process facilitated by black protest and liberal reform. Between the time that Powell entered Congress in January 1945 and the time that Bond entered the Georgia legislature in January 1967, the number of black elected officials increased more than tenfold from fewer than sixty to well over six hundred. And by the late 1960s, a select few, like Powell, who held the gavel to the House Committee on Education and Labor, were rising to positions of prominence undreamed of just a few years before.[4] Second, they demonstrated the power and transformative effects of the white backlash on U.S. electoral politics. Many liberal and moderate white elected officials were forced to support the exclusion votes in response to white popular anger at the civil rights and Black Power movements. Others opportunistically mobilized that anger through controversies like the Bond and Powell exclusions to generate a racial realignment within the two-party system. By 1968, these elected officials and party operatives had succeeded in drawing a majority of white Americans out of the Democratic Party and creating a white majority coalition that would eventually find a home in the GOP.

Whites and blacks viewed the exclusions in uniquely different ways. Most whites saw the exclusions as just punishment for Bond's and Powell's alleged misdeeds and ignored or denied the role of race in the controversies. Blacks, on the other hand, "saw white legislators as practicing a double standard of justice and acting unnecessarily harshly."[5] These conflicting views would come to shape debates over harassment for the remainder of the post–civil rights period.

Black Protest, Liberal Reform, and the Rise of Black Elected Officials

In the mid-1960s, civil rights activists and liberal reformers achieved a series of legislative and judicial victories securing the basic rights of citizenship and suffrage for African Americans. In July 1964, Congress passed the CRA, effectively outlawing Jim Crow segregation in American public life. The elaborate legal system of separate and unequal that had defined southern life for half a century subsequently began to collapse. That same year, the Supreme Court extended the maxim of "one voter, one vote" to all congressional districts in *Westberry v. Sanders* and to all state legislative districts in *Reynolds v. Sims*. Mass reapportionment of state and federal legislative districts ensued.[6] Although reapportionment is given relatively short shrift in explorations of the black freedom movement, it was arguably one of the more important reforms of the era. African Americans' access to elected office increased markedly as a result of reapportionment. An excellent example of the impact of *Westberry v. Sanders* and *Reynolds v. Sims* on black communities can be seen in Julian Bond and Martin Luther King Jr.'s home state of Georgia.

To look at a Georgia legislative and congressional district map in 1960, one would have to assume that the vast majority of the population resided in the rural counties. Rural counties boasted the same number of legislators as did urban, and the Peach State's only metropolis could scarcely be discerned from a small village in the state house or in Congress. For instance, the Fifth Congressional District, which contained the city of Atlanta, had a population of 823,680 according to the 1960 census. By comparison, the Ninth Congressional District, a rural area northeast of Atlanta, contained only 272,154 residents. Both had roughly the same representation in the Georgia legislature, the U.S. Congress, and, due to the existence of a "county units" system — a county-based state electoral system similar to the Electoral College — a proximate role in determining statewide offices.[7] Though seldom as extreme as in Georgia, this state of affairs reigned across the country. In 1960, every single state in the Union had at least a 2 to 1, rural to urban disparity between the population and the way votes were counted in state and federal legislative districts. Because those African Americans who had access to the franchise were concentrated in cities during the post–World War II period, this disparity had a disproportionately negative effect on blacks' access to political power.[8]

On June 19, 1964, four days after the Supreme Court ruled on *Reynolds*, a three-judge federal panel ordered the Georgia General Assembly to reapportion the state's legislative districts and hold special elections to fill the newly created seats. Reapportionment dramatically altered the composition of the general assembly. Rural areas experienced a net loss of seats, while most urban areas doubled and tripled their representation. In the most remarkable instance, Fulton County, home to Atlanta, gained twenty-one new house seats, bringing its total to twenty-four.[9] Although state legislators did their best to gerrymander the black population, the sheer size of the city's African American community made such impossible. One-quarter of the newly created state house districts in Fulton County contained black majorities. In the special election to fill the newly drawn seats, Atlanta blacks elevated seven of their number — Julian Bond among them — to the Georgia House of Representatives and two to the state senate. Additionally, the increasing strength of local black voters convinced the majority-white Muskogee County Democratic organization to run an African American for the seat for the 110th House District. The eight blacks elected to the house would become the first African Americans to enter the chamber in nearly a century. Similar transformations occurred across the country. In 1964 alone, court actions mandating reapportionment were handed down in thirty-nine states.[10]

At the same time that reapportionment made elected office more accessible to urban blacks, the VRA gave many southern blacks (and many of these, rural) access to the franchise for the first time since Reconstruction. Unlike in the rim-South and some southern cities, where black voter registration had been growing at a steady clip since World War II, in the Deep South and many rural counties black registration rates remained abysmally low. But with passage of the VRA and the subsequent dispatch of federal registrars to the covered jurisdictions, southern black voter registration increased dramatically. In the two years following passage of the VRA, black registration in Georgia jumped from 27.4 to 52.6 percent of the voting-age population. In other Lower South states, the change was even more dramatic. In Mississippi, where only 6.7 percent of eligible blacks were on the rolls in 1964, 59.8 percent were registered by 1967. In Alabama, the numbers jumped from 19.3 to 51.6 percent. The number of African Americans on the rolls in Louisiana doubled during the same period, moving from 31.6 to 58.9 percent. The percentage of new registrants was more modest in the Upper South, where large numbers of African Americans were already on the roles. Nevertheless, by 1967, fully one-half of southern African Americans were registered to vote.[11]

African Americans used new legislative districts and their newly secured franchise to score a dizzying number of electoral breakthroughs in 1966–67. In the first state elections following redistricting, African Americans integrated the all-white California Senate, Georgia House of Representatives, Kentucky Senate, Louisiana House of Representatives, Mississippi House of Representatives, Nevada Assembly, Texas Senate, and the Virginia House of Delegates. In 1967, the "Year of the Black Mayor," African Americans entered the mayor's race in six major cities. Two of them, Carl Stokes and Richard Hatcher, won the races in Cleveland, Ohio, and Gary, Indiana, respectively. Adding to the tally, President Lyndon Johnson appointed Walter Washington mayor-commissioner of the nation's capital. Chuck Stone, in his study *Black Political Power in America*, noted that African Americans were also active on the local level, running for and winning "offices as disparate as . . . the Seattle city council, a Waterloo, Iowa, court judgeship, and a school commission in Pittsfield, Massachusetts."[12] In short, in the two years following passage of the VRA, black voters were on the march, using their newly won franchise, newly created legislative districts, and the racial unity stimulated by the civil rights and Black Power movements to create black political power.

The White Backlash

The accelerated pace of reform generated by the black freedom movement provoked fear, insecurity, and countermobilizations by white Americans, North and South. Seeking to capitalize on whites' increased anxieties, segregationists, reactionaries, and opportunists positioned themselves in opposition to the civil rights movement and the liberal state that had aided in its successes.

In 1964, Alabama governor George Wallace (D), an up-and-coming leader of the segregationist South, entered the Democratic presidential primary in Wisconsin, Indiana, and Maryland. Running on a platform of opposition to liberal social reform, embodied most immediately in the CRA then before Congress, he received a third of the vote in Wisconsin and Indiana and nearly won the primary in Maryland. Wallace's success demonstrated the resonance of his anti–civil rights, anti–liberal reform message among working-class white ethnics and the white, suburban middle class of the Northeast and the Midwest.[13]

Senator Barry Goldwater (R-Ariz.) echoed much of Wallace's rhetoric in the Republican primary. Following Vice President Richard Nixon's loss to Senator John F. Kennedy (D-Mass.) in the 1960 presidential election, Goldwater had become convinced that the Republican Party "was not going to get the Negro vote." The GOP's only alternative, he reasoned, was to "go hunting where the ducks are" — meaning among whites opposed to civil rights reform. In order to do so, he believed, the Republican Party must side with the white South, and increasingly with white suburbanites and urban white ethnics, in the battle over desegregation. Taking his own advice to heart, Goldwater, who had supported the civil rights acts of 1957 and 1960, opposed the Civil Rights Act of 1964. He justified this about-face on the grounds that the CRA would create a "federal police force of mammoth proportions" and an "informer psychology" that would rend the fabric of American democracy. Goldwater's "modern racial conservatism" — the rejection of federal efforts to address racial inequality on the grounds that such activities were beyond the proper purview of federal power — would come to form the basis of Republican racial politics for the next four decades.[14]

Goldwater's opposition to the CRA drew legions of segregationists into the GOP. On the eve of the Republican National Convention, white southerners purged Negro "Black and Tan" stalwarts from the state delegations, effectively creating a home for segregationists in the party of Lincoln. Of the 375 southern delegates to the Republican convention, all were white and 366 were for Goldwater.[15] In the general election, Goldwater campaigned heavily in the South, often using the noted segregationist Senator Strom Thurmond (D-S.C.) as a stump speaker. As a result, he won Alabama, Georgia, Louisiana, Mississippi, and South Carolina — the first Republican victories in the Deep South since Reconstruction. Additionally, the Republican Party picked up eight congressional seats in the South — again, the first since Reconstruction. Goldwater's appeal, however, did not extend beyond the region. The senator's reputation as an extremist and warmonger moved many white Americans to remain with the Democratic Party. As a result, Johnson won every state outside the Deep South except Goldwater's home state of Arizona and crushed his GOP challenger by nearly 16 million votes. The Democratic Party as a whole benefited from Johnson's landslide, racking up staggering majorities in the House (295–140) and the Senate (68–32).[16] Americans, it appeared, stood firmly behind Johnson's liberal reform agenda, including civil rights reform.

But appearances were deceiving. Just two years later, GOP and Democratic conservatives, buoyed by the white backlash, staged striking comebacks. In the 1966 midterm election, the Republican Party picked up forty-seven seats in the House and three in the Senate, almost all at the expense of liberal Democrats. Notably, congressional Democrats experienced the fewest losses in the South, where most ran against the president and his reform agenda.[17] Republican gains allowed the old conservative coalition of southern Democrats and conservative Republicans to reassert itself in Congress, thereby grinding civil rights reform to a halt. Many state races brought similar results. Across the country, opponents of civil rights won or narrowly missed election to high government office. In Arkansas, Jim Johnson, founder of the state Citizens' Council, won the Democratic gubernatorial nomination by defeating five racial moderates. In Maryland, George P. Mahoney's opposition to open-housing legislation earned him the Democratic gubernatorial nomination. In a move that would become painfully ironic two years later, Baltimore's black population threw their weight behind his Republican challenger, sending Spiro Agnew to the governor's mansion. In Illinois, three-term incumbent Senator Paul Douglass's support of open-housing legislation led to his defeat by Republican Charles Percy. White antagonism toward open-housing legislation was so strong that even the legendary machine boss Richard Daley had trouble turning out votes for Douglass in Chicago. In Alabama, George Wallace, who was barred from running for governor by term limits, ran his wife, Lurleen, as a stand-in candidate. Mrs. Wallace defeated nine challengers with more-moderate racial platforms in the primary and went on to defeat the segregationist Goldwater Republican, Representative James Martin (R-Ala.), in November. And in perhaps the most significant contest of the year, Ronald Reagan, a Goldwater supporter who had opposed the CRA and the VRA and backed an effort to repeal California's open-housing legislation, was elected governor of the Golden State. Measuring the political winds following the election, the arch-segregationist Senator James Eastland (D-Miss.) declared, "The sentiment of the entire country now stands with the southern people." While Eastland overstated his case, one could certainly argue, as has historian Harvard Sitkoff, that a "voting majority pledged to preserve social order had superceded the coalition to promote social change."[18] It is in this atmosphere of black political insurgency and white backlash that Julian Bond and Adam Clayton Powell Jr. were denied seats in their respective legislatures.

Harnessing the Backlash in the South: Julian Bond

Perhaps no case more clearly reveals how state repression of a black elected official both reflected and accelerated the backlash than that of Julian Bond. Bond came to political maturity and public prominence as the spokesman for the Atlanta Committee on Appeal for Human Rights (COAHR), which coordinated the Atlanta sit-in protests and voter registration campaigns of 1960. Slight of stature, soft-spoken, a lover of tweed jackets and the life of the mind, Bond had entered college with the intention of becoming a poet. But before he could graduate, he was swept up in the ferment of the civil rights movement. In April 1960, he led the COAHR contingent of student protesters to Shaw University, where he became a founding member of SNCC. In 1961, SNCC executive secretary James Foreman tapped him to become the communications director for the fledgling civil rights organization. Over the course of the next five years, Bond distinguished himself as an eloquent voice for nonviolence and racial justice.[19]

In 1965, SNCC capitalized on the court-ordered reapportionment of the Georgia legislature by running Bond for the seat from the newly drawn 136th House District, a 95 percent black enclave abutting the Atlanta University Center. The district, which came within blocks of SNCC's Auburn Avenue headquarters, provided the young civil rights activists with the perfect opportunity to apply the lessons of Black Power organizing learned in Mississippi and Alabama (with the Mississippi Freedom Democratic Party in 1964 and the Lowndes County Freedom Organization in 1965–66) to an urban context. With high name recognition and nearly a decade of constant residence in the district, Bond was the obvious choice to run for the new seat. SNCC veteran Ivanhoe Donaldson urged his initially reluctant colleague to enter the race. When Bond relented, the SNCC Executive Committee loaned him the money to pay his filing fees and open a campaign headquarters. SNCC veteran Charles Cobb served as Bond's campaign manager, and a small army of SNCC volunteers registered voters, hung signs, knocked on doors, and ferried residents to the polls.[20] In short, the Bond campaign was a civil rights campaign.

The campaign was fabulously successful. Bond beat his primary election opponent by a margin of 2 to 1, and his general election opponent by a margin of 4 to 1. Perhaps most importantly for Bond and his colleagues in SNCC, who believed strongly in participatory democracy, turnout in the general election was the highest of any legislative district in the state: 82 percent. For many Atlanta blacks, indeed for many young movement activists across the country, Bond's election fulfilled the promise of the VRA and reapportionment and signaled the tremendous progress of the southern civil rights movement.

Despite many SNCC activists' participation in the Bond campaign, Bond's involvement with SNCC waned during his run for office. By the time of the November election, he had not done any work for SNCC in months. Nonetheless, Bond had not resigned his post as communications director. It was not surprising, then, that reporters contacted him for a comment when SNCC released a January 6, 1966, statement on the war in Vietnam.

For several months, SNCC activists had been debating whether to issue a statement on the war in Vietnam. They knew that blacks were disproportionately represented among draftees and that the war was draining money from domestic reform efforts, and they suspected that southern draft boards were being used to neutralize activists by sending them overseas. They had not spoken out previously because some members feared losing funding from anticommunist northern liberals and political support from the Johnson administration. Incidentally, they would be correct on both counts. Despite the political risks, they drew up a statement that SNCC chairman John Lewis read at a January 6 press conference.[21] Drawing a direct link between the suppression of the Vietcong in Southeast Asia and the federal government's refusal to protect civil rights workers from racial terrorists in the American South, Lewis stated: "We believe the United States government has been deceptive in its claims of concern for the freedom of the Viet Namese people, just as the government has been deceptive in claiming concern for the freedom of colored people in the United States." And in light of this deception, Lewis expressed "sympathy with, and support" for "the men in this country who [were] unwilling to respond to the military draft which would compel them to contribute their lives to United States aggression in Viet Nam in the name of the 'freedom' [they found] so false in this country."[22]

Ed Spiva of radio station WGST was the first reporter to reach Bond for comment on the evening of January 6. Spiva questioned Bond vigorously about his support for the SNCC statement and his personal feelings about the war. "Do you endorse the release made by the SNCC group today?" Spiva queried. Bond did. Asked to elaborate on his reasons for doing so, Bond stated: "I agree with this statement for the reasons set forth in it — because I think it is sorta [sic] hypocritical for us to maintain that we are fighting for liberty in other places and we are not guaranteeing liberty to citizens inside the continental United States." To Spiva, like many white Georgians — indeed like many white Americans — the SNCC statement smacked of treason. In 1966, public discussion of American foreign policy was circumscribed by the cold war logic of unquestioning patriotism versus treason. With this in mind, Spiva questioned Bond about his fitness for office, particularly his ability to take the oath of office with a "clear conscience." Perhaps unaware of the impact of his words, Bond shrugged off Spiva's queries: "What does the oath require? That you uphold the Constitution of Georgia and the Constitution of the United States of America, right? . . . I don't see anything in this statement that conflicts with that."[23] Many white Georgians, however, did.

The Atlanta press reacted to the SNCC statement and Bond's endorsement by publishing wave after wave of what Bond would later call "vicious, rabid, scare headlines." On January 7, the *Atlanta Journal* printed two front-page articles on the subject with the headlines "Rights Leader Charges 'Murder' in Viet Nam" and "Loyalty of Bond Faces Challenge." Bond would remain on the cover of the *Journal* through January 18. The January 7 issue of the *Atlanta Constitution*, on the other hand, focused on SNCC with the front-page article "Defy Draft Call, SNCC Chief Urges." The headline of the jump article on page 12 referred to Bond: "SNCC Leader and Legislator Back Draft Card Burnings." Although relegated to the twelfth page that morning, Bond and his endorsement of the SNCC statement would dominate the front page of the *Constitution* for the following seven days. In nearly all this coverage, the careful nuance of the SNCC statement and Bond's endorsement was stripped away. Sympathy with those who "seek alternatives to the draft" became a call to "defy" the draft and "burn draft cards."

The local radio station WGST also inflamed white public anger. Spiva repeatedly aired his exclusive interview, and talk radio discussed the SNCC statement and Bond's endorsement ad nauseam. Most guests agreed that Bond should not be allowed to assume his duly elected seat in the legislature. Bond recalls that "the local radio station, which ran a short talk program, propagandized all that weekend saying 'People have a right to say what they want to, but in this particular case this young man should not be in the legislature.'"[24]

Seeking to capitalize on the controversy and goaded by the media, local white politicians rushed to denounce SNCC and Bond. Upon hearing a Friday-morning newscast describing the SNCC statement and Bond's endorsement, Representative Jones Lane (D-Statesboro), a leader of the chamber's segregationist bloc, began organizing his colleagues to oppose Bond's being seated. Independent of Lane, Representative James "Sloppy" Floyd (D-Rome), the powerful chairman of the Georgia House Appropriations Committee and a leader of the rural block that had opposed reapportionment, began to organize his house colleagues as well. Though segregationists like Lane and Floyd would emerge as the driving force behind the effort to exclude Bond, they were not alone in expressing their outrage over Bond's endorsement of the SNCC statement. On January 7, the racial moderate state senator James Westberry (D-Atlanta), who had filed the suit that led to *Westberry v. Sanders* and, subsequently, to the reapportionment of the Georgia House, stated to reporters that it was the "duty" of the house to exclude Bond. And these state elected officials were joined by Atlanta representatives of the federal government. Over the weekend, the Atlanta office of the FBI announced that it was sending a copy of the SNCC statement to the DOJ for "further study" — a clear signal that local agents believed the statement to be subversive.[25]

On Monday, January 10, Bond arrived at the Georgia House amid a storm of controversy. The public commentary surrounding his endorsement of the SNCC statement had so saturated political discussion over the weekend that one commentator described it as "one of the most explosive issues ever to hit an opening session of the Georgia legislature."[26] As early as Saturday it had become clear that Lane and Floyd would attempt to exclude Bond from the house. They did not disappoint, gathering over seventy-five signatures on a petition demanding that Bond not be seated. At ten o'clock the house came to order. Following the certification of elected members' victories, the clerk stated: "I will ask representative-elect Bond to stand aside. There have been several petitions filed to this office challenging his right to a seat."[27] The other members of the house stood and took the oath of office as Bond remained seated at his desk. The question of Bond's fitness for office would be placed before the House Rules Committee later that afternoon.

Although petition organizers like Lane repeatedly stated that they sought Bond's ouster "not because of his race," but "because of [his] un-American attitude," their choice of a lawyer for the Rules Committee debate revealed that their outrage over the SNCC statement was a proxy for racial backlash. The petitioners chose former legislator Denmark Groover to present their case.[28] Groover had a long and distinguished record of hostility to black citizenship. As Democratic floor leader in the mid-1950s, he ushered bills through the Georgia House replacing the red and white stripes of the Georgia flag with the stars and bars of the Confederacy; requiring the closing of public schools if federal courts ordered desegregation; allowing for the privatization of public property like schools, parks, and swimming pools threatened with integration; and a host of other legislation geared toward the maintenance of segregation. Newly empowered by post–World War II voter registration drives, the black voters of Macon had forced Groover into early retirement in 1956 and, following a 1962 political comeback, again in 1964.[29] Like Lane, Groover was careful to present the case against Bond in the color-blind language of loyalty to country. In his presentation to the House Rules Committee, Groover argued that Bond's endorsement of the SNCC statement gave "aid and comfort to the enemies of the United States" — the legal definition of treason — and as such, he could not take the oath of office, which required that he swear allegiance to the Constitution in good faith. Bond's lawyer, Howard Moore, defended his client using the first amendment: "Mr. Bond has a right to speak and that is purely and simply all that this case is about." Groover's argument carried the day. The overwhelmingly white Rules Committee voted 23 to 3 to recommend that Bond not be seated. Only the two newly added black legislators and Fulton County delegation chairman Jack Ethridge favored seating.[30]

Though Lane and Groover were able to veil their racial motives, most petition signers were not. In the debate before the full house on the Rules Committee report, Representative George Bagby (D-Dallas) blamed the entire affair on SNCC. SNCC, he claimed, had staged the controversy in order to buoy its flagging fund-raising efforts and reclaim its national profile. No matter, he defiantly declared. Although he knew that the legislature was "being used," he was voting for expulsion. Though absurd, Bagby's allegations were widely held by many white Georgians. The following day, *Atlanta Constitution* editorialist Eugene Patterson devoted his entire column to expounding on the Dallas representative's theory. Indeed, for years segregationists across the region had been arguing that civil rights activists planned instances of white repression, from fistfights, to bombings, to murder, for the purpose of gaining publicity and raising money. Representative Bobby Pafford, a veteran of the house and a leader of the "rural bloc," followed Bagby to the well. His statement revealed a hostility to reapportionment and the civil rights movement that exceeded his rejection of Bond's criticism of American foreign policy. In a veiled reference to integration, Pafford lamented, "Not only our state, our counties, but the Legislature itself has been invaded by one whose 'Snicking' pursues not freedom for us but victory for our enemies." Bond's presence was all the more galling, Pafford continued, because "his [Bond's] chair was emptied by a court edict which threaten[ed] to tear at the very heart of this nation as founded by [the] forefathers, for many great and noble Georgians . . . [were] gone." There were even those who believed the SNCC statement to be immaterial. Civil rights activists themselves were the problem. Justifying his vote for exclusion to a reporter, Representative Arthur J. Funk (D-Savannah) stated, "I don't care if he's innocent of making those remarks. All those people tend to think that way, and every day he's on this floor is a disgrace."[31]

The Bond controversy all but eliminated the already narrow space available to white racial moderates. Several legislators, particularly those from the Atlanta metropolitan area, had hoped to seat Bond and then censure the young legislator elect. "There was a lot of sentiment for seating him and censuring him," Representative Robert Farrar (D-Atlanta) told reporters, "but the way it was handled we had no opportunity to vote on that." For most legislators, however, the option of censure would not have mattered. Representative Richard Starnes (D-Rome) noted that he had received more mail and phone calls from his (white) constituents regarding Bond in the previous four days than he had on all issues before the legislature in the past six months. The communications were "unanimous," Starnes confided, "'If he stays in, don't you bother coming home.'" That afternoon, Starnes joined the 183 other white legislators who voted to deny Bond his seat. Only 12 legislators, 5 of them black and all of them from the Atlanta metropolitan area, voted against the exclusion.[32]

Just as many Georgia whites understood that race was a critical element of the move to deny Bond his seat, so too did the state's blacks. On January 9, James Forman, former executive secretary of SNCC, declared that the effort to exclude Bond was a "racist act" that "if implemented . . . would make all previous civil rights legislation pointless." The following day, Martin Luther King Jr., a resident of Bond's 136th District, argued that the controversy had "obvious racial overtones." To drive home the point, he noted, "Many of the persons who voted to refuse Mr. Bond his seat were and are the very persons who have consistently defied the law of the land through their irresponsible acts and statements. . . . There was never an outcry [from these individuals] for unseating the members of the state legislature who in 1954 so blatantly advocated defying, evading and circumventing the U.S. Supreme Court's school desegregation decision." King was not engaging in hyperbole. Fourteen of the legislators who had voted for interposition in defiance of *Brown v. Board* still sat in the legislature in 1966, and all of them voted to exclude Bond.[33] And many ordinary Georgia blacks concurred with these civil rights activists' statements. On the afternoon of January 11, five hundred black students rallied in support of Bond at the Atlanta University Center. Later that evening, five hundred African Americans attended a mass meeting at the Mount Moriah Baptist Church, only blocks away. Four days later, King led approximately one thousand demonstrators in a march on the state capitol chanting, "We want Julian Bond. We want Julian Bond."[34]

And Bond too believed that race was the primary issue in his ouster. In the several days between the release of the SNCC statement and January 10, Bond had remained silent on the advice of his lawyers. He broke that silence at a press conference outside the house chamber following the clerk's refusal to administer the oath of office. In his remarks to the press that day and in subsequent discussions the following year, Bond linked the exclusion vote to the civil rights movement. "Negroes have died for the right to vote in Georgia," Bond stated to reporters. "Now they are saying, what good does it do to get the vote, to elect representatives, if those elected must face 'attitude tests' and loyalty oaths?" Bond often repeated this argument during the hundreds of speeches he gave to support his family in the year that he was barred from the house.[35] Bond also linked the Georgia House's action to Reconstruction. Tucked into Bond's coat pocket on January 10 was a speech by Rev. Henry McNeil Turner, delivered to the Georgia Legislature ninety-eight years before when he and his fellow black legislators were expelled by their white colleagues. Bond had changed the names to portray himself as the ejected black Reconstruction legislators and Denmark Groover as their white antagonists. Though Bond did not get the chance to deliver Turner's address before the house, he did communicate the sentiment therein to the public. Approximately one year after his initial exclusion, Bond wrote an article for *Ramparts* magazine in which he reprinted excerpts of the Turner address. "Mr. Groover, let me say this to the young men of Georgia," Bond wrote. "The black man cannot protect a country if the country does not protect him. And if tomorrow a war should arise, I would not lift a finger or raise a musket to defend a country where my manhood is denied, nor lift a finger in defense of Georgia unless Georgia acknowledges that we are men and invests us with all the rights of manhood."[36] Bond also recited this speech for Roger Williams, who included it in his 1971 Bond family biography. In subsequent years, Bond expanded on this metaphor. Speaking at the Institute for Black Elected Officials in September 1969, he compared the late 1960s to the late 1870s: "We find ourselves in a similar period. Rutherford B. Hayes ended the first Reconstruction in Washington at the Wormley Hotel in 1877. Richard Nixon is trying to strangle the short-lived second Reconstruction with a deal made in Miami Beach in 1968." The details of the two counterrevolutions were not exact, Bond conceded. But the implications for African Americans were the same.[37] Bond's civil rights and "second post-Reconstruction" metaphors would be, in the coming decades, an attractive framework for understanding harassment, with early antiharassment activists like Mervyn Dymally, C. Delores Tucker, and Mary Sawyer employing them in their own studies and public statements.

Within days of the Georgia House vote, Bond sought relief before the courts. He was joined in his suit by 136th District residents Arel Keyes and Martin Luther King Jr. In the following months, Bond won a February special election called to fill his seat, was denied his seat three months later by an unrepentant house, won the September 1966 primary, and won the November general election. All the while, the controversy was front-page news in Georgia and often in the national dailies, making Bond a national celebrity—and thereby amplifying his depictions of the Georgia House's actions. By early fall, Bond's suit had made its way to the Supreme Court in the form of *Julian Bond et al. v. James "Sloppy" Floyd et al.* There, both sides repeated polished versions of the arguments first heard before the Georgia House. On December 5, a unanimous Court found in favor of Bond. Writing for the Court, Chief Justice Earl Warren noted that Bond's endorsement of the SNCC statement was protected under the First Amendment, and that the Georgia House had no constitutional authority to expand on the qualifications for office enumerated in the Georgia Constitution and deny Bond his seat. The Court also commented on the racial aspects of the case. Brushing aside the state's claim that race had nothing to do with the expulsion vote, Warren wrote, "It would be completely unrealistic not to recognize the racial background of the current dispute." Georgia "did not engage in a wholesale expulsion of the Negro members of its legislature, as in 1868," Warren continued. "But it does have a long contemporary history record of discrimination against the Negro in many fields and the representative excluded in the instant case is a Negro representing a Negro constituency who presumed to express himself openly on a matter of domestic and foreign policy." The Court ordered that Bond be awarded back pay for the year that he was barred from the legislature and that he be sworn in with his colleagues on the tenth of January 1967.[38]

Speaking to reporters after he heard news of the decision, Bond stated, "What the Supreme Court set up was a precedent — in the future, no legislature will ever be able to do this kind of thing again." He would prove incorrect. Bond was seated on the morning of January 10, 1967, without incident.[39] Later that very day, however, the U.S. House of Representatives voted to deny Representative Adam Clayton Powell Jr. (D-N.Y.) his duly elected seat in Congress.

Harnessing the Backlash in the Nation's Capital: Adam Clayton Powell Jr.

If the Bond exclusion demonstrates the way in which repression of black elected officials became one key arena of the white backlash against the southern civil rights movement, the House of Representatives 1967 vote to exclude Adam Clayton Powell Jr. illuminates the role of repression in the white backlash against Black Power. Just as important, Powell's expulsion helps us to understand the complicated nature of that repression. Not even Powell would claim that he was innocent of the crimes with which he was charged. And yet, to quote a member of one of the House committees charged with investigating Powell, "the effort to exclude the gentleman from New York could not have succeeded, and might not have been attempted, had Adam C. Powell done everything he is accused of doing, but had he been — to coin a phrase — 'less colorful.'"[40]

Born in 1908, the first son of Mattie Fletcher Powell and the up-and-coming preacher Adam Clayton Powell, Adam Jr. came of age the pampered son of one of the leading families of Harlem, New York. Despite his pedigree, Powell, who, fresh out of college, became an assistant pastor at his father's Abyssinian Baptist Church, developed a strong following among the poor southern migrants of Harlem during the Great Depression. He led rent strikes against slum lords and boycotts of discriminatory merchants and distributed aid to the destitute and hungry. He also distinguished himself as a voice for the dispossessed through a weekly column in the *Amsterdam News*. The African American voters of Harlem rewarded Powell for his activism and advocacy with a seat in the newly formed city council in 1941. When the New York legislature created a majority-black congressional district centered on upper Manhattan in 1944, Harlemites made him only the third African American elected to Congress in the twentieth century.[41]

Powell arrived in Washington, D.C., intent on doing two things: desegregating federal programs and acting as a spokesman for the national black community, particularly the black poor. In his first two years in Congress, Powell introduced bills establishing a permanent Fair Employment Practices Commission (FEPC), making lynching a federal crime, barring segregation in interstate travel, and a host of other desegregation initiatives. All were ignored. A racial and ideological minority in a majoritarian institution, he was powerless to enact a legislative agenda. Seeking a way around the powerful southern committee chairmen who regularly killed his legislation, Powell created what became known as the "Powell Amendment." Beginning in 1946 and continuing for the next fourteen years, Powell attached his amendment, which barred discrimination in federally funded programs, to any major legislation that passed his desk. The Powell amendment forced every member of the House to go on record as supporting or opposing segregation in federal programs. Such a move was politically risky. By raising southern Democratic opposition to liberal federal programs, Powell often alienated the backers of those programs, his most likely allies. Thus, early on, Powell set a precedent of exercising independent black political power — albeit the power to obstruct.

Powell had far more success as a spokesman for the national black community. From the House floor, he loudly denounced segregation and lambasted its supporters. His rhetoric became a major concern of the Truman and later the Eisenhower administration because it threatened to undermine American claims to be the leader of the free world in the cold war era. It was also a source of intense pride for African Americans. Although South Side Chicago blacks had sent a black representative to Congress since 1928, not since Oscar DePriest (R-Ill.) left the chamber in 1932 had an African American spoken out so forcefully from the floor of the House in support of black equality. Thus, for the first sixteen years of his congressional career, Powell's white colleagues viewed him, in biographer Charles Hamilton's words, as a "congressional irritant," an obstacle to be circumvented in both Democrats' and Republicans' efforts to pass legislation. To many African Americans, on the other hand, he was "Mr. Civil Rights," a fearless crusader for black equality within the white power structure.[42]

Aside from his outspoken advocacy of black equality, the congressman from Harlem was best known for his breaches of congressional ethics. From the moment he set foot in Washington, Powell recognized that kickbacks, bribes, misuse of office and committee funds, personal travel on the public dollar, and various other forms of graft were so widespread as to constitute an institutional culture. Selfish, arrogant, and accustomed to a lifestyle of privilege, Powell readily adapted to the mores of the midcentury Congress. Soon after being sworn in, the freshman congressman began collecting salary kickbacks from his secretary, Hattie Dobson. He would continue to do so until 1954, when a DOJ investigation sent Dobson to jail, because she refused to betray her employer. Also in 1945, Powell placed his first wife, Isabel Powell, on the congressional payroll, even though she did not perform work for his office, and pocketed her paychecks. He was forced to remove her name in 1946 when the two were estranged. Throughout the 1950s and into the 1960s, Powell took midsummer junkets to Europe, where he attended the International Labor Organization meeting in Geneva. His itineraries invariably included more sightseeing and recreation than meetings. Powell also chronically underreported his taxes, moving the U.S. attorney in Manhattan to indict him for tax evasion in 1958. Although the subsequent trial ended in a hung jury, Powell was forced to pay several thousand dollars in back taxes to the IRS. And to this list could be added numerous other instances of petty graft chronicled by his biographers.[43] Powell was by no means the worst offender in Congress. In 1967, reporter Jack Anderson published *Washington Exposé*, a muckraking investigation of the illegal, or at least dishonest, activities of the Washington elite. In the nearly five-hundred-page study, Powell's name graced only four pages.[44]

Powell's advocacy of civil rights and his embrace of graft earned him criticism from friend and foe alike. Opponents of civil rights and liberal reform focused on his alleged misdeeds, calling for investigations and seeking to link these two aspects of Powell's politics in the public mind. Criticism also came from friends, primarily blacks but also liberal whites, who believed that Powell's antics detracted from his civil rights advocacy. These criticisms were often expressed privately for fear of invoking a verbal blast from the mercurial preacher or injuring the cause. Interestingly enough, what drew the public rebuke of foes and the private criticism of friends made Powell a hero to a majority of working-class African Americans. They reveled in what they saw as Powell's defiance of white authority and exposure of white hypocrisy. What "whites regard[ed] as Powell's violation of elemental ethics," Kenneth Clark writes in *Dark Ghetto*, "Negroes view[ed] as effective and amusing defiance." This defiance, Clark continued, "is a caricature, a burlesque, of the personal exploitation of power. . . . His [Powell's] behavior merely focuses on the fact that certain respectable white congressmen, too, may use public funds for personal junkets or put their wives on the public payroll. The white power structure never successfully calls him to account and the Negro sees this and applauds."[45] Thus, for Powell and many African Americans, his violation of congressional ethics was a form of racial protest.

When challenged on his behavior, Powell made this criticism of white America explicit. He did so in two interconnected ways. First, Powell charged his accusers with racism. When Senator Homer Capehart (R-Ind.) the arch-conservative chairman of the Senate Banking Committee, sought to uncover graft in the Federal Housing Administration, he called Powell before his committee to explain two three-thousand-dollar "loans" he had received from a Queens housing developer — one of the few developers building integrated housing in New York — in 1952 but had failed to pay back. Powell fought back by labeling Capehart's investigation a "Republican sponsored drive to destroy what little non-segregation [had] been started in housing." Second, Powell claimed that many of his colleagues engaged in similar forms of graft. If pressed, he was willing to name names. Sitting before Capehart, demonstrably nonplussed by his power, Powell wondered aloud about "what money *he* [had] loaned, what money *he* [had] borrowed, and under what conditions." The investigation was subsequently dropped.[46] Charles Hamilton explains the dilemma Powell's defenses caused for his antagonists. "In order to get at him," Hamilton writes, "it was necessary to come to grips with the larger problems he both exposed and reflected." Few in Congress, however, were dedicated to racial equality in the 1950s, and fewer still were willing to rid the institution of graft. Their reluctance, Hamilton continues, "was his [Powell's] greatest protection, as paradoxical and vexing as that was to those who resented this maverick politician from Harlem."[47]

Between 1960 and 1966, however, four events shifted the political ground beneath Powell's feet. First, in January 1961, Powell ascended to the chair of the House Committee on Education and Labor. Not since he had entered Congress in January 1945 had he held any real institutional power.[48] Powell's elevation to the chairmanship made him a crucial element of House Democratic leadership. Between 1961 and 1966, Presidents Kennedy and Johnson made social reform legislation, most of which would pass through the Education and Labor Committee, a centerpiece of their domestic policy agendas. In this second phase of his legislative career, Powell became, for many African Americans, a symbol of the more conservative definition of Black Power. Because Powell was a member of party leadership with control over a half-million-dollar staff budget and some of the centerpiece legislation of two Democratic administrations, congressional Democrats expected him to curtail his more controversial behavior. The same circumstances that led others to expect more of him, however, provided Powell with more opportunities for graft. Second, substantial swings in voter allegiance between 1958 and 1966 added dozens of freshman members to Congress spread across both parties. The 1964 Democratic landslide, for instance, brought a class of seventy-one freshman liberal Democrats into the House. Many of these freshman members were intent on cleansing the lower chamber of the graft that Powell and many of his colleagues had come to accept as a way of doing business. With no skeletons in their own closets, these young Turks were immune to Powell's primary defense of charging his detractors with hypocrisy.[49] Third, and perhaps most importantly, the white backlash against the civil rights and Black Power movements greatly strengthened the conservative coalition that had opposed liberal racial reform. The 1966 election brought forty-seven freshman Republicans into the House. When they arrived in Washington, these freshman Republicans joined the chamber's bipartisan conservative coalition, which was then crafting a political language that linked race to crime and the alleged wastefulness of the welfare state. For these legislators, Powell was a propaganda issue just waiting to be exploited. Last, between 1960 and 1966 Powell was embroiled in a series of controversies that left him particularly vulnerable to attack.

Powell's legal troubles began at the very same time that he assumed the chairmanship of the Committee on Education and Labor. In January 1960, Powell commenced a campaign against the numbers racket in Harlem, singling out the New York Police Department for its complicity in the multimillion dollar business. As part of the campaign, Powell fingered Esther James, an elderly Harlem widow, as a "bag woman" who extorted payoff money from numbers runners and delivered it to the police. Powell's accusations were no idle fishing expedition. Subsequent investigations of New York City Police Department complicity in organized crime confirmed almost all of them. James, however, filed a defamation of character suit against Powell seeking one million dollars in damages. Ignorant of her extensive criminal record, several New York editorialists lionized her as a sweet old lady who had been attacked by an irresponsible congressman. Powell ignored her, comfortable in the fact that he possessed credible evidence of her criminal activity. Evidence of James's guilt, however, turned out not to be the decisive issue in the subsequent trial. Powell never attended a single hearing. After three years of delays orchestrated by his lawyers, an all-white jury (despite Manhattan's 50 percent black and Puerto Rican population) found him guilty and awarded James over two hundred thousand dollars in damages on April 13, 1963.[50]

While the jury was deliberating in New York, Powell was suffering from the fallout of an altogether different controversy in Washington. During the winter recess of 1962, Powell and two of his committee staffers embarked on an eight week "codel" (short for congressional delegation overseas trip) to England, France, Greece, and Italy. The official reason for the trip was to study the working conditions of women in the NATO countries. In actuality, Powell had organized the trip as a romantic getaway for himself and Education and Labor Committee staffer Corrine Huff, with whom he was then having an affair. The other staff member had been brought along to provide cover for the vacationing lovers. In December 1962, New York Times columnist Drew Pearson published an editorial detailing the party's itinerary, setting off a media firestorm back home and forcing Powell to cut short his trip.[51]

This latest controversy provided the perfect opportunity for conservative Republicans to attack the liberal reform agenda of the Kennedy administration by attacking Powell. On February 5, Senator John Williams (R-Del.) criticized Powell from the Senate floor. Federal agencies, Williams alleged, were "shoveling the taxpayer's money out" to Powell, sometimes "scrambling around to see who could give Mr. Powell the most favorable deal." Though Powell owed several years in back taxes, Williams declared, the IRS had not made an honest attempt to collect the money. "Powell and his associates," he continued, had received a large number of questionable loans from the Department of Health, Education and Welfare and the Home Finance Agency at interest rates below market value. And, Williams continued, "on the front page of every newspaper [were] accounts of Mr. Powell's European vacation with his lady friends, where he attended all the night spots of the European capitals on a tax paid junket that was financed through the State Department."[52] The senator's remarks violated congressional protocol, which forbade attacks on the "character or reputation" of fellow members. Accordingly, Senator Wayne Morse (D-Ore.) introduced a resolution to strike his colleague's remarks from the record the following day. In a remarkable gesture of defiance, Williams opposed the measure and used the occasion to make several more accusations against Powell. "I made the remarks and I stand behind them," Williams stated. "I did not discuss this person's conduct in the House of Representatives. I never said one word yesterday, nor will I today, about this person having relatives on the public payroll who are not working. . . . Neither will I say that he is not fulfilling his duties and is guilty of a great deal of absenteeism."[53] Powell was then in Puerto Rico seeking to convince his third wife, Yvette Marjorie Flores, that the news reports about his relationship with Corrine Huff were untrue. He would respond at a February 20 press conference upon his return.

Powell's response, given to reporters in committee chambers, was familiar to those who had followed his career. "I say unequivocally that Williams' attack on me was motivated by racial prejudice because I am a Negro," he declared. To buttress his point, Powell detailed Williams's opposition to several civil rights bills and noted that the senator owned a home with a racially restrictive covenant. Reporters had heard such charges from the Harlem congressman before. They wanted him to address Williams's allegations. Powell refused, sticking instead to his normal line of defense. In response to reporters' questions about his being spotted in expensive nightclubs and restaurants with his two aides during his most recent trip to Europe, Powell stated that several members of the House and the Senate had been in those same venues. "Ask some of my colleagues what they did in Europe the same night I was there," he quipped. When asked about his wife being on the Education and Labor Committee payroll, Powell again referenced the actions of his colleagues: "Over 100 members of the House of

Representatives have their relatives on payroll that we know about." Summing up, Powell declared, "I wish to state very emphatically that I will always do just what every other congressman and committee chairman do in the House."[54] Powell had been pushed to the wall. As he had shown in the past, he would label his detractors as racists and expose the corruption of his fellow members of Congress in his defense.

Powell's defense of his actions violated the code of silence that surrounded the topic of congressional ethics. Certainly, other members behaved as he did, but they were more discreet. By trumpeting their exploits, Powell threatened to undermine public confidence in the institution. And members of Congress were particularly concerned about protecting their image in early 1963. The previous year, a series of congressional scandals had focused public attention on the issue of corruption. Of most immediate concern to members was the publication of two spring 1963 articles in *Parade* magazine on the unethical and illegal behavior of congressmen by reporter Jack Anderson.[55] Powell's defense threatened to exacerbate the controversy. Also Powell's charges were particularly disturbing to the chamber's younger members, who had not been in Washington long enough to engage in graft. Both the guilty and the innocent had been tarred by Powell's February 20 press conference. By casting such a wide net, Powell had managed to stimulate his detractors and alienate his supporters.

Within weeks of the press conference, Rep. John Ashbrook (R-Ohio), an arch-conservative Goldwater supporter and member of Powell's Education and Labor Committee, criticized his chairman for airing the Congress's "dirty linen." He resented Powell's claim that every other congressman did just as he did, and determined to call his bluff. Ashbrook claimed that Powell had mismanaged committee funds, constructed a large and inefficient staff, and gave generous contracts to friends and political allies. He concluded by requesting a reduced committee appropriation for the coming Congress. Ashbrook's speech broke the dam. Several of his Republican colleagues rose to thank him for "doing something that many Members have felt needed to be done."[56] Democrats, many of whom had begun to receive a not-insignificant volume of constituent mail demanding that Powell be disciplined, were largely silent.[57]

The Republican salvo had its intended effect. Powell had requested a committee appropriation of $697,000 for the Eighty-eighth Congress. Following the Williams and Ashbrook speeches, he received approximately $550,000. Far more noteworthy, however, was the manner in which those funds were allocated. Three-fourths of the funds were dispensed directly to the five subcommittees, thereby depriving Powell of direct control over the majority of his committee budget.[58] This last move was obviously a vote of no confidence in Powell by the Democratic Party leadership, a not-so-subtle demand that he get his affairs in order.

Powell did not heed the warning. Instead of settling the libel suit brought by Esther James, he continued to ignore the courts. After countless delays, two New York judges issued civil contempt warrants against him in 1964. Again, rather than respond, Powell simply sidestepped this latest obstacle by restricting his time in Manhattan to Sundays — the only day of the week that civil warrants could not be served. In November 1966, a frustrated New York Supreme Court judge handling the James case ordered Powell arrested any day of the week that he set foot in New York City.[59] Back in Washington, Powell continued to antagonize his congressional colleagues. He used committee funds for travel to his home in Bimini (since he could not return to New York) and kept his estranged wife, Yvette Marjory Flores, on the congressional payroll. During Labor Day weekend in 1966, Powell held a closed-door Black Power conference in his committee chambers, a move loudly opposed by several committee members. And that summer, he held up several pieces of antipoverty and labor legislation of particular importance to the president and many congressional liberals, arguing that they were too timid in attacking the problems of the black poor. Frustrated by Powell's inaction on pending legislation and alleged misuse of committee funds, members of the Education and Labor Committee staged a revolt. On September 22, 1966, committee members voted 27 to 1 to curtail Powell's power to control legislation and the committee budget.[60]

The committee revolt quickly reverberated into the larger House. With news of Powell's legal troubles and alleged malfeasance splashed across the front pages of the nation's newspapers and a growing number of calls from constituents to discipline the Harlem congressman, the House voted on September 26 to have the House Administration Committee investigate his handling of Education and Labor Committee funds. The unpleasant task of chairing the committee fell to Representative Wayne Hays, Democrat of Ohio. Over the course of the following three months, the Hays Committee held a series of open and closed-door hearings that proved particularly damaging to Powell. Hays invited Powell to testify, but the congressman refused. His participation, he claimed, was contingent on Hays conducting a "comparative analysis of the travel vouchers of staff members of other full committees and subcommittees, including [Hays's] own" and a "comparable analysis of the travel undertaken by all other Committee and Subcommittee Chairmen."[61] Powell, however, was in no position to make threats. Hays refused his request and completed the report without his testimony. Issued on January 3, 1967, the Hays Committee report confirmed that many of the allegations made against Powell were indeed true. Powell, his son Adam Clayton Powell III, and several of his aides had used assumed names to conceal their use of committee funds for personal travel. Though it could not be confirmed, the committee held a "strong presumption" that the congressman's estranged wife had not performed work for the salary she received as his congressional secretary (Powell had been receiving and depositing her checks into his personal bank account) and recommended that she be dropped from the payroll. Lesser offenses were also listed among the committee's twelve conclusions.[62]

Issued only six days before the start of the ninetieth congressional session, the Hays Committee report set in motion a chain of events that quickly led to Powell's exclusion. As the committee conducted its investigation in fall 1966, many House Democrats hotly debated ways of disciplining Powell. This discussion raged most intensely within the Democratic Study Group, the largest subgroup within the House Democratic Caucus. A coalition of Northeastern and Midwestern liberals advocated denying Powell his committee chairmanship in the hope of heading off an attempt to deny Powell his seat altogether. This latter position was being championed by Representative Lionel Van Deerlin (D-Calif.), a second-term congressman from San Diego, California. Van Deerlin proposed to have Powell step aside at the start of the Ninetieth Congress while a special committee ascertained his fitness for seating. His position gained the support of many southern Democrats and Republicans. More importantly, Van Deerlin gained a substantial national following among white Americans who saw Powell as the embodiment of Black Power in Congress and the corruption of the liberal welfare state.

Powell did little to dispel this notion. Indeed, in a last-ditch effort to blunt the growing support in the Democratic Caucus and among the public for denying him the chairmanship of the Education and Labor Committee — for Powell did not believe that Congress would deny him his seat — he framed the effort to discipline him as an attack on black America. On January 5, Powell issued a press release titled "15 Facts" from his Washington office. True to form, he refused to address the conclusions of the Hays Committee, focusing instead on what he referred to as his colleagues' authorization of "two standards of conduct — one for white Congressmen and one for Negro Congressmen." After citing several cases in which white congressmen accused of wrongdoing had escaped punishment, Powell queried:

> How much is race — the fact of my being a Negro — the singularly most important issue in the efforts within the House of Representatives and editorials against me?
>
> To what extent are they motivated by the desire to politically castrate one of America's most powerful Negro politicians of his power?
>
> How much does all of this represent the convulsion of change — the beginning of the new era of the rejected Negro, an organized turning of white America's back on its black brothers?

Offering his own answer, Powell leveled a startling allegation that perhaps revealed his growing desperation: "The . . . facts, taken in concert, unequivocally permit the conclusion that a political conspiracy of enormous dimensions involving certain influential members of the press, and I deeply regret, a number of my colleagues in Congress, has not only been mounted against Adam Clayton Powell, but against black political leadership, black people and black progress."[63] Though many congressmen would have shrunk before Powell's accusations in the past, they confronted them now. Hays responded to Powell's charge of a double standard by arguing, "I suspect that if Powell were white he would have been investigated earlier." Representative Alphonzo Bell (R-Calif.), a junior member of Powell's Education and Labor Committee, argued that the move to discipline Powell was less an attempt to single out a black member than an effort to force Powell to "recognize the same standard of ethical behavior that cover[ed] all other members."[64] Though these allegations were questionable, in the context of the white backlash, when many white Americans believed that African American lawbreakers were being coddled by the liberal state, they went largely unchallenged.

When the Democratic Caucus met on January 9, the liberals won out. By a voice vote, the caucus adopted a motion to deny Powell the chairmanship of the Education and Labor Committee for the entire Ninetieth Congress.[65] Rather than head off a Republican–southern Democratic effort to unseat Powell, however, the liberals' move demonstrated that the Democratic Party was split and Powell vulnerable. The following day, when Speaker McCormack conducted the swearing-in ceremony, Representative Van Deerlin rose to object to the oath being administered to Powell. Under House rules, Powell was forced to stand aside.[66] Following the seating of the other members, the same coalition of Democratic liberals who had stripped Powell of his chairmanship the day before fought hard to have him seated. They were overwhelmed, however, by a coalition of southern Democrats and Republicans who coalesced around a carbon copy of the Van Deerlin proposal, House Resolution 1, offered by minority leader Gerald Ford (R-Mich.). The resolution, which denied Powell his seat until an investigation determined what, if any, punishments should be imposed for his alleged misdeeds, passed by a vote of 363 to 65 with all Republicans and all southern Democrats voting in the affirmative.[67]

Within days of the January 10 exclusion vote, House Speaker McCormack assembled a special nine-member committee under the leadership of Judiciary Committee chairman Emanuel Celler (D-N.Y.). The Celler Committee was charged with the rather opaque task of determining "the question of the right of Adam Clayton Powell to be sworn in as a Representative from the State of New York in the Ninetieth Congress, as well as his final right to a seat therein as such Representative."[68] The committee majority quickly came to the realization that they had no constitutional right to exclude Powell. Only one month before, the Supreme Court had ruled in the case of *Julian Bond et al. v. James "Sloppy" Floyd et al.* that the Georgia House of Representatives did not have the constitutional authority to expand on the requirements for office enumerated in the Georgia Constitution. The same rule held for Congress.[69] Deferring to the Court, the Celler Committee, in its February report, recommended that Powell be seated, censured, forced to pay a forty-thousand-dollar fine, and stripped of his seniority. The recommendations defied precedent. Never had the House or the Senate imposed a penalty as severe as that recommended for Powell. Representative John Conyers (D-Mich.), the only African American member of the committee, noted as much in dissenting remarks.[70]

Lawyers all, the members of the Celler Committee had produced a report that adhered to the relevant statutes. They had not, however, debated the merits of the case free of political influence. During the committee's deliberations, members were subjected to intense pressure from the black and the white communities. Committee members were deluged with mail from their white constituents concerning Powell. Much of the mail, Representative Conyers stated, was "bitter and harsh," advocating exclusion on openly racist grounds. Representative Celler stated that the mail contained "uninhibited expressions of hate and vindictiveness." Representative Charles Teague (R-Calif.) agreed. The mail that he and his colleagues received was "100–1" in favor of "throwing the rascal out."[71] The mail was representative of white public opinion. In January and February, Harris polls indicated that over 80 percent of white Americans believed Powell "should not be given his seat in Congress." In a stark demonstration of the racial divide that characterized the controversy, an equal number of black Americans believed that Powell should be seated.[72]

While many white Americans expressed their views through the mail, many African Americans expressed their views through civil rights organizations, public demonstrations, and face-to-face discussions with black members of Congress. On January 10, the day that the House voted to exclude Powell, approximately one thousand protesters gathered on the House steps chanting, "We want Powell back in the chair," "No Powell, no vote," and "No Powell, no Johnson." Following the vote, Powell mounted the steps to address the group. Picking up on familiar themes, he declared, "You are looking at the first black man who was ever lynched by Congress!" As the crowd responded with shouts of "Tell it!" and pumped their fists in Black Power salutes, Powell pointed to the building behind him and shouted, "This building houses the biggest bunch of elected hypocrites the world has ever known."[73] The crowd again roared in approval. And seemingly with one voice, black leadership, radical and moderate alike, reaffirmed Powell's characterization of the Democratic Caucus and

House votes. On January 9, following the Democratic Caucus vote, SNCC and Representative Julian Bond issued a statement condemning the vote as "consistent with the high-handed manner that the Democratic Party has always used towards Afro-Americans in this country." Floyd McKissick of the Congress of Racial Equality deemed the Democratic Caucus's action a "political castration of the black people." On January 23, Roy Wilkins, Whitney Young, Martin Luther King Jr., Bayard Rustin, and A. Philip Randolph issued a joint statement: "We do not close our eyes to the shortcomings of Mr. Powell or of any other congressman. . . . We ask only that Mr. Powell be judged by standards equally applied to all Congressmen."[74] In the weeks and months following the exclusion vote, many of these leaders visited Powell at his island home in demonstrations of solidarity. Martin Luther King Jr. traveled there, as did Representative Bond. Also among Powell's visitors was a young California state senator by the name of Mervyn Dymally (D-Compton/Watts).[75] In the late 1970s, Dymally would emerge as the primary sponsor of harassment research. Powell also received support from former SNCC chairman turned Washington, D.C., community activist Marion Barry. Speaking before a community meeting in the Shaw neighborhood of northwest D.C., Barry stated: "Regardless of whether Adam Clayton Powell is good or bad, regardless of whether he is flamboyant or not, regardless of whether he goes to Bermuda or not, we should support him in this issue because he is being attacked by racists."[76] Twenty-four years later, Barry would use a similar line of defense when federal investigators prosecuted him for drug possession.

No member of the Celler Committee felt the tensions implicit in this racial split more than John Conyers. Despite his misgivings about the extraordinarily harsh punishment prescribed by the committee, Conyers joined his colleagues at a press conference endorsing the committee recommendations. Yet Conyers soon found that there was little support for his position within the black community. Soon after the Celler Committee announced its recommendations, Whitney Young, executive director of the Urban League, stated, "In this nation you can be white and wrong and make it. You can be black and right and perhaps be successful, but it is obvious that you cannot be both black and wrong." NAACP executive director Roy Wilkins was equally blunt: "Unless Congress metes out equal justice to all offenders regardless of their race, religion, party, regional or national origin, it will validate the charge that Mr. Powell, despite his highly irregular conduct, has been singled out personally for special treatment." Conyers returned to his district to hear these sentiments echoed on the streets of black Detroit. In order to deflect his constituents' anger, indeed the anger of much of black America, Conyers called a press conference where he backed away from his initial support of the Celler Committee report. With a nod to many African Americans' belief that Powell was the victim of a double standard, Conyers announced that he would seek to hold congressional investigations on the alleged wrongdoings of white members of Congress. Several days later, Conyers held another press conference where he announced that he would ask Congress to drop the loss of seniority and forty-thousand-dollar fine that the Celler Committee had recommended be levied against Powell.[77]

Though Conyers was receptive to the outrage of the black community, his white colleagues were not. Rather, they paid attention to the mail from their white constituents. During the debate over the Celler Committee report, in fact, members made little effort to disguise the fact that white popular opinion was the primary factor in determining their votes. Before the debate even began, one member exclaimed, "My people don't want him." During the debate itself, members' references to the mail became more exact. Arch Moore (R-W.Va.), ranking Republican on the Celler Committee, noted, "If we only read [the mail] which is presently on our desks . . . it would have been easy for us to have come and recommended that the member elect be excluded." Speaking in favor of the committee report, Clark MacGregor (R-Minn.) concurred, arguing that a recommendation for expulsion "would have been highly popular in the emotionalism of the moment. Emotionalism [was] rampant in the communications addressed to each member of [the House]."[78] And the mail had its intended effect. Although most members of the Celler Committee were willing to privilege the Constitution over politics, many of their colleagues were not. For them, a vote to exclude Powell was a vote to stay in Congress. Representative Teague, who had spoken to many of these members, stated, "Several members on both sides of the aisle have told me in the last few days that they are satisfied and the recommendations of the committee should be adopted, but they were afraid that they could not vote to do so" and secure reelection. Representative Andy Jacobs underscored this point in his chronicle of the episode, *The Powell Affair*, when he noted that several dozen "members of Congress . . . approached [him] . . . to say privately that they thought the committee's recommendations were right, but that a vote for seating would have meant their own unseating in the next election."[79]

Recognizing how widespread these attitudes were among the white electorate, minority leader Ford maneuvered to have Powell excluded despite the constitutional constraints. During the Celler Committee's deliberations, Ford directed Republican members to delete from the committee report any mention of the constitutional requirement that Powell be seated. Committee Democrats agreed to his request in return for Republican leadership's support of the committee recommendations. Writing about the episode several months later, Representative Jacobs recalled, "And so we struck a deal. We would fail to inform the Congress that it would be violating the Constitution if it refused to seat Adam Clayton Powell in return for the Republican leadership's support of our recommendation that Powell be sworn in."

In the week following the release of the report, Republican leadership abandoned their deal with committee Democrats. The Republican Caucus chairman, Representative Melvin Laird (R-Wis.), told his party colleagues that they did not have to support the Republican leadership's endorsement of the report. Supplementing Laird's advice was Ford himself. During the floor debate over the report, Ford disingenuously fulfilled his end of the bargain by stating that he *personally* would vote for the committee recommendations. He qualified this endorsement, however, by devoting the majority of his remarks to the issue of Congress's right to exclude a member-elect. Lamenting the fact that the committee did not address this subject in its report — the omission, Representative Jacobs derisively noted, was made "at the special request . . . of none other than Mr. Ford" — Ford argued that Congress did have the power to exclude duly elected members. Ford then demanded a recorded vote on the committee report, thereby depriving members of the political cover they would need if they were to follow the law.[80] Subsequently, the House rejected the Celler Committee report by a margin of 222 to 202. As the House Clerk tallied the votes, Ford and his lieutenants hurriedly drafted an amendment in the form of a substitute expelling Powell from the Ninetieth Congress. With the strong backing of Republicans and southern Democrats, it passed by the margin of 307 to 116. The members of the Ninetieth Congress had made history. Never before had the House rejected the recommendations of a special committee in the matter of disciplining a member only to impose instead a more stringent penalty.

Powell countered the House's unprecedented action with one of his own, by filing a lawsuit challenging his exclusion. Like the Bond suit before it, Powell's challenge would find its way to the Supreme Court. Meanwhile, the governor of New York scheduled a special election for April to fill Powell's seat. Though Powell did not travel to Harlem to campaign, he won with 86 percent of the vote. The vote demonstrated Black Harlemites' determination to thumb their noses at the white congressmen who had excluded Powell. But rather than travel to Washington, D.C., to present this newest certificate of election to the House, and likely be excluded once more, Powell remained in Bimini. While waiting for his case to make its way through the courts, Powell embarked on a college speaking tour, delivering militant speeches in which he espoused Black Power, criticized the war in Vietnam, and, of course, denounced his congressional colleagues as racists and hypocrites. In the fall of 1968, Powell again ran for reelection, believing that he had to remain the sole heir to the seat from Harlem if his court challenge was to succeed. Again he won, though by a uniquely low margin in the Democratic primary. Immediately after the election, African

American representatives John Conyers and Charles Diggs (D-Mich.) began negotiations with Republican and Democratic leadership to ensure that Powell would this time be seated. Their job was made easier by the decline in public attention to the Powell controversy. Unlike two years before, members were no longer being deluged with mail. Public attention had shifted to the remarkable political events of 1968, and away from the exiled congressman from Harlem. Nonetheless, some members remained determined to exclude Powell. On January 10, 1969, conservative Republican H. R. Gross of Iowa demanded that Powell stand aside, then submitted a motion to ban him from the Ninety-first Congress. It was defeated. Emanuel Celler then introduced the Conyers and Diggs compromise motion whereby Powell would be seated, stripped of his seniority, and fined twenty-five thousand dollars. The motion passed by a vote of 252 to 160. Twenty-four years after he first entered the chamber, Powell was sworn in as a freshman member of the House of Representatives.[81]

The following June, Powell and the Celler Committee were vindicated when the Supreme Court ruled that the House of Representatives could not add to the constitutionally stipulated requirements for membership and had acted unconstitutionally by excluding him. Writing for the majority, Chief Justice Warren argued that the House's decision to exclude Powell contained "racist overtones."[82]

Despite Powell's seating and the Supreme Court ruling, a small number of conservative representatives continued to advocate for expulsion. Representative Bill Dickinson (R-Ala.), one of the five Republicans swept into office by the 1964 Goldwater (congressional) landslide in Alabama, led a campaign to expel Powell from the chamber. Although in September 1970 *Washington Post* columnist Jack Anderson reported that Dickinson "may have violated the bribery and kickback laws himself," the Alabama congressman continued to advocate for Powell's removal. Only Powell's 1970 primary election defeat at the hands of state senator Charles Rangel (D-Harlem) ended the campaign.[83]

The Powell affair was finally over, but few African Americans would forget the way the House of Representatives had treated "Mr. Civil Rights."

Racial Realignment

The significance of the political struggles surrounding Julian Bond and Adam Clayton Powell Jr. were realized within months of their respective exclusions. In September 1966, segregationist Lester Maddox captured the Democratic nomination for governor of Georgia by handily defeating former governor and national Democratic Party stalwart Ellis G. Arnall in a runoff election. Two years before, Maddox had become something of a celebrity among segregationist Georgians when he refused to abide by the public accommodations section of the CRA and desegregate his Atlanta restaurant, the Pickrick Restaurant. On one occasion he brandished an ax handle against a group of African Americans demanding service. News of the incident spread quickly, and in the ensuing months Maddox sold hundreds of autographed ax handles, which he called "Pickrick drumsticks," to admiring whites.[84] Despite his popularity, Georgia liberals were stunned by his victory. "Only eight to ten months ago," the *New York Times* editorialized following the runoff, "white liberals were coming out of political retirement, convinced that the South had rounded the corner in race relations. But in recent months almost all of them have been overwhelmed, not simply by ordinary, run of the mill segregationists, but by some of the most militant segregationists to have emerged in the South in this century." In a written statement on the election issued from the Southern Christian Leadership Conference (SCLC) office in Atlanta, Martin Luther King Jr. could barely conceal his disgust: "Georgia is a sick state," he lamented.[85] A Goldwater supporter in 1964, Maddox faced a Goldwater Republican, Representative Howard "Bo" Callaway (R-Ga.), in the general election. That November, liberal white and black Georgians found themselves trapped between the right wings of the Democratic and the Republican parties. Neither Maddox nor Callaway received a clear majority, however, which threw the election into the Democratic-controlled state legislature. There, the men who had denied Bond his seat twice in the previous year and were, on that day, grudgingly accepting the legislator-elect into their ranks under court order, voted to award Maddox the governorship.[86]

Political developments following Powell's ouster from Congress proved equally bleak for the advocates of liberal racial reform. In 1967, the conservative coalition that had begun the year by denying Powell his seat reemerged as a dominant force in the House of Representatives. In the Eighty-ninth Congress (1965–66), the coalition had a success rate of only 39 percent. This was the liberal-dominated Congress that had passed the VRA and much of President Johnson's Great Society legislation. In the Ninetieth Congress (1967–68), however, the coalition was successful in 68 percent of the votes on which it took a stand. In one mean-spirited demonstration of Congress's growing hostility to liberal federal programs that helped blacks, congressional conservatives succeeded in defeating a 1967 rat abatement bill, with opponents laughingly dubbing a "civil rats bill." The 1968 election would further swell the coalition's ranks.[87]

The 1968 election also signaled the reassertion of conservative forces in presidential politics. Employing a "sunbelt strategy" that would come to define Republican politics for the next three decades, Richard Nixon triumphed over Democrat Hubert Humphrey and American Independent Party candidate George Wallace. Critical to Nixon's election was the backlash vote, which he roused with appeals to "law and order" and attacks on "forced busing" and "permissiveness." Though Nixon won big in the border South, the West, and the middle-class suburbs (nationwide), he was denied a majority by George Wallace's capture of the old Confederacy. Wallace polled nearly 10 million votes (13.5 percent of those who voted) and won Alabama, Arkansas, Georgia, Louisiana, and Mississippi. Though the overwhelming majority of Wallace voters were Democrats, a majority counted Nixon as their second choice.[88] Together Nixon and Wallace garnered 57 percent of the total vote. Though this vote did not constitute a mandate for any particular program, it was a clear rejection by a majority of white voters of the national Democratic Party and its Great Society and civil rights reform policies. Humphrey, a liberal closely identified with the reform efforts of the past decade, garnered only 38 percent of the white vote nationally.[89]

Had matters ended there, Powell's and Bond's exclusions would be footnotes in the story of the civil rights and Black Power movements, moments of intolerance in the crucible of the white backlash. But matters did not end there. Powell and Bond were just the more famous representatives of a new generation of black elected officials. In the years after 1967, the number of black voters and elected officials continued to grow in leaps and bounds. They became a critical new layer of the black revolt of the late 1960s and early 1970s. Over time, they evolved into the most dependable constituency within the Democratic Party and came to control critical parts of the party machinery. During that same period, large groups of white voters joined a slow but steady migration (begun as early as 1948) out of the Democratic Party in response to the liberal reforms of the Great Society and the rise of black voting and office-holding. Over the course of the next decade, some of the same elected officials who had engineered Bond's and Powell's exclusions gathered these disaffected white voters under the Republican banner, thereby transforming a racial realignment into a partisan realignment. These groups would continue to do battle into the new century, with the conservative coalition often using the repressive tactics evident in the expulsions of Bond and Powell to attack liberal Democrats, and black Democrats in particular.

With the shift of racial conflict from the streets to the state — or as Bayard Rustin so famously put the matter in 1965, "from protest to politics" — black elected officials searched for language to explain the continued resistance they encountered in the post–civil rights era. Between 1965 and 1995, hundreds, possibly thousands of black elected officials — most less duplicitous than Powell, almost none as innocent as Bond — experienced a string of politically motivated surveillance and counterintelligence, IRS audits, and official corruption investigations at the hands of a newly conservative state. In the mid-1970s, they identified Bond's and Powell's exclusions as the opening shots in a running battle between themselves and the state and the white news media. They used Bond's formulation of a "second post-Reconstruction" and Powell's notion of a "conspiracy" and a "racial double standard" to frame their understanding of what was happening to their ranks. Thus, rather than footnotes in the history of the backlash, Bond's and Powell's ejections became, for these black elected officials and many of their constituents at least, a prologue to a pattern of government harassment of black elected officials that would come to blanket the post–civil rights period.

It can be comfortably predicted that whites will continue to resist black political advancement, not solely on the basis of race, but also because no group enjoys the surrender of power. If race tensions escalate . . . then black political breakthroughs will be resisted by both the white population and white politicians who now serve predominantly black constituencies or districts with a significant percentage of black people.

— Chuck Stone, *Black Political Power in America*

In the short run, the Nixon Administration was simply interested in smearing and destroying . . . dissenters; in the long run, it wanted to use attacks on dissenters to turn the "silent majority" into the basis of a lasting Republican coalition.

— Gary Powers, *Secrecy and Power: The Life of J. Edgar Hoover*

CHAPTER TWO

Black Elected Officials, White Resistance, and the Surveillance State, 1965–1974

WRITING HIS DOCTORAL DISSERTATION in 1979, Huey P. Newton, cofounder and chairman of the Black Panther Party, reflected on the government repression visited upon him and his comrades in the late 1960s and early 1970s. State repression of dissident factions, particularly of African Americans, Newton observed, was a staple of modern American governance. Yet in the late 1960s, this repression reached a level unseen since the 1920s: "Under the leadership of Nixon," Newton wrote,

Americans in their majority—when they were confronted by widespread protest over both domestic and foreign policies—issued to the government and its agencies what appeared to be blanket approval of the squelching of dissent by means legal or illegal. This led inexorably to a vast and pernicious campaign of no-holds-barred conspiracies and extra-legal acts designed by law enforcement agencies to "neutralize," contain, and/or destroy organizations and individuals thought to be enemies of the American government (or the status quo), merely because they dared to disagree openly with the existing order and its policies.[1]

Newton and his Black Panther Party bore the brunt of this crackdown. By 1969, the FBI had targeted the Panthers in over 230 separate COINTELPRO, or counter-intelligence, actions, and in that year alone, police killed several Panthers and arrested over 740 more.[2] The breadth and violence of the police and intelligence community crackdown on the Black Panther Party has occupied historians' attention since the late 1970s, and the more extreme instances of repression, like the police assassinations of Chicago Panthers Mark Clark and Fred Hampton, have come to define our collective understanding of state repression during this period.[3]

But as Newton so astutely observed, the authorities targeted not just the Panthers but rather "organizations and individuals thought to be enemies of the American government (or the status quo)." One such targeted group to which historians have paid little attention is black elected officials. The oversight is understandable. The primary state responses to black electoral insurgency were not repression but incorporation, co-optation, or neglect. Black elected officials' efforts to channel the black revolt into the electoral system shielded them from the more aggressive forms of repression directed at radicals like Newton. Yet state repression of black elected officials was remarkably widespread in the late 1960s and early 1970s, touching perhaps a majority of their ranks at all levels of government.[4]

State repression of black elected officials unfolded during the late 1960s and early 1970s in several overlapping and mutually reinforcing patterns that corresponded to state attacks on the black freedom movement. In the years following passage of the VRA, newly enfranchised African Americans sought self-determination through the ballot. In so doing, they threatened to displace the white elected officials and political organizations that had ruled over their communities for generations. Whites in these areas used the state agencies at their disposal to prevent blacks from getting elected, assuming office once elected, and/or challenging their legitimacy once in office.

In many instances, these whites received help from a rapidly expanding and decidedly white supremacist municipal, state, and federal intelligence apparatus. In response to the popular unrest of the period, a host of government entities expanded their surveillance and counterintelligence activities, and many set their sights on black elected officials. In the Deep South, several states created "sovereignty" or "peace" commissions for the purpose of defending segregation.

These agencies placed most of the black political community in these states under surveillance, including black elected officials. In most major cities, police intelligence squads developed to combat organized crime and Communists in the 1950s and 1960s shifted their focus to civil rights, Black Power, antiwar, and student activists in the mid-1960s. Because many black elected officials were associated with or sought to speak for these groups, they too were targeted for surveillance and counterintelligence. On the federal level, the FBI also expanded its surveillance and counterintelligence apparatus to control popular unrest. Viewing black political activism as subversive in and of itself, the bureau placed perhaps a majority of black elected officials under surveillance and targeted a substantial number for counterintelligence. Supplementing the FBI's activities were the IRS, Central Intelligence Agency (CIA), and Military Intelligence, all of which spied on black elected officials in the late 1960s.

The high incidence of surveillance and counterintelligence directed at black elected officials was also a product of the Nixon administration's attempts to crush dissent and forcibly realign the United States' party system. Prior to 1968, neither political party held a monopoly on state repression. Although Republicans had a well-deserved reputation as Red-hunters, southern Democrats and big-city Democratic machines were equally prolific in their use of surveillance and counterintelligence against dissidents and political opponents. But in January 1969, the initiative shifted to the Republican-controlled White House. That month, Richard Nixon entered office promising to impose "law and order" on an increasingly assertive and unruly reform movement. True to his word, he dramatically increased state surveillance and counterintelligence against civil rights activists, black radicals, antiwar protesters, and a host of other dissident groups. Additionally, Nixon endeavored to forcibly realign U.S. politics by using the instruments of repression against his political opposition. Nixon undertook this latter project at the very time that black voters achieved majority enfranchisement and black elected officials were rising within the Democratic Party apparatus. As the most loyal members of the Democratic coalition and the most outspoken critics of the new president, black elected officials became some of the primary targets of the president's surveillance, counterintelligence, and "dirty tricks." Only the Watergate controversy and the subsequent state and federal investigations of "government lawlessness" put an end to the crackdown.

The Continued Black Political Insurgency, 1968–1974

In his study of black politics since 1941, *Running for Freedom*, historian Steven Lawson argues that newly enfranchised blacks "considered the franchise ... as a weapon for destroying racist institutions and encouraging liberation." Indeed, it was on this point that the many and querulous factions of black activists that proliferated in the ten years following passage of the VRA agreed. By the late 1960s, Manning Marable writes, "nationalists of every kind, from the nihilistic 'cultural nationalists' or 'black fascists' . . . to the socialist-oriented nationalists on the left, to Black Capitalists, [joined integrationists to create] . . . institutions and groups which influenced electoral politics."[5] Some of these groups, like the already well-established Voter Education Project, focused on increasing black voter registration and providing technical support for black candidates. Others, like the Freedom Now Party and the Lowndes County Freedom Organization (also known as the Black Panther Party), were third-party efforts designed to provide more-radical alternatives to the two major parties. But by far the majority of African Americans waged insurgent campaigns within the Democratic Party itself, often building their own campaign infrastructure independent from, and in opposition to, white-dominated Democratic organizations. Notable examples of this strategy are the Mississippi Freedom Democratic Party, the National Democratic Party of Alabama, and the many black Democratic clubs created by black activists and elected officials across the country. And their efforts met with stunning success. By 1975, 3,499 African Americans held elected office across the country. Blacks increased not only their share of political offices but the caliber of those offices as well. By 1975, 18 blacks sat in the House of Representatives and 1 in the Senate; another 281 served in state legislatures or executives; and 152 served as mayors, including in the major cities of Flint, Michigan (1966), Gary, Indiana (1967), Cleveland, Ohio (1967), Newark, New Jersey (1970), Los Angeles, California (1973), Detroit, Michigan (1974), Atlanta, Georgia (1974), and Washington, D.C. (first elected, 1975).[6]

Fired by the ideology of Black Power, these black elected officials attempted to work together to determine and achieve group goals. In 1969, black members of Congress created the Democratic Select Committee, later to become the Congressional Black Caucus (CBC), for the purpose of "organizing a black national constituency." In 1972, the National Black Assembly, a broad coalition including nearly every major black political formation in the country, hosted the National Black Political Convention in Gary, Indiana, at which delegates drew up a "National Black Political Agenda." Some of the participants went on to create the National Black Independent Political Assembly to carry on the gathering's work. Far less ambitious, though critically important, were the three (1967, 1969, and 1975) National Institutes for Black Elected Public Officials. These gatherings served as networking and skill-building events for black elected officials.[7] Although these efforts at national cooperation around a black agenda failed to achieve some of their more ambitious goals, they helped to create a modern black political identity rooted in ideas of racial cooperation and group agenda setting. And these ideas were implemented in microcosm at nearly every level of government. By the late 1970s, black elected officials had created the CBC, the National Black Caucus of State Legislators (NBCSL), the National Black Caucus of Local Elected Officials (NBC-LEO), the National Conference of Black Mayors (NCBM), the National Association of Black County Officials, and black caucuses in the legislatures of nearly every state with a sizable black population. These organizations provided a forum for crafting a black political agenda and providing services and support to members. Thus, by the mid-1970s, black elected officials constituted a relatively cohesive block of insurgent elected officials seeking to alter U.S. politics in order to benefit their constituents. They were by no means revolutionaries. In fact, many black elected officials were a petty bourgeois faction that, in the words of Manning Marable, sought "clientage and accommodation to one of the major capitalist parties."[8] Whether they planned to fundamentally alter the society or not, black elected officials were a potential threat to white elected officials and political organizations in those areas where blacks constituted a majority or substantial minority of the population. At stake were power, patronage, government services, and each community's real and perceived relationship to the state. It is not surprising then that many whites regarded the rise of black elected officials with suspicion, anxiety, or dread.

Those emotions often manifested themselves in various forms of repression. In his work on black politics in the post–civil rights period, political scientist Robert Smith notes that there are five possible system responses to insurgent political formations: "neglect, symbolism, substantive policy, co-optation and political repression." These responses, he argues, are not mutually exclusive but rather frequently occur in combination. Indeed, Smith writes, "formal cooptation often occurs simultaneously with political repression." In making this claim, Smith was arguing, like most historians of the late 1960s and early 1970s, that the system response to the black political revolt of the late 1960s was co-optation of moderate elements (black elected officials) and repression of radical elements (black nationalists and leftists).[9] Smith's formulation is generally correct. "Radicals" or "militants" received the lion's share of state repression in this period. But black elected officials were by no means immune to repression. Smith's formulation overlooks the difficulty of categorizing black protest in the late 1960s and early 1970s. Sometimes radicals ran for office. Other times whites viewed moderate black elected officials as radicals because they did not practice the politics of deference. Still other times moderate black elected officials worked with radicals to win office (as with Kenneth Gibson in Newark) or to create a black united front (as with the 1972 Gary convention). Put differently, both black and white definitions of radical and moderate were fluid. As such, the repression so liberally applied to black radicals during the period was often also directed at black elected officials. During the Nixon years, when the repressive apparatus that had been used against the New Left was turned against the president's "political enemies," the distinction was muddied further still.

State and Local White Resistance

Writing in 1968, journalist and former aide to Representative Adam Clayton Powell Jr. (D-N.Y.) Chuck Stone outlined the difficulties that would accompany the rise of black political power in predominantly black areas: "It can be comfortably predicted that whites will continue to resist black political advancement, not solely on the basis of race, but also because no group enjoys the surrender of power. If race tensions escalate . . . then black political breakthroughs will be resisted by both the white population and white politicians who now serve predominantly black constituencies or districts with a significant percentage of black people."[10] In the years after 1968, racial tensions did increase, and many white elected officials used the white public's increasing racial anxieties to resist blacks' efforts to win elected office. This resistance, not surprisingly, was most intense in the Black Belt counties of the Deep South and the majority-black cities of the industrial North.

Some of these efforts took the form of increased white registration for the purpose of offsetting the upsurge in black registration and/or efforts to purge blacks from the rolls. In the years following passage of the VRA, southern whites flocked to the registrar's office, constituting 60 to 70 percent of the new enrollees. This spike in white registration was sometimes orchestrated by white elected officials. In Alabama during the 1966 gubernatorial campaign, Governor George Wallace (D) worked hard to register one hundred thousand new white voters for the express purpose of nullifying black gains. White elected officials in other states attempted to scrub newly registered blacks from the rolls. In 1971, the State of Mississippi ordered the reregistration of voters in thirty counties that had witnessed a marked increase in black voting. In the cities, whites used similar tactics to beat back black challenges to white incumbents. In 1967, city councilman Richard Hatcher overcame voter fraud and threats of violence by Gary, Indiana, white Democrats to secure the 1967 Democratic nomination for mayor. Immediately following the primary, the defeated white Democratic machine came out in support of the Republican candidate Joseph Radigan, and together Gary's white Democrats and Republicans commenced an ambitious campaign of voter fraud designed to steal the general election. White registrars purged several thousand black voters' names from the roles while simultaneously registering several thousand "ghost voters" in white precincts. On Election Day, teams of "iron workers" and "prostitutes," under the direction of the Democratic machine, were to travel from precinct to precinct, voting these ghost voters' names. With the help of several investigative reporters and the DOJ, Hatcher headed off the scheme and emerged victorious on Election Day. In 1970, Morgan State University professor and antipoverty administrator Parren Mitchell challenged eight-term incumbent Samuel Friedel (D-Md.) for the seat from the Seventh Congressional District in Baltimore. The election was a squeaker with each candidate claiming victory by a margin of only several hundred votes. Subsequent investigations by the U.S. Civil Rights Commission determined that members of the Baltimore City Board of Supervisors of Elections loyal to Friedel had engaged in a host of fraudulent activities that disfranchised several hundred black voters. After a number of recounts, Friedel conceded the election to Mitchell in early October.[11]

Even in defeat, some whites refused to accept the reality of black electoral victories. For example, in the first election held after the VRA went into effect, the black voters of Hancock County, Georgia, elevated voting rights activist Robert Ingram to a place on the all-white county school board. When Ingram presented himself for seating, the board chairman, who was then still leading local white resistance to the implementation of *Brown v. Board*, charged that Ingram was ineligible to serve because he had been convicted for a liquor-law violation (possession) in 1945. Ingram was forced to wait for one month while the attorney general examined his case. Several months later, the board's white majority again sought to remove Ingram, who worked at the Milledgeville State Hospital, using a law that barred elected officials from holding state jobs. Ingram was subsequently forced to find alternative employment.[12] Ingram's experience was by no means an isolated incident. In 1969, following the election of future Mississippi congressman Bennie Thompson and two other African Americans to the Bolton, Mississippi, Board of Aldermen in the Democratic primary, local whites asked the Democratic Executive Committee to void the election. They charged that Thompson and his supporters had violated the Mississippi Code by constantly checking the voter rolls and arguing with white poll workers if black voters' names were not properly listed. When the executive committee refused to act, these whites sued in county court. Thompson countersued in federal court, alleging that local whites had violated provisions of the VRA. Following a six-month legal battle, Thompson and his slate emerged victorious and were seated. Four years later, when Thompson and his all-black slate swept the mayor's office, the board of aldermen, and the Democratic Executive Committee, white incumbents again attempted to void the election and keep their seats, first before the white-dominated, lame-duck Democratic Executive Committee and then, when Thompson and his slate challenged the committee's ruling, in county court. Thompson again succeeded in having the case removed to federal court, where his slate again emerged victorious, this time after only four months.[13]

Once black elected officials assumed office, many white voters and elected officials worked to frustrate their ability to govern by making spurious allegations of mismanagement or fraud. Bennie Thompson recalled that during his tenure as a member of the Hinds County Board of Supervisors the state auditor's office "would get complaints every year filed by [white] citizens." As Thompson related, "A disproportionate number [were] filed against you because you're Black. . . Well, you know, it may or may not have been true. But it was always Johnny on the Spot by the Auditor's Office when those complaints were called in on me. But when similar complaints were called in on my white counterparts they just said, 'Well, if they keep it up, let us know.'"[14] In Macon County, Alabama, Sheriff Lucius Amerson, the first African American to hold that title in the South since Reconstruction, complained that county whites had made a "concerted effort to discredit Blacks in office so that they [were] unable to keep voter support [of both blacks and whites] in coming elections." In Amerson's case, Macon County whites had spread rumors that he was cheating on his wife with a white woman; that his wife, an employee of the local Head Start program, had mistreated local children; and that the jail under Amerson's stewardship was unsanitary and dangerous. The latter complaint stimulated an inquiry by the FBI, which had not much cared about the state of the Macon County jail prior to Amerson's election. Sometimes these false allegations were made by representatives of the state. In March 1968, two white representatives of the Mississippi Alcohol Beverage Control Division demanded that Wilkinson County, Mississippi, supervisor James Joliff allow them to search his business without a warrant. He refused and was promptly indicted for obstruction by the local district attorney. Despite "the testimony of six black witnesses that contradicted the agents' claims," historian Christopher Danielson writes, a majority-white jury (ten whites and two blacks) found him guilty. As a convicted felon, Joliff was forced to resign his position as county supervisor, a result, the county leader of the NAACP and Deacons for Defense argued, that local whites had been pursuing all along. The Mississippi Supreme Court later confirmed Joliff's claim when it overturned the verdict, arguing that the agents had acted illegally. Joliff was subsequently reelected by the black voters of Wilkerson County in 1971. His case was unique only in degree. In 1973, political scientist Lester Salamon found that half of the Mississippi black elected officials he interviewed stated that whites subjected them to some form of obstruction upon entering office.[15]

Allegations of fraud designed to remove blacks from office were not peculiar to the Black Belt South. The experiences of Cleveland, Ohio, mayor Carl Stokes (D) are instructive. Writing in his 1972 autobiography *Promises of Power*, Stokes states: "I was investigated by everyone from Cleveland's lowliest Polish housewife to the highest agencies of the United States government: my own Police Department, all of the Cleveland-area papers, the strike force set up to fight organized crime, the Justice Department, the Internal Revenue Service, were all in Cleveland and anywhere I'd ever been, investigating me because of rumors, allegations and accusations."[16] The former mayor did not overstate his case. In 1969, reporters for the *Willoughby News-Herald*, a small newspaper headquartered in the Cleveland suburbs, and the *Cleveland Plain Dealer*, Cleveland's paper of note, traveled to the Bahamas to investigate rumors that Stokes had financial ties with the underworld figures then building casinos and hotels on the islands. Upon their return, the *Plain Dealer* reporters filed an internal memo stating that they were unable to find any evidence to confirm the allegations. Upon her return, Doris O'Donnell, of the *News-Herald*, wrote a four-part series on the subject of underworld figures investing in the Bahamas, the lead article of which insinuated that Stokes was somehow tied to these individuals. She had no evidentiary basis for the claim. In response, Stokes filed a two-million-dollar libel suit, forcing the paper's editor to enter into negotiations for a settlement.[17] Between 1968 and 1971, the Cleveland Organized Crime Task Force conducted multiple investigations of allegations of illegal conduct by Stokes and members of his administration. Not a single accusation, investigators stated in an April 1971 press conference announcing the conclusion of the investigation, proved true. Several members of the task force conceded that they expected such an outcome when they first opened the cases, as all the accusations were made by Stokes's political opponents and based on rumors and hearsay. The task force nonetheless pursued these spurious allegations for the better part of Stokes's two terms in office.[18] Stokes also found his administration being investigated by the Cuyahoga County prosecutor's office. County prosecutor John Corrigan, who had held the office since 1956, had, as far as Stokes could recall, "never investigated the activities of the Democrats who [had] dominated the county commissioner's office for decades . . . [and] never investigated the activities at City Hall until the Stokes administration." During Stokes's two terms, Corrigan, who often fought with the mayor over control of the county Democratic organization, conducted two wide-ranging probes of the administration. The political battles that stimulated these investigations became so bad that in 1972 Stokes determined not to run for reelection, claiming that the political atmosphere had become too poisonous.[19]

Whites also worked hard to undercut black efforts at self-determination by making unfounded allegations of fraud against black-led War on Poverty Community Action Programs. In the late 1960s and early 1970s, African Americans used the Office of Economic Opportunity's Community Action Program and similar foundation-run programs to reduce their dependence on white economic and political elites. Often the black activists who worked to build these programs were one and the same with those who were building black political power. A number of recent studies have uncovered evidence that southern white powerbrokers regularly used allegations of fraud against antipoverty programs to undermine black efforts to gain economic independence and political power. Many of these investigations directly implicated black elected officials.[20] In Hancock County, Georgia, which hosted the largest antipoverty program in the South, the East Central Committee for Opportunity (ECCO), allegations of fraud made by local whites sparked a series of audits and investigations that ultimately doomed the program. Between 1973 and 1976, the ECCO was audited by the Office of Economic Opportunity at the request of Governor Jimmy Carter (D), the General Accounting Office (GAO) and the DOJ at the request of Senator Sam Nunn (D-Ga.), the IRS, and the Oconee Regional Narcotics Squad. In 1976, these multiple investigations led to the indictment of ten ECCO-affiliated elected officials and program employees.[21] Although only one of the individuals indicted was convicted outright, the investigations irreparably damaged the organization. By 1976, nearly all of the ECCO's government and foundation funding was revoked, all but ending its experiment in black economic self-determination.

Though political struggles such as those seen in Hancock County may have characterized the rise of black political power in the Black Belt, they were by no means the dominant trend for the country. The primary means of repression directed at black elected officials during this period was not the overt repression of the Black Belt South but the covert repression of the surveillance state.

The Surveillance State

The black revolt of the 1960s stimulated a number of related social uprisings within other segments of the U.S. population. Inspired by the sacrifices of civil rights activists and the dash of Black Power militants, students, women, Native Americans, Chicanos, gays, and a host of other groups staged their own revolts. And almost every member of this New Left lent their voices to the growing outcry against the war in Vietnam. By the late 1960s, authority figures of every stripe — police; federal, state, and municipal government; the armed forces; the upper classes; men; whites — were being challenged in new and increasingly threatening ways. To many of these political and socioeconomic elites, it appeared that the very fabric of American society was being torn asunder.[22] In response to the unrest generated by these social uprisings, municipal, state, and federal authorities initiated a dramatic expansion of state surveillance and counterintelligence.

A wildly disproportionate share of this state surveillance and counterintelligence was directed at black activists. While African Americans' outsized role in the social uprisings of the period was a contributing factor, the primary reason for this disparity was the U.S. intelligence community's long history of defining nearly all black activism as subversive. No other organization was more central to creating this definition and spreading it to the rest of the domestic intelligence community than the FBI. Bureau attitudes toward African Americans were shaped during World War I, when the Wilson administration defined all criticism of the war effort as subversion and white supremacy was a cornerstone of U.S. politics. In this atmosphere, Kenneth O'Reilly writes, the bureau defined "every black dissident as subversive." This initial response to black protest was reinforced when J. Edgar Hoover was named director of the fledgling bureaucracy in 1924. Hoover harbored a strong personal preference for racial segregation, a sincere conviction that blacks were inclined to subversion, and a dogged determination to hold his agency aloof from federal efforts to protect black civil rights. For the next fifty years, Hoover exercised a near-total domination of the bureau, and during that time he inculcated the agency with his personal racial politics. With African American demands for an end to white supremacy defined as a threat to national security, the bureau settled into a steady regimen of surveillance and counterintelligence during the Jim Crow era. Agents measured and filed annual reports on black public opinion, built dossiers on black activists, and disrupted black radicalism. Simultaneously, they studiously ignored flagrant violations of black civil rights, North and South.[23]

The bureau made little distinction between black protest leaders and black elected officials during this period. Indeed, bureau spying tended to increase when black protest leaders sought political office. In June 1942, for example, Hoover turned his attention to Adam Clayton Powell Jr., directing the New York field division to open a file on the young city councilman. The director sought "background information on Powell, his connections and affiliations, radical activities into which he [had] entered and his connection with the Communist party," in light of "strong indications of Communist affiliation on the part of Powell." Powell, however, had been "linked" with the Communist Party (CPUSA) on several previous occasions. The New York field division had written numerous reports to Washington, connecting Powell with the CPUSA and alleged communist-front organizations as early as the mid-1930s, reports that Hoover acknowledged in his June 29 memo. The director's actual reason for concern had come only days before, on June 16, 1942, when Powell announced his intention to run for the newly drawn, majority-black Twenty-second Congressional District. Powell's winning campaign, which was shadowed by bureau surveillance of almost all of his fund-raising events and speeches, inaugurated twenty-six years of nearly unbroken FBI surveillance.[24]

During the black revolt of the 1960s, the FBI dramatically increased surveillance and counterintelligence against black activists and, by extension, black elected officials. The catalyst for this development was the March on Washington for Jobs and Freedom. In the early years of the movement, Hoover had done his best to avoid civil rights enforcement, hoping that the movement would collapse if left to face the repression of state and local white authorities on its own. But the march, O'Reilly argues, "convinced Hoover that the civil rights movement would not wither away on its own, that he would have to smash it before it irreparably damaged his America." Immediately following the march, Hoover directed the FBI to conduct a counterintelligence campaign against the civil rights movement designed to "expose, disrupt or otherwise neutralize" activists. Two years later, when urban rebellions flared in several of America's major cities and Black Power became the rallying cry of a new generation of activists, Hoover dramatically expanded FBI attacks on the black community by constructing "a pervasive two-track surveillance system." He directed his agents to "smash the vanguard (black political activists of liberal and radical views) and to keep track of the masses (the everyday people who lived in black communities)." To these ends, in 1967 the bureau initiated a series of COIN-TELPROS against black activists and organizations. Simultaneously, the FBI and many police departments cultivated an army of "racial ghetto type informants" who reported on any and every form of black political activity. In 1968 there were thirty-three hundred such informants operating under the direction of the FBI in black communities across the nation. By 1972, that number had reached seventy-five hundred.[25]

Because of their connection to target constituencies, black elected officials experienced heavy FBI surveillance and counterintelligence during this period. From 1968 to (at least) 1974, the FBI placed California state assemblyman Leon Ralph (D-Los Angeles) under surveillance, wiretapping his office, stealing documents, and photographing others. Ralph was by no means a radical. He appears to have been targeted for no other reason than that he represented the black communities of Watts and Compton.[26] In the early 1970s, the office phones of Representative Ronald Dellums (D-Calif.) were tapped for various periods of time, and his Berkeley congressional office was, as he recalled, "trashed, firebombed and vandalized on at least five occasions." Dellums, a congressional icon of the New Left, suspected that the bureau was the culprit and declared as much at an April 1973 press conference.[27] In the early 1970s, FBI surveillance of Chicago black nationalists led them to create an intelligence file on Representative Ralph Metcalfe (D-Ill.). Metcalfe's crime, in the bureau's eyes, was being seen at meetings with militant black leaders.[28] In 1972, the FBI classified Birmingham, Alabama, city councilman Richard Arrington (D) as a "Key Black Extremist" who would be summarily arrested in the case of a national emergency. The pretext for this classification was Arrington's alleged association with the Black Panther Party and the Alabama Black Liberation Front, groups with which the politically moderate former zoology professor had no association. Arrington's active opposition to the Birmingham Police Department's brutal treatment of black city residents, on the other hand, appears to have been what brought him to the bureau's attention.[29]

In 1967, as protest increased across the country, the FBI was joined in its domestic spying efforts by a host of other federal agencies. That year, the CIA, the National Security Agency (NSA), and Military Intelligence commenced extensive domestic spying campaigns. Though to a far lesser degree than the FBI, these organizations also spied on black elected officials. The phones of Detroit representative John Conyers (D-Mich.) were tapped by the FBI and CIA. Following the 1968 riots in Washington, D.C., Military Intelligence monitored the activities of Mayor Walter Washington (D) and most of the city's other black political leaders. The FBI and Military Intelligence collected surveillance information on Maryland state senator Clarence Mitchell III (D-Baltimore). Georgia state representative Julian Bond was placed under surveillance by the FBI, Military Intelligence, and the CIA for his antiwar speeches and frequent criticisms of the Nixon administration. His fellow Atlanta elected official, city councilman Hosea Williams, was also subjected to FBI and CIA surveillance.[30]

Black elected officials were also subject to surveillance and counterintelligence by state and municipal police intelligence units during this period. Seeking to fill the void left by the FBI's intelligence focus on the old Left and in reaction to the uniquely local problems of civil rights agitation, urban rebellions, campus unrest, and antiwar protests, hundreds of states and municipalities created intelligence units in the mid-1960s. By 1972, approximately five hundred such units existed across the country. Trained in surveillance and counterintelligence by federal agencies as diverse as the CIA, the FBI, Military Intelligence, and the IRS, and subject to minimal oversight, these "miniature FBI's," as one historian has called them, targeted "everyone and anyone involved in protest activities."[31] And no one received more attention from these groups than African Americans.

At the root of police intelligence unit repression of black elected officials was police hostility to the black community. For the first half of the twentieth century North and South, police assumed the role of maintaining a racially unjust status quo. They patrolled the boundaries of the ghettos in the North and enforced segregation and disfranchisement in the South. In the 1950s and 1960s, when African Americans commenced a sustained assault on those boundaries, police attitudes hardened against the black community. In a 1966 DOJ report exploring the racial attitudes of police officers in Boston, Chicago, and Washington, D.C., researchers noted that 72 percent of the patrolmen they interviewed *volunteered* statements expressing "extreme prejudice" or "considerable prejudice" against African Americans.[32] It is noteworthy that these attitudes were registered *before* the major riots of 1967 and 1968, for during the riots, police attitudes toward African Americans reached a new low. Researchers argue that police developed a "siege mentality" during the conflagrations. Believing that they were outmanned and outgunned by an insurgent black population, many police determined that they were in a war setting in which they and the black community were the combatants. Among these officers, "'law and order' became a coded battle cry," Frank Donner tells us, "as the police were transformed into an army defending white power and the status quo."[33] This hostility toward the black community was easily transferred to its representatives in government, black elected officials.

Many black elected officials' names first entered police intelligence organizations' files in response to their civil rights or Black Power activism. As Manning Marable notes, "Most black reformist leaders and community leaders with histories of involvement in social protest movements fell under local police scrutiny years before they sought public office."[34] But whether blacks engaged in protest or electoral activity, and regardless of whether they were radicals or moderates, many of these organizations placed them under surveillance just the same. As Donner writes in his study of police intelligence units, "the heavy surveillance of blacks . . . not only in large cities but even in smaller ones and towns, was considered self-justifying."[35] A brief look at police intelligence unit surveillance of the black congresspeople during this time is instructive. In the early 1970s, the Michigan State Police intelligence unit placed Representative John Conyers (D-Mich.) under surveillance. Around the same time, the intelligence unit of the Houston Police Department created a noncriminal intelligence file on Representative Barbara Jordan (D-Tex.). In the early to mid-1970s, the intelligence division of the New York State Police created noncriminal intelligence files on Representatives Charles Rangel (D-N.Y.) and Shirley Chisholm (D-N.Y.). Between 1968 and 1974, the Inspectional Services Division of the Baltimore Police Department, an intelligence unit closely tied to the FBI, placed Representative Parren Mitchell (D-Md.) under twenty-four-hour surveillance, illegally bugged his home and office telephones for eight months, and placed paid informers in his congressional campaigns.[36]

Though these intelligence units generally refrained from conducting counterintelligence against black elected officials, the very reality of surveillance was, for many of the targets, a frightening revelation. On more than one occasion, Representative Mitchell was threateningly informed by Baltimore police commissioner Donald Pomerleau that he and many of his colleagues in Baltimore's Left-liberal political coalition, including his nephew state senator Clarence Mitchell III (D-Baltimore), were being watched. Recalling Inspectional Services Division surveillance from the vantage of the late seventies, Mitchell noted that it had a "psychological impact" on him that he could only describe as "surrealistic."[37]

In the Deep South, these police intelligence operations were supplemented by the avowedly segregationist "sovereignty" and "peace" commissions created by southern state governments in the years after *Brown v. Board*. In 1956, the Mississippi legislature created the Mississippi Sovereignty Commission (MSC), a propaganda and surveillance organization charged with the task of performing "any and all acts and things deemed necessary and proper to protect the sovereignty of the State of Mississippi" — that is, segregation. Throughout the late 1950s and the 1960s, the MSC funneled state monies to the Citizens' Councils, spied on black activists, and fed pro-segregationist propaganda to the local and national media. Following the Magnolia State's example, Louisiana, Georgia, and Alabama created similar organizations in the early 1960s. In 1968, these four states created a short-lived Interstate Sovereignty Association to promote regional cooperation in resistance to the civil rights movement. Though sometimes comically inept in their surveillance activities — the MSC, for instance, never had any bugging equipment, did not purchase cameras for its investigators until the early 1960s, and relied on private detective agencies to do much of its spying — these organizations nonetheless created massive libraries of intelligence dossiers on southern "subversives." For instance, the MSC gathered intelligence dossiers on alderman Bennie Thompson (D-Bolton), Mayor Charles Evers (D-Fayetteville), Representative Fred L. Banks Jr. (D-Jackson), and a host of other Mississippi black activists and elected officials. In the early 1970s, the Alabama Peace Commission placed Macon County sheriff Lucius Amerson (D), Birmingham city councilman Richard Arrington (D), and state senator J. Richmond Pearson (D-Leroy) under surveillance. By the early 1970s, due in large measure to the moderating influence of black voters, these agencies fell out of favor with white southern elected officials and were shuttered.[38]

Though it was not an intelligence organization, a politicized IRS subjected black elected officials to surveillance and counterintelligence in the decade following passage of the VRA. Since the early days of the twentieth century, presidents had used the IRS on a case-by-case basis to gather information on and harass their political enemies and individuals who they believed posed a threat to the social order. At the suggestion of a young J. Edgar Hoover, President Herbert Hoover began the practice in 1931, and nearly every president to follow him into the Oval Office up to (at least) 1976 used the nation's tax service in a similar manner. Lyndon Johnson was no exception to this rule.[39] For example, in January 1967, newly elected California state senator Mervyn Dymally (D-Watts) attended a White House reception for Democratic Party activists. During the reception, a *Washington Post* reporter asked Dymally his thoughts on the Vietnam War, to which he offered strong criticism of the White House's policy in Southeast Asia. The following day, much to the chagrin of the Johnson administration, Dymally's remarks were published in the *Post*. Days later, back in his California office, Dymally received a visit from representatives of the felony unit of the IRS who had just opened a criminal investigation of his tax returns. He was subsequently audited three times over the course of the next several years. "One year," Dymally recalls, "they got me for about six dollars. Another year, they got me for per diem. In California, all legislators receive the equivalent of what was the standardized federal allowance for travel every day. There had been a gentlemen's agreement in effect between the IRS and the legislature that we did not pay taxes on our per diem, but now they said I had to pay those taxes." Though none would proceed to indictment, the tax investigations took a financial toll on the state senator. Between the three investigations, Dymally spent several thousand dollars on his legal defense. There was little doubt in his mind that the Johnson administration had ordered the investigations in retaliation for his comments to the *Post*. Considering Johnson's prolific use of the FBI and the IRS to attack critics of his Vietnam policy, Dymally's suspicions are amply justified by the record. The president, had, in fact, asked the FBI to run Dymally's name — along with that of thirty other prominent black Democrats attending the same White House reception — through FBI files prior to his visit. The check of Dymally's file uncovered undisclosed "derogatory information," which was passed on to the president.[40]

Examples of executive misuse of the IRS abound in the years before 1969. But before Richard Nixon entered the White House, attempts to use the IRS as a political weapon were, in the words of Frank Donner, "for the most part, reactive, sporadic, and directed at particular targets rather than a class or category of taxpayers."[41] In the summer of 1969, however, the IRS, under intense pressure from the Nixon White House and the Permanent Subcommittee on Investigations of the Senate Government Operations Committee, chaired by Senator John McClellan (D-Ark.), created a secret counterintelligence unit called the Special Services Staff (SSS). The mission of the SSS was to aggressively audit "predominantly dissident and extremist organizations," with the intention of diverting resources and manpower from their political activities. In its four years of operation, the SSS opened files on 8,585 individuals and 2,873 organizations. Fully 41 percent of these files focused on African American activists and organizations. Although it is unclear how many of these individuals were black elected officials, without question they were included in this group. In 1971, for instance, the SSS placed Congressman Charles Diggs (D-Mich.), then the most senior African American in Congress, on a "special watch list for examination of his taxes." The SSS was abolished on August 7, 1973, one day after *Time* magazine revealed its existence to the public.[42]

Around the same time that the SSS was shut down, the IRS created another intelligence operation. In May 1973, tax bureaucrats created the Intelligence Gathering Retrieval Service (IGRS), a computer database designed to house material with "potential tax consequences" on dissident individuals and organizations. The rationale for the IGRS was that the IRS should be ready to assist law enforcement if "subversive" individuals or organizations broke the law. To this end, the IGRS used tax forms, news reports, and intelligence gathered by a small army of spies and informers to build dossiers on over 460,000 individuals and organizations. Donner notes that in the California regional office, the IGRS was used almost exclusively to spy on liberal elected officials, African Americans, and left-wing political leaders: "The IGRS political thrust is confirmed by a selective printout of 102 names of IGRS file subjects leaked to the public in late spring 1975. . . . The printout is crowded with political figures — a few conservatives but mostly liberals of assorted hues, anti-war activists, ghetto leaders, and the like." Mayor Thomas Bradley (D-Los Angeles) and Congressman Augustus Hawkins (D-Calif.), then the most powerful African American elected officials in California, were on the leaked IGRS list. Like the SSS, the IGRS was shuttered after its existence was exposed by the news media in early 1975.[43]

Although IRS officials in Washington engaged in a remarkably high degree of political targeting, they were far outstripped by their counterparts in regional IRS offices. Reporter Jason Berry outlined this pattern in a 1976 article for *The Nation* magazine titled "The IRS Bullies the New South." Having worked as Fayette, Mississippi, mayor Charles Evers's press secretary during his 1971 run for governor, Berry had glimpsed southern IRS offices use of the tax system to repress black leadership firsthand. Evers had faced a state tax audit in 1970 and a federal audit in 1972. The federal audit led to a criminal investigation and then an indictment for tax evasion in 1975. During the initial federal investigation, twenty-six members of the black-led Mississippi Loyalist Democratic Party, of which Evers was a leader, were audited as well. Four days into Evers's trial, the judge declared a mistrial in response to the improper testimony of an IRS agent. The guilt or innocence of Evers and his compatriots aside, Berry found such a high incidence of audits among such a small number of black activists highly suspicious. In 1975, he sought to discover how widespread the use of the IRS for political purposes was in the South.[44] When Berry published his findings in the spring of 1976, the recently concluded Watergate hearings and congressional hearings on the U.S. intelligence community had already uncovered evidence that the federal executive branch had employed the IRS as a tool to punish its political enemies. Following the pronouncements of the Church Committee, many Americans believed that the politicization of the nation's tax service began at the top. "That is true in the case of Richard Nixon's Enemies List, and the Special Services Staff (SSS) of the IRS," Berry wrote. "But the real erosion of the Internal Revenue Service as a purely tax-collecting agency began in the 1960s, at the bottom, in regional districts and local offices." Southern elites, Berry argued, had employed the IRS in their assault on the civil rights movement long before

Nixon had pressured the Washington office to engage in similar forms of repression. Unlike the Washington office, however, which had ceased political audits following news media exposure of the sss and the IGRS, southern regional offices had continued to employ them against "black elected officials, activists, liberals, and businessmen" through 1976.[45]

A close look at the southern states that Berry cites in his report supports his contention. In Alabama, for instance, state senator U. W. Clemon (D-Bessemer) was audited every single year between 1968 and 1974. The audits appeared to be for purposes other than revenue collection. "They don't get money," Clemon stated to Berry, "but they just keep coming back." Clemon's colleague in the lower chamber, Representative Thomas Reed (D-Tuskegee), was also targeted by the IRS due to his civil rights and political activities. In 1976, Reed told one interviewer that his state and federal tax returns had been audited four times in the previous twelve years. In all, five of the thirteen African Americans in the Alabama legislature and two black Alabama sheriffs were audited by the IRS in the early 1970s.[46]

The pattern was the same in Georgia. In October 1970, only days after he helped to stage the Mohammed Ali–Jerry Quarry fight in Atlanta, state senator Leroy Johnson (D-Atlanta) received a visit from representatives of the felony unit of the IRS. "Two days after the fight, IRS agents came to my home at 7:30 a.m.," Johnson told journalist Carl Rowan, "and they've been after me ever since." Following a four-year investigation, a grand jury indicted Johnson on four counts of tax evasion in May 1974 — only months before the August primary in which he was up for reelection. Unable to recover from the indictment, Johnson lost the primary to a black challenger. In the ensuing trial, the weakness of the government's case was revealed when two of the counts were dismissed and the jury of nine whites and three blacks acquitted Johnson on the two remaining counts. During the trial, it was learned that Johnson had overpaid his taxes for the years under investigation. He was subsequently refunded six thousand dollars.[47] Jurors found Johnson guilty, however, of the obscure felony charge of allowing a false affidavit to be given to the IRS on his behalf. Following the exhaustion of his appeals, Johnson reported to prison in October 1976. Because of the felony conviction, Johnson, only years before one of the most powerful black elected officials in the South, was barred from practicing law or holding government office upon his release. There was little question that the IRS investigation of Johnson was part of a larger attack on Atlanta black elected officials. Between 1974 and 1976, the tax returns of Georgia state senator Julian Bond, Representative Henrietta Canty, Representative Hosea Williams, Representative Ben Brown, Representative Douglass Dean, Representative James McKinney, city councilman Ira Jackson, and city councilman Carl Ware — all black Democrats of Atlanta — were audited by the IRS.[48]

In all, Berry found that "more than fifty prominent members of black liberal alliances in Deep South states [had] been audited or investigated" between
1973 and 1976. Noting that only about 2 percent of Americans were audited
annually by the IRS in the early 1970s, Berry determined that "the statistical
probability that such a pattern of audits could be legitimate is highly unlikely."
When he further considered that "Southern activists who were audited paid
few adjustments, and those who did were assessed under highly questionable
IRS decisions," Berry concluded that "in Mississippi, Tennessee, Georgia, and
Alabama [the four states he covered in his study] the IRS function[ed], in effect,
as an arm of political systems which [were] trying by economic means to keep
blacks out of power."[49]

Disturbed by the audits of the Mississippi Loyalist Democratic Party,
which sparked the Berry article, Congressman Charlie Rangel (D-N.Y.) asked
the House Ways and Means Committee, Subcommittee on Oversight, to investigate in late 1975. The subcommittee directed the General Accounting Office
to conduct an investigation. The GAO's findings, published in 1978, exoner-
ated the Mississippi IRS agents but did not explain the high incidence of audits. Investigators discovered that twenty-four of the activists in question (the
original news story had listed twenty-eight) had been audited a collective total
of forty-five times between 1970 and 1975, fully 28 percent of the 161 tax returns that they had filed during that period. A year-by-year breakdown shows
that in 1972, more than 50 percent of the activists' tax returns were audited.
The GAO nonetheless dismissed Berry's charges as "unsupported." It came to
this conclusion through voluntary interviews with members of the Jackson,
Mississippi, regional office and an examination of their field notes. Though federal investigators concluded that the opportunity for abuse did exist, they could
not find any affirmative evidence of the same.[50] No action was taken against
the IRS officials in Jackson or any of the other southern states covered in the
Berry article.

The Nixon Administration and the Hyperpoliticization
of Surveillance and Counterintelligence

From the time he entered office, Richard Nixon coupled the covert repression
of the police and intelligence agencies with an overt appeal for "law and order."
In the political lexicon of the Nixon administration, student protesters, black
militants, civil rights activists, and young adherents of the counterculture became enemies of the state. These groups were responsible for the "growth of
permissiveness" in American society. Simultaneously, Nixon worked to con-
nect these groups to the "northeastern liberal elite" of the Democratic Party.
As Kenneth O'Reilly has argued, "Nixon had an answer to the decade's basic

paradox: Why had ghetto riots and a rise in crime, welfare dependency, illegitimacy, drug abuse, and joblessness followed the Great Society's civil rights revolution and expanded social service entitlements? His answer was a simple one: There were no structural problems of race or class, only 'excesses' caused by 'the malaise of affluence' and bleeding heart liberalism." Thus liberal Democrats, perhaps even more than political dissidents, were a threat to the social order because they had loosed an assortment of "hardcore unemployed . . . laggards . . . muggers . . . rapists . . . welfare cheats . . . [and] street punks," in Nixon's words, upon the hard-working, tax-paying white middle and working classes. In exchange for their votes, Nixon promised to protect "the silent majority" from these criminals, social degenerates, and their fellow travelers in the Democratic Party.[51]

In 1968, Nixon had used these themes to transform white middle- and working-class disaffection with liberal reform into a rejection of the national Democratic Party. His victory, however, had been remarkably slim because he had shared the disaffected white vote with George Wallace, who captured much of the old Confederacy. Once in office, Nixon sought to bring these Wallace voters into the Republican Party and in so doing create a realignment of American politics. Always the shrewd campaigner, Nixon used the 1970 midterm elections to begin building the political coalition that he hoped to amass in 1972. Early in the campaign season, the president dispatched Vice President Spiro Agnew on a multistate tour targeting the administration's detractors in the Senate. The tour, in Agnew's words, was to be a "national campaign to determine the leadership of the seventies . . . a second critical phase in the historic contest begun in the fall of 1968 — a contest between the remnants of the discredited elite that dominated national policy for forty years and a new national majority, forged and led by the President of the United States."[52] Agnew's attacks on "radical-liberals," "permissiveness," "forced busing," and "welfare cheats," however, did not pay dividends. Democrats lost only two seats in the Senate and gained nine in the House. In an election postmortem, White House special counsel Charles Colson argued, "Except in the urban Northeast, we did not succeed in making the public believe that Democratic, Liberal permissiveness was the cause of violence and crime. . . . We didn't sell the point that violence and disorder in our society are caused directly by the rhetoric, softness, and catering to dissidents which the Democrats have engaged in."[53]

As described above, Nixon responded to this information by putting increased pressure on the intelligence community to expand federal surveillance and counterintelligence of dissident groups and his political opponents. Although the federal intelligence community continued to expand to meet the White House's intelligence and counterintelligence demands, Nixon and his aides were dissatisfied with the pace and effect of these agencies' actions.

Determined to overcome these bureaucrats' seeming timidity, the White House sought first to guide their hands and then, as the 1972 election campaign loomed, to go around them by creating an independent surveillance and counterintelligence operation answerable only to the president.

In August 1971, John Dean, counsel to the president, delivered a memo to President Nixon suggesting a strategy for dealing with his political enemies. In the memo, Dean suggested that the president create a list of his critics and political opponents — "a small list of names — not more than ten" — to be targeted for political repression. The list would be turned over to a "project co-ordinator" (Lyn Nofziger, deputy assistant to the president for congressional relations, is mentioned as the "most knowledgeable and the most interested") who would be charged with "determin[ing] what sorts of dealings these individuals [had] with the federal government and how [the administration could] best screw them (e.g. grant availability, federal contracts, litigation, prosecution, etc.)." Nixon enthusiastically accepted Dean's suggestion and created several lists containing approximately seven hundred names. In his testimony before the Senate Watergate committee, Dean indicated that the administration had directed the IRS to use tax audits to harass and intimidate the individuals on the lists. Historian John Andrew estimates that approximately half the people on the lists were, in fact, audited by the IRS and a lesser percentage were investigated by the FBI.[54]

The most famous of Nixon's "enemies lists," as they came to be called, included the names of two hundred Democratic elected officials, fund-raisers, donors, journalists, celebrities, and academics who had criticized the administration. Of the two hundred persons on the list, twenty-three were African American — twelve of those being members of the CBC. Members of the CBC included on the list were Ronald Dellums, Charles Diggs, Shirley Chisholm, William Clay, George Collins, John Conyers, Augustus Hawkins, Ralph Metcalfe, Parren Mitchell, Robert Nix, Charles Rangel, and Louis Stokes. Dellums and Conyers also appeared on a special sublist of "priority" targets sent to White House counsel John Dean on September 9, 1971, by Charles Colson. Attacking Dellums, Colson wrote, "might help [Nixon's reelection chances] in California next year." Conyers, he believed, was more of a direct threat, noting that the Detroit congressman was "emerging as a leading black anti-Nixon spokesman." His "known weakness for white females," Colson offered, might provide an avenue for discrediting him.[55] In 1971, the CBC consisted of thirteen legislators, making the president's list a declaration of war on the voting representatives of the national black community. D.C. delegate Walter Fauntroy — the only sitting member of the caucus to escape inclusion on the list — was a nonvoting member of the House of Representatives. He was nonetheless subject to federal surveillance. In the 1960s, the Secret Service had opened a dossier on Fauntroy in his capacity as director of the Washington bureau of the SCLC. Fauntroy's file remained active until 1975, three years *after* he was elected to Congress.[56]

Though the bureaucracy was responsive to White House requests to repress black Democrats and nonstate actors, it often hedged when directed to attack high-ranking white Democrats or engage in overtly partisan behavior for which it could not manufacture a national security rationale. Frustrated by federal bureaucrats' reticence and fearing a tough challenge in 1972 from Senator Edwin Muskie (D-Maine), the White House created a political espionage unit within the Committee to Reelect the President (CRP) for the purpose of conducting spying and "dirty tricks" against Democratic presidential candidates. Using a motley assortment of thirty former spooks, police officers, and party hacks, the CRP infiltrated Democratic primary campaigns, stole confidential information, bugged the offices of opposition candidates, and spread malicious rumors about Democratic candidates in the press and among target groups of voters. Because they were directed at Democratic presidential candidates, few of these operations targeted black elected officials. Representative Shirley Chisholm, who was then conducting an ill-fated campaign for the Democratic nomination, appears to have been the only black target.[57]

These measures proved to be unnecessary. In a bruising and chaotic primary, made all the more so by CRP's activities, Democrats nominated Senator George McGovern (D-S.Dak.) as their standard-bearer. McGovern's strength in the primaries had been his support by student and antiwar activists, some of the very people Nixon was seeking to build an antireform majority against. Upon discovering that McGovern had secured the nomination, Nixon confided to his diary that Republicans had a "chance not just to win the election, but to create the New Majority [they] had only dreamed of in 1970."[58] The only remaining threat to Nixon's dream of a party realignment was George Wallace. In 1968, Wallace had siphoned off many of the white Democratic voters who would have crossed party lines and joined the Republicans. A possible third-party run by the Alabama governor threatened to draw an even larger share of the "silent majority" away from Nixon in 1972. But on the afternoon of May 15, all the president's fears evaporated when Wallace was shot three times by Arthur Bremer, a lone assassin desperate to make a name for himself. Wallace would live, but the shooting had effectively ended his quest for national office.[59] With Wallace out of the race, Nixon eagerly swept up his constituency. In November, he secured all eleven states of the formerly Democratic South and received 61 percent of the popular vote. Aside from the white South, Nixon won the support of a majority of blue-collar, Catholic, and urban whites.[60] Although Nixon's victory did not translate into a realignment in Congress, he had succeeded in making the racial realignment of the presidential election of 1968 a party realignment in 1972.

The Scope of the Repression

The collective effect of the overlapping surveillance and counterintelligence programs and the resistance some whites showed to black office-holding discussed above was a uniquely high incidence of state repression of black elected officials. The experiences of the African Americans who sat in Congress during this period give us a picture of black elected officials' experiences in microcosm. Between 1965 and 1975, twenty-one African Americans served in Congress, twenty in the House and one in the Senate. Of those twenty-one congresspeople, sixteen, or 76 percent, experienced some form of state surveillance, counterintelligence, or politically motivated criminal investigation or were excluded from office. To the targeted elected officials, the repression appeared to come from nearly every facet of a hostile white-controlled state. In 1967, Congress denied Adam Clayton Powell Jr. his seat in the House of Representatives. President Nixon placed twelve of the thirteen then-sitting members of the CBC on one of his enemies lists in 1971. State and municipal intelligence units gathered noncriminal intelligence files on five black members of Congress. The FBI, the IRS, and the CIA spied on eight. And the DOJ conducted criminal investigations of five. Only one of these five members was indicted, and none was convicted. In the wake of her 1972 presidential campaign, Shirley Chisholm was charged with four violations of federal campaign financing laws by the Federal Election Commission (FEC). After a short investigation, a DOJ spokesman announced that the charges of misconduct were unsubstantiated and that other alleged violations had been resolved.[61] Only Representatives William Dawson, Edward Brooke, Yvonne Burke, Cardiss Collins, and Harold Ford escaped some form of government scrutiny during this period.

Law enforcement and intelligence community repression also touched a number of future congresspeople in the years between 1965 and 1975. Judge George Crockett was placed under surveillance by the FBI for his affiliation with Communists and radical labor groups; state senator Mervyn Dymally (D-Los Angeles) was audited by the IRS, ostensibly for his criticism of the Johnson administration's policy in Vietnam; civil rights activist John Lewis was placed under surveillance by the FBI for his work in SNCC; Bobby Rush was placed under surveillance by the FBI in his capacity as the deputy minister of defense for the Chicago chapter of the Black Panther Party; Bennie Thompson was placed under surveillance by the Mississippi State Sovereignty Commission and harassed by local white political elites in his positions as alderman and mayor of Bolton, Mississippi; and state senator Harold Washington (D-Chicago) was audited following his protest of Vice President Spiro Agnew's speech before the Illinois State Legislature. Few would forget these experiences when they reached Capitol Hill in the 1980s and 1990s.[62]

The remarkably high incidence of state surveillance and counterintelligence of black elected officials during this period led a choice few to suspect that they were being targeted for repression. Speaking to reporters during the FEC investigation that followed her 1972 presidential bid, Representative Chisholm stated that Adam Clayton Powell Jr. had warned her that she would be scrutinized for her assertive political style. "He said, 'Shirley, if you are a simple, quiet black woman and you don't speak out against inequities, they'll leave you alone. But if you become outspoken, they will get you.'"[63] This notion was, of course, widespread when discussing black protest leaders. But only a handful of black elected officials were aware that they were being targeted for surveillance and counterintelligence before Watergate exposed the activities of the surveillance state to the public. In the mid-1970s as the scope of state repression became known to the public, perhaps a majority of black elected officials began to apply Powell's admonition to themselves.

The Fall of the Surveillance State

"Given Nixon's massive electoral mandate of November 1972," Manning Marable has written, "it is entirely possible that even greater criminal acts against black nationalists, Marxists, community organizers, elected officials, and ministers would have transpired during his second term in office."[64] This was undoubtedly true. Immediately following the election, Nixon ordered White House counsel Dean to draw up "comprehensive notes on those who tried to do [the administration] in (in the 1972 election)." Nixon's directive gives a clear picture of what he had in mind: "They didn't have to do it. If we had a close election and they were playing the other side I would understand this. No — they were doing this quite deliberately and they are asking for it and they are going to get it. . . . We have not used the Bureau [FBI] and we have not used the Justice Department but things are going to change now."[65] Given black elected officials' role in stumping for McGovern, they were bound to experience a disproportionate share of this planned crackdown. The president, however, never got the chance to implement his scheme. By the time of his January inauguration, local, federal, and news media investigations of the preelection break-in by CRP operatives at Democratic National Committee headquarters in the Watergate Hotel were threatening to derail his presidency. Although a White House cover-up held off investigators for over a year, by the summer of 1974 all evidence pointed to Nixon's involvement. On August 8, as the House of Representatives held impeachment proceedings across town, Nixon became the first U.S. president to resign from office. Former House minority leader Gerald Ford (R-Mich.), who had ascended to the vice presidency following Spiro Agnew's 1973 resignation amid charges that he had accepted bribes from Maryland construction companies, was sworn in later that day.[66]

Watergate did far more than just end Richard Nixon's political career; it lifted the veil of secrecy surrounding the surveillance state. The Watergate investigation revealed that the Nixon administration had used the FBI and the IRS to attack his political enemies. Americans also discovered that five of the seven burglars captured at the Democratic National Committee headquarters were CIA veterans and that the agency had provided CRP with equipment for earlier political espionage projects.[67] Information of FBI, CIA, IRS, and DOJ targeting of political dissidents had surfaced repeatedly in the late 1960s and early 1970s. With popular support for the surveillance state and the Nixon administration running high, the media and most Americans had largely ignored it. In 1972, for instance, the CBC had held hearings on government lawlessness. During the proceedings, investigative journalist Jack Anderson presented leaked FBI files demonstrating conclusively that prior to FBI director J. Edgar Hoover's death earlier that year, the bureau had placed at least five thousand black activists under surveillance. Few in the media batted an eye.[68] In the aftermath of Watergate, however, such information was taken seriously by a newly adversarial press and reenergized liberals in Congress. And new revelations would keep the public's attention focused on the misdeeds of the surveillance state in the years to come. In December 1974, *New York Times* reporter Seymour Hersh revealed the existence of a then-defunct CIA domestic spying program. In response to Hersh's articles, President Ford created a White House blue ribbon commission to investigate. The House and the Senate too created special committees to investigate Hersh's allegations. Before investigators were even able to settle into their work, Ronald Kessler of the *Washington Post* uncovered evidence of FBI spying on members of Congress and Martin Luther King Jr. The following month, February 1975, CBS's Daniel Schorr disclosed that the CIA had attempted to carry out several assassinations of foreign leaders. Then in March 1975, the *Miami Herald* uncovered an IGRS program that had targeted most of the high-ranking elected officials in the Miami-Dade area. The investigations, in turn, expanded to cover the new revelations. In so doing, they pulled back the curtain of secrecy on much of the federal surveillance apparatus. Spurned by the lawsuits of targets and civil liberties groups, many state legislatures opened their own investigations into the activities of state and municipal intelligence units. These investigations uncovered levels of political repression and lawlessness similar to that of their federal counterparts.[69]

Faced with congressional and state legislative investigations, widespread public mistrust, and the threat of lawsuits from their targets, many of the intelligence agencies dramatically curtailed or shut down their domestic spying and counterintelligence operations and destroyed their files. The FBI, for instance, trimmed its internal security target list to 17 organizations and 130 individuals by the fall of 1977. Many municipal and state intelligence outfits followed suit. In Baltimore, the files of the Inspectional Services Division were taken into an alley and burned (only weeks before a Maryland state legislative committee commenced a 1975 investigation of its activities).[70] Subsequently, police and intelligence community surveillance and counterintelligence operations against black elected officials, like those against all political dissidents, declined precipitously.

Watergate also stalled the party realignment that Nixon had so recklessly pursued. Initially, it appeared as though Gerald Ford might be able to maintain the new Republican majority. Ford had joined the administration after the 1972 campaign and was therefore not tainted by Watergate. He entered office with a 71 percent approval rating and the good will of an American people desperate for honest leadership. In a bungled attempt to put Watergate behind the nation, however, Ford squandered this goodwill by granting Nixon an unconditional pardon. Democrats took full advantage of Ford's misstep. In the 1974 midterm elections, Democrats picked up forty-nine seats in the House and four in the Senate, ballooning their majorities to a veto-proof margin in the House and filibuster-proof margin in the Senate. In the 1976 presidential election, Democrats continued to use Watergate to make gains. Georgia governor Jimmy Carter distinguished himself from a crowded field in the Democratic primaries as an outsider who could "clean up the mess in Washington." In the general election, Carter hammered home the issue of trustworthiness, campaigning under the slogan "I will never lie to you." Disillusioned with the scandal-tainted Republican Party, a critical minority of the white Democrats and Independents who had voted for Nixon in 1972 decided to cast their vote for Carter. In November, Carter defeated Ford by slightly over 1.6 million votes.[71]

Ironically, it was during this moment of Democratic resurgence, when state surveillance and counterintelligence of the black community was on the wane, that black elected officials discovered "harassment."

Those who consider the charge of national conspiracy against black elected officials as silly must explain why 50 percent of all Blacks in the U.S. House of Representatives are under investigation for criminal activity and not 50 percent of the White Representatives. Certainly they are not contending that Black members as a group are more criminally inclined, less principled, more corrupt, less moral?

— Congressman William L. Clay (D-Mo.)

This study began with reports of scattered incidents of harassment of black elected officials. It started out asking if there were a pattern of harassment. For a time, there was doubt of sufficient evidence to make a case for patterns; entertainment of the question of conspiracy was totally declined. But as the volume of known cases mounted, as the issues they raised were delved into more deeply, a radical shift in thinking occurred.

The conclusion is that there is substantial harassment. There are patterns. There is conspiracy.

— Mary Sawyer, *The Dilemma of Black Politics: A Report on the Harassment of Black Elected Officials*

CHAPTER THREE

Discovering "Harassment" in the Post-Watergate Period, 1975–1980

ON OCTOBER 11, 1977, the two highest-ranking black state lawmakers in the country, California lieutenant governor Mervyn Dymally (D) and Colorado lieutenant governor George Brown (D), traveled to Washington, D.C., for the purpose of releasing *The Dilemma of Black Politics: A Report on the Harassment of Black Elected Officials*, by Mary Sawyer. For nearly two years, dozens of high-ranking black elected officials had been alleging that they were being "harassed" by the state and the news media, that they were subject to a "double standard" in the judgment of their actions, that the country was going through a "second post-Reconstruction" period in which blacks were being swept from office, or that they were the targets of a "national conspiracy" to silence dissent. At Brown's request and with Dymally's support, Sawyer had gathered these black elected officials' claims together into a three-hundred-page report in which she claimed to have uncovered evidence of "substantial harassment" — which she defined as "a continuum of deliberate activity to damage Black officials' effectiveness and credibility" — occurring at "all levels of government" and "throughout the country."[1]

Though Sawyer had achieved the impressive goal of creating the first report on black elected officials' allegations of "harassment," the October 11 press conference exposed some of the limitations of her work. Reporters raised the question of how to determine harassment from law enforcement. Sawyer argued that black elected officials' allegations of harassment should be given equal weight as reporters' and prosecutors' allegations of misconduct. In actuality, she privileged black elected officials' version of events. Reporters were also wary of her claims that the instances of surveillance, audit, and investigation listed in *Dilemma* were an "indication of a broad, coordinated conspiratorial attack on influential Black officials." With the increased public concern with ethics in government following Watergate, some argued, state and news media investigations of elected officials were increasing across the board. Could black elected officials be reading race into a race-neutral crackdown on official corruption? In light of recent revelations of government repression of the black freedom movement and strong anecdotal evidence, Sawyer doubted as much.[2] These same questions had vexed some of the black elected officials whom Sawyer had interviewed for *Dilemma*. Most had resolved them by inferring the ill intent of government investigators and journalists. Sawyer had adopted their claims uncritically.

With Brown's and Dymally's help, Sawyer spent the years following the publication of *Dilemma* lobbying civil rights and black political organizations to fund continued research on harassment and create a legal defense and advocacy organization for black elected officials. Although ultimately unsuccessful, her efforts spread "harassment ideology" to much of the black political community. And despite the methodological flaws in harassment research, harassment ideology would influence black political thought for decades to come.

George Brown and the Genesis of "Harassment"

On October 15, 1975, members of the National Association of Human Rights Workers (NAHRW) gathered in Portland, Oregon, for the closing dinner of their annual conference. Conference participants assembled that evening to hear one of their own, the former executive director of the Metro-Denver Urban Coalition (1969–75) and newly elected lieutenant governor of Colorado, George Brown, deliver the keynote address. As the first African American elected to a lieutenant governorship in the history of the United States (in the same year as

Mervyn Dymally of California), Brown had become a symbol of the success of black political incorporation. During his first several months in office, he had crisscrossed the country delivering speech after speech about the remarkable distance the country had come in the short ten years since passing the VRA.[3] Before the NAHRW, however, Brown delivered a very different message. The lieutenant governor's remarks that evening were devoted to identifying what he had come to believe was a growing threat to black and brown political leadership, indeed to American democracy. "There are many disturbing things happening in America today," Brown began. "And that is particularly true for me. When I examine what's happening to black and brown political leadership, black and brown professionals, black religious leaders, and black businesspeople . . . I know for certain that if black leaders and brown leaders are harassed and discredited, before they fall, that poor whites, and yes, middle America, is not far behind." Brown conceded, "[I do not have] proof that there is a deliberate effort to knock down certain folks. I can't prove that." But he asserted, "The list of fallen black leaders is growing," and "there are some folks in this nation who are rejoicing because of it."[4]

The lieutenant governor's remarks before the NAHRW were rooted in the complex interplay between Brown's personal experiences of the previous two months, the growth of adversary journalism, and the growing effort to police elected officials' ethics in the aftermath of Watergate. In late August, Brown had attended the Lieutenant Governors' Conference in Point Clear, Alabama. At the gathering, he delivered an impassioned speech on the topic of his relationship to Alabama and contemporary U.S. race relations. Although he had trained in Alabama during World War II as a Tuskegee Airman, he had not returned since. His reluctance stemmed from a crash during a 1943 training exercise. In the crash, Brown claimed, he was knocked unconscious and discovered by a white farmer. Rather than help the young pilot, this alleged member of the Ku Klux Klan, chained, beat, and branded Brown on the chest with a *K*. In a dramatic flourish, Brown ripped open his shirt exposing a keloid "K": proof, he claimed, of the alleged assault. Brown then stated that his ability to return to Alabama as the lieutenant governor of Colorado showed how far the country had come in the past three decades. The speech electrified the conference. Soon after Brown stepped from the podium, the assembly elected him vice chairman.[5]

The following day, reporters from the *Denver Post* began to check Brown's facts. Brown had worked at the *Post* for fourteen years, and no one in the newsroom could recall him having told such a story. Under scrutiny, the lieutenant governor's tale began to unravel. Brown had been branded not by a white farmer in Alabama during World War II but by his Kappa Alpha Psi fraternity brothers, at his own request, in college. The revelation created a media firestorm in Colorado. Backtracking in the face of the criticism, Brown claimed that his words were misconstrued, that he had mistakenly conflated a story of his having been beaten with that of another pilot who had been branded. "The incidents I referred to were correct," Brown stated to reporters. "I told of an incident of a cadet who was branded. I told a personal incident of how I was badly beaten." He apologized if "there was any merging [of the stories], either actual or implied." Brown's mea culpa may have ended the controversy if it were true, but it was not. Though several had been threatened and insulted, no Tuskegee Airman was ever branded in Alabama during World War II. Though he did not say so at the time, in a 2002 interview with the author Brown admitted that the branding story was a rumor that circulated among black Army Air Corps cadets stationed in Alabama. "I heard it," Brown said. "I didn't know whether it was true or false." Brown's speech and his subsequent refusal to admit that he had misled his listeners were headline news in Colorado newspapers for over two weeks. The controversy caused tremendous embarrassment for Brown and the state Democratic Party. Indeed, it caused so much concern that on September 8 Colorado governor Dick Lamm (D) publicly demanded that Brown "set the record straight."[6]

In the midst of the branding controversy, Brown was blindsided by another scandal. On September 9, Martyn Butler, chairman of the Clear Creek County Republican Party, sent a letter to Governor Lamm listing Brown's travel vouchers for the first six months of his tenure. Butler complained that the majority of the trips for which Brown had submitted travel vouchers did not pertain to official state business and requested an investigation of this alleged misuse of taxpayer money. Butler also forwarded his missive to the state's major dailies, the *Rocky Mountain News* and the *Denver Post*, both of which published stories on Brown's travel the following day. Brown had charged $4,090 to the state for travel, and of that amount approximately $3,600 had been spent on personal trips, primarily speaking engagements before civil rights organizations out of state. When reached by reporters, Brown admitted that the figures contained in the letter were correct. The charges, he argued, were the product of a policy, used for the first six months of his tenure, whereby his office charged all his travel to the state, then reimbursed the state for the private travel. The woman in charge of scheduling and billing Brown's travel, administrative assistant Josie Johnson, told reporters that she had adopted the practice on the advice of several veteran staff when she arrived in the capital in January 1975. She had discontinued the policy in June when it produced multiple accounting irregularities. Claiming that the matter was an honest mistake, Brown stated that he welcomed an inquiry in order to clear his name.[7]

Brown's missteps could not have come at a worse time in post–World War II U.S. political history. By the mid-1970s, the deceptions of the Johnson and Nixon administrations about Vietnam and Watergate and the then-ongoing

Church Committee investigation of the FBI and the CIA made Americans increasingly distrustful of political elites. In the ten years preceding Watergate, historian Kathryn Olmstead writes, "the percentage of people who distrusted the government had risen from 22 to 62 percent. [In 1974,] forty-five percent of Americans polled believed that there were 'quite a few' crooks in government, up from 29 percent in 1964."[8] Attuned to the changes in the public perception of government, the media adopted an adversarial stance toward government and elected officials in particular. Political scientists Benjamin Ginsberg and Martin Shefter argue that this new form of journalism capitalized on the growing mistrust of government not so much by engaging in the hard work of investigative journalism as by taking "a hostile posture toward the government and public officials."[9] And many elected officials and government bodies took their lead from public opinion and the media. Congress and many state legislatures adopted ethics legislation and created ethics committees; ambitious prosecutors sought to ferret out government corruption; and the two political parties worked to tar each other with the label of corruption.[10] In this atmosphere, allegations of official misconduct, no matter how small, often ballooned into scandals as investigators rushed to open inquiries, journalists made the allegations front-page news, and the public believed the worst about the elected official under investigation.

This was certainly the case in Denver. On September 9, the same day that the *Denver Post* and the *Rocky Mountain News* ran articles on Butler's allegations, state controller Dan Whittemore announced that he was conducting an administrative review of Brown's travel records. The following day, Colorado Republicans, seizing the opportunity to injure the state's first Democratic administration in twelve years, called for a legislative investigation in the Republican-dominated state House of Representatives. Hoping to outflank state Republicans, Governor Lamm ordered Denver district attorney Dale Tooley to investigate. Local reporters covered the political wrangling over the Brown scandals closely, and their editors often made these findings, no matter how minute, front-page news.[11] The controversies also moved the *Denver Post* to reprint "Court Records Show Much Financial Woe in Brown's Past," an article detailing Brown's personal finances that it had first published during the 1974 primary election. The September 11, 1975, article stated that Brown possessed few assets and had for many years failed to pay his bills on time, and that his inability to properly manage his finances had led to fourteen separate judgments against him in Denver County District and Superior Courts. *Post* editors appear to have reprinted the article in an attempt to give context to the travel-voucher scandal — either to demonstrate that Brown was negligent when handling money or to suggest a motive for Brown's alleged theft of state funds.

Denver African Americans viewed the state and news media scrutiny of Brown not as just criticism of a high-ranking elected official but as a racialized attack on the most powerful black elected official in the state of Colorado. This belief was reinforced by their observation that such high levels of scrutiny were not applied to earlier generations of white elected officials. On September 13, six Colorado black elected officials, Representative Arie Taylor (D-Denver), Representative Wellington Webb (D-Denver), Denver city councilman Bill Roberts (D), Northglenn mayor pro tem Odell Barry (D), Boulder mayor Penifield Tate (D), and Senator Regis Groff (D-Denver), issued a joint statement taking issue with the *Denver Post* for its September 11 exposé on Brown's finances, which they termed "distasteful," "non-relevant," and an "attempt to destroy" Brown's character. "These facts that are being reprinted [information on Brown's finances] were fully recognized by the voters [in the 1974 election]," the elected officials stated, and "to the credit of Colorado voters . . . wealth is not a requirement for public office." Several days later, an interracial group of Brown supporters again criticized the *Denver Post* article, noting that Brown's personal finances had "nothing to do with the travel vouchers." Unlike Brown's Denver and Boulder supporters, the NAACP criticized the travel-voucher inquiry itself. On September 19, the NAACP issued a press release stating that Brown was being investigated "under the guise of justice" and offering the association's support for his defense. Speaking to reporters in Denver, NAACP regional director Ina Boon expressed the association leadership's belief that Brown was being singled out for scrutiny because he was a high-ranking black elected official, stating that Brown's "integrity was questioned only after he became lieutenant governor, a pivotal spot in state government."[12]

Though initially contrite in the face of the branding and travel voucher scandals, by mid-September Brown had come to similar conclusions. Like the Denver and Boulder black elected officials who had organized to defend him, Brown believed that the *Denver Post*'s September 11 article on his finances was meant to imply that he had a motive for stealing state funds. He also believed that his speech before the lieutenant governors' conference had been misquoted. And as Brown argued in an interview with the author, "it wasn't the first time [he had] been misquoted" by the Denver press. In 1970, the *Rocky Mountain News* had reported that a group of African Americans, assembled to protest the shooting death of a black community college professor by a white gas-station attendant, "cheered lustily" as then-state senator Brown (D-Denver) exhorted them to retaliate violently against white Coloradoans. Brown filed a five-hundred-thousand-dollar libel suit, claiming that the story was untrue and had irreparably damaged his prospects for statewide office. The trial ended in a hung jury.[13] Brown was particularly disturbed by the press scrutiny because he had been something of a darling of the Denver press prior to 1974. "When I first went into office the media was just extremely friendly," Brown recalled. As a working reporter — Brown remained with the *Denver Post* for several years after he was elected to the state legislature — he appears to have been treated with the deference afforded a colleague during his years in the state senate. "But after I became lieutenant governor," Brown claimed, "suddenly, I guess I was, I don't like to use the word 'threat' but maybe that's it." In the same interview, Brown noted that there was an alternative explanation for the news media coverage of the "branding" and travel-voucher scandals: "After Watergate, every writer, every person in the media was looking for that Watergate story. And the rumor became the headline . . . even if you had to write the headline and the rumor and then three or four paragraphs in the story point out it wasn't true. The headline sold papers . . . made the news."[14] Because President Nixon had resigned only three months before Brown was elected, it was impossible for Brown to determine if the change in the way the Denver press treated him was a product of the post-Watergate rise in adversary journalism or a belief that his new position now made him a "threat." Brown's interactions with other high-ranking black elected officials that summer, however, convinced him that it was the latter.

As a prominent member of the Black Caucus of the National Democratic Committee, Brown was regularly in contact with a large network of black elected officials and party organizers. Two of these individuals were Pennsylvania secretary of state C. Delores Tucker (D) and Gary, Indiana, mayor Richard Hatcher (D). Brown referred to both in his remarks before the NAHRW. In February 1975, the *Philadelphia Inquirer* had accused Tucker of conflict of interest regarding her acceptance of honoraria for several speaking engagements before chapters of the NAACP. Tucker's office exercised oversight of tax-exempt organizations in Pennsylvania, including the state NAACP. Tucker refuted the charges, labeling the *Inquirer*'s claims "an attempt to discredit [her]." The allegations triggered a month-long investigation by Governor Milton Shapp's newly created Board of Ethics. The board cleared Tucker of any wrongdoing that March — she had only accepted honoraria from out-of-state branches of the NAACP — and the state senate confirmed unanimously her appointment to a second term that July.[15] At the same time that Tucker was defending her job in Pennsylvania, the administration of Mayor Hatcher was being investigated by a grand jury in Hammond, Indiana. The grand jury had reportedly convened to investigate corruption in Lake County, which contains Gary, but nearly all its energies focused on Gary exclusively. Although the U.S. attorney never stated that Hatcher was a subject of the investigation, indictments of his close associates and employees and the tone of the U.S. attorney's questioning of those individuals indicated that the DOJ was, in fact, targeting the mayor. Brown believed that the U.S. attorney's investigation was a form of harassment.[16] Hatcher was never indicted.

Brown also referred to his California counterpart, Lieutenant Governor Mervyn Dymally (D), during his October 15 remarks. Brown and Dymally had met in late August at the National Lieutenant Governors' Conference and become fast friends. They shared a tremendous amount in common. Both were members of Kappa Alpha Psi fraternity and former journalists, and both had become the first black state senators and lieutenant governors in their respective states. One of the places where they believed that their careers diverged was in their relationship with the media. Brown was still something of a media darling in August 1975. Dymally, on the other hand, was in the midst of a bitter fight with the *Los Angeles Times*. On July 3, 1975, the *Times* had published a lengthy article accusing Dymally of misusing funds and nepotism while chair of the board of the Urban Affairs Institute (UAI), a then-defunct nonprofit he cofounded in 1968 to increase the number of minority youth in government. Dymally, who had admitted to sloppy bookkeeping when the institute closed its doors two years before, attacked the *Times* article as "columns of inaccuracies, innuendoes, and outright falsehoods," written in a spirit of "vendetta journalism." After reading press reports of the then-ongoing IRS investigation of Fayette, Mississippi, mayor Charles Evers (D) and the Atlanta news media's scrutiny of Mayor Maynard Jackson (D), Dymally came to believe that his situation was symptomatic of a larger pattern of state and news media attacks on black elected officials. Speaking to reporters on August 24, only four days before he met with Brown in Alabama, Dymally claimed that the *Times* story was part of "a wave of repression" of black elected officials "unprecedented since Reconstruction."[17] During their August 28 meeting, he impressed his views on Brown.

Viewing these investigations in tandem with his own ordeal, Brown adopted Dymally's belief that they formed a "pattern." He first made this argument one week after the travel-voucher story broke in a September 18 speech in Dallas, Texas. Citing the recent and ongoing investigations of Mayor Evers, Secretary of State Tucker, and Lieutenant Governor Dymally, Brown claimed that high-ranking black elected officials were subject to a pattern of "harassment."[18] One week later, Brown and Dymally traveled to Washington, D.C., to discuss "fighting . . . a deliberate pattern of official harassment of black elected officials" with representatives of the Joint Center for Political Studies.[19] In mid-October, Brown brought his campaign to the NAHRW.

Having outlined his understanding of the problem, Brown sought to enlist the NAHRW in his effort to address it. "I would like to propose a new mission," Brown told his audience.

A part of this new mission of yours might be to consider how you can start a nation-wide monitoring or evaluation system that moves in when a person of leadership is harassed or their credibility otherwise attacked. . . . We need to be about creating within our system of government some means, some commission, some function of a group that would move in to do the proper kind of answering to whatever the charges might be. Maybe your Association can be the nucleus of such a group.[20]

His audience listened intently and sympathetically. Few, however, were ready to assume so controversial a task for themselves or their organization. The lone exception was Mary Sawyer, a young white woman then working as an assistant to the city manager of Berkeley, California, and a member of the NAHRW Board of Directors.

Mary Sawyer, California Lieutenant Governor Mervyn Dymally, and the Committee on the Status of Minority Elected Officials

Mary Sawyer grew up in a small, all-white town in rural Nebraska. Much of her young life revolved around the local Presbyterian church, where she adopted a social-justice theology. "The message I got from this little church," Sawyer recalls, "was all people are created equal; all people are the children of God." When Sawyer left the monochrome environs of her hometown to enroll at Colorado State University (CSU) in the fall of 1962, she learned that many of her fellow white Americans rejected this credo when it came to nonwhites. At CSU, Sawyer befriended several black students from Denver, and, as she recalls, "learn[ed] about discrimination" for the first time in her life. Unable to reconcile the racial inequalities of American society with her religious beliefs, she participated in civil rights activism in the hopes of correcting the former. "I was just appalled," Sawyer remembers thinking to herself. "Here are all these white adults going around saying that they are Christian, and they're not. The dishonesty of that propelled me into the movement."[21] The conduit for Sawyer's entrance into civil rights activism was state senator George Brown (D-Denver).

During her freshman year, Sawyer attended a CSU Young Democrats meeting at which Brown was the featured speaker. Unable to remember the subject of his speech, Sawyer nonetheless recalls its impact: "I have never been affected, ever, by a speaker like I was by him," she stated nearly forty years later. Following the speech, Sawyer wrote to Brown about racial discrimination on campus, requesting his advice on what to do about it. She was surprised to receive a return call. At the time, Brown was the director of the Denver chapter of the National Urban League and a veteran civil rights activist. He encouraged Sawyer to organize students and faculty to address the problems outlined in her letter. Later that semester, Sawyer organized several faculty and students to form a campus chapter of the Congress of Racial Equality (CORE).[22] Although they would not meet again for several years, Brown had made a lasting impression on Sawyer.

In 1974, soon after Brown was elected lieutenant governor, Sawyer, then a member of the NAHRW Conference Committee, convinced her colleagues to secure him as the keynote speaker for their 1975 annual conference. Like his speech before the Young Democrats, Brown's remarks before the NAHRW challenged and inspired Sawyer. Two days after the banquet, at the first board meeting of the new NAHRW administration, she offered a motion to establish a special committee to devise strategies for carrying out the lieutenant governor's request. The motion carried, creating what would soon become the Committee on the Status of Minority Elected Officials (CSMEO) and charging it with studying the problem outlined by Brown. Soon afterward, Sawyer was appointed chairperson.[23]

Now at the helm of the CSMEO, Sawyer developed a plan of action. First, she set parameters for the study. Brown had stated that the entire spectrum of "black and brown political leadership" was under attack. Sawyer decided, however, to limit the study to black elected officials only. She knew that black elected officials possessed the institutional capacity, through their many caucuses and the Joint Center for Political Studies, to facilitate a study of the type Brown proposed. More importantly, however, Sawyer believed that black elected officials were the "spearhead of the struggle for liberation."[24] They should, then, in her mind, take priority in any investigation of alleged attacks on black and brown leadership. Second, Sawyer determined that the committee's primary objective would be to create a report on what she was now calling "harassment," borrowing the term from Brown. Data for the report would be collected through a "national clearinghouse" structure composed of local NAHRW chapters, civil rights organizations, and black political organizations. The committee would begin this research by "building a data file and documenting a pattern" of attacks on black elected officials. The data would be supplemented by interviews with "a sampling of individuals who [had] been subjects of harassment."[25] Sawyer hoped to produce a report within two years.

In 1975, when each week brought new revelations of government lawlessness, often directed at the black freedom movement, Sawyer found ample support among black elected officials for her research. She began her project by contacting Eddie Williams, president of the Joint Center for Political Studies. Williams, who had discussed harassment with Brown and Dymally just two months before, invited Sawyer to attend the Third National Institute for Black Elected Public Officials in Washington, D.C., for the purpose of making the contacts that would facilitate her research. The institute was the third national gathering of black elected officials since 1967. It was designed to operate as a networking, skill-building, and strategy-development session for the 3,503 black elected officials then holding office.[26] Sawyer attended the conference as an official representative of the NAHRW. During a workshop titled "Black Politics and the Mass Media," she made a brief presentation, outlining her proposal for a clearinghouse and requesting support and cooperation from the elected officials in attendance.[27] As Williams had predicted, conference participants reacted enthusiastically to her remarks. A brief description of the two black elected officials on the "Mass Media" panel explains why. At the time that the institute met in Washington, a Maryland State Senate investigative committee was putting the finishing touches on its report on illegal surveillance of citizens by the Inspectional Services Division (ISD) of the Baltimore Police Department, a municipal intelligence unit closely tied to the FBI. Investigators had uncovered a massive campaign of surveillance and counterintelligence against the state's Left and liberal political organizations. The moderator of the panel, Maryland state senator Clarence Mitchell III (D-Baltimore), featured prominently in the committee's findings. From 1966 to 1974, the ISD regularly monitored Mitchell's personal and political activities, wiretapped his phones, placed informers in several organizations of which he was a member, and stole or photographed files from his office.[28] Mitchell was joined on the panel by former Cleveland, Ohio, mayor and NBC News commentator Carl Stokes. Stokes had experienced multiple district attorney, newspaper, and DOJ investigations during his four years in Cleveland City Hall. Nearly all the investigations had been stimulated by his political opponents, and none implicated the mayor in wrongdoing.[29] Having been the subjects of the kind of state and news media "harassment" of which Sawyer spoke, both Mitchell and Stokes embraced her proposal. Sawyer also received help from Lieutenant Governor George Brown, who was on hand at the panel discussion. Encouraged by the response to Sawyer's presentation, he submitted a proposal to the Institute Steering Committee calling on member organizations to support the work of the CSMEO. Without debate, the committee voted unanimously to adopt the proposal.[30]

Despite this promising beginning, the CSMEO was beset with logistical and financial difficulties that almost derailed the project. In January 1976, Sawyer assembled a group of fifty NAHRW members to canvass black elected officials and conduct secondary-source research in their respective areas. The clearinghouse, it appeared, was up and running. But by October 1976, Sawyer had heard from only three of the fifty clearinghouse volunteers despite numerous communications requesting an update on their efforts. That same month, she discovered that clearinghouse participants in New York, Ohio, and Illinois had dropped out of the project entirely, leaving three of the states with the largest number of black elected officials uncanvassed.[31] Many, it appears, had been enthusiastic about the project when Sawyer solicited their help in January but were not willing to devote the time and energy necessary to conduct the research.

Also, the CSMEO was unable to secure a stable source of funding. The NAHRW did not possess the resources to support the clearinghouse, leaving the job of fund-raising to the committee. Most foundations, however, rebuffed Sawyer's requests for funding. Chastened by the political backlash against their support for civil rights, antipoverty, and black political organizations in the decade following passage of the VRA, most large foundations shunned overtly political or politically controversial projects by the mid-1970s. The CSMEO was both overtly political and politically controversial, and all the major foundations rejected Sawyer's requests. In 1976, Sawyer applied for over thirty different grants but received only three, the largest being a fifteen-hundred-dollar award from the Third World Fund.[32] Operating on a proposed budget of roughly ten thousand dollars, Sawyer kept the project afloat through these small grants, in-kind donations, and periodic infusions of her personal income. This state of affairs, however, would soon begin to weigh on Sawyer. Not only did she need money, but she needed time off from work to conduct research. In May 1976, Sawyer made the connection that would provide the CSMEO with both, at least indirectly.

That month Sawyer traveled to Sacramento to interview Lieutenant Governor Mervyn Dymally. Born in Trinidad, Dymally had traveled to the United States for college. After earning his degree in 1954, he taught special-needs children during the day and dabbled in local politics in the evenings. Moving quickly through the ranks of the Los Angeles Democratic Party, in 1962 Dymally ran for and won the state assembly seat for South Central Los Angeles and part of Watts then being vacated by Assemblyman Gus Hawkins (D). Four years later, he capitalized on a court-ordered reapportionment to become the first person of African descent to sit in the California Senate. After an active career in the senate in which he distinguished himself as an advocate for women and youth, Dymally ran for the lieutenant governorship in 1974. Polling more votes than winning gubernatorial candidate, Democrat Jerry Brown, Dymally won the seat, making him the first person of (black) West Indian descent to be elected to a lieutenant governorship in U.S. history.

Despite his remarkable successes and wide electoral support, Dymally felt besieged when Sawyer arrived in the state capital. He was in the midst of a continuous four-year battle with the Los Angeles and Sacramento press — a saga that he shared with the young researcher. In 1972, the *Los Angeles Times* had published two articles accusing Dymally of conflict of interest and calling for the Senate Legislative Ethics Committee to investigate his involvement with Batick Wine and Spirits Company, a "black capitalist" attempt to integrate the California wine industry. Although he was eventually cleared of these charges, the investigation marked the beginning of a nearly unbroken string of newspaper inquiries.[33] "That was the beginning," Dymally told Sawyer. From that point forward, Dymally considered himself to be in open conflict with the *Times*, the *Sacramento Bee*, and several other white California news organizations. By Dymally's estimation, in his first two years as lieutenant governor he was the subject of twelve investigations by the *Times* and at least five by the *Bee*. Dymally's conflict with the Los Angeles and Sacramento press became particularly intense right after his meeting with Sawyer. In September 1976, the *Bee* published an article titled "Campaign Fund Donations? Dymally Is Linked to Controversial Pharmacist," claiming that Dymally had ties to a Los Angeles pharmacist convicted of illegally selling prescription drugs. In the article, the *Bee* suggested that the pharmacist had bought influence from Dymally with a series of campaign donations. Released over the AP and UPI wire services, the story was reproduced throughout California as "Dymally Crime Link Revealed," "Dymally Dope Dealer Tie Probed," "Dymally Linked to Ex-Opium Dealer Bared," and "Report Details Dymally Association with Known L.A. Crime Figure." The *Bee* story, and the controversy that it spawned, was the last straw as far as the lieutenant governor was concerned. On November 3, 1976, Dymally wrote an editorial for the *Bee* outlining his difficulties with the press and announcing a new policy of refusing to speak to reporters. The lieutenant governor was unsure if the press scrutiny directed at him was the product of "the fact that [he was] black and the powers that be in a racist society are obliged to discredit — if not destroy — a high level black official who has obtained . . . the semblance of power" or of "sloppy reporting and editing, and a tendency among some reporters, once they have decided on a story, to select only those facts that support their conclusions and disregard the rest." Like Brown, Dymally recognized the difficulty of interpreting reporters' intent in the post-Watergate era. He nonetheless erred on the side of self-defense and accused critical reporters of "vendetta journalism."[34]

Although Dymally had been critical to George Brown's early thinking on harassment, he had had no hand in the establishment and early work of the CSMEO. That changed following his interview with Sawyer. A dedicated proponent of black political development — he was an organizer of the three National Conferences of Black Elected Officials; cofounder of the UAI in 1968 (disbanded in 1973); and editor of the anthology *The Black Politician: His Struggle for Power* in 1969 — Dymally was gravely concerned about the implications of Sawyer's research for his colleagues. As the subject of what he understood to be a four-year campaign of news media harassment, Dymally had a distinct personal investment as well. He offered Sawyer his unqualified support. Several weeks after the interview, Sawyer moved to Sacramento to take a job as a consultant to the California Commission on Economic Development, which was housed in the lieutenant governor's office. Working part-time for the commission, Sawyer devoted her free time to the CSMEO. Dymally provided the committee with a desk, phone, copier, and the occasional intern.[35] He also lent his name to CSMEO projects. For instance, when the clearinghouse collapsed, Sawyer reproduced its work by sending a questionnaire to black elected officials inquiring if they had ever been harassed. Dymally wrote a cover letter, encouraging his fellow black elected officials to participate in the study.[36] This crucial support allowed Sawyer to finish the study by the summer of 1977. Indeed, Dymally's support for Sawyer's research set a pattern. From 1976 through the late 1980s, Dymally was the primary sponsor of harassment research and the most consistent advocate of antiharassment activism among black elected officials.

"Is There a Conspiracy?"

In January 1976, as Sawyer was beginning her research, *Ebony* magazine published "Is There a Conspiracy against Black Leaders?" by journalist and Washington insider Carl Rowan. Rowan's article expanded discussions of harassment beyond the small groups of black elected officials and political activists discussed above and introduced it to the larger black community. It also made a strong argument that the source of black elected officials' difficulties was a white "conspiracy" against black leadership. This assertion and the reaction it elicited in the black community would have a critical influence on Sawyer's methodology and conclusions.

Rowan's article was, in part, a product of his tumultuous relationship with the FBI. In the late summer of 1975, the congressional investigations of the intelligence community were evolving into a public-relations nightmare for the bureau. In an effort to repair the damage, newly appointed director Clarence Kelley was doing his best to cultivate friendly African American media contacts. After years of bloody wars with the black Left, and in the wake of media revelations of FBI spying on Martin Luther King Jr., the bureau's profile among African Americans had hit a new low. In the 1960s, Bill Sullivan, head of domestic intelligence under J. Edgar Hoover, had worked with Rowan, feeding him FBI propaganda and providing him with scoops. In 1968–69, however, Rowan turned sharply against the bureau when he came to believe that the FBI had a hand in Martin Luther King Jr.'s assassination. Following the assassination, Rowan recalls, he suspected "that someone in the U.S. government had put out a contract to 'neutralize' [King] — 'neutralization' being almost synonymous with a death sentence in the argot of the intelligence community." Rowan raised his concerns with Sullivan in 1969 but received what he described as "garbage answers." Kelly hoped to bring the veteran black journalist back into the fold. Rowan had other ideas. When Kelley approached him in 1975, Rowan saw the opportunity to finally answer some of the questions he had put to Sullivan six years before, questions that had been raised anew in the then-ongoing Church Committee hearings. He asked that Kelly give him access to the King file as a show of good faith. Determined to prove that the FBI had turned over a new leaf, Kelley agreed and allowed Rowan to review thousands of pages of the King dossier at FBI headquarters. Reading through the file, Rowan became convinced that the FBI, which had worked so assiduously to destroy King's character while alive, had, in fact, been a party to what, in his 1991 memoir, he called "a conspiracy to kill King."[37]

Around the same time that he gained access to the King file, Rowan began seeing increasing numbers of news reports detailing investigations of wrongdoing against high-ranking black elected officials. With notions of an FBI conspiracy to assassinate King fresh in his mind, he began interviewing these black elected officials for the purpose of writing an article. He conducted in-depth interviews with Representative Shirley Chisholm (D-N.Y.); Georgia state senator Leroy Johnson (D-Atlanta); Representative Ralph Metcalfe (D-Ill.); California lieutenant governor Mervyn Dymally (D); Colorado lieutenant governor George Brown (D); and Representative William Clay (D-Mo.); and more-abbreviated interviews with Pennsylvania secretary of state C. Delores Tucker (D); Vice Mayor William Chenault (D-Cincinnati); Berkeley, California, city councilman D'Army Bailey (D); and Tennessee state senator Avon Williams (D), all of whom claimed to be the targets of undue state and/or news media scrutiny, a "double standard" in the judgment of their actions, or worse, a "conspiracy" to destroy black leadership. In the ensuing article, the interviews were presented as case studies, in which Rowan provided a brief biography of the elected officials and a brief synopsis of their experiences. Rowan also made passing mention of the difficulties of state senator Julian Bond (D-Ga.), Fayette, Mississippi, mayor Charles Evers (D), and deceased former representative Adam Clayton Powell Jr. (D-N.Y.), figures whose cases he believed were so well known as not to require even an abridged recounting. Additionally, in an effort to show continuity in the government's actions over time, Rowan provided a detailed discussion of southern state governments' attempts to discredit Martin Luther King Jr. long before J. Edgar Hoover set his sights on the martyred civil rights leader. Working from these fourteen cases, Rowan conflated the documentable fact that "a lot of the most heralded black officials [were] being thrown out of office on criminal charges and others [were] fighting desperately for their political lives" with these black elected officials' allegations that the country was "going through a new post-reconstruction era where whites [were] engaged in a vast conspiracy to drive blacks out of power and back into bondage." Adopting this analysis uncritically, Rowan concluded, "Any blacks who achieve exceptional power had better realize that extraordinary efforts will be made to discredit, even convict, them."[38]

Despite the forcefulness with which he made his argument for a conspiracy against high-ranking black leaders, Rowan noted the problems with his allegations. "This is not to say that all black officials being indicted or otherwise accused these days are innocent of any wrongdoing," he wrote. "Some black officials are betraying the trust placed in them by voters, black and white alike." This fact, Rowan recognized, "poses some serious questions for black Americans:

- How do we determine which officials are victims of conspiracies to deprive them of power and which ones are crooks who deserve the contempt of the black community?

- How can we ensure that black officials are not subject to more rigid standards of conduct than their white peers?

- What mechanisms can black Americans devise to protect black officials once an honest investigation of the facts leads responsible blacks to conclude that a certain official is being framed, railroaded or punished for some minor transgression that white officials have been getting away with for generations?"[39]

These questions went to the heart of any allegations of harassment and efforts at defense. Rowan was unable, however, to answer a single one. He rejected as unworkable George Brown's suggestion that African American's create an investigatory committee that could closely examine suspicious cases and determine if they were harassment—the only plan put forward by a black elected official to address the problem. Rowan was much more comfortable with a uniquely unworkable solution. First, he suggested that black elected officials "make themselves as immune as possible to . . . attacks" by remaining ever vigilant of the "special surveillance they face, the extra harsh judgments they must endure." He then assigned a watchdog role to the black community writ large, insisting, "Black Americans must study the evidence closely in the cases that truly matter. And where it is clear that a black politician has violated the trust and the hope that we as a people have placed in him, we must denounce him and applaud his prosecution." Rowan believed that by limiting their antiharassment advocacy only to those cases in which blacks were determined to be innocent of wrongdoing, such advocacy would be made "powerfully effective."[40] Rowan did not, however, explain how blacks would determine what standards they would use for distinguishing law enforcement from harassment, which cases "truly matter," or what mechanisms blacks would use to defend black elected officials who were unfairly investigated.

Rowan should perhaps not be faulted for refusing to wrestle with the difficult task of answering the questions he posed to his readers. In the twenty years that black elected officials considered these questions, none came up with a workable answer. But Rowan can be faulted for not even following his own, ambiguous advice. He presented the case studies of the several black elected officials he interviewed for his article as a list of "recent assaults on black leaders" and "efforts to strip them of power." These "assaults," however, included the disputed cases of Mervyn Dymally's battle with the *Los Angeles Times* and George Brown's travel-voucher scandal. They also included a description of the then-ongoing federal investigations of Representative William Clay (D-Mo.) in which Rowan admitted, "[I have] no idea what he is or is not guilty of, if anything."[41] Like Brown and Dymally before him, Rowan was making an accusation of state repression while at the same time acknowledging the possibility of benign alternative explanations of the events in question. This ambiguity, however, was lost in Rowan's alarmist title and repeated assertions of a conspiracy.

Rowan's article introduced the idea of harassment, albeit in the name of "conspiracy," to black America, where it resonated with a black community deeply suspicious of American governing institutions in the wake of Watergate and the congressional hearings on the intelligence community. Rowan was keenly aware of this mistrust. As he noted in the article: "Anyone who followed the Watergate hearings or is abreast of current congressional probings of the nation's intelligence agencies has surely become aware of one reality: for the last several years no black leader was so radical, so moderate, so Uncle Tommish, that he was not a target for wiretapping, bugging, tailing by the FBI, CIA, DIA, IRS, or some other agency of government." The public response to Rowan's article underscored the appeal of his claims within the black community. In the months after the article was published, *Ebony* received an avalanche of letters to the editor, all concurring with Rowan's thesis. Many exhibited a deep-seated mistrust of government institutions rooted in a long memory of slavery and segregation. Douglass Springs, writing from Cincinnati, Ohio, stated, "Hell yes, I believe there is a conspiracy against black leaders. We blacks have been plotted against since we first came to this country in chains." Charles Davis of the Bronx, New York, echoed his remarks: "There is no doubt in my mind that there has been some degree of conspiracy against blacks who speak out about injustice in our society." Others related their own experiences, alleging state-sponsored attacks on local projects funded with Great Society grants. Writing from Tallahassee, Florida, James Scruggs offered: "I wish to acknowledge that this conspiracy cuts deeper at the [level of] less visible black administrators. A close look at service programs financed by government (soft monies) will show an even more vigorous operation." And many like Dwaine Powell of Chicago, Illinois, ignored the nuance of Rowan's argument concerning defense efforts, arguing that blacks should "show [whites] how we feel by reelecting our officials."[42] Regardless of the specifics, these African Americans were in general agreement: black leadership was under siege, and blacks should close ranks behind black elected officials who allege harassment.

African Americans' embrace of Rowan's conspiracy allegations was neither remarkable nor singular in the mid-1970s United States. The notion of conspiracy pervaded public discourse on government lawlessness in the years after 1971. With almost daily revelations of government plots to deceive the American people about the war in Vietnam (Pentagon Papers, 1971); spy on and harass American dissidents (media exposés of IRS intelligence activities and the FBI's COINTELPRO program, 1971, 1973, 1975); evade campaign finance laws and disorganize the major opposition party through "dirty tricks" (Watergate, 1972–74); and even assassinate foreign leaders (congressional investigations of the CIA, 1975), the secret hand of a malevolent government seemed omnipresent. The Watergate investigation and the congressional hearings on the intelligence community, rather than dispel these concerns, only multiplied them. High-ranking elected officials like President Nixon refused to cooperate with investigators and were eventually shielded from prosecution. Intelligence community bureaucrats appeared to be hiding as much as they revealed. The investigations, therefore, as historian Robert Allen Goldberg notes, "intensified the cynicism of the deceived and confirmed conspiracy theories of a shadow government manipulating events."[43] The popular allure of conspiracy theory among Americans in the mid-1970s is best seen in Congress. In 1976, the House of Representatives created the Select Committee on Investigations to examine allegations that the assassinations of President John F. Kennedy and Martin Luther King Jr. were the result of conspiracies.[44] Rowan's use of the term "conspiracy," then, reflected the language and popular concerns of the times. What distinguished Rowan's ideas from those of the larger U.S. population was their appeal to the black popular memory of racial oppression (and the reality of continuing racial hostility). Though many white Americans were embracing conspiracy theory in the late 1970s, they were simultaneously moving away from their already-tenuous commitment to racial redress. Thus, despite the popular embrace of conspiracy theory, Rowan found little white support for his claims of a conspiracy against black leaders.

Rowan's article also influenced the as-yet-unsettled debate about what exactly was happening to black elected officials. When George Brown spoke of harassment before the NAHRW, he used the term as a default. He did not know if there was a "deliberate effort" to discredit black elected officials; he knew only that "the list of fallen black leaders [was] growing and that there [were] some people in this nation who [were] rejoicing because of it." In her interview with Rowan, C. Delores Tucker had variously claimed that black elected officials were the victims of a news media "double standard" and the targets of a "national conspiracy on the part of the political establishment to preserve the status quo," two distinctly different things. Others, like Ralph Metcalfe, had blamed their troubles on local power struggles with white political machines — in this case the Daly machine with which Metcalfe had recently broken ranks. Rowan's article, specifically his choice of title, amplified the voices of those black elected officials who believed that their troubles were the product of a national conspiracy. Convincing as Rowan's argument might have been to many African Americans, it might never have caught on were it not for a series of news media and government investigations of Representative William Clay (D-Mo.) between 1974 and 1977 and his repeated claims that these investigations were evidence of a national conspiracy.

William "Bill" Clay came to political prominence as a civil rights activist working with the St. Louis chapter of CORE in the 1950s. In 1959, Clay was elected alderman of the Twenty-sixth Ward running on a civil rights plank. His abrasive demands for black access to jobs alienated many in St. Louis's Democratic machine and the black submachine. One such protest outside the Jefferson Bank in 1963 landed him in jail for violating a court injunction against picketing and brought forth angry calls by the *St. Louis Globe Democrat* that he be stripped of his elected position. Although not openly hostile to black civil rights, the *Globe Democrat* editors, like many St. Louis whites, viewed the assertive black power politics that Clay was coming to symbolize as a threat to peace and public order. The bank protest may have made Clay a villain to local whites, but it made him a hero to local blacks. It also convinced the young politician that he needed to build a black power base to wrest concessions from the machine. By 1968, Clay had used his newfound fame to gain control of patronage from the machine in North St. Louis and secure a seat in the U.S. House of Representatives.[45]

Weakened by the demographic changes engulfing the city, the machine made its peace with Clay. The *Globe Democrat*, however, did not. Beginning in July 1974, it published a series of adversarial articles designed to spark law enforcement investigations of Clay and in the process discredit him on the eve of the August 6, 1974, Democratic primary. The articles variously accused Clay of being associated with a heroin dealer, using his clerk hire funds for political purposes, and hiring a "hit man" to murder his opponent.[46] A representative example of the dishonesty of the *Globe Democrat*'s reporting is the August 5 article "Hoodlum Support for Clay," which featured a picture of Clay standing uncomfortably next to two men with extensive criminal records. The picture was taken in the late 1960s at a ward fund-raiser at which North St. Louis residents paid two dollars to be photographed with then-alderman Clay. The article detailed the criminal pasts of the two men, Fred Parker and Earl Davis, and alleged that Clay had a relationship with both. Though the title made it appear as though the two men were supporting Clay in the 1974 Democratic primary, in actuality, at the time the article was published, Davis was dead and Parker had been in prison for several years.[47] The following day, Clay defeated his *Globe Democrat*–endorsed opponent. When he returned to Washington, D.C., Clay sent a "dear colleague" letter to his fellow members of Congress detailing the *Globe Democrat* "conspiracy" to defeat him.[48]

In the post-Watergate frenzy to catch corrupt elected officials, the *Globe Democrat*'s preelection attack on Clay became fodder for a series of interlocking federal investigations. In the months following the 1974 election, the DOJ, the FBI, the GAO, the IRS, the St. Louis Crime Task Force, and the *Wall St. Journal* all began investigations of Clay's office that lasted over three years, cost Clay thousands of dollars in legal fees, and gave him an undeserved reputation for criminality. The first of these investigations involved the *Globe Democrat*'s allegations of clerk hire violations. For twelve months, federal investigators (from the U.S. attorney's office in St. Louis and the GAO in Washington) questioned several dozen of Clay's present and former employees. The case was eventually dropped for lack of evidence.[49]

The following December, while the clerk hire investigation was still ongoing, attorneys for the St. Louis Crime Task Force introduced Clay's name into the narcotics trial of John Conley Jr., a former state representative and Clay ally from North St. Louis. In a pretrial brief, chief prosecutor Liam Coonan alleged that Conley told undercover agents who were discussing a drug transaction that he "knew they were alright and would introduce them to William Clay." To support this claim, Coonan secured the testimony of paid government informer Robert Stuart, who stated that Conley was "with Mr. Clay" during a discussion of a drug deal. The allegations were given heavy coverage by the *Globe Democrat* and soon found their way into newspapers around the country.[50] Unable to defend himself in court — Clay had not been charged, only identified as an unindicted coconspirator in the trial of another person — Clay wrote thirteen different letters to attorney generals William Saxbe, Lawrence Silberman (acting), and Edward Levi requesting that either he be indicted or his name be removed from the brief. He also issued a press release charging that a "conspiracy" existed between the "*Globe Democrat* and the U.S. Attorney to Destroy Congressman Clay." Only when Clay mobilized eighty-four members of Congress, including House Speaker Thomas "Tip" O'Neill (D-Mass.), to pressure Attorney General Levi to expedite the case did the DOJ commence an internal investigation of Coonan's allegations. Rather than focus on Coonan's actions, however, investigators focused on Clay. FBI agents poured over his tax returns and interviewed friends and associates in Washington and St. Louis. They also interviewed several prison inmates, including Fred Parker, the man listed in the August 5, 1974, *Globe Democrat* smear article. The investigation found Coonan's claims to be unfounded, and after thirteen months, the case was dropped. No members of the St. Louis Crime Task Force were ever disciplined.[51]

Three months after Coonan first made his allegations in March 1975, the *Globe-Democrat* ran a front-page article charging Clay with failing to report three thousand dollars in political contributions to his 1974 campaign committee. This article stimulated yet another investigation, with the FBI visiting the offices of the contributors and photographing the checks in question. Federal investigators quickly discovered that the contributions had in fact been reported. The investigation, like the others, was dropped for lack of evidence.[52]

In fall 1975, as the FBI was wrapping up its investigation of campaign contributions, St. Louis banks began receiving summonses from the IRS demanding all files they possessed on Clay and his wife, Carol Ann Johnson. Although it is difficult to determine when or why the IRS began its investigation, it continued for the next year and a half.

The multiple investigations triggered by the *Globe Democrat* created a feeding-frenzy effect, and soon other newspapers were conducting investigations of Clay. In March 1976, the *Wall Street Journal* believed it had found the ever-elusive evidence of Clay's criminality when it published the front-page article "How a Congressman Billed Government for Phony Travel: Rep. Clay of Missouri Claimed Trips to Different Cities during Same Time Periods." The article accused Clay of falsifying congressional travel records for the years 1971 to 1975 and, in the process, defrauding the government of several thousand dollars. Clay claimed that the *Journal* was making much to do about clerical errors in his travel reimbursement requests and charged that this latest investigation was the product of a "national conspiracy against black elected officials." He was joined in this assessment by CBC chairwoman Yvonne Braithwaite Burke (D-Calif.), who stated that the *Journal* had "joined what [was] looking more and more like a conspiracy between certain federal agencies and some elements of the media to undermine the integrity, and ultimately the effectiveness, of black leaders." Subsequent developments in the travel-voucher controversy did little to dissuade Clay and Burke of their beliefs. Approximately one month after publishing the Clay story, the *Journal* published "Federal Travel Expenses Net Some Congressmen Thousands of Dollars," another front-page article accusing nine white congresspeople of travel violations similar to those leveled at Clay. The article noted that confusion over recent changes in reimbursement guidelines and member's lax attitude about keeping detailed travel records made such travel reimbursement irregularities widespread in Congress. Ignoring the second article, in June 1976, Alan Hollander, a Buffalo, New York, law student filed suit against Clay in federal court. Hollander sought damages for the government using an 1863 statute that permitted "any citizen to sue a federal official in the name of the United States for knowingly making false claims against the government." In a remarkable instance of selective prosecution, the DOJ amended the case, adding the claim that Clay owed the government $186,000 for the allegedly fraudulent travel, but did not take any action against the nine white members of Congress who were named in the second article. Clay settled the case for $1,754, after government investigators found that his staff had mistakenly requested reimbursement for eight trips under the mileage (driving) as opposed to the airfare designation. The nine white members of Congress named in the second article quietly submitted similar reimbursements.[53]

Despite the settlement with the DOJ in the travel-reimbursement case, Clay remained under investigation. In October 1977, the IRS expanded its ongoing probe with a request for Clay's financial records from the House of Representatives. The Clerk of the House refused, citing a House resolution prohibiting him from complying with such requests. Undaunted, the IRS worked with the U.S. attorney in St. Louis to convene a grand jury for the purpose of subpoenaing the House clerk. In effect, the IRS was using the grand jury as a shell to obtain Clay's records despite legal restrictions on its ability to do so. Speaking with reporters about the investigation in March 1977, Clay framed the inquiry as the latest in an ongoing campaign of harassment: "I've been subjected to investigations and harassment for three years. This is part of a continuing practice." Displaying the wit that made him such an effective public speaker, Clay continued, "If they attempt to frame me on income tax fraud, they had better have witnesses that are more credible than the $100-a-day junkie that they used in an attempt to frame me on narcotics charges." Clay filed suit against the IRS and the U.S. attorney later that month, alleging that the two were improperly using the grand jury to obtain his tax records. The following July, the IRS and the U.S. attorney agreed to end the probe. In a parting shot at his tormentors, Clay ridiculed the investigation as a "circus act" that was part of an "ongoing plot" to silence him.[54] With the end of the IRS controversy, and for the first time in three years, Clay was no longer "under investigation."

The multiple federal investigations stimulated by the *Globe Democrat* and the *Wall Street Journal*, and Clay's forceful and repeated denunciations of the investigations as a "plot" or "conspiracy" to destroy his career, lent tremendous credence to Rowan's January 1976 charges of a conspiracy to destroy black leadership and, in the process, influenced Sawyer's research. Writing in the May 1976 issue of *Focus*, the magazine of the Joint Center for Political Studies, she noted, "In national publications, in keynote addresses, in conference programs, in informal discussions — the question is repeatedly asked, 'Is there a conspiracy against black elected officials?'" The question was so often repeated following the publication of Rowan's article that Sawyer felt compelled to title her article "Is There a Conspiracy?" Although Sawyer raised the issue of conspiracy as a question, Rowan's assertion that a conspiracy did in fact exist and black elected officials belief in the same penetrated her methodology, thereby influencing her conclusions.

The Dilemma of Black Politics

By the summer of 1977, Sawyer had collected nearly one hundred case-studies of harassment from across the nation. Her subjects ranged from small-town school board members to the mayors of America's largest cities. Their combined stories told a harrowing tale of state and news media scrutiny and persecution that spanned the previous decade and touched black elected officials at every level of government. Using a lyrical writing style and a keen understanding of black politics, Sawyer assembled these case studies into a three-hundred-page report titled *The Dilemma of Black Politics: A Report on the Harassment of Black Elected Officials. Dilemma* would become the most influential statement on harassment ever written, shaping black elected officials' understanding of their relationship to the news media and the state for decades to come.

Sawyer arranged *Dilemma* into three large sections. The first, "Grievances," lists ninety-five case studies of black elected officials who claimed to have suffered harassment. Like Rowan, Sawyer provided several in-depth case studies followed by a longer list of abbreviated case studies. The case studies cover both by-then familiar figures like former representative Adam Clayton Powell Jr.; Representative William Clay; and Lieutenant Governor George Brown and more obscure figures like Benton Harbor, Michigan, mayor Charles Joseph (R); Macon County, Alabama, sheriff Lucius Amerson; and Memphis, Tennessee, state senator John Ford (D). Sawyer presents this data as "neither exhaustive nor comprehensive," but rather as "a spot check" on black elected officials then holding office. She saw the report as an incomplete data set presented in the hopes of alerting the public to "a very real problem of critical significance" and, in turn, stimulating further research and corrective action.[55] This disclaimer aside, Sawyer's case studies are quite thorough. In 1976, the number of African Americans holding high government office was still very small, allowing for a relatively comprehensive study at the state and federal level. Only six African Americans held statewide office in 1976: California lieutenant governor Mervyn Dymally, Colorado lieutenant governor George Brown, Pennsylvania secretary of state C. Delores Tucker, Michigan secretary of state Richard Austin, Massachusetts senator Edward Brooke, and Connecticut state treasurer Henry Parker. Sawyer notes that four of the six had experienced a news media investigation, and that three of those four had been subjected to government ethics investigations. None were found guilty of wrongdoing.[56] Similarly, Sawyer discovered that three-quarters of the 16 African Americans serving in Congress in 1976 had experienced a random assortment of police and intelligence community surveillance and counterintelligence, grand jury investigations, media investigations, IRS audits, and/or been placed on Nixon's enemies list in the previous ten years.[57] Although her data was incomplete, Sawyer could say with certainty that at least 10 percent of the 276 African Americans serving as state legislators in 1976 had been subjected to state and/or news media scrutiny — the vast majority by the IRS. Sawyer's figures for other state and local offices are more qualitative than quantitative. She provides approximately fifty case studies for these groups.[58]

The second section of the report, "Methods, Meanings, and Motives," explores the forms of harassment, describes its perpetrators, and places it in historical context. For Sawyer, like Rowan, harassment was characterized not by a specific modus operandi or group of perpetrators but rather by its effect on black elected officials. It took a multiplicity of forms, including "lack of coverage, biased coverage, investigations, and unfounded criminal accusations by the white media; audits and investigations by the IRS; surveillance, bugging, burglaries and covert disruptive activity by intelligence agencies; and inquiries, Grand Jury investigations and allegations by law enforcement agencies."[59] Sawyer identifies three institutions as the principal perpetrators of harassment: the white news media, the intelligence community, and the law enforcement community. Over the course of the previous decade, she argues, the law enforcement and intelligence communities had engaged in targeted attacks on the black freedom movement, black elected officials included. Harassment, then, was "in part an extension of the attacks instigated by the intelligence community in the Sixties against civil rights workers, against poverty programs, against Black Power advocates. It [was] in part a continuation of the program designed and developed by the Nixon administration to eliminate black activists." With Nixon's 1974 resignation, Sawyer asserts, harassment took on a new form. "Since Watergate," Sawyer writes, "this nation has exploded in a new level of consciousness and indignation at the revelations of corruption in our governmental system." This popular indignation, however, was being used disingenuously by government investigators and reporters "as a tool for attacking Black politics under the guise of abolishing corruption."[60] What unified these state and news media actors and the methods they used, indeed what made their actions harassment, Sawyer argues, was their goal or effect: to discredit, disrupt, or imprison black elected officials.

Harassment was not, in Sawyer's eyes, a seemingly timeless attack on all powerful African Americans. Sawyer viewed harassment broadly as the age-old reaction to "the intrusion of Blacks on the prerogative of white values, white power, and white control."[61] The primary reason that black elected officials were harassed, then, was because of the "threat" they posed to white political power. This was a marked departure from Rowan's claim of a blanket attack on all black leadership. Black leadership, Sawyer was saying, had a choice. They could cooperate with the system of what she called "traditional white politics," by which she meant brokerage politics, or they could attempt to change that system to benefit their black constituents by adopting "black politics," by which she meant antiracist, redistributive politics. This was the "dilemma" to which Sawyer referred in her title. If black elected officials adopted "black politics," they were likely to be harassed. Only if they abandoned "black politics," and thereby betrayed what Sawyer understood as their reason for being, could they ensure against being targeted for repression.[62]

Despite its remarkable insights, *Dilemma* is characterized by several notable methodological failings that would reinforce black elected officials' misperceptions about harassment and be exploited by critics when the report was released. First and most importantly, Sawyer adopted the ambiguous definition of harassment used by her subjects. Although most black elected officials understood "harassment" to mean political repression perpetrated by the state and the news media, many others used it as an umbrella term to describe all manner of unwanted scrutiny, political or policy opposition, and repression directed at black elected officials. Looking at several of Sawyer's case studies, one can see the problems that this definition poses. For instance, Sawyer writes that former Iowa state representative June Franklin (D) was harassed when Republican state representatives "gerrymandered . . . her district boundaries . . . in such a way as to preclude a successful bid for reelection." In another case study, Sawyer writes that when Manhattan borough president Percy Sutton ran for mayor in 1971, he received the "silent treatment" from the white New York news media, and what coverage he did receive was "almost exclusively of a negative character." In a third case study, Sawyer discusses Baltimore city councilman Michael Mitchell, whose "office was broken into and files disturbed on three separate occasions," by the ISD of the Baltimore Police Department. Only pages later, Sawyer describes the "hate mail" received by a school district trustee who asked to remain anonymous, as harassment.[63] Thus, harassment could mean illegal, state-sanctioned counterintelligence, perfectly legal partisan politics, a news media snub, and the vigilante activities of a private citizen. The only thing that united these disparate phenomena was their real or perceived negative effect on the black elected officials in question. This definition was, at its worst, almost entirely subjective.

Second, Sawyer adopted uncritically black elected officials' allegations of repression. Sawyer never spoke to representatives of the many media organizations and government entities she accused of harassment. Her only primary sources of information were black elected officials. And her regard for these sources shaped the way in which she received their allegations of repression. Sawyer had traveled to these individuals' homes and offices and spoken with them at length about their difficulties. Many had shared with her the immense personal and professional burden that the various instances of surveillance, investigation, audit, and negative media coverage had taken on their personal and professional lives. Some broke down and cried. These interviews deeply affected Sawyer. "One can marvel at the strength and fortitude of officials who continue to carry out the duties of their offices in a responsible fashion even as they are being unfairly accused of irresponsibility," she wrote of the interviews, "but one cannot listen to the accounts and watch the progression of such events without also responding in the depth of your being to the spiritual burden imposed." Having felt that burden through her interactions with these elected officials, Sawyer could make no claim "of an absence of bias." This bias, however, caused her to sidestep the question, first posed (and ignored) by Rowan, of whether her subjects were "crooks" or "victims of conspiracies."[64] She would assume the latter.

Third, Sawyer incorporated aspects of Rowan's, Tucker's, and Clay's conspiracism into her findings. Taking their claims seriously, Sawyer had searched for a "single national or international conspiracy in the sense of a plot being masterminded to destroy the institution of Black politics through the systematic discrediting and elimination of change-oriented Black elected officials." She did not find any evidence to confirm the existence of such a conspiracy. She refused, however, to abandon the concept, stating, "*Neither does it* [the study] *determine that there is not such a conspiracy.*" Rather than discard the theory proffered by several of her subjects but unsupported by her research, Sawyer retained it in altered form, settling for the claim that "conspiratorial activities transpire within certain newspapers; among businesses and corporations; between Federal agencies; and among intelligence, law enforcement, and judicial operations."[65] These claims added nothing to Sawyer's conclusions. The first rested on the impossible presumption that one can find evidence of nonexistence. The second gave a sinister spin to the regular workings of government. There was no question that federal, state, and local police and intelligence agencies had cooperated in their investigations of black elected officials, but there was nothing *necessarily* untoward about government agencies working together. As early as 1978, Sawyer would regret her focus on conspiracy and de-emphasize the claim in her writings.[66] By then, however, critics had already seized on the term, using it to dismiss her research as "conspiracy theory."

The last section of *Dilemma*, "Toward Resolution," provides action items for those interested in ending harassment. Here Sawyer gives a laundry list of corrective action for everyone from the "the federal government" and "the mass media" to "the public — white and black." It is perhaps a function of her faith that Sawyer believed that the very people whom she was accusing of illegal or racist activity would consider her recommendations for reform. They did not. I wish to focus, then, on Sawyer's recommendations for black elected officials and civil rights organizations, for it is they that Sawyer would lobby in the years to come to address harassment. Here, Sawyer laid out two major action items. First, she called for the creation of a "national advocacy organization with paid staff to counter harassment." This organization, Sawyer hoped, would also collect information on harassment, thereby absorbing or supplanting the CSMEO. Second, Sawyer called for the creation of a "legal defense fund either through an existing civil rights organization or a newly established organization."[67] Based on the response she had received from black elected officials to date, Sawyer believed that her study would stimulate a flurry of activity around the topic of harassment, making the creation of such a defense organization a real possibility. It did not. *Dilemma* turned out to be the first and only large-scale investigation of harassment. Though a number of antiharassment advocacy organizations were created in the 1980s and early 1990s, no national legal defense fund ever took shape.

Sawyer had produced a critically important document. A majority of her case studies documented instances of illegal state repression of black elected officials; her interviews gave readers insight into black elected officials' evolving understandings of these attacks; and the document itself served as a rallying point for black elected officials as they searched for ways to understand and address their plight. Unfortunately, though, Sawyer had synthesized and refined rather than confronted the inconsistencies of Brown's, Dymally's, and Rowan's ideas. Although she hoped that other researchers would supplement and complicate her work, none ever did. As such, Sawyer's research shaped discussions of state and news media attacks on black elected officials for the remainder of the century. Evident in those discussions were both the insights and the methodological failings of *Dilemma*.

With the help of People's Temple Church in San Francisco, which absorbed the cost of production, Sawyer printed eight hundred copies of *Dilemma* and prepared for its October 1977 release.[68]

The Dilemma of Harassment

The public response to *Dilemma* in the year following its release revealed the racial divide that characterized late-1970s U.S. politics and Sawyer's methodological failings. African Americans embraced the report, employing it in multiple efforts to defend black elected officials accused of misconduct. Whites, on the other hand, ignored or rejected it, often seizing on Sawyer's methodology to justify their opposition. This racial divide demonstrated the dilemma antiharassment activists faced in their attempts to identify harassment and defend targeted black elected officials. And this dilemma was on full display in 1978, when the two highest-ranking black elected officials in Congress lost their seats in what many African Americans believed were cases of harassment.

The mainstream white press greeted the release of *Dilemma* with what *Black Enterprise* magazine called a "thunderous silence," while local white papers in Colorado and California viciously attacked Brown and Dymally for their roles in producing the report. Of the national dailies, only the *New York Times* and the *Los Angeles Times* covered the October 11 release of *Dilemma*. The *New York Times* article, all of four hundred words, was buried on page 44. The *Los Angeles Times* was only slightly more generous, placing its article on page 24.[69] Local newspapers in California and Colorado were far more attentive to the release of *Dilemma*, publishing a number of articles in the week following the press conference. These reporters' assessment of *Dilemma*, however, was uniformly negative. Criticism of the report took two forms. First, these reporters attacked Sawyer's methodology of only talking to black elected officials and not their alleged tormentors, as one-sided. Second, reporters seized on Sawyer's discussion of conspiracy to discredit her findings. With titles like "Prove It Doesn't Exist," "Non-Existent Conspiracy," and "New Witch Hunt," they lampooned Sawyer's argument (reported as Dymally's in California and Brown's in Colorado) that while she did not uncover evidence of a national conspiracy, she would not rule out its existence.[70]

In sharp contrast to the silence and hostility of the white press, the black press gave *Dilemma* widespread and positive coverage. The *Minority News Digest* included coverage of the report in its October 10 and December 5 releases. The National Newspaper Publishers Association serialized Sawyer's press release, forwarding it to all member newspapers. These papers, in turn, published a number of articles that presented *Dilemma* as cutting-edge research and a warning of impending attacks on black elected officials. The black weekly magazine *Jet* published a favorable article, and the now defunct *Sepia* invited Sawyer to write a full-length feature article the following February. Of the dozens of articles written by black publications, only *Black Enterprise* uttered a word of caution about Sawyer's methodology. Arguing that the report "lacks documentation of some of its most serious charges" and "fails to give those it brands as the persecutors of black elected officials any opportunity to reply within its pages," *Black Enterprise* feared that the report "was far less effective than it might have been" in presenting a subject of critical importance to the black community.[71]

The racial divide was equally distinct among black and white elected officials. Black elected officials used *Dilemma* in their efforts to defend themselves from state and news media investigations, while white elected officials, Republican and Democrat alike, ignored the report. In November 1977, Atlanta black elected officials and civil rights activists used *Dilemma* to make their case that local news coverage of their ranks was racially biased. In June 1978, Herman Starks, president of the NBC-LEO, wrote to President Jimmy Carter and Attorney

General Griffin Bell expressing "strong opposition to prejudicial attempts to discredit black leadership in this country." He requested that the administration "use [its] offices to put an end to these prejudicial acts."[72] The following year, representatives of the NCBM met with FBI director William Webster to discuss "apparent harassment of blacks across the country."[73] According to the NCBM president, Mayor A. Jay Cooper (D-Prichard, Ala.), who took notes during the meeting, Webster listened attentively to the delegation's complaints and agreed that the bureau was investigating a large proportion of the NCBM's membership. Cooper recorded that Webster estimated that number to be 40 percent of sitting black elected officials. Webster did not offer any assurances that existing investigations were being conducted in a racially neutral manner.[74] The meeting only served to further undermine the board's confidence in the FBI. Within days of leaving Washington, the NCBM board voted to hire a private investigator to determine if the bureau had unlawfully placed its membership under surveillance.[75]

The civil rights community also embraced *Dilemma*. No organization was more enthusiastic in its response than the NAACP. In May 1978, the NAACP convened the National Leadership Summit Conference with the stated intention of charting a course for the future of black political and economic development. Nearly one thousand delegates and spectators attended the gathering in downtown Chicago. Among them was Sawyer, who had been invited to participate in the "Political Arena" discussion. She submitted a position paper to the gathering titled "Sustaining Black Leadership," which outlined several strategies for continued study of harassment and the defense of black elected officials. Sawyer's paper drew considerable attention, consuming three hours of debate during the workshop. The panel adopted her recommendations for action wholesale and published her position paper in its final report. Later that summer, the association placed the issue of harassment on its national agenda. As a result, the association's leadership used its syndicated opinion columns to popularize the issue with national program director Kenyon Burke, former executive director Roy Wilkins, and Benjamin Hooks writing columns on the topic.[76] The NAACP again called on Sawyer in June 1979 for its Seventieth Annual Convention in Louisville, Kentucky. Organizers had created a workshop titled "Harassment of Black Elected Officials and Civil Rights Leaders," in response to the level of interest in Sawyer's position paper one year before. The panel attracted over three hundred participants, demonstrating the continued popular appeal of harassment two years after the publication of *Dilemma*.[77]

By the winter of 1978, Sawyer was in high spirits. Her efforts had been a remarkable success. Although the white press and white elected officials had ignored or belittled *Dilemma*, the black press, many black elected officials, and the civil rights community had greeted the report with enthusiasm. Back in her Sacramento office, requests for *Dilemma* exceeded supply and invitations for speaking engagements were piling up on her desk.[78] Yet many African Americans' embrace of *Dilemma* masked harassment ideology's enduring flaws. Two years before, Carl Rowan had raised the questions of how to distinguish harassment from law enforcement, how to ensure that blacks are not subject to a double standard, and what mechanisms blacks could use to defend black elected officials. Sawyer had wrestled with only the last of these three questions. This oversight would be put on full display in the spring of 1978, when the two highest-ranking black elected officials in Congress, Representative Charles Diggs (D-Mich.) and Senator Edward Brooke (R-Mass.) lost their seats in the midst of news media and government investigations.

In March 1978, Representative Diggs, dean of the CBC, chairman of the House Committee on the District of Columbia, and chairman of the House Foreign Relations Committee, Subcommittee on Africa, was indicted by the Washington, D.C., U.S. attorney on thirty-five counts of mail fraud, making false statements, and receiving salary kickbacks from his congressional staff. Following a short trial that October, Diggs was convicted of all but six of the counts and sentenced to three years in prison plus a stiff fine. His lawyers filed an appeal, allowing the congressman to remain free on bail. Weeks later, the residents of the First Congressional District of Michigan, apparently believing Diggs's claims that he was a victim of "selective prosecution," resoundingly reelected the veteran legislator to Congress. Existing House rules did not bar congressmen who had been convicted of a felony from taking their seats and voting if they were elected after their conviction, and Diggs was sworn in with his colleagues in January. Following the trial, however, he was forced to surrender his institutional power and resigned his committee and subcommittee chairmanships under pressure from several of his colleagues in the Democratic Caucus.[79]

Like the Powell case before it, Diggs's legal problems began with a legitimate investigation of his misuse of clerk hire funds but were quickly exploited by conservative Republicans for political purposes. On January 9, Republican House leaders announced that they would seek Diggs's expulsion from Congress. Members of the Republican old guard like House minority leader John Rhodes (R-Ariz.) hoped to achieve this end by working through the Committee on Standards of Official Conduct (Ethics Committee). Others, like the group of conservative young Turks lead by freshman representative Newt Gingrich (R-Ga.), sought to force an immediate vote on expulsion. Responding to the old guard's complaints, the Ethics Committee began an inquiry in early February. Unsatisfied with the pace of the investigation, Gingrich announced in a February 22 letter to Diggs that if he attempted to vote on any matters before the House, he would move to have him expelled. Diggs voted on a bill to increase the public debt the following week. True to his word, Gingrich offered a resolution to expel him from Congress. Speaking to reporters after submitting his resolution, Gingrich begged the American public to share in his outrage: "Yesterday, a convicted felon voted on a $38 billion debt limit. We are permitting a convicted felon to vote on the laws of the United States!" The freshman Republican's resolution was referred to the Ethics Committee by a vote of 322–77, where it was tabled and subsequently died.[80] In June of the following year, the Ethics Committee filed formal charges against Diggs for violating House rules and began negotiations for an admission of guilt. The committee called for censure rather than expulsion following Diggs's agreement to formally apologize to the House and make restitution.[81] Eleven days after the report was issued Representative Dan Lungren (R-Calif.), another conservative young Turk, attempted to force another vote on expulsion. The motion was tabled by a margin of only eight votes (205–197). A breakdown of the vote demonstrated the regional tensions within the Democratic Caucus and the strategy of Gingrich and Lungren: 193 Democrats and 12 Republicans voted to table Lungren's motion, while 134 Republicans and 63 (almost exclusively southern) Democrats voted to bring the measure to the floor. The following day, July 31, the House voted 414–0 to censure Diggs, with four members voting "present."[82] Though Gingrich's and Lungren's efforts proved futile in the short run, they forecast a strategy that the Republican Party would use to remarkable effect in the late 1980s and early 1990s as part of its effort to split the Democratic coalition and wrest control of the House of Representatives from the Democratic majority.

Within months of the Diggs indictment, in May 1978, Senator Edward Brooke (D-Mass.), the only African American in the upper chamber, became the subject of intense media coverage that ultimately led to his defeat in the fall general election. The centerpiece of these stories was a discrepancy between Brooke's financial disclosure report to the Senate and sworn statements he made during his 1977 divorce proceedings. At issue were forty-nine thousand dollars in loans recorded in Brooke's divorce proceedings but absent from his disclosure reports. Under questioning from reporters, Brooke conceded that he had fabricated the loan during the divorce proceedings in order to conceal family assets from his then-estranged wife. Responding to the news reports, the Senate Ethics Committee and the Massachusetts state district attorney opened investigations. That November, Brooke, tainted by scandal and under investigation, was defeated by Democrat Paul Tsongas in his bid for reelection. Soon after the election, both investigating bodies concluded that there were no grounds for legal action against the former senator.[83]

That summer, leading African American intellectuals and political activists identified Diggs's and Brooke's legal troubles as cases of harassment. In his weekly column, former NAACP executive director Roy Wilkins wrote, "Black

Leadership is under fire. The cloud over the political future of Sen. Edward Brooke is a case in point."[84] One month later, Wilkins's successor, Benjamin Hooks, wrote an editorial of his own in which he opined that both Diggs and Brooke were the victims of "a deliberate campaign of harassment."[85] In an April 1979 article for *Encore American and World News*, political activist Herschelle Challenor claimed that Diggs was a "victim of selective justice." In 1976 and 1977, Challenor noted, white representatives James Hastings (R-N.Y.), Wayne Hayes (D-Ohio), and John Young (D-Tex.) were all found to have violated House clerk hire rules. The DOJ had declined to prosecute in each instance. Indeed, Challenor wrote, *never* before in the history of the Republic had the DOJ indicted a member of Congress for violation of clerk hire rules. Why Diggs? (Challenor's claim was not true. Just two years before, in December 1976, Representative Hastings had been convicted of receiving kickbacks from his staff.)[86] The previous June, political scientist and former Diggs staffer Ronald Walters suggested a political motivation for the Diggs investigation. Noting that the investigation was begun shortly after the congressman delivered a blistering attack on President Gerald Ford's policy toward the Marxist government of Angola, Walters argued in the pages of *Africa* that it was likely retribution for his break with the administration.[87]

The Diggs and Brooke cases exposed the weaknesses of harassment ideology. Although Challenor, Hooks, Walters, and Wilkins acknowledged the existence of a post-Watergate increase in official corruption investigations and the increased popularity of adversary journalism, they nonetheless were inclined to define the Diggs and Brooke investigations as harassment. Yet a closer look suggests that the Diggs and Brooke investigations were a product of the very forces that these writers dismissed. Diggs was among the first wave of high-ranking elected officials who were caught up in the anticorruption investigations that followed Watergate. Between 1975 and 1978, seventeen members of Congress were indicted for bribery, conspiracy, soliciting sex, reckless driving, mail fraud, and a number of other crimes as federal prosecutors and special counsels launched a torrent of official corruption investigations against high-ranking elected officials. This was a larger number of indictments of members of Congress in a four-year period than at any previous time in American history.[88] Senator Joseph Biden (D-Del.) pointed to this phenomenon when he rose on the Senate floor to speak out in defense of Senator Brooke: "All the special counsels we appoint think they are [Watergate prosecutor] Leon Jaworski. All see themselves as though somehow they are about to be knighted for uncovering great corruption. . . . It worries the heck out of me . . . that we seem to be falling into a situation where we can be tried in the press, we can be tried outside the normal channels of jurisdiction of both the Senate and the courts of law in this country."[89] Diggs was also one of the first casualties in what would become a decades-long ethics war between the Democratic and the Republican parties. Democrats had used the Watergate scandal to paint the Republican Party as the party of corruption, and in the process won big in the 1974 midterm elections. In subsequent elections, a group of conservative Republicans affiliated with Newt Gingrich sought to turn the tables on the Democrats by leveling their own allegations of corruption, and Diggs became one of their first targets. The Brooke case, on the other hand, was quite obviously not an instance of selective prosecution, racial targeting, or any other nefarious motivation. Brooke had purposefully attempted to conceal money from his estranged wife at a time when public indignation about such activity by elected officials was at an all-time high. In the midst of the resulting controversy, he lost to a strong Democratic challenger in an increasingly Democratic state. Diggs's defenders too had little grounds for alleging harassment. Following his conviction, the Detroit congressman admitted that he was guilty of receiving kickbacks from his staff for several years before he was eventually caught.

The contradictions inherent in the Diggs and Brooke cases did not cause antiharassment activists to rethink harassment ideology. In July 1978, Sawyer penned a letter to Diggs stating that she was "immensely pleased" with Walters's article on the Diggs controversy, arguing that "the analysis [was] right on target." That same day she wrote to Brooke, offering to send additional copies of *Dilemma* to help with his defense efforts.[90] In the meantime, Rowan's questions continued to go unanswered.

The End of the Committee for the Study of Black Leadership

More than challenge Sawyer's research, the events of 1978 deprived her of access to the prestige and institutional support of the Colorado and California lieutenant governors' offices, events that she both rightly and wrongly attributed to repression. Exhausted by four straight years of antiharassment research, and lacking even the meager support that she had received from Dymally and Brown, Sawyer closed the newly renamed Committee for the Study of Black Leadership (CSBL) in 1979.[91]

The first of Sawyer's patrons to leave office was George Brown. In June 1978, Colorado Democrats gathered in Denver to ratify a party slate for the upcoming elections. Brown had announced his candidacy for reelection two months before despite Governor Lamm's well-known preference that he be dumped from the ticket. Lacking the incumbent governor's support and suffering from three straight years of negative news coverage, Brown faced bleak prospects. In the field of five vying for his post, he was expected to finish last. When his turn came to have his name placed in nomination, Brown strode to the podium for what most in the room expected to be a campaign speech. In a move designed for maximum publicity, the lieutenant governor shocked the audience by withdrawing his candidacy. Citing constant and vicious "media harassment" during his tenure as lieutenant governor, Brown claimed that he could not put his family through another four years of such treatment.[92]

Reading news reports of Brown's announcement in Sacramento, Dymally wrote his friend a sympathetic letter in which he jokingly paraphrased former President Richard Nixon: "They only have me to kick around now."[93] Unlike Brown, Dymally *was* running for reelection, and despite intermittent battles with the *Los Angeles Times* and an ongoing FBI investigation, he was a strong candidate. In most polls he led his Republican challenger, Los Angeles record executive Michael Curb, by five to ten percentage points.

In early October, however, a bizarre chain of events involving a gross misuse of office by Evelle J. Younger, the California attorney general and a Republican gubernatorial candidate, derailed the Dymally campaign, sending the lieutenant governor down to defeat. On October 5, a reporter from the *Los Angeles Times* approached Michael Franchetti, an investigator in the California attorney general's office, to inquire about a "low-grade rumor" that Dymally was going to be indicted by federal prosecutors. It was true that the FBI was investigating Dymally for possible misuse of office. The U.S. attorney, however, had no evidence to indict, and never would.[94] Following the meeting, Franchetti wrote a memo to his supervisor detailing his conversation with the *Times* reporter, expressly identifying the inquiry as based on a rumor. Soon afterward, a member of the attorney general's office — many California Democrats have argued that Franchetti was the culprit — forwarded the memo to Bill Stout, a news anchor at CBS affiliate KNXT. Stout's wife worked for the Curb campaign. Using excerpts from the memo, Stout announced on the October 10 evening news: "There is a state investigator's report saying the U.S. Department of Justice has the evidence for indictments of both Dymally and Hugh Pike, his one-time finance chairman."[95] Stout either did not know or refused to state that the "report" was actually a memo concerning questions about a rumor.

Rather than condemn the announcement as an improper leak from his office, Attorney General Younger exploited it in his bid for the governorship, hoping that so doing would help him to defeat incumbent Governor Jerry Brown (D). Three days after the Stout broadcast, Younger penned a letter to U.S. Attorney General Griffin Bell accusing him of obstructing the indictment of "a particular state officeholder" against whom the FBI had secured "evidence of numerous indictable counts," and leaked it to the press. In subsequent public statements and off-the-record conversations with reporters, Younger encouraged speculation that Dymally was the unnamed state officeholder.[96] Subsequently, Curb made these allegations a centerpiece of his campaign. In a series of appearances in late October, Curb made repeated assertions that Dymally was not only under investigation but had committed crimes in office. Speaking in Redlands, Curb claimed that Dymally "used public funds in private business deals" and "diverted funds into his own pocket." During a press conference in San Jose, Curb opined, "I think he [Dymally] will be indicted and I think he is guilty of criminal offenses in office." Pressed by reporters, Curb conceded that he had no specific knowledge of Dymally's alleged misdeeds. Determined to make the story stick, Younger disingenuously endorsed Curb's assertions by referring back to the improper leak from his office: "I don't have any quarrel with the charges made by Mr. Curb. . . . He can hardly be faulted for repeating what a couple of million people saw and heard [on the *CBS Evening News*]."[97]

The incumbent lieutenant governor tried in vain to contain the impact of the CBS broadcast. He dared Curb and Younger to produce evidence of his alleged misdeeds and filed criminal slander complaints against Curb in Redlands and San Jose. Despite these efforts, Dymally narrowly lost the election on November 7.[98]

Dymally's defeat and the ongoing FBI investigation deprived Sawyer, and by extension the CSBL, of a source of income. Sawyer had become Dymally's administrative assistant shortly after releasing *Dilemma*. Now she was out of a job. Soon after the election, Dymally created Voter Education and Research Action Inc. (the VERA Center), a research and consulting firm located in Sacramento. He hired Sawyer as a consultant, saving her, she claims, from the unemployment line. Simultaneously, the FBI investigation of the former lieutenant governor intensified. His clients were sometimes contacted by the FBI directly, thereby frightening them into ending their relationships with Dymally. As a result, the VERA Center retained only a handful of clients in 1979. "It had gotten to the point in '79 where I was damn near broke because nobody would touch me," Dymally recalled.[99] As the investigation frightened more and more of the center's business away, Sawyer — who had not taken a second job so as to devote all her free time to the CSBL — was forced to apply for unemployment after all. Because the CSBL had depended on periodic infusions of Sawyer's salary and the office space and materials provided by Dymally, the VERA Center's inability to retain clients starved it of the resources necessary to operate effectively. The financial strain on Sawyer also threatened to deprive the CSBL of its chairman and only full-time volunteer.[100] Writing to NAHRW president Larry Groth in August 1979, Sawyer confided that she was "pretty much committed to staying with the work of the Committee until October 1980," explaining, "At that point, I will need to assess what has been accomplished, and how much assistance and support there is from other groups and individuals on this issue. I will have to assess my own strength, resources, direction, and whether to continue, or move on to other involvements."[101] That support would not materialize.

Since the publication of *Dilemma*, Sawyer had penned a number of letters to foundations, civil rights groups, and black political organizations begging them to fund or adopt the CSBL, all to no avail. Foundations continued to shun the CSBL. Civil rights and black political organizations had been enthusiastic about of the committee's work, and Sawyer believed that they might be more receptive to her entreaties. They were not. In 1978, Sawyer wrote to NAACP executive director Hooks imploring him to adopt the CSBL. Although Hooks and the NAACP were extremely supportive of the committee as discussed above, he was not willing to commit money and personnel to the project. Sawyer made similar inquires with the CBC and the SCLC later that year. They, like that to the NAACP, were rejected.[102]

In fall 1979, Sawyer looked to the NAHRW as a last resort, a move that would lead to the closure of the CSBL. Writing in her October 1979 annual report, she challenged the board of directors to transform the NAHRW to meet the staff and funding needs of the CSBL: "Consideration should perhaps be given to phasing out the Committee within a year unless the status and character of NAHRW is radically transformed."[103] Sawyer envisioned a more activist NAHRW with an expanded membership and paid staff, capable of supporting the committee's work. Board members, however, had neither the resources nor the desire to alter the nature of the NAHRW to meet the needs of one of its committees. Lacking alternatives, Sawyer fastened on the notion that the NAHRW's engagement with harassment had inadvertently provided other organizations with an excuse not to take up the issue themselves. During the October 16, 1979, board meeting, she shared these feelings with her colleagues: "There is a possibility that if we phase out, an independent effort will be made by another group that has a vested interest in the issue." Adopting Sawyer's logic, the board voted to phase out the CSBL over the following twelve months.[104] Later that winter, Sawyer closed the CSBL bank account and archived its files.

In just a few short years, the issue of harassment had moved from the quiet lament of several individual black elected officials to a widely accepted interpretation (among blacks) of black leadership's relationship to the news media and the state. Black elected officials and their supporters now had a language and a body of research for understanding and describing the surveillance, counterintelligence, audits, and criminal and news media investigations that so many had experienced. They had not, however, coordinated a system for legal defense, research, or information sharing as Sawyer had counseled. No civil rights or political organizations stepped forward to take up the issue of harassment following the dissolution of the CSBL. As such, *Dilemma*, which Sawyer had envisioned as a catalyst for "dialogue" with "neither intent nor presumption that this [would] be the final statement on the matter of harassment," became just that. Just as importantly, black elected officials had not resolved the internal contradictions and unanswered questions of harassment ideology. As such, they entered the Reagan and Bush years with a popular but theoretically flawed interpretation of what was happening to their ranks and what they should do to defend themselves. This interpretation would provide them with a rallying point as they attempted to defend themselves against the disproportionate, and sometimes selective, prosecution that plagued black elected officials under the DOJ of the Reagan and Bush years. Conversely, it led some black elected officials into the realm of conspiracy theory, thereby undermining their credibility with whites and blacks alike.

The Public Integrity Section was created by Attorney General
Levi for good and valid reasons. Even so, however, it is
remarkable how fast such units, established to supervise and
coordinate a key area of enforcement, can be transformed into
subtle instruments of political harassment.

— David Burnham, *Above the Law: Secret Deals,
Political Fixes, and Other Misadventures of
the U.S. Department of Justice*

In the eighties, politics as well as ambition, intersected with
the remnants of bigotry. And this time, the government
officials black leaders had to worry about most were the federal
prosecutors, in increased numbers.

— Mary Fischer, "The Witch Hunt"

CHAPTER FOUR

Prosecution as Political Warfare
in the Reagan and Bush Years,
1981–1992

IN 1981, NEWLY APPOINTED Associate Attorney General Rudy Giuliani sat
down for an interview with representatives of the Presidential Accountability
Group, a Ralph Nader–affiliated watchdog organization that monitored executive appointments. Though Giuliani had been working in Washington for almost a year, he was best known for his role in the 1973 prosecutions of corrupt
New York City Police Department detectives later immortalized in the film
Prince of the City, which was then in theaters. As a young assistant U.S. attorney
in the Nixon DOJ, Giuliani inherited the case of Robert Leuci, a New York City
police officer who had been caught taking bribes and pocketing cash recovered
from drug dealers. Giuliani "flipped" Leuci into a government informant, forcing him to wear a wire and implicate his fellow officers in similar forms of corruption. The investigation led to dozens of prosecutions of corrupt New York
City cops.[1] In his interview with the Presidential Accountability Group, Giuliani

claimed that undercover operations were the key to successful official corruption investigations and insisted that the methods he had used in the Leuci case would work with state and federal elected officials. "I used to think when I was a prosecutor that one of the things that would have been very useful is if we would have caught one or two lobbyists for income tax evasion or some serious crime, get them to cooperate and run an undercover investigation the way we did in the New York City Police Department," Giuliani explained. "Congress really needed that. And the New York State Legislature needs that."[2]

Giuliani was not stating a passing fancy. He was describing administration policy. With primary oversight of the DOJ, Criminal Division, Giuliani set the tone for the department's approach to "official corruption" investigations for the next eleven years.[3] Using a battery of new weapons for prosecuting fraud by public officials created in the aftermath of Watergate, in particular undercover and "sting" operations, the DOJ increased the number of official corruption prosecutions per year by 50 percent between 1980 and 1984. Though Giuliani only stayed on as associate attorney general until 1983, the outlook he expressed in this 1981 interview guided the DOJ in the arena of official corruption investigations through the end of the George H. W. Bush administration. By 1991, the department was prosecuting twice as many public officials per year as it had in 1980.

Giuliani presented his plans for an official corruption crackdown as the desire of a disinterested public servant for clean government, and in many respects, he was sincere. In the absence of strong ethics guidelines and law enforcement attention, official corruption had flourished in the pre-Watergate era. The ethics reforms of the mid-1970s had eliminated some of the most blatant forms of graft, yet much remained when Giuliani arrived in Washington.[4] But the official corruption crackdown was not carried out by disinterested public servants. Rather, it was carried out by ideologically conservative Republican partisans who transformed the DOJ into what Thomas and Mary Edsall have called the "heart and mind of the Reagan revolution." While many U.S. attorneys conducted their offices in a professional manner, others enforced the law in ways that furthered the political transformation that facilitated their rise. The majority of official corruption investigations of the Reagan and Bush years targeted Democratic lawmakers. In particular, the U.S. attorneys directed a disproportionate amount of their prosecutorial attention toward African Americans who had emerged as some of the primary advocates for the welfare state, the base of the Democratic coalition, and, as the decade wore on, the most assertive and effective opponents of Reaganism.[5] Put differently, many Republicans used the official corruption crackdown as a political weapon against the Democratic Party and its most loyal constituency, African Americans.

Republicans did not enter office in January 1981 with the intention of using the official corruption crackdown as a political weapon; rather, the transformation occurred gradually through conflicts between Democrats and the Reagan and Bush administrations and internal struggles within the GOP.[6] Before Giuliani even came to Washington, members of Congress from both parties had expressed serious concern about federal prosecutors' new post-Watergate investigatory powers and the potential threat they posed to the rule of law. Following the 1980 election, however, high-ranking Republican elected officials excused the excesses of government investigators and encouraged the DOJ to expand the official corruption crackdown in ways that disproportionately targeted Democrats. In the late 1980s, journalists and black elected officials exposed a stark racial disparity in investigations. The DOJ responded by expanding the crackdown. Simultaneously, many high-ranking members of the Republican Party used these investigations to generate a public impression of Democratic corruption, an impression they then used as a partisan issue in every election between 1988 and 1994. By the second half of the Bush presidency, these two campaigns had generated an impressive symmetry that produced the highest number of official corruption investigations in U.S. history and a pronounced public awareness of the same. Thus what began as an effort at good government reform in the years after Watergate was, under the administrations of Presidents Reagan and Bush, transformed into a racial and partisan political weapon by certain segments of the DOJ and the Republican Party.

Acutely sensitive to the possibility of government repression and having, just years before, created a complex ideology for understanding "harassment," black elected officials became some of the earliest and most persistent critics of the official corruption crackdown and Republican attempts to use it to their political advantage. Granted, a significant number of the black elected officials investigated by the DOJ during the 1980s and early 1990s were found guilty, and rightfully so. Black elected officials were no more immune to corruption than their white counterparts. But for black elected officials, guilt or innocence was not the key issue. They objected not to the Reagan and Bush administrations' efforts to curb corruption but to stings that verged on entrapment and leaks from the grand jury designed to put pressure on targets. And most importantly, they objected to the racially and politically disproportionate manner in which the official corruption crackdown was being implemented.

Using the Official Corruption Crackdown as a Political Weapon

In the years after Watergate, the DOJ and Congress created potent new weapons for prosecuting bribery, extortion, and other acts of official corruption. In 1976, the DOJ created the Public Integrity Section to coordinate its efforts to combat fraudulent practices by government officials. The following year, the FBI pioneered a new investigative technique called the "sting" — a law enforcement–sponsored criminal enterprise designed to attract those "predisposed" to illegal behavior — for the purpose of uncovering hard-to-detect corruption. Congress, too, joined the fight against corruption. The Ethics in Government Act, passed in 1978, required high-level government officials to file annual financial disclosure forms. The law also established procedures for the appointment of special prosecutors (later called independent counsels) to investigate alleged malfeasance by executive branch officials. Two years later, Congress passed the Judicial Councils Reform and Judicial Disabilities Act, which allowed for the disciplining of federal judges by their peers and the transmission of impeachment recommendations to Congress. Such was the zeal of congressional reformers that in 1984 they gave federal investigators the power to pursue allegations of theft, fraud, and bribery by any state or local government entity that received as little as ten thousand dollars in a given year from the federal government, thereby opening nearly every state and local government entity in the country to federal scrutiny. And between 1981 and 1992 Attorney Generals William French Smith, Edwin Meese, and Richard Thornburgh doubled the staffs of the U.S. attorneys and gave them increased autonomy to wield these new investigatory tools against alleged corrupt public officials. Thus, by the end of Reagan's first term, the DOJ had the statutory authority, the investigative tools, and the manpower to aggressively pursue allegations of corruption by public servants at nearly every level of government. And despite Reagan's stated aversion to an intrusive federal government and calls for a more robust federalism, his DOJ planned to use these new powers to root out corruption from the U.S. Congress to the town council.[7]

These anticorruption policies went into effect at the very time that the two major political parties became locked in a "grinding political stalemate." Despite intense party competition for all branches of government in the late 1960s and early 1970s, Democrats maintained a hammerlock on the House of Representatives and many statehouses while Republicans emerged as the party of the presidency. The Senate remained up for grabs. Seeking to break the stalemate, and unable or unwilling to defeat each other through electoral mobilization, the two parties turned to nonelectoral forms of contestation. Both parties worked to use the government institutions they controlled, political scientists Ginsberg and Shefter tell us, to "undermine and disrupt institutions controlled by their rivals." Thus Republicans sought to expand the powers of the president and increase presidential control over the executive agencies. Democrats, in turn, attempted to strengthen Congress by working to check presidential authority. In this atmosphere, the official corruption reforms of the late 1970s and early 1980s became "weapons of political warfare." Between 1981 and 1992, Republicans used the DOJ and the FBI to investigate the Democratic-controlled

Congress, state legislatures, municipal governments, and the judiciary. By the late 1980s, the Republican House minority also started using the Committee on Standards of Official Conduct to investigate House Democrats. Conversely, Democrats used the independent counsel and Congress's subpoena power to investigate the Reagan administration. Mobilizing the news media and the judiciary to supplement their efforts, both parties RIPed — an acronym Ginsberg and Shefter use to describe the process of "revelation, investigation, and prosecution" — their political opponents. This political warfare would come to define U.S. politics into the new millennium.[8]

The Reagan administration struck first and with the greatest effect. Between 1981 and 1992, the DOJ dramatically increased the number of official corruption investigations. Following the creation of the Public Integrity Section in 1976, the number of DOJ official corruption indictments doubled from an average of 220 for the first half of the 1970s to an average of 500 for the second. This initial increase was a product of the heightened suspicion of public officials fostered by Watergate. Although public consciousness of official corruption subsided in the early 1980s, official corruption prosecutions increased by 80 percent under Reagan. In Reagan's first term, the number of official corruption prosecutions jumped from 727 in 1980 to 1,076 in 1983. Following a slight dip to 931 in 1984, prosecutions jumped to 1,157 in 1985 and topped 1,200 through 1988. In the late 1980s and early 1990s, when party contestation for control of Congress and many statehouses reached a fever pitch, the number of prosecutions increased yet again. In 1989, DOJ official corruption prosecutions jumped to 1,349 and in 1991 reached the startlingly high figure of 1,452. In DOJ prosecutions of federal officials, the only area where the department has exclusive jurisdiction, the increase was even more striking. During the Reagan and Bush years, the number of official corruption investigations of federal officials increased fivefold, from 123 in 1980 to 624 in 1992. In 1991, the high point of DOJ official corruption investigations in U.S. history before or since, the number of prosecutions of federal officials spiked, reaching 803.

This official corruption crackdown targeted scores of public officials at every level of government from both political parties, but a majority of those targeted were Democrats.[9] Congress received early and repeated attention, with the DOJ conducting wide-ranging investigations of a "Capitol Hill drug ring" (1983–84), "no-show" or "ghost" employees (1988–89), abuse of the House bank (1991–92), and abuse of the House post office (1991–92) — in addition to U.S. attorney investigations of individual members. These probes led to the indictment of sixteen congresspeople between 1981 and 1992, nine of whom were Democrats. Though they were not indicted, the investigations also implicated a large number of powerful Democrats, most notably House Speaker Jim Wright (D-Tex.); Democratic whip Tony Coelho (D-Calif.); and chairman of

Department of Justice Official Corruption Prosecutions of Federal, State, and Local Officials, 1970–2009

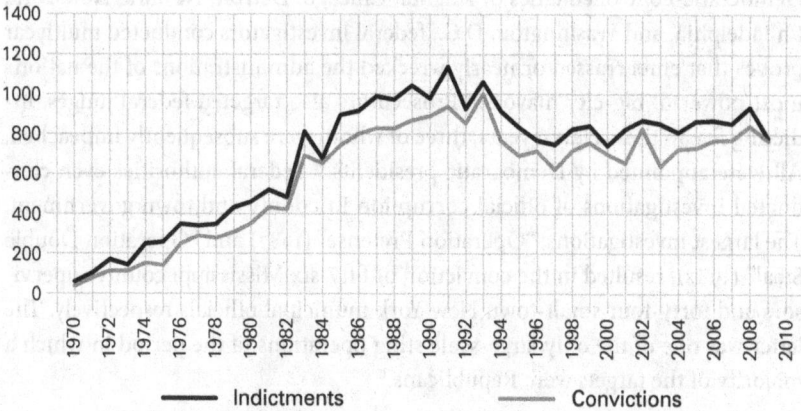

Legend: —— Indictments —— Convictions

Public Integrity Section, Criminal Division, Department of Justice, *Report to Congress on the Activities and Operations of the Public Integrity Section* (Washington, D.C.: U.S. Government Printing Office, 1978–2009). The Public Integrity Section entered the following footnote next to the 1984 figures: "The 1983 figures were reviewed to attempt to identify the reason for the substantial jump in prosecutions of federal officials. The explanation appears to be two-fold; first, there clearly was a greater focus on federal corruption nationwide, but there also appears to have been more consistent reporting of lower-level employees who abused their office, cases that may have been overlooked in the past."

the Democratic Caucus Bill Gray (D-Pa.).[10] State legislators; county, town, and municipal governments; even judges also found themselves subject to new levels of federal scrutiny between 1981 and 1992. Political scientists Kenneth Meier and Thomas Holbrook have found that "prosecution of corrupt officials was more intense in Democratic states than in Republican states during the Reagan years." Indeed, during this period, federal investigators carried out major sting operations targeting state legislators in Alabama, Arizona, California, Kentucky, New York, South Carolina, Texas, Tennessee, and West Virginia. These investigations led to the indictment of a number of high-ranking elected officials, most prominent among them president of the West Virginia Senate Larry Tucker (D); New York State Assembly speaker Mel Miller (D); and Kentucky House speaker Don Blandford (D). Not only did these investigations ensnare high-ranking legislators; they also led to the indictment of large percentages of legislators. "Operation Lost Trust" (1990) and "Operation Boptrot" (1992), for instance, led to the indictment of fully 10 percent of the sitting members of the South Carolina and Kentucky legislatures respectively.[11] Notably, of the states listed above, only Arizona had a Republican majority in its state legislature, but even here a majority of the legislators targeted in Operation Azcam were Democrats.[12] Federal investigators also targeted municipal governments. In the Democratic-controlled cities of Atlanta, Chicago, Detroit, Newark, New York, Philadelphia, and Washington, D.C., federal investigators conducted multiyear probes that embarrassed or nearly wrecked the administrations of the nation's most powerful big-city mayors.[13] Prosecutors also targeted federal judges, indicting five in these eleven years, three of whom were subsequently impeached. All were appointed by Democratic presidents.[14] Federal authorities even conducted investigations of official corruption in county and town government. The largest investigations, "Operation Pretense" (1987) and "Operation Double Steal" (1987), resulted in the conviction of fifty-six Mississippi county supervisors and forty-four small-town New York municipal officials respectively. The latter was one of the only large-scale sting operations of the period in which a majority of the targets were Republicans.[15]

Reagan Revolution / Rainbow Rebellion

The partisan warfare of the 1980s and early 1990s had a pronounced racial dimension, a product of the nature of the Reagan revolution and African Americans' reaction to it. As the 1970s came to a close, the American electorate was in a foul mood. Inflation and unemployment were rising in tandem, gas lines snaked out of service stations, the inner cities were crumbling, crime was at an all-time high, and in international affairs, the United States appeared impotent in the face of the Iranian hostage crisis and Soviet aggression in Afghanistan. The popular reaction to the turbulence of the late 1970s took many forms. Among them was a white backlash against African Americans and the government institutions believed to serve their needs. On the political fringe, the backlash took the form of increased hate-group activity. White vigilante organizations like the American Nazi Party and the Ku Klux Klan swelled with new members, and racist violence ranging from burned crosses to lynchings increased markedly. The majority of whites, however, expressed their anger through mainstream politics: staging raucous protests against busing; filing a bevy of lawsuits against affirmative action and minority set-aside programs; staging a revolt against taxes, which many believed were being redistributed via welfare programs to lazy and undeserving blacks; and abandoning the Democratic Party, now widely identified as the party of African Americans, in droves. This last phenomenon was particularly acute in areas where blacks had succeeded in gaining control of the local Democratic Party apparatus. Nearly all the mayoral races that included a black candidate in traditionally Democratic cities during the 1970s and early 1980s featured deeply polarized electorates with a majority of white Democrats switching to the GOP in the general election. Assessing the racial landscape in 1980, Jesse Jackson argued, "Racism has become fashionable again and feelings of guilt have turned to feelings of hostility."[16]

Enter former California governor Ronald Reagan. During the 1980 election, Reagan succeeded in gathering the disparate elements of this new white backlash into the Republican Party and, in the process, becoming the first conservative president since Herbert Hoover. Since the 1950s, Reagan had been a darling of the political right. As a General Electric pitchman, he had traveled the country, warning GE workers that the welfare state constituted creeping socialism and liberals a fifth column in the battle with Soviet totalitarianism. Applying this antistatist philosophy to the civil rights rebellion then engulfing the nation, Reagan joined segregationists in their opposition to civil rights reform, arguing that it constituted an unconstitutional expansion of government control over citizens and their businesses. In 1966, Reagan rode the white backlash into the California governor's mansion. There he refined a political philosophy that shunned all forms of government regulation of private and business life, at least with regard to race. Though he was never close with Richard Nixon, Reagan's hostility to the reform movement and racial libertarianism dovetailed with the president's strategy of using race to build a white voting majority within the GOP. During his time in Sacramento, Reagan energetically repressed the New Left and railed against lawbreakers, welfare cheats, and liberal elites. Perhaps most importantly for the modern racial conservative movement, Reagan did all of this without making explicit reference to race. Thomas and Mary Edsall note that "Reagan paralleled Nixon's success in constructing a politics and a strategy of governing that attacked policies targeted toward blacks and other minorities without reference to race—a conservative politics that had the effect of polarizing the electorate along racial lines."[17]

In 1980, during his own quest for the White House, Reagan made a conscious effort to reassemble Nixon's white majority coalition of 1972. Courting what one of his campaign strategists called "George Wallace inclined voters," Reagan voiced his support for "states' rights," expressed his strong opposition to busing as a remedy for segregation in public schools, derided affirmative action as "quotas," claimed that civil rights law posed a threat to the liberties of white Americans, and portrayed the welfare safety net as an expensive government handout to undeserving black women. As in his 1968 and 1976 runs, Reagan received grassroots support from members of the old Citizens' Councils and various other segregationist holdovers.[18] Come Election Day, huge numbers of white Democrats and independents joined an energized Republican base in voting for the GOP nominee. Indeed, the only element of President Jimmy Carter's 1976 coalition that did not witness substantial defections to the Republican Party in 1980 was African Americans.[19]

The white backlash of the late 1970s swept not just Reagan but a whole new generation of Republican elected officials into office. Republicans picked up 12 seats in the Senate, thereby giving them control of the upper chamber for the first time in twenty-six years. In the House, the GOP gained 33 seats, shrinking the Democratic majority from 273 (159 Republicans) to 242 (192 Republicans). Republicans also scored major victories on the state level, picking up four governorships and 189 state legislative seats.[20] Many Republicans interpreted the 1980 contest as a realigning election that signaled the rise of a Republican majority in national politics. Republican National Committee (RNC) chairman Bill Brock called the 1980 contest "the breakpoint election in bringing about a party realignment." Even those conservatives who did not use the language of realignment believed that the election had given them the green light to disassemble the welfare state. Like Reagan's chief of staff Edwin Meese III, they argued that Reagan and conservatives had a "mandate."[21]

Once in office, Reagan and his appointees did as they had promised and worked assiduously to reverse the liberal public policies designed to remedy racial discrimination. William Bradford Reynolds, Reagan's pick to be assistant attorney general for civil rights, "put in prodigious hours," biographer Ronald Wolters has noted, "to review and modify the legal briefs prepared by [his liberal] staff lawyers, making sure that 'equal rights' had not been twisted into 'special preferences.'" To Reynolds this meant dramatically decreasing voting rights enforcement and regularly interpreting civil and voting rights cases to the benefit of whites. Clarence Thomas, Reagan's African American pick to head the Equal Employment Opportunity Commission (EEOC), refused to bring class-action discrimination lawsuits — the agency's most successful instrument for forcing compliance with nondiscrimination statues — and instead brought several suits for alleged "reverse discrimination" on behalf of white men. Reagan gutted the U.S. Civil Rights Commission, replacing several of its liberal members with conservatives. In subsequent years the commission abandoned its historic function as a national civil rights watchdog and toed the administration's "color-blind" line. The president also slashed funding to cities, cut social services, and shifted the tax burden to the poor and the working class — all with devastating effects for African Americans, who were concentrated in the cities and among the poor and the working class.[22]

In the face of the Reagan revolution, African Americans emerged as the core of the Democratic opposition and some of the most effective opponents of Reaganism. In 1982, African Americans staged a series of protests that forced Reagan to back away from his opposition to renewal of the VRA. In 1984 and again in 1988, Jesse Jackson ran for president in the Democratic primaries, providing an eloquent critique of Reaganism and forcing his Democratic rivals to sharpen their attacks on the popular incumbent. More than provide a rhetorical counterpoint to the Reagan administration, Jackson struck at the GOP's emerging base by registering tens of thousands of reliably Democratic black voters in the increasingly Republican South. In 1983–84, for instance, the Jackson campaign and related black and left-leaning voter registration efforts added between 2 and 2.5 million voters to the rolls nationally, including 183,000 to the rolls in Georgia, Alabama, North Carolina, Louisiana, and South Carolina.

These overlapping black counterinsurgencies, what Manning Marable has called a "Rainbow rebellion," slowed the Reagan revolution. In 1985, Alabama black political organizers and elected officials temporarily put the brakes on Reagan's efforts to stack the federal judiciary with conservative ideologues by convincing the previously compliant Senate Judiciary Committee to reject Reagan nominee Jefferson Sessions for a seat on the U.S. District Court for the Southern District of Alabama. Sessions became the first Reagan judicial nominee to be rejected by the Senate. The following year, African American anti-apartheid activists and their friends in Congress handed Reagan his first major foreign-policy defeat when they overrode his veto of divestment legislation. In 1986, African American activists again handed Reagan a bitter loss when delegate Walter Fauntroy (D), who was also president of the National Black Leadership Roundtable (NBLR), mobilized black voters in ten closely contested southern Senate races. These black voters provided the margin of victory to Democratic senatorial candidates in Alabama (Richard Shelby), Georgia (Wyche Fowler), Louisiana (John Breaux), and North Carolina (Terry Sanford). Strong black support also provided the margin of victory for incumbent Senator Alan Cranston (D-Calif.). Thanks in no small part to the NBLR and Fauntroy, the Democratic Party retook the Senate by a margin of 55–45, and, in the process, ground Reagan's assault on the welfare state to a halt.[23]

As the specter against which Reagan had built his winning coalition and the most assertive opponents of Reaganism, African Americans became the primary targets of Republican-directed political warfare. White voters and elected officials in areas where they had been displaced by local blacks regularly made allegations of corruption to Republican U.S. attorneys against black Democratic elected officials and voting rights activists. White businessmen, long accustomed to a good-old-boy network that gave them an inside track on government contracts alleged corruption and cronyism against black elected officials who attempted to implement affirmative action and minority set-aside programs. FBI agents, many nursing their own racial grievances, appear to have fed a disproportionate number of allegations against black elected officials into the federal investigatory apparatus. A series of class-action lawsuits filed in the late 1980s and early 1990s reveal that white FBI agents exhibited a deep-seated racism that was often tolerated by their supervisors. Considering the degree of discretion allowed agents in undercover and sting operations, these attitudes likely affected target selection. Yet even when agents did not exhibit racial bias, their target-selection criterion guaranteed a disproportionate racial result. The FBI's "profile" for public servants who might be "predisposed" to criminal behavior flagged elected officials who were not independently wealthy, which disproportionately identified African Americans. The U.S. attorneys energetically pursued these many allegations of fraud against black elected officials despite scant evidence of wrongdoing and the obvious bias of the sources. Others investigated the same black elected officials over and over again, using the steady stream of allegations from local whites as justification for their activities. Conversely, some of these same Republican U.S. attorneys ignored allegations of corruption against their political allies.[24]

These developments led to significant levels of racially disproportionate targeting in federal official corruption investigations. In 1988, *Washington Post* reporter Gwen Ifill found that while African Americans constituted only 3 percent of all elected officials, they were the targets of 14 percent of DOJ official corruption investigations between 1983 and 1987. African Americans were thus five times more likely to be investigated than their white counterparts.[25] Investigations of members of Congress reflected this disparity. Ten of the thirty-six African Americans who served in the House of Representatives between 1981 and 1992 were investigated by the DOJ; two were indicted.[26] To match this figure, several hundred white congresspeople would have had to have been investigated and several dozen indicted. Only 171 federal legislative branch officials were prosecuted between 1981 and 1991, the overwhelming majority being staff, not members. Fourteen white congressmen were indicted.[27] The numbers were even more lopsided for black federal judges. Two of the five federal judges indicted by the DOJ during this period were black; one of the three judges who were impeached was black, and another black judge, Robert Collins of the U.S. District Court for the Eastern District of Louisiana, resigned under threat of impeachment in 1993. Yet during the 1980s, African Americans constituted less than .5 percent of federal judges. Put differently, black federal judges were several hundred times more likely than their white counterparts to be indicted by the DOJ or impeached during the Reagan and Bush years.[28]

The Crackdown Hits Black Elected Officials

As early as 1983, black elected officials became aware of the racially disproportionate nature of the official corruption crackdown. On July 19, 1983, Representative George Crocket (D-Mich.), a former Wayne County Recorder's Court judge and a member of the House Judiciary Committee, penned a letter to his chairman, Representative Peter Rodino (D-N.J.), complaining about what he and many of his constituents perceived as the deliberate targeting of black elected officials by federal investigators. Crockett feared that under President Reagan "the federal prosecutor and the federal grand jury [were] being used to besmirch the good name of black leaders in an effort to destroy their political potential." Over the course of the previous several months, Crockett explained, federal grand juries had investigated charges against the highest-ranking black elected officials in Detroit, Michigan; Newark, New Jersey; and Tchula, Mississippi. Additionally, a grand jury led by Associate Attorney General Giuliani was then investigating a senior member of the CBC. And a Miami grand jury had indicted the only black federal judge in the state of Florida, "the first such time a sitting federal judge [had] been so charged," Crockett noted.

While Crockett did not dispute federal prosecutors' right to investigate allegations of wrongdoing against public officials, he was disturbed by the manner in which the investigations were being conducted. The investigations featured "massive leaks to the press . . . of grand jury evidence prior to indictment." The airing of grand jury evidence, Crockett argued, "can prejudice a person's right to a fair trial as well as destroy a person's reputation and position in the community prior to — or, in some cases, instead of — an indictment or trial." He requested that Rodino conduct hearings to ascertain whether federal prosecutors were using the grand jury process to attack black Democratic elected officials. Crockett's was the first allegation of harassment made by a member of Congress since the late 1970s. Two days later, Rodino received a letter from the newly elected congressman from South Central Los Angeles, Mervyn Dymally (D-Calif.), applauding Crockett's initiative and urging the chairman to conduct hearings on the "harassment of black elected officials."[29]

The five cases that Representative Crockett cited in his letter provide a window into the manner in which the official corruption investigations about which black elected officials complained were conducted in the early 1980s. They featured ambitious, at times overzealous, prosecutors and investigators who vigorously pursued targets despite weak or inconclusive evidence, sloppy investigative work that fell apart at trial, and massive leaks to the press. Many also featured a proclivity of federal investigators to cooperate with white reactionaries. It is primarily for these reasons that all but one of the black elected officials cited in Crockett's letter saw the charges against them dropped, were acquitted, or had the cases reversed on appeal.

Take the Newark case, for example. There, Mayor Kenneth Gibson (D) and city council president Earl Harris (D) — the first African Americans to hold those positions — were indicted on a combined total of 141 counts of conspiracy, neglect of official duty, misconduct in office, official misconduct, and obtaining municipal funds by false pretenses, theft, and deception, after it was discovered that the man hired to conduct security at Newark's primary source of drinking water, former city councilman Michael Botempo (D), was a "no show" employee. In the ensuing trial, Judge Paul Huot dismissed 118 of the counts, arguing that they did not apply. During the remainder of the trial, Huot repeatedly admonished the prosecution for not sufficiently supporting its charges against Gibson and Harris. Prosecutors could not prove that Gibson and Harris had conspired to hire Botempo as a no-show employee, or that they had received anything in return if they did. The jury apparently shared Huot's misgivings about the prosecution's case. On October 21, they acquitted Gibson and Harris on the charge of conspiracy and deadlocked on the charge of misconduct in office.[30]

Federal prosecutors were similarly overzealous in preparing their case against Judge Alcee L. Hastings, the Florida judge in Crockett's letter. In 1981, William Dredge, a felon with ties to the mob, strolled into the U.S. attorney's office in Miami and alleged that Hastings was part of a bribery scheme. Hoping to get a deal on drug charges pending against him in Baltimore, Dredge claimed that Hastings was soliciting bribes in order to fix cases through attorney William Borders. One case in which Borders had solicited a bribe for Hastings, Dredge claimed, was *United States v. Romano*. A jury had found Thomas and Frank Romano guilty of racketeering before Hastings in 1980, and he had sentenced the pair to three years in jail and ordered one million dollars of their assets seized under the Racketeer Influenced and Corrupt Organizations Act (RICO). Dredge claimed that Borders had promised to have Hastings release the Romanos' assets in return for $150,000. Within days of this meeting, the U.S. attorney negotiated a plea bargain reducing the charges against Dredge and set up an undercover investigation targeting Hastings, codenamed "Apple Eye."

The ensuing sting produced circumstantial evidence against Hastings. The FBI had retired agent Paul Rico pose as Frank Romano, whom Borders had never met, and agree to accept Borders's bribe solicitation. Wearing a wire, the agent negotiated with Borders about the terms of the bribe and tried to gather evidence implicating Hastings in the scheme. Although he secured a large body of indisputable evidence against Borders, Rico was not able to gather anything solid against Hastings.[31] Rico had failed in his initial attempt to implicate Hastings, but he had one last chance to do so when he delivered the final bribery payment to Borders in Washington, D.C., on October 9, 1981. Just days before, Hastings had signed an order returning the majority of the Romanos' assets — a ruling he had been required to issue by two higher court rulings earlier that summer restricting the scope of RICO forfeitures — thereby sealing the deal. Rather than wait to see if Borders would deliver some of the money to Hastings, FBI agents arrested him on the spot. Two months after the arrest, the U.S. attorney in Miami indicted Hastings and Borders for bribery and conspiracy.

The flawed investigation came to light during the trial. Hastings argued that the evidence presented by the government represented a classic case of Borders's "making rain," or claiming that he could influence a judge even though he had no actual plans to try to do so, not conspiracy. Paraphrasing his defense in a 2001 interview, Hastings stated,

> When I went on the bench . . . , we were lectured by the then eight judges. And among the things they talked about was "rainmaking" and the fact that everywhere all over the United States of America people say that they got to the judge. Lawyers will say it. You know, "If you give me an extra $10,000 then I'll get the judge . . . to do this, that or the other." And if it goes your way then, you know, everything is fine. If it doesn't go your way, the guy either goes to jail or you get your $10,000 [or] give him [his] $10,000 back. And you say, "You know, that sucker wouldn't take the money. Man, you know, I tried."[32]

Rainmaking was apparently so common that even Dredge was aware of it. When Borders first approached him with a bribery solicitation, he refused to take him seriously, explaining, "Well here's another guy smoking Ajax. . . . I have heard for years that people had federal judges in their pocket." The jury found Hastings's explanation plausible and acquitted him in February 1983. Looking back on the case in 1989, one of the prosecutors, Assistant U.S. Attorney Martin Raskin, argued that the FBI's decision to arrest Borders on the spot rather than wait to see if he would transfer the money to Hastings had made it impossible to determine with certainty whether Hastings was guilty or innocent.[33]

The investigations were also marked by massive and detailed leaks from federal investigators to the press. Representative Ron Dellums (D-Calif.) — the member of the CBC mentioned in Crockett's letter — discovered that he was under investigation by the DOJ from the March 15, 1983, *CBS Evening News*. Since July 1982, a special DOJ task force led by Associate Attorney General Rudy Giuliani had been investigating allegations that a "drug ring" operated on Capitol Hill. Federal investigators had developed their case against Dellums from a single witness, Robert Yesh, a longtime employee of the House door-keeper's office. The previous year, Yesh had been arrested for a drug offense, and in return for reduced charges, he testified to the grand jury that he had sold cocaine and marijuana to Dellums and one of his aides on six separate occasions — one of them on the House floor. These were the charges that were leaked to CBS. Although no evidence corroborating Yesh's testimony ever surfaced, and Dellums was never even formally charged, he was forced to endure months of negative media coverage and the threat of indictment.[34]

The leaks were even more extensive in Detroit. In late 1982, the *Detroit Free Press* and the *Detroit News* began carrying detailed leaks from the then-ongoing grand jury investigations of high-ranking officials in the administration of Mayor Coleman Young (D) — a political ally of Representative Crockett. The investigations focused on the city's sludge-hauling contract with Vista Disposal Inc. and the city's bus fuel contract with the Magnum Oil Company — both minority-owned businesses. Leaks from the investigation were so detailed that the *Detroit News* was able to obtain quotes from the six-month federal wiretap on Coleman Young's home phone. In an article exploring the leaks, the *Detroit Metro Times* argued that "the sheer numbers and widespread availability of leaks over the past year suggest[ed] that if the sources were not actually encouraged to maintain their intimate relationship with the press [by the U.S. attorney], no serious effort was made to prevent their continuation."[35] When, during the trial that resulted from the case, prosecutors asked the judge to name Young as an unindicted coconspirator, the judge rejected the request on the grounds that the prosecution had not provided sufficient evidence to warrant such a move. Though the prosecution had not assembled a case that would hold up in court, the U.S. attorney had nonetheless succeeded in trying Young in the court of public opinion.[36]

Last, and most disturbing to Crockett, in some of these investigations federal prosecutors worked with reactionary white local elected officials to prosecute black elected officials. In Tchula, Mississippi, federal prosecutors prepared two cases against Mayor Eddie Carthan (D) in the midst of a vicious racial power struggle in which local whites were using the criminal justice system to attack his administration. Tchula is a town of approximately two thousand, situated in Holmes County along the southern rim of the Mississippi Delta. In 1977, Eddie Carthan, a twenty-seven-year-old small businessman and former school board president, was elected mayor, and four African Americans secured seats on the five-member board of aldermen. For the first time since its founding in 1826, the 81 percent black town had a majority-black government.[37] In response, local white farmers and merchants, whose families had run the town as a personal fiefdom since the antebellum period, initiated a multifaceted campaign of repression that eventually led to Carthan's imprisonment. They began this process by forcing one of Carthan's allies on the board of aldermen to resign, thereby creating a biracial board majority under the leadership of the one remaining white alderman, John Edgar Hayes.[38] Under Hayes's direction, the three passed several bills designed to limit Carthan's control of town finances and personnel, reduced Carthan's salary, raised property taxes on his supporters, refused to pay the travel and phone bills he incurred in the course of doing city business, locked him out of city hall for eight weeks, and replaced several of his black appointees with whites.[39] The board majority also made repeated contacts with the local district attorney, the Mississippi attorney general, and the U.S. attorney for the Southern District of Mississippi, requesting investigations of Carthan's alleged abuse of power and misuse of federal grant moneys. Carthan responded in kind, refusing board requests for information, repeatedly vetoing board votes (a questionable move since Tchula had a weak mayor form of government), and refusing to speak with the Hayes faction. By early 1980, the escalating struggle between the mayor and the board majority ground town business to a halt.

This struggle escalated in 1980–81, when the local district attorney indicted Carthan and several of his supporters for felony assault on a police officer. In April 1980, the board majority attempted to seize the office of the police chief by voting to replace the sitting, Carthan-appointed police chief with Jim Andrews, a white former police chief and brother-in-law to local white power broker and former mayor B. T. Taylor. That same night, and although he had not been sworn in or bonded, Andrews got his old uniform and gun and went to the town hall, where he assumed his new position. In response, Carthan accompanied by the sitting police chief, Alderman David McLaurin, and four black "police auxiliaries," went to the town hall and demanded that Andrews surrender his gun and leave the building. Andrews refused and drew his weapon, whereupon Carthan and his companions forcibly disarmed him and ejected him from the building. The group also found off-duty African American police officer James Harris, whom Andrews had brought with him to secure the building, hiding in a back room. They demanded that he leave, and he did so voluntarily. Several days after the incident, Andrews and Harris filed charges of "aggravated assault against a police officer" against Carthan and his companions. In the ensuing trial, Carthan and his companions were found guilty of simple assault on a police officer — a felony. Carthan was sentenced to three years in prison, and his codefendants received probation and hefty fines. Carthan and McLaurin were forced to resign their elected offices immediately.

Following the trial, a mountain of information surfaced that revealed the illegal nature of the proceedings. First, two black jurors wrote letters to Governor William Winter (D) alleging that they had been "confused, tricked, and misled" by the presiding judge's instructions. One of the jurors, Cornelius Brooks, wrote: "In my most sincere honest opinion these 7 men are innocent of what they're convicted of. I only changed my conviction under pressure and know that what I did was wrong." Second, Harris recanted his story on WLBT-TV3 (Jackson) and claimed that he was paid to file charges against Carthan. There was ample evidence to support his second story. Following the trial, Harris began working in B. T. Taylor's convenience store and, despite his meager salary, managed to secure a new Lincoln Towncar from a lot owned by Andrews's cousin. Defense lawyers also located a witness to the altercation at city hall, James Rhyne, who swore that the seven defendants had not assaulted Harris. The district attorney had interviewed Rhyne before the trial but told him not to testify because "his testimony would be helpful to the defense." Rhyne had not come forward during the trial, he said, because he feared that he would lose his job working for Alderman Hayes.[40] On the strength of this information, Carthan appealed the decision.

In an effort to head off any possibility of a comeback, District Attorney Frank Carlton manufactured murder charges against the former mayor and Joseph Carthan, his brother. In June 1980, just three months after the "Tchula 7" had been convicted of assault, two men, later identified as Vincent Bolden and David Hester of East St. Louis, Illinois, walked into B. T. Taylor's convenience store with Roosevelt Granderson, one of Carthan's black opponents on the board of aldermen. They cleaned out the store's cash register and safe, securing five thousand dollars. Before leaving, Bolden pumped two slugs into the back of Granderson's head, killing him instantly. After fleeing in several stolen cars, robbing several Holmes County banks, and engaging in a shootout with police on the streets of Tchula, the two men were apprehended by police. Following their capture, Carlton offered Bolden and Hester a deal: give him evidence of Carthan's involvement in the murder, and they would receive dramatically reduced sentences. Hester agonized over the decision. He did not know Carthan and was sure that Bolden did not either. He refused to implicate the former mayor. Bolden, on the other hand, had multiple felony charges pending above and beyond the Granderson robbery and murder and was looking at a possible death sentence. He took the deal and signed an affidavit alleging that Carthan and his brother had hired him to murder Granderson. In April 1981, Carlton indicted the Carthans for capital murder, basing his entire case on Bolden's affidavit. The defense, on the other hand, called Hester to the stand to testify that neither he nor Bolden knew Carthan and produced alibis for all the times when the former mayor had allegedly met with the shooters to plot the execution.[41] An all-black jury found the state's evidence unconvincing and acquitted Carthan in November 1982.

Considering that the trial of the "Tchula 7" was marred by false and coerced testimony and misleading instructions from the judge, and the murder charges against Carthan and his brother were quite simply fabricated, one would expect that federal authorities would have steered clear of the racial power struggle in Tchula. Instead, the U.S. attorney for the Southern District of Mississippi, George Phillips, developed two fraud cases against Carthan in 1981–83. The first involved a loan Carthan had secured to fund a town day-care center in 1979. He had received state aid for the project, and as he prepared to order equipment for the center, he received a call from Robert Bolden (no relation to Vincent), director of the state Office of Minority Affairs under Governor Cliff Finch (D). Using a simple fraud scheme that he later alleged had "been going on for years . . . in Mississippi," Bolden convinced Carthan to buy the day-care equipment through a firm owned by his friend Harold Foreman.[42] Bolden and Foreman then secured a loan for the price of the equipment from a Jackson bank, forged

Carthan's name on delivery receipts, delivered only a fraction of the equipment ordered, and pocketed the rest of the money at the City of Tchula's expense. When authorities apprehended them for the scheme, Bolden and Foreman implicated Carthan in return for dramatically reduced sentences. (The two had faced up to ninety years in prison each for their crimes. For their cooperation, Bolden received five months in federal prison, and Foreman received a three-year suspended sentence and a ten-thousand-dollar fine.) No tangible evidence tied Carthan to the scheme. Prosecutors relied exclusively on Foreman's and Bolden's claim that Carthan agreed to let them forge his name on the delivery receipts in return for a kickback. A jury of nine whites and three blacks convicted Carthan of two counts of giving false information to an FDIC-insured bank. He was sentenced to three years in prison and fined five thousand dollars.

At the same time that he was prosecuting Carthan for bank fraud, Phillips was preparing a second fraud case concerning the Tchula free-food program. In the 1981 indictment, Phillips charged that Carthan had submitted receipts to a federally funded free-food program for food that had never been delivered. In 1983, however, the U.S. attorney abandoned the case when his primary witness, Koai Meuchy, the owner of the corporation that delivered food to the Tchula food program, was killed during a shootout with police in nearby Canton, Mississippi. "The police were trying to apprehend Meuchy," John Kincaid writes, "for killing a nineteen year old pregnant woman and shooting three other people." Meuchy had testified against Carthan in return for leniency when sentenced. He had been convicted of issuing false receipts to the federal government in an unrelated case.

By 1983, when Phillips dropped the food program charges against Carthan, the multiple prosecutions of the mayor and his allies — and the national attention they were drawing — were proving an embarrassment to the state. Before the year was out, all the pending charges against Carthan were dropped and his sentences were suspended or reduced to time served. Though the former mayor had escaped an extended jail sentence, the prosecutions had achieved their intended effect. By the time Carthan emerged from prison, four whites, led by Alderman Hayes, dominated the town board, and B. T. Taylor was again the mayor of Tchula.[43]

Excusing Repression

The concerns raised by black elected officials about the selective and unfair nature of the official corruption crackdown did not, in the early 1980s, lead to any formal hearings or national press attention. Rodino, whose district included parts of Newark, responded positively to Crockett's request. He scheduled hearings for November 1983 and invited witnesses, among them Mary Sawyer. The proceedings were canceled at the last minute, however, for reasons unknown.[44] Yet the kinds of excesses that were evident in these prosecutions did become the subject of congressional concern in the early 1980s, as the House Judiciary Committee launched a series of hearings between 1980 and 1984 on the FBI's use of undercover and "sting" operations. Although these hearings would reveal serious problems with prosecutors' use of these techniques, congressional Republicans rejected all efforts at reform, demanding instead that Congress defer to the executive branch.

The vast majority of DOJ official corruption investigations between 1977 and 1992 revolved around FBI undercover or "sting" operations. Official corruption crimes, like bribery and influence peddling, are difficult for law enforcement to detect. They involve spoken agreements between parties that are familiar with one another, often leaving a convoluted paper trail and no witnesses. Under J. Edgar Hoover, the FBI had ignored such crimes, seeking to protect its image by focusing on cases that were easier to prosecute and less politically risky. After Watergate, however, the bureau was pressured to find new ways to catch corrupt politicians. In an effort to fulfill this new mandate, the bureau increased its employ of undercover operations and created the sting. Federal investigators instantly took to the new techniques, increasing their use sixfold in a seven-year period. In 1977, the FBI budgeted $1 million for its fifty-three undercover and sting operations. In 1984, the bureau was conducting over three hundred such operations at a cost of $12.5 million, figures that would only grow in the years ahead.[45]

The first large-scale FBI sting aimed at public officials was Operation Abscam. Between 1978 and 1980, FBI agents posed as representatives of an Arab sheik and offered over thirty elected officials bribes in exchange for political favors. Revealed to the public on February 2, 1980, by the *NBC Nightly News*, Abscam created a storm of controversy for the thirty targeted lawmakers, the vast majority of whom were never indicted. The operation raised a significant number of difficult questions, questions to which Congress demanded answers because so many of its members had been targeted, and tainted, by the investigation. Congresspeople wanted to know how the FBI determined who was targeted for the sting, how aggressively agents pursued targeted congresspeople once they were selected, if the individuals who were ensnared in the scheme were entrapped, and how the pretrial leaks would affect the targeted congressmen — both those who were indicted and those who were not. Soon after news of Abscam broke, the House Judiciary Committee, Subcommittee on Civil and Constitutional Rights, tried to answer these questions in a series of hearings. Rather than focus only on Abscam, the subcommittee explored the conduct of FBI undercover and sting operations in general.[46]

During one of the subcommittee's first hearings, representatives of the FBI and the DOJ acknowledged that their increased use of undercover and sting operations presented a potential danger to the rule of law. Targets of these investigations could be entrapped or tried in the press, they admitted. Public faith in government institutions could be undermined. Both claimed, however, that they had created "safeguards" to ensure that the dangers inherent in undercover and sting operations were not realized. First, the safeguards required that agents "only initiate investigations . . . when [the agencies] reasonably suspect[ed] that criminal activity of a given type or pattern [was] occurring or [was] likely to occur." Second, agents were required to make "clear and unambiguous to all concerned the illegal nature of any opportunity used as a decoy." Last, agents were required to model their decoy operations "on the real world as closely as [they could]," so as not to create a criminal opportunity so enticing that it would attract individuals who otherwise would not be predisposed to illegal behavior. In addition to these safeguards, all undercover operations were subject to approval and renewal by a joint DOJ-FBI Undercover Operations Review Committee. With these guidelines in place, the bureau and the DOJ argued, federal investigators could employ a needed investigative device while at the same time ensuring that individuals would not be targeted for arbitrary reasons, and targeted individuals would not be entrapped. Subcommittee members were asked to "wait and see how [the new guidelines] work[ed] in real cases" before passing judgment.[47]

The subcommittee did just that, delaying the release of its final report until June 1984 so that it could observe the DOJ's conduct under the new guidelines. What it found undermined nearly all the DOJ's and the FBI's assurances. Following an in-depth review of "Operation Corkscrew" — an FBI sting on the Cleveland Municipal Court conducted between 1978 and 1982 — the subcommittee concluded that "the safeguards in practice were little more than rhetoric, offering at best limited constraints upon the investigators, and little or no protection to the public." In Operation Corkscrew, FBI agents and informers targeted the judges of the Cleveland Municipal Court without reliable evidence of their predisposition for criminal behavior, used unrealistically large bribes to entice targets to engage in criminal behavior, and never clarified for the targets the illegal nature of the criminal opportunities they created. When the U.S. attorney reviewed the evidence gathered in the sting, he found it so weak that he refused to present it to a grand jury. Seeking to justify their efforts, and their budget, with indictments, agents went around the U.S. attorney and presented their case to the local district attorney. When he too refused to present it to a grand jury, the agents leaked it to the press in hopes of forcing local prosecutors' hands. The subcommittee judged Operation Corkscrew a "failure," noting "the integrity of an entire court system was impugned; the only prosecutions

obtained were for crimes which would not have occurred but for the undercover operation; innocent parties were injured; and previously respected public
servants were tainted and have suffered grave personal harm." The subcommittee noted as well that these violations were not limited to Operation Corkscrew.
Indeed, the subcommittee found that in all the sting and undercover operations they studied between 1980 and 1984, "virtually every one of the principal
safeguards was either directly violated, ignored, or administratively construed
in a manner inconsistent with their stated purposes." To address these issues,
the subcommittee recommended judicial review of undercover and sting operations and congressional action to determine "which of the more sensitive
techniques used in undercover operations [were] to be permitted and under
what circumstances they [might] be used."[48]

Committee Republicans disagreed with the Democratic majority's conclusions in a strongly worded dissent. They dismissed the report as a "slanted and
biased document that [was] aimed at closing down an effective and almost in-
dispensable tool in combating organized crime, drug operations, fencing operations, and political corruption." In making their case, Republicans dismissed
Operation Corkscrew and the other botched sting operations covered in the
report as aberrations. They focused instead on an FBI report that demonstrated
the "accomplishments" of undercover operations. Using the bureau's aggregate
figures, Republicans argued that in 1983, undercover operations had lead to 1,328
indictments and $81,506,583 recovered through fines and forfeiture of prop-
erty. These figures more than justified whatever risks undercover operations
might pose, they posited. What Republican's failed to mention, however, was
that only three of the indictments and $77,445 cited in the FBI report resulted
from undercover and sting operations targeting public officials. These numbers
were essentially no different from those for the years when undercover operations and the sting were not employed. Ignoring these disaggregated figures
and Democrats' concerns, the Republicans argued, "[The] executive branch,
charged with the duty of enforcing our laws, should be given the widest discretion to use whatever means at its disposal — within constitutional means — to
fight what is becoming an increasingly sophisticated criminal element in our
society."[49]

The Judiciary Committee hearings demonstrated a startling development
(that black elected officials had been discussing for more than a year). FBI agents
were sometimes targeting public officials for undercover and sting operations
based on rumors or erroneous assumptions of their alleged participation in or
predilection for criminal activity. Once investigations were begun, agents and
their informants seemingly stopped at nothing to ensnare the targets. And the
entire process featured weak oversight despite demonstrated patterns of abuse.
Just as importantly, the hearings exposed Democrats' and Republicans' deep

disagreements about the value of the DOJ's aggressive pursuit of official corruption. While Democrats affirmed the DOJ's stated goal of ferreting out official corruption, they raised serious concerns about the possibility that certain aggressive law enforcement techniques could lead to entrapment or undermine public confidence in federal law enforcement agencies. Republicans, on the other hand, doggedly defended the Reagan administration and its law enforcement initiatives. Not surprisingly, Democratic suggestions for legislative reform went nowhere, and the Reagan DOJ not only continued but increased its use of undercover and sting operations after 1984.

1987–1988: A Crisis of Legitimacy at Justice

In President Reagan's second term, the DOJ continued its official corruption crackdown. And like during his first term, these prosecutions disproportionately affected black elected officials. Unlike in the early 1980s, however, several of these investigations burst onto the front pages of the nation's newspapers. Most of the black elected officials targeted in the early 1980s did not have a national profile, and their cases occurred in small media markets. In 1987, however, the DOJ brought a series of high-profile cases in large media markets, thereby bringing national attention to black elected officials' allegations of harassment. Specifically, these cases highlighted the disparate ways in which black Democrats and white Republicans charged with similar crimes were treated by the Reagan DOJ.

The first major case of the year occurred in April 1987. Following eleven months of detailed leaks of grand jury testimony to the *Washington Post* and the *Baltimore Sun*, the U.S. attorney in Baltimore indicted state senator Clarence Mitchell (D-Baltimore) and his brother city councilman Michael Mitchell III (D) on multiple charges of fraud and conspiracy, the most serious in connection with the wide-ranging federal investigation of the Wedtech Company — a then-defunct defense contracting firm that had bilked the federal government out of several million dollars in minority set-aside or 8(a) contracts. Prior to the indictment, federal investigators told the *New York Daily News* that the Mitchell brothers' uncle, Representative Parren Mitchell (D-Md.), chairman of the House Committee on Small Business, which oversaw the minority set-aside program, was also a subject of the investigation. Representative Mitchell hastily arranged a press conference, denied that he was the subject of the investigation, and denounced the DOJ for the leak. His action forced the U.S. attorney in Baltimore to declare that the story was in fact untrue.[50] During the Mitchell brothers' trial, prosecutors could not produce evidence that they had done anything illegal for the money they received from Wedtech. The Mitchells claimed that they were paid for legitimate consulting services and produced signed contracts that stated as much. In a liberal interpretation of federal conspiracy statutes, however, prosecutors argued that they did not have to prove that the Mitchells actually did anything illegal for the money they received from Wedtech, only that they had led Wedtech officials to believe that they would. The evidence presented at trial to support even this contention was circumstantial.[51] Nonetheless, the jury voted to convict the Mitchells for wire fraud in connection with the alleged conspiracy but acquitted them of the charge of conspiracy. The split verdict led many legal experts to term the jury's decision "inconsistent" and "confused." Clarence Mitchell III was more direct, arguing that the prosecution "bamboozled the jurors" into supporting a racial and partisan attack on one of the country's most prominent black political families.[52] The Mitchell brothers were sentenced to several years in prison each. Their political careers were over.

The Wedtech case revealed the selective nature of the official corruption crackdown. Although the DOJ doggedly pursued its rather weak case against the Mitchell brothers and other Democratic elected officials connected to the disgraced defense contracting company, it was far less aggressive in its pursuit of the powerful white Republicans who had ties to the same firm. On April 8, 1987, just six days after the Mitchell indictments were handed down, Attorney General Edwin Meese recused himself from all Wedtech-related cases amid news reports that he had exercised his influence on behalf of the company in 1981–82 in his capacity as counsel to the president. In the following days, reporters discovered that Meese had extensive contacts with Wedtech including a substantial financial partnership with Franklyn Chinn, a former consultant and board member of the corporation. The reports moved the chairmen of the House and Senate Judiciary Committees to call for an independent prosecutor's investigation of Meese's ties to the firm. Bowing to the pressure, Meese requested that special prosecutor James McKay, who was already investigating former White House aide Lyn Nofziger's ties to Wedtech, add his name to the investigation.[53] In June, the Mitchell brothers filed a pretrial motion arguing that Meese's professional and financial relationship with Wedtech "created a blatant conflict of interest" and demanding that the case against them be dismissed. When it was denied by the presiding judge, the Mitchells filed an emergency motion with the Supreme Court. That motion was denied by William Rehnquist, who, despite the testimony of Clarence Mitchell III against his elevation to the high court in 1971 and to the position of chief justice in 1986, refused to recuse himself from the case.[54]

On July 5, 1988, McKay issued his report for the Meese investigation. In it, he concluded that Meese "probably violated" three federal laws in his dealings with Wedtech and in other matters. He declined, however, to indict the attorney general, citing "lack of evidence." To the contrary, a close look at the report suggests that McKay was simply not willing to use the evidence he had found. For instance, McKay found that at the same time that Meese's college friend Richard Wallach was being paid several hundred thousand dollars by Wedtech and bragging that he had influence with the then-counselor to the president, Meese had used his influence to secure a military contract for the Bronx defense contracting company. Meese claimed that the McKay report completely "vindicated" him. He nonetheless announced that he would be stepping down from his post as attorney general in the coming months.[55]

The Mitchell brothers' claim that they had been singled out for investigation was reinforced by a series of high-profile DOJ prosecutions of black elected officials in 1987–88. Within weeks of the Mitchell indictments, a grand jury in Knoxville, Tennessee, indicted Representative Harold Ford (D-Tenn.) on nineteen counts of mail fraud, conspiracy, and influence peddling. Prosecutors alleged that Ford had accepted over one million dollars in bribes from a prominent Tennessee banking family — disguised as bank loans — in order to finance an "extravagant and lavish life style, well above his personal means." The indictment forced Ford to relinquish his position as chairman of the House Committee on Ways and Means, Subcommittee on Human Resources. He would not be tried until 1990.[56] In May 1987, the U.S. attorney for the District of Columbia executed a number of raids targeting the administration of Mayor Marion Barry (D) and several black businesses holding city contracts. Built on a seventeen-month sting operation, the raids led to dozens of arrests, and agents seized thousands of documents — the whole operation floodlit by the klieg lights of local and national media. Despite the media splash created by the raids, it took prosecutuors some time to build their case. The delay fueled rumors encouraged by Barry and openly discussed in the black community that the entire affair was a setup. In so doing, he broke with a DOJ policy of not discussing ongoing investigations.[57] The following October, the U.S. attorney in Atlanta indicted Fulton County commissioners Reginald Eaves (D) and Charles Williams (D) and neighboring DeKalb County's only African American commissioner, John Evans, for extortion and conspiracy. During the course of a three-year undercover investigation, the indictment claimed, the commissioners had solicited and accepted several thousand dollars in bribes from undercover FBI agents posing as developers seeking zoning changes.[58] This last set of indictments became a flashpoint for controversy less because of its content than its timing. Only six months before, Alice Bond, wife of former state senator Julian Bond (D-Atlanta), had told Atlanta police that her estranged husband was a drug addict who used cocaine "at least every two hours on a daily basis." In response to officers' questions about possible drug use by Mayor Andrew Young (D) and other prominent Atlanta African Americans, Bond stated that she had no direct knowledge of such activity but had been "told" that Young had used drugs. In a summary of the interview that the officers later leaked to the press, the officers wrote that "Mrs. Bond claim[ed] to have seen Mayor Andrew Young using cocaine." When news of her allegations broke, Bond received a call from Mayor Young, who told her that "if she was just telling passing rumors . . . she shouldn't do anything in a fit of emotion." Subsequently, the U.S. attorney in Atlanta began a grand jury investigation of Young for possible witness tampering.[59]

By the time Eaves, Williams, and Evans were indicted, Atlanta black elected officials, indeed many black elected officials across the nation, felt themselves under siege. Following the Fulton and DeKalb counties indictments, SCLC chairman Joseph Lowery announced that he had directed aides to examine the sting to determine if federal investigators had engaged in selective prosecution. Mayor Young raised similar concerns of racial targeting before departing for Memphis to attend a rally in support of Representative Ford. And city councilman Hosea Williams compared the indictments to Redemption, stating, "What happened to us 100 years ago, is happening to us all over again," before joining the Mitchell brothers in leading a small march protesting "selective prosecution" in downtown Atlanta.[60]

Ironically, Attorney General Meese used these allegations of selective prosecution to seek revenge against Congress for demanding a special prosecutor investigation of his relationship to Wedtech and, in the process, sparked yet another investigation of a prominent black elected official. Only hours before leaving office in early August 1987, Meese issued DOJ order 1297–88. The order stipulated that the attorney general must launch a fifteen-day "initial investigation" whenever he received "information from any source" indicating that a U.S. congressperson may have committed a criminal act. If the investigation determined that "the information [was] specific and from a credible source," a "preliminary investigation" — limited to ninety days — must be undertaken to determine if there was "reasonable ground to believe that further investigation [was] warranted." If the attorney general determined that further investigation was warranted, he was required to appoint a special independent prosecutor to conduct the investigation. Responding to claims that the DOJ had become politicized under his leadership, Meese claimed the order would "remove any real or apparent concern that a particular investigation [might] be politically motivated . . . since the decision whether to prosecute [would] be made by an individual who [had] no long-term affiliation with the Department or any branch of government." The claim, on its face, was absurd. The order left the discretion to investigate and the choice of the "independent" prosecutor to the attorney general. It was, therefore, no guarantee against a politically motivated investigation. If anything, the order allowed the attorney general to mask political investigations beneath the veneer of an ostensibly objective, mandated process. Among the Washington press corps, the order became known as "Meese's revenge" (on Congress, as the order specified no other political body).[61]

The first person to be investigated under the new order was the African American Washington D.C. delegate Walter Fauntroy (D-D.C.). In fall 1988, Associated Press reporter Richard Keil published a series of articles concerning Fauntroy's employ of Thomas Savage, son of African American Chicago congressman Gus Savage (D-Ill.), on his congressional staff.[62] The reports alleged that Fauntroy employed Savage as a favor to his father and that the younger Savage may not have performed the work for which he was paid. Under the Meese order, Keil's articles triggered a DOJ investigation. During the "preliminary investigation," the FBI and the DOJ, Office of Professional Responsibility (OPR), balked at receiving information from Fauntroy's attorneys and conducting interviews with members of his staff.[63] Despite having refused this volunteered information, newly appointed attorney general Richard Thornburgh extended the investigation for sixty days, citing his desire to consult the Bush administration about rescinding order 1297-88 and "to give investigators additional time."[64] Thornburgh may not have been disingenuous. Meese's order had become a source of embarrassment to the new attorney general. Although Thornburgh suspended the order on April 13, his action did not end the Fauntroy investigation. Instead, the case was handed over to the U.S. attorney for Washington, D.C.[65]

Despite the increasing public discussion of possible DOJ malfeasance generated by the 1987-88 cases and Meese's resignation, the DOJ not only continued but expanded the official corruption crackdown in 1989. Determined to break the political stalemate of the past decade, conservative House Republicans used the widening crackdown to attack the Democratic leadership of the House of Representatives.

From Excusing to Exploiting the Official Corruption Crackdown

In the November 1988 presidential election, Vice President George H. W. Bush pulled off a stunning victory over Democrat Michael Dukakis, sweeping the Electoral College (426-111) and carrying every section of the country. At first blush, Bush's victory appeared to consolidate the Republican realignment. Not since 1836 had a sitting vice president been able to secure a third consecutive term for his party. But Bush also had the dubious distinction of being the first winner of a presidential contest since John Kennedy to see his party lose seats in both houses of Congress. The election results moved Tom Edsall of the *Washington Post* to conclude that "despite three solid presidential victories in this decade, political realignment [had] proven an elusive goal for the GOP."[66]

Since at least 1972 — and perhaps as far back as 1968 — conservative Republicans had embraced the idea that the American electorate had realigned itself squarely behind conservative political positions. As such, Nixon's liberal reforms, Watergate, and Ford's loss to Carter seemed like freak accidents that betrayed and postponed the inevitable conservative ascendance. After the election of 1980, in which Ronald Reagan carried forty-four states and the GOP claimed huge victories in Congress and in statehouses across the country, Republicans were sure that the long-overdue realignment was taking place. As such, the Reagan administration and congressional conservatives moved aggressively to reorient public policy to match what they believed was a popular mandate.[67] Initially, they received help from conservative southern Democrats in the House of Representatives, effectively creating a unified conservative federal government. In 1982, however, House Democratic leadership regrouped and went on the offensive. Following the 1982 midterm elections, Speakers Tip O'Neill (D-Mass.) and later Jim Wright (D-Tex.) reigned in errant southern Democrats and used increasingly restrictive rules to limit GOP input in legislation. By mid-decade, Republicans were effectively shut out of the decision-making process in the House of Representatives. Simultaneously, Tony Coelho (D-Calif.), Democratic whip and chairman of the Democratic Congressional Campaign Committee, used strong-arm tactics to squeeze huge campaign contributions out of corporate donors who had bankrolled the Republicans in 1980. Coelho's initiative was so successful that by the end of the decade, House Democratic incumbents were receiving a majority of corporate campaign donations.[68] In 1986, Senate Democrats made a similar comeback, retaking the chamber for the first time since 1980. Democrats' congressional rebound and Bush's 1988 victory reinforced a two-decade-old trend of Republican control of the presidency and Democratic control of Congress.

The prospect of continued political gridlock in a split government raised the profile of Republican partisans determined to break the Democrat's hammerlock on Congress. Foremost among them was Representative Newt Gingrich (R-Ga.). Since he first entered the House in 1979, Gingrich had used ethics — or, more specifically, the alleged ethical lapses of the Democratic leadership — to attack the House majority. Within weeks of his being sworn in as a freshman member of Congress, Gingrich had executed this strategy against veteran African American Representative Charles Diggs (D-Mich.) — who had been convicted of a felony and subsequently reelected as he appealed the case — calling for his expulsion. For the next fifteen years, Gingrich employed the same formula in his quest to wrest control of the House of Representatives from the Democratic majority. In 1983, Gingrich and several other conservative junior Republicans, all from the South and the West, cofounded the Conservative Opportunity Society (COS), an organization that journalist John Barry has aptly described as "a marketing device to achieve power." At Gingrich's behest, the COS waged its battles on the ethics front, sending members to the well every day to deliver one-minute harangues against the alleged ethical lapses of the House Democratic leadership. Gingrich and his colleagues also used the House Ethics Committee to attack the Democratic Party. Between 1980 and 1988, the committee investigated eighteen members of Congress for nonsexual offenses. Of that number, fifteen were Democrats, including House Speaker Jim Wright (D-Tex.). In many of these cases, the initial complaint that triggered the investigation was submitted by Gingrich or one of his COS colleagues.[69]

For much of the 1980s, Gingrich and the COS were restrained in their attacks on House Democrats by a moderate House Republican leadership and a disinterested press. In 1987–88, however, the ethics issue emerged as a preoccupation of both major political parties and the news media. Throughout President Reagan's two terms in office, administration officials had been dogged by allegations of graft and ethical violations. By 1987, well over two hundred administration officials had been accused of wrongdoing in the press, and several dozen had been convicted of crimes. As the 1988 election season approached, reporters began to talk of the administration's "sleaze factor." Congressional Democrats were all too willing to remind the public of the administration's alleged ethical lapses, with Representative Patricia Schroeder (D-Colo.), chairwoman of the House Subcommittee on Civil Service, going so far as to compile a list of all the news stories of executive branch corruption. Fearful that the ethics issue could damage their prospects in the upcoming presidential election, John Barry writes, "Republicans were desperate to find Democrats with problems to neutralize this sleaze factor."[70] Gingrich, not surprisingly, was the first to act. In the spring of 1988, the Georgia Republican assigned an aide, full-time, to search the Texas and national press for negative news stories about House Speaker Jim Wright. He then had the aide forward these articles to editors and writers across the country encouraging them to investigate these allegations of wrongdoing, some as much as a decade old. Throughout, Gingrich kept the House Republican leadership informed of his efforts, and they, in Gingrich's words, "were quite willing for me to do this. No one asked me to stop."[71]

More than give Gingrich a free hand, Republican Party leaders adopted his strategy. In June 1988, the Republican National Congressional Committee (RNCC) conducted a survey testing the benefits of using allegations of Democratic corruption in the upcoming election. They found that 51 percent of Democratic swing voters who were informed about ongoing investigations by the House Ethics Committee against fourteen House Democrats said that they would vote Republican in order to replace a corrupt Democratic leadership.[72] At the Republican National Convention a few months later, congressional conservatives added to the party platform a section titled "Ethics and Congressional

Reform," which lamented the loose ethical standards and graft that had engulfed the House of Representatives after "36 years of one-party rule."[73]

Although the ethics issue did not pay dividends for Republicans in the 1988 election, the election strengthened the hand of so-called bomb throwers like Gingrich, who were determined to use the ethics issue to weaken congressional Democrats. In the postelection party reorganization in January 1989, current and former members of the COS secured four of the eight Republican leadership positions in the House of Representatives, with Gingrich being elected minority whip. Additionally, Lee Atwater, manager of the Bush-Quayle campaign who had used "negative theory" — the idea that the way for Republicans to win in a majority Democratic electorate was to generate a negative impression of the Democratic candidate in the public mind — became head of the Republican National Committee. Bare-knuckle political strategist Ed Rollins was selected to chair the Republican National Campaign Committee. Additionally, in February 1989, leading Republicans meeting in Washington, D.C., announced that they would use the wedge issues of drugs, crime, education, and political corruption to extend their party's success in presidential elections "down into the precincts."[74]

Gingrich's strategy dovetailed with the DOJ's existing focus on official corruption. Indeed, the two fed off each other. As the DOJ leaked information from ongoing investigations of Democratic elected officials, Republicans used the leaks to make the case for Democratic corruption and the need for additional investigations. And in the months following the 1989 party reorganization, as the Republican Party amplified its allegations of corruption, the number of leaks from DOJ investigations of high-ranking Democratic elected officials spiked. As in the previous eight years, a disproportionate number of these investigations focused on black elected officials.

1989: Leaks Become a Flood

"The flood of trouble that has engulfed Democratic leaders in the House of Representatives grew even wider and deeper tonight." With that, *CBS Evening News* anchorman Bob Schieffer turned the story over to Rita Braver. Earlier that day, May 30, 1989, Braver had learned from three "Justice Department sources" that House Speaker Jim Wright (D-Tex.), who was then under investigation by the House Ethics Committee, would now be facing a "preliminary criminal investigation" by the DOJ. Shocking as this information was, the focus of Braver's report was not Wright but House Democratic Caucus chairman, Representative William Gray (D-Pa.), the highest-ranking African American in Congress. Braver's DOJ sources had informed her that Gray was the subject of a criminal investigation by the FBI. Though they gave her few details, the sources told Braver that "FBI agents visited Gray [that] weekend to ask for his cooperation in the investigation, which was not forthcoming." In light of Gray's refusal to cooperate, Braver continued, "subpoenas in the case [were] expected in the next few weeks."[75]

The CBS report capped a catastrophic week for the Democratic Party. Within a matter of just five days, DOJ leaks to the press had revealed criminal investigations of three of the top four Democrats in the House of Representatives. On May 25, the *Los Angeles Times* had published a report stating that the DOJ had initiated preliminary criminal inquiries into the financial dealings of House Democratic whip, Representative Tony Coelho (D-Calif.), and Los Angeles mayor Tom Bradley (D), who may have received preferential treatment from Drexel Burnham Lambert Inc. in the purchase of "junk bonds." By the time CBS broadcast its story on Gray, Coelho had already announced his resignation, stating that he did not want to subject his family or his party to a drawn-out investigation of his personal financial affairs.[76] Though his concerns were self-serving, they were not misplaced. One year before, Representative Gingrich had filed ethics charges against House Speaker Wright, and though every single one of Gingrich's charges was thrown out, during the course of its investigation the Committee on Standards of Official Conduct discovered that Wright had violated several other House rules.[77] The FBI investigation leaked to CBS was an outgrowth of those findings. Weakened by the ethics investigation and, after May 30, facing a preliminary criminal investigation, Wright determined that his career could not be salvaged. On June 1, he tearfully announced his resignation to the House. At the very same time that Wright was speaking to his colleagues, the House clerk received a subpoena for the clerk hire records of Delegate Walter Fauntroy (D-Washington, D.C.), who was then under investigation by the U.S. attorney in Washington for hiring the son of Representative Gus Savage (D-Ill.).[78] Details of the Fauntroy grand jury investigation had repeatedly been leaked to the Washington press, leading to widespread speculation about the investigation and its repercussions for the solidly Democratic, majority-black city's only representative in Congress. Of the six Democratic elected officials mentioned in this series of leaks, only Wright and Coelho were white.

Republicans mobilized to exploit the leaks. On May 28, RNCC spokesman John Buckley and Gingrich hit the Sunday talk shows to make the case that the Wright and Coelho resignations were symptomatic of a larger pattern of Democratic corruption. "The double resignation of two top Democrats shows that there is a greater problem than Jim Wright," stated Buckley. "There's a systemic problem that has to do with one party controlling Congress for 35 consecutive years and the resignations of the No. 1 and No. 3 Democrats are the bitter fruit of that." Speaking on *Face the Nation*, Gingrich predicted that as many as "another 9 or 10" House Democrats might face investigation. For

Gingrich, this was a purely partisan issue. When majority leader Tom Foley (D-Wash.) called for bipartisan ethics reform, Gingrich rejected him, announcing that Republicans would introduce their own package in an effort to show the American people that they were the "party of reform." Seeking to keep the Wright and Coelho cases in the national spotlight, RNC Chairman Lee Atwater stated that he believed the two should be prosecuted by the DOJ despite their having resigned. Gingrich also worked behind the scenes to make a clean sweep of House Democratic leadership, directing his staff to disseminate a rumor (created weeks before by a Democratic staffer in the office of Speaker Wright) that majority leader Tom Foley (D-Wash.) was gay. The press did not pick up on it, perhaps finding it too distasteful.[79]

Republican efforts to capitalize on the DOJ leaks of May 1989 encountered a serious complication in the figure of Representative Gray. Only minutes after the *Evening News* went off the air, Gray held a press conference outside his Capitol Hill office. The normally mild-mannered Philadelphia preacher glowered at reporters as he attacked the leak, denouncing it as "an outrageous lie about [him] that [had] no basis in fact [then] or at any time." Gray stated that although he had spoken with FBI agents and the U.S. attorney over the weekend, he had been told that a staff member, not he, was the subject of the investigation. He insisted that he had offered his full cooperation. The leaks and their inaccuracy, Gray posited, suggested a sinister motive, and he publicly called on the DOJ to disclose the full nature of the investigation so as to clear his name. Additionally, Gray demanded that Attorney General Thornburgh initiate an independent counsel investigation to discover the source of the leak.[80]

Gray's aggressive response to the CBS leak emboldened House Democrats. The following day, three senior Democratic members of the House Judiciary Committee called on Attorney General Thornburgh to "take clear and aggressive steps to stop these leaks" claiming that people in the DOJ were using them "for political purposes against House Democrats." If Thornburgh refused to act, they argued, they would have to conclude that those making the leaks had his support. From the House floor, Representative Barney Frank (D-Mass.) voiced similar concerns. "Either this is an extraordinary coincidence," he sardonically remarked, "or the most egregious case of prosecutorial misbehavior that I've ever encountered." Delegate Fauntroy chimed in, stating that Thornburgh did not have "control of his agency." And in a demonstration that Republicans were divided in their opinion of Gingrich's hard-charging campaign, Representative Robert Michel (R-Ill.), the conciliatory House minority leader whom Gingrich was then trying to displace, wrote Thornburgh, "It is hard to imagine anything more irresponsible."[81]

In the face of this outcry, Thornburgh was forced to commence an internal investigation. But rather than assuage critics' concerns, his actions only heightened them. The day after the *Los Angeles Times* published its story on Bradley and Coelho, Thornburgh had initiated an investigation of that leak. Normally, the OPR handles cases of alleged misconduct by DOJ officials. But instead of assigning the leak investigation to the semiautonomous OPR, Thornburgh assigned it to the Criminal Division — a division over which he had direct control. On June 1, Thornburgh broadened the existing Criminal Division inquiry to include the leaks concerning Gray, Wright, Fauntroy, and Savage.[82] Thornburgh later claimed in his autobiography that he assigned the probe to the Criminal Division because he was "furious" about the proliferation of leaks from his department and wanted a "special, high-powered investigation" to determine who the culprits were. "After the Wright and Coelho investigations, this was the last straw," Thornburgh writes. "I was livid and responded in the worst possible manner in my determination to find out who was responsible for this one [the Gray leak]."[83] But the attorney general's recollection of the investigation does not conform to the facts. He had begun the Criminal Division investigation on May 26, four days before the Gray and Wright leaks. On June 1, Thornburgh added the new leaks to the existing investigation. Only if his moment of anger stretched backward in time could Thornburgh have decided to commence a Criminal Division investigation of the Gray leak in a fit of rage. Thornburgh's actions raised Democrats' suspicions that he was attempting a cover-up, and his conduct during and after the inquiry did nothing to alleviate their concerns.

Taken as a whole, the Gray leak investigation suggests that the attorney general not only condoned but also sought to cover up the series of leaks that were devastating House Democratic leadership in 1989. The Criminal Division probe lasted six months before Thornburgh pulled the plug, claiming that investigators had been unable to determine the source of the leak. But reporters for the *New York Times* later discovered that Thornburgh was covering up for his two top aides. During the probe, the FBI submitted Thornburgh, his press secretary David Runkel, and his executive assistant Robert Ross to polygraph tests. Each official was asked if he had contact with CBS reporters prior to the Gray leak. Both Runkel and Ross gave evasive answers and, in response to certain questions, lied outright. Runkel is reported to have told FBI investigators that he was not involved with the leak prior to taking the polygraph test. After failing the test, he revised his statement to say that he had played a role in confirming the leak. The polygraph machine noted that Ross was probably lying when he told the FBI that he had no contact with CBS reporters during the period that the network is believed to have formulated the story. He would later change his statement to a claim of nonrecollection. Thornburgh is reported to have passed the polygraph test.[84] When the controversy over the Gray leak first broke, Thornburgh had pledged to fire anyone involved, but he only transferred his aides. Moreover, when the *Times* report revealed their involvement, Thornburgh sought to justify their actions by claiming that they had acted "in an authorized manner . . . following [his] standing instructions that no one in the department mislead the media."[85] Considering the DOJ's long-standing practice of refusing to answer questions about ongoing investigations, and sometimes even to acknowledge their existence, this explanation rang hollow.

When incensed congressional Democrats demanded an independent review of the investigation in light of the *New York Times* report, Thornburgh continued to stall. Insisting that a DOJ official conduct the review, he gave the assignment to Solicitor General Kenneth Starr. Though he would later be characterized as a rabid partisan, Starr was then considered a fair-minded jurist, and Democrats reluctantly agreed to Thornburgh's terms. Nearly one year after the leak controversy began, Starr delivered his opinion to Thornburgh in the form of a confidential report, which Thornburgh refused to release to the press. Subsequently, Thornburgh issued a press release in which he claimed that Starr did not recommend any disciplinary action against any DOJ official and counseled that the matter be closed.[86] Even high-ranking DOJ and Bush administration officials raised questions about Thornburgh's handling of the investigation and his interpretation of the Starr report. Most notably, Deputy Attorney General Donald Ayer resigned in protest, claiming that Thornburgh had repeatedly tried to block the OPR from investigating his aides. Also the *New York Times* reported that several senior Bush administration officials questioned Thornburgh's characterization of the Starr report, suggesting that it was "narrowly worded" and "failed to describe fully the extent of concerns expressed by Mr. Starr."[87]

Yet despite the criticism from members of the administration and his former number two man, Thornburgh held his ground. "I'm not trying to hide anything," he declared when asked about the allegations. Eventually, he simply stopped talking, telling reporters in May 1990: "The matter is closed. . . . I'm not going to comment on it further."[88] After one year of stonewalling by Thornburgh and his aides, the Gray leak investigation was abandoned.

Expanding the Crackdown amid a Crisis of Confidence

On the evening of January 18, 1990, Mayor Marion Barry (D-Washington, D.C.) visited Hazel Diana "Rasheeda" Moore at her room at the Vista International Hotel in Northwest, Washington, D.C. The mayor, whose infidelities were common knowledge in the District, had come that evening in hopes of having sex with his one-time girlfriend. Rejecting his overtures, Moore asked instead that Barry smoke crack cocaine. Barry had been using cocaine since the early 1980s.

Despite this history, he hesitated. Moore, however, was persistent, asking him to smoke the drug seven times and implying that she would have sex with him once he had done so. Barry took the pipe, put the lighter to it, and inhaled. Moments later, agents of the FBI and the Metropolitan Police Department burst into the room, handcuffed the mayor, and declared him under arrest. The entire episode had been captured on FBI surveillance video.[89] The Barry arrest was only the most famous of a string of controversial DOJ stings of black elected officials in the years between 1990 and 1992.

Despite the scandals of 1987–89 that forced one attorney general from office and another to submit to a lie detector test, the DOJ dramatically expanded the official corruption crackdown in 1990–92. Indeed, in 1991 the DOJ indicted the highest number of public officials in U.S. history. Like the Barry investigation, many of these cases featured aggressive stings that crossed the line into entrapment, weak evidence that fell apart at trial, and legally dubious prosecutorial maneuvers that often drew the ire of presiding judges. As Republicans accelerated their efforts to capture the House of Representatives and many statehouses across the country, they also stepped up their efforts to use DOJ official corruption investigations of Democrats as one of their primary political weapons. In the House of Representatives, Newt Gingrich and his allies continued to use the Ethics Committee to attack Democrats and spark DOJ investigations. And in 1992, Gingrich and his partisans were successful in inserting the claim that the "Democratic leadership of the House [had] been tainted with scandal and [had] resisted efforts to investigate scandals once disclosed" into the Republican Party platform. The only way to "restore integrity to the House of Representatives," it continued, was to elect a Republican majority. State Republicans were also quick to capitalize on the official corruption crackdown. When a wide-ranging sting on the bingo business in Tennessee implicated many Democratic state legislators, the executive director of the Tennessee Republican Party made clear that the GOP would try to use the issue to retake control of the Tennessee House.[90] Regardless of prosecutors' intent, the Republican DOJ was, in effect, creating crimes and then prosecuting Democratic lawmakers for those crimes on a grand scale while Republican political operatives and elected officials used those prosecutions to precipitate a forced realignment. As in earlier periods, these investigations disproportionately targeted black elected officials.

A quick perusal of some of these investigations demonstrates why they continued to produce a racially disproportionate result. Several of these stings were the product of allegations of fraud made by disgruntled white businessmen in majority-black jurisdictions. For example, in Winston Salem, North Carolina, black alderman Patrick Hairison, lobbyist Rodney Sumler, and community activist Rev. Lee Faye Mack were convicted in May 1992 for bribery and conspiracy in the letting of city contracts. The convictions were a product of

"Operation Mushroom Cloud," an FBI-IRS sting begun after a local white businessman, who had just been fined by the city for violating a minority-hiring statute championed by the town's black aldermen, alleged that several black aldermen were demanding bribes in return for city contracts. That same year, the FBI concluded a sting against black elected officials in Compton, California. Representative Walter Tucker (D-Calif.), who was a former Compton mayor, and city councilwoman Patricia Moore (D) were later indicted for bribery and conspiracy in 1994. The sting that netted Tucker and Moore had originally targeted Representative Mervyn Dymally (D-Calif.). It too was begun after a disgruntled white businessman whose proposal to locate a trash incinerator in the heart of the city had been voted down by the city council alleged that Dymally had threatened to kill the project if he was not paid a bribe.[91]

Other stings conducted during this period featured disproportionate targeting of black elected officials in majority-white political bodies. In "Operation Lost Trust," the largest official corruption investigation in South Carolina since Redemption, the FBI enlisted Ron Cobb, a well-known Columbia lobbyist and former state legislator, in a sting on the state legislature. Cobb offered legislators between $1,000 and $1,300 in cash for their support of an FBI-created bill that would allow pari-mutuel betting on horse and dog tracks in the state. Cobb disproportionately targeted African American legislators. Although indictments were roughly proportional across partisan lines — five of the eighteen state legislators indicted in the heavily Democratic general assembly were Republican — African Americans were overrepresented among the accused. Of the eighteen legislators indicted, 40 percent were black, while blacks comprised only 12 per cent of the state legislature.[92] Cobb had targeted more black legislators than were indicted. During the sting, Cobb had offered black state senator Theo Mitchell (D-Greenville) a $1,000 "campaign contribution." Mitchell rejected the money, however, when Cobb turned the conversation toward the pari-mutuel bill.[93] This evidence of disproportionate targeting was all the more disturbing because Cobb had not followed the FBI guidelines for conducting stings. When offering legislators bribes, Cobb had not made the criminal opportunity presented in the sting "clear and unambiguous," often calling the money he offered legislators "campaign contributions." Representative Ennis Fant (D-Greenville), one of the eight indicted black lawmakers, recalled that the offer Cobb made him was ambiguous. "He told me it was a campaign contribution and never mentioned a bill," Fant stated. "I knew something was fishy about it, and I filed it in the official records right away." Several of the other indicted legislators made similar claims, and a majority reported the money to the relevant legislative committee soon after receiving it.[94]

Cobb's questionable handling of the sting and the U.S. attorney's subsequent attempts to conceal his misdeeds during the trials of the Lost Trust defendants sparked two investigations by the OPR and a rebuke from one of the presiding judges. In 1997, U.S. District Court judge Falcon Hawkins, who had presided over several of the Lost Trust cases, dismissed the government's case against five of the legislators — three of them black. In his ruling, Hawkins claimed that prosecutors had engaged in selective prosecution, concealed evidence from the defense, and allowed false testimony by Cobb. In one notable charge, Hawkins asserted that the U.S. attorney's office had refused to pursue strong evidence that Republican governor Carroll Campbell's close friend Dick Greer was "heavily involved in payoffs." "The court is convinced," Hawkins concluded, "that the totality of the government's actions in these matters rises to the level of egregious prosecutorial misconduct . . . so outrageous as to offend the sensibilities of the court." Although a higher court reversed Hawkins's decision and forced the defendants to endure yet another trial, his ruling forced even the prosecution to admit that it had made a number of "mistakes" both during the investigation and at trial.[95]

Not all the official corruption investigations from this period were stings. Many were developed from more traditional investigatory techniques. But even these gave many black elected officials a feeling that they were being unfairly targeted. In August 1990, Queens, New York, U.S. attorney Andrew Maloney indicted African American representative Floyd Flake, who was also the pastor of Allen AME Church, on seventeen counts of tax evasion, fraud, and conspiracy for allegedly embezzling $141,000 from federally supported church programs to fund his "lavish lifestyle."[96] The Flake indictment was the second "lifestyle" prosecution of a black member of Congress, the first being that of Harold Ford (D-Tenn.) in 1987. Though a grand jury had uncovered substantial evidence of sloppy bookkeeping and questionable accounting practices by Allen AME personnel, the prosecution's case fell apart in the early days of the March 1991 trial. The prosecution's argument hinged on the nature of a church fund that it alleged was a "sham" account used to embezzle tens of thousands of dollars for Flake's personal use. The defense argued that the account was a legitimate ministerial expense fund, common in many large churches. Three weeks into the proceedings, Judge Eugene Nickerson informed prosecutors that their case was "shaky" and issued several rulings that narrowed the charges to tax evasion.[97] Recognizing that he would not be able to convince the jury of even these counts, Maloney made a motion to dismiss all the remaining charges the following month. He was wise to do so. All the jurors who submitted to interviews after the trial stated that prosecutors had not proven their case. One argued that there was "no evidence" against Flake and his wife, while another suggested that "there may have been racial motivations" for the indictment. Indeed, two jurors gained such positive impressions of the Flakes during the trial that they decided, independently of each other, to attend services at Allen AME the first Sunday after the case was dismissed.[98]

After twelve straight years of Republican rule, former Arkansas governor Bill Clinton (D) won the 1992 presidential election, ending the official corruption crackdown and with it the disproportionate prosecution of black elected officials. Clinton received 83 percent of the African American vote. Though this was a lower percentage of the black vote than the three previous Democratic nominees had garnered, it still constituted Clinton's margin of victory. Black elected officials complained loudly of disproportionate prosecution to incoming attorney general Janet Reno, and soon after the transition, Reno demanded the resignations of all sitting U.S. attorneys and replaced them with administration appointees. She also ordered the FBI to scale back its use of the sting and shifted the department away from its focus on official corruption.[99] Whether Reno took these steps in response to black elected officials' complaints is impossible to determine. Most incoming administrations fire their predecessors' political appointees, and many white Democrats had also complained about the official corruption crackdown of the Reagan and Bush years.[100] What can be said with certainty is that Reno's actions led to a dramatic decline in DOJ investigations of black elected officials. Only three of the fifty-four African Americans to serve in Congress between 1993 and 2000 were investigated by the DOJ. Of the three, all were convicted or resigned to avoid prosecution.[101] By comparison, more than 30 percent of the CBC was investigated during the Reagan and Bush years, of whom two were indicted and none convicted — an indictment to conviction rate of 0 percent.

Viewing the official corruption crackdown and some Republicans use of the same as a weapon of political warfare from above, the picture is necessarily confused. The aggregate numbers undoubtedly demonstrate disproportionate partisan and racial prosecution. But the DOJ is a large and decentralized bureaucracy, and while many federal investigators used the crackdown as a racial and/or partisan weapon, others did their jobs without partisan or political bias. Conversely, while some black elected officials charged with corruption were innocent, others used harassment ideology to mask their misdeeds. To gain some clarity and appreciate its complexity, we must view the official corruption crackdown at the state, county, and municipal level. In the following chapter, I explore Republicans' use of the crackdown as a racial and partisan weapon in the state of Alabama.

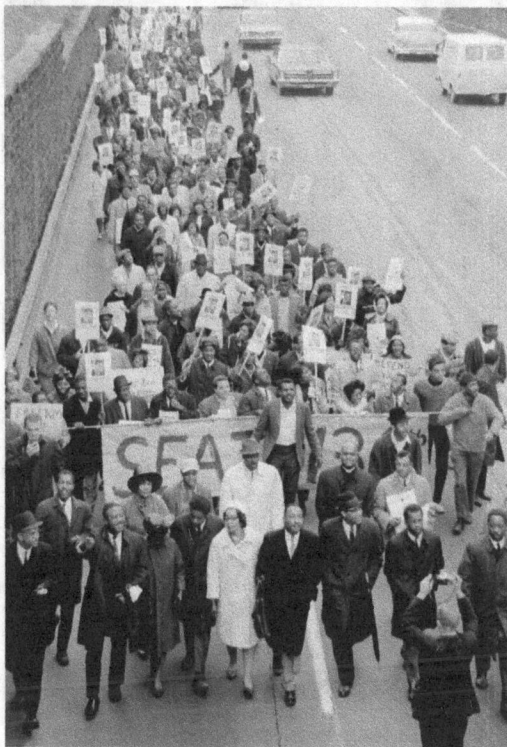

Martin Luther King Jr. leading a march on the Georgia state
capitol protesting the Georgia House's refusal to seat Julian
Bond. © Bettmann/CORBIS.

Adam Clayton Powell Jr. speaking with reporters shortly after being stripped of his chairmanship of the House Committee on Education and Labor. In his hand is Jack Anderson's *Washington Exposé*, which chronicled the unethical and illegal behavior of the Washington elite. Francis Miller / Time and Life Pictures, Getty Images.

Lieutenant Governor George Brown
of Colorado.

Lieutenant Governor Mervyn Dymally of California.

Above left: Secretary of State C. Delores Tucker of Pennsylvania. *Above right:* Mary Sawyer, author of *The Dilemma of Black Politics: A Report on the Harassment of Black Elected Officials* (1977) and *The Harassment of Black Elected Officials: Ten Years Later* (1987). Courtesy of Mary Sawyer.

William "Bill" Clay with Fred Parker (second from left), Earl Davis (third from left), and unidentified man at a Twenty-sixth Ward Democratic organization fundraiser in the late 1960s. The *St. Louis Globe Democrat* published this picture only days before the 1974 Democratic primary under the title "Hoodlum Support for Clay" in the hopes of tying Clay to Parker's and Lewis's known records of violence and drug dealing. From the collections of the St. Louis Mercantile Library at the University of Missouri–St. Louis.

Charles Diggs speaking with reporters outside the U.S. District Courthouse in Washington, D.C., after being convicted of accepting kickbacks from his congressional staff. Courtesy of the District of Columbia Public Library, Star Collection, © Washington Post.

Below: Flyer, issued by the African American Legal Defense Fund, urging supporters of Judge Alcee Hastings to rally at the Capitol in protest of his impending impeachment. Courtesy of Representative Alcee Hastings.

STOP THE LYNCHING !!!
Come to the
"RALLY FOR JUSTICE"
When: Wednesday, October 18
Where: U.S. Capitol Steps (West Side)
Time: 11:00 A.M.

Hear Judge Alcee Hastings just prior to making his final arguments before the U.S. Senate concerning his impeachment hearing. Several national leaders and elected officials will also be present.

National Campaign
To Free Mayor
Eddie James Carthan
and the Tchula Seven
and to Preserve
Black Political
Rights

It's one thing for a black to win
an election in a small Southern
town. It's another to use the
power of that office.

POLITICAL PRISONERS
IN AMERICA

SENATORS
CLARENCE and MICHAEL

MITCHELL

These

Outstanding

PUBLIC SERVANTS

for over

30 YEARS . . .

NEED YOUR HELP
NOW!

*". . . Clarence and Michael have been convicted for
offenses they did not commit."*
Congressman Parren J. Mitchell

Above left: Flyer for the National Campaign to Free Mayor Eddie James Carthan and the Tchula 7.
The image depicts Carthan flanked by two unidentified little girls. *Above right:* Flyer for the Mitchell
Defense Fund. Clarence Mitchell III stands to the left and Michael Mitchell to the right. Courtesy of
Clarence Mitchell III.

[The Department of] Justice has made a complete turnaround on the enforcement of voting rights and is now assisting whites to take away what political gains blacks have made.

— School Board chairman Wendell Paris
(D-Sumter County)

Most blacks are Democrats. I think if you can destroy the reputation of black elected officials, if any good accrues to anybody it is to the Republican Party. And what has not been lost on me is the fact that this [official corruption investigation of Birmingham-area black elected officials] has been carried out largely by Republican Administrations.

— Mayor Richard Arrington, (D-Birmingham, Ala.)

CHAPTER FIVE

The "Selective Prosecution" of Black Elected Officials in Alabama, 1981–1992

ON OCTOBER 30, 1989, Birmingham, Alabama, mayor Richard Arrington (D) traveled to Washington, D.C., to deliver a luncheon address titled "The Federal Government and the Harassment of Black Elected Officials" at the NAACP's "Conference on the Present Crisis."[1] Grounding his subject in the "context of the overall black freedom struggle," Arrington began: "In Alabama, in places like Montgomery, Selma, and Birmingham, . . . our people persevered against great odds and overcame them. Out of those struggles . . . came landmark civil rights legislation in public accommodations, voting rights and housing. We paused to celebrate, but quickly learned that the struggle was not over. We had simply finished one battle, often times at great sacrifice, only to face a new obstacle." That new obstacle, Arrington argued, was the realignment of federal authorities with the enemies of black progress under Presidents Reagan and Bush. "Agencies and institutions which once stood with us in our struggle have sometimes realigned themselves with our opposition. . . . A Justice Department that had been a defender of civil rights of minorities abandoned that role in the eighties . . . with Reagan, [Attorney General Edwin] Meese and [Assistant Attorney General for Civil Rights] Reynolds in the forefront."[2] This realignment, Arrington continued, had taken two specific forms in Alabama. First, the DOJ under Reagan and Bush had commenced a concerted effort to roll back liberal civil rights policy. In 1981, Arrington had worked with career attorneys in the DOJ to craft a consent decree mandating affirmative action programs in the Birmingham Fire Department, which had long discriminated against blacks in hiring and promotion. Just two years later, however, political appointees in the DOJ reversed course and joined seven white firefighters who sued the city claiming that the consent decree violated their right to equal protection. In June 1989, the new conservative majority on the Supreme Court, created through Reagan's appointments, sided with the firefighters and invalidated the consent decree in *Martin v. Wilks*.[3] Second, Arrington told the crowd, the Reagan DOJ was seeking to force a state-level political realignment by using its law enforcement powers to attack black (Democratic) voters, voting rights activists, and elected officials.

As in several other parts of the country, the Reagan revolution coincided with the rise of black political power in Alabama. Between 1978 and 1985, Alabama blacks used sophisticated get-out-the-vote techniques to win control of county and municipal governments across the Black Belt — a crescent-shaped belt of twelve counties stretching across the middle of the state where African Americans constituted anywhere from 40 to 80 percent of the population — and in Birmingham. Their efforts elicited a swift counterattack by local white political elites. Turning first to their allies in state government, these whites mobilized state law enforcement to prosecute black activists for vote fraud and, in the process, turn back the tide of black electoral insurgency. When that effort failed, they turned to their newfound friends in the Reagan DOJ. In 1984, the Alabama U.S. attorneys federalized the local vote fraud investigations first commenced by white state prosecutors. Despite weak and contradictory evidence, they worked with local white investigators, political organizers, and registrars to build cases against black voting rights activists and elected officials in *all* the black-controlled counties in the western Black Belt. Following the vote fraud investigations, the U.S. attorneys shifted their attention to the numerous allegations of fraud and corruption made by white residents against the black political leadership of Birmingham and Montgomery. Though these allegations were rooted less in evidence of misconduct than in political and policy disagreements between racial-partisan factions, Alabama federal investigators conducted a string of investigations and sting operations targeting a *majority* of the black elected officials in these areas. Simultaneously, federal authorities ignored documented evidence of fraud by high-ranking white Republican elected officials, moving black elected officials to term the investigations in which they were targeted "selective prosecution."

In the 1980s Alabama boasted what was arguably the best-organized black political community in the nation. The overwhelming majority of politically active Alabama blacks were members of the NAACP, the SCLC, the Alabama Democratic Conference (ADC), and after 1986, the Alabama New South Coalition (ANSC). Although the leadership of these groups sometimes feuded, they constituted effective tools for mounting a counteroffensive to the Reagan and Bush DOJ investigations.[4] In 1984–85 and 1989–92, Alabama voting rights activists and black elected officials created counterpropaganda and defense organizations to combat state and federal investigators. In each instance, they were successful in shining a national spotlight on investigators' actions, raising funds for legal defense, and organizing the black community to defend its advocates and elected representatives at the ballot box and in the streets.

In the three years following his speech to the NAACP, Arrington mobilized Alabama's black political leadership to fight the Alabama U.S. attorneys to a legal and public relations standstill. This effort made him a leading figure in the antiharassment groundswell that captured the black popular imagination in the late 1980s and early 1990s and exposed what was arguably the most ambitious attempt to transform the official corruption crackdown into a tool of political warfare. Only the Democratic transition in 1993 ended the stalemate.

State Investigations of Black Voting Rights Activists in Alabama, 1978–1982

Following the passage of the VRA, African American voter registration increased exponentially across Alabama. Between 1964 and 1969, the percentage of eligible blacks on the rolls shot up from 19.3 to 61.5 percent. In the Black Belt counties, the increase in black registration forecast an end to white-minority rule. African Americans, however, had limited success in electing representatives of their choosing to county government. This was, in large measure, a product of local whites' successful attempts to undermine black registration and voting. In the late 1960s and the 1970s, white registrars intimidated blacks seeking to register, purged the voter rolls, and placed the polls in hard-to-reach or all-white areas. White employers forced blacks to work through polling hours or offered them overtime on Election Day. Others were more brazen, simply paying blacks to vote for the white candidates or not to vote at all. But by far the most useful weapon for Black Belt whites in their attempts to maintain political control was the absentee ballot.[5]

Alabama's twelve Black Belt counties posed unique problems for voting rights organizers. With their aging population, lack of public transportation, and substantial number of migrant workers, large numbers of residents were unable to get to the polls on Election Day. Thus turnout became the decisive factor in many closely contested elections. In the 1970s, African American political organizations focused on getting their partisans to the polls, thereby writing off the homebound and migrant workers, a substantial segment of the black electorate. Local white political organizations, on the other hand, mobilized every conceivable white vote in the county by mastering the absentee ballot system. When these votes were not enough to ensure a white voting majority, white registrars and political operatives illegally solicited and submitted absentee ballots from whites who no longer lived in the county.[6] These absentee ballots were the margin of victory in many closely contested countywide races. "Observers of the region," former NAACP Legal Defense Fund attorney Lani Guinier writes, "were fond of noting that black politicians went to bed thinking they had won the election, but in the morning, after the absentee ballots had been counted, they would always learn they had lost."[7] By the late 1970s, therefore, Black Belt whites' use and abuse of the absentee ballot system became local black voting rights activists' number one concern.

Initially, these activists took their complaints to the DOJ. Selma (Dallas County), Alabama voting rights activist J. L. Chestnut, (then) a hard-drinking, razor-tongued voting rights attorney, recounts one such meeting with DOJ officials in 1978 in his autobiography *Black in Selma*. After listening to Chestnut's complaints, the attorneys stated that they could not help him. Fraud in a county or state election, they argued, was a matter for the Alabama secretary of state or the local district attorney. The DOJ had a standing policy of leaving state and local vote fraud cases to local district attorneys, focusing their energies on federal elections instead. Even in the case of vote fraud in federal elections, the DOJ only tended to step in when the alleged fraud might have determined the outcome of the election or when government officials were implicated in the alleged wrongdoing. "Shit," Chestnut exclaimed. "You're saying we should go to [Alabama governor] George Wallace." The DOJ attorneys knew that Wallace had appointed the registrars who were committing the fraud about which blacks were complaining. They were, however, hamstrung by DOJ policy.[8] Instead, they counseled Chestnut to match his opponent's strategy — legally. "They told me that with so many black people in these counties, we shouldn't be leaning on Washington," Chestnut recalls. "We should master the absentee system ourselves."[9]

Lacking any alternative, Chestnut and his fellow voting rights activists returned to Alabama intent on using the absentee ballot system to increase black turnout. Within months of their return, Chestnut writes, "each of the little Black Belt county organizations had two or three people in charge of nothing but absentee ballots."[10] These activists would identify potential absentee voters among migrant workers, the elderly and shut-in, the illiterate, and students away at college; go to their homes to help them fill out absentee ballot applications; return to their homes to provide voter assistance and pick up the ballots; notarize the ballots; and then take them to the post office to be mailed to the registrar (activists learned that if they mailed the absentee ballots from local mail drops, white mail carriers would throw them out). The operation was extremely complex and time consuming. As Perry County Civic League president Albert Turner explained, "You got to know the laws, you got to have dedication. You've got to get up off your ass and get out there and go to them folks' houses. This ain't no playtime."[11]

Black Belt African Americans' employ of the absentee ballot reversed their political fortunes in the years between 1978 and 1984. With black turnout reaching 80 percent in some counties, African Americans elected a majority of the countywide officeholders in Greene (since 1969), Perry (1978), Lowndes (1980), Wilcox (1982), and Sumter (1982) counties and gained seats on two other previously all white county commissions. Additionally, in 1982, Black Belt African Americans elected Jenkins Bryant (D-District 68) and James Thomas (D-District 69) to the Alabama House of Representatives and, following a 1983 court-ordered redistricting championed by Black Belt voting rights activists, Lucius Black (D-District 87) to the house and voting rights attorney Hank Sanders (D-District 23) to the state senate.[12] For the first time since Reconstruction, the Black Belt had black representatives in Montgomery and in a majority of the county seats.

Having lost the elections at the ballot box, local whites sought to invalidate them in court and to undermine local blacks' ability to reproduce them in the future. The opening shot of this white counterinsurgency was fired in 40 percent black Pickens County in 1978. There, following complaints from local white political activists, District Attorney Presley Johnson (D) indicted Maggie Bozeman, president of the Pickens County branch of the NAACP, and Julia Wilder, president of the Pickens County Voters League on thirty-nine counts of voter fraud, one for each of the absentee ballots they had mailed on behalf of elderly African American Pickens County residents in the 1978 primary election. An all-white jury found them guilty of all thirty-nine counts on the strength of a single witness — and despite the countervailing testimony of all the other witnesses in the case. Judge Clatus Junkin gave Wilder the maximum sentence, five years in prison, while Bozeman was sentenced to four years in the penitentiary. The sentences were the stiffest for vote fraud in the history of Alabama. Although the sentences were reduced in 1982 by Governor Fob James (D), whose 1980 election had hinged on the black vote, the prosecution was successful. Not a single African American held countywide office in Pickens in 1982.[13]

Local white elites also fell back on more traditional methods of voter suppression to stem the tide of black electoral insurgency. In 1981, white state legislators from Perry, Wilcox, and Sumter counties introduced reregistration bills in the Alabama House. Though the legislators stated that the bills were designed to clean the county voter rolls — and, indeed, the voter rolls in these counties were filled with the names of former county residents and the deceased — the intended effect appeared to most blacks to be more sinister. Representatives Preston Minus (D), sponsor of a reregistration bill for Sumter County, had passed similar legislation covering Choctaw County in 1978. At the time that the legislation was passed, there were 6,679 whites registered in Choctaw County and 5,369 African Americans. Following reregistration, 5,200 whites returned to the rolls compared with 3,000 blacks. The Alabama legislature has a "local legislation" rule through which members are able to introduce and vote on legislation affecting their district only. Only members whose districts are affected by the legislation can vote on these bills. Thus, Minus and his colleagues were able to introduce, debate, and pass their reregistration bills with their white counterparts in the Senate. They could not, however, implement them without clearance from Washington. Section 5 of the VRA requires that all voting changes introduced by covered jurisdictions be "precleared" by the DOJ. DOJ lawyers have sixty days to object to a proposed voting change under section 5. Perry and Wilcox county authorities were barred from implementing their reregistration plans when DOJ attorneys filed objections. DOJ attorneys failed, however, to file an objection in the Sumter County case before the sixty-day deadline, thereby allowing county authorities to implement the new law.[14]

White Black Belt elites also used the law enforcement apparatus to attack ostensibly nonpolitical organizations that had stimulated the black political revolt. In the spring of 1979, Black Belt whites launched an investigation of the Federation of Southern Cooperatives, a black-led nonprofit organization coordinating more than one hundred agricultural cooperatives and credit unions throughout the rural South. In 1976, black voter registration in Sumter County spiked. Two years later, black candidates staged strong challenges to local whites' political dominance. Many of the blacks who had organized the voter registration drives and run for office in Sumter County were affiliated with the federation, which was based in the Sumter County town of Epes. Local whites began to allege — though they could produce no proof — that the federation was funding local black political activity. In May 1979, over one hundred influential white Sumter County citizens and elected officials met at the Cotton Patch Restaurant in neighboring Greene County for the purpose of initiating a federal investigation of the federation's alleged misuse of government grants. Among those gathered at the meeting were state representative Preston Minus (D), whose district covered Sumter and Choctaw counties; Mayor I. Drayton Pruitt (D) of Livingston, the Sumter County seat; Sumter County School Board chairman Robert Upchurch (D); Sumter County probate judge Sam Massengill; Sumter County tax assessor Joe Steagall; U.S. representative Richard Shelby (D), whose district included Sumter County; staff representatives of Alabama's two U.S. senators; several lower-level white elected officials; and local newspaper editor John Neel, who had for some time been editorializing that the federation was misusing federal and foundation monies. Local blacks would later dub this meeting the "Cotton Patch conspiracy." The group was successful in initiating a GAO investigation of the federation. GAO investigators found no wrongdoing and dropped the matter. Undaunted, local whites persuaded the U.S. attorney in Birmingham, J. R. Brooks, to take up their cause. Brooks subsequently undertook an eighteen-month investigation during which he subpoenaed over twenty-two file drawers worth of federation records and had the FBI interview approximately two hundred individuals associated with the federation — a process that local blacks charged was little more than an effort to intimidate black voters. Brooks was forced to drop the investigation in 1981 due to lack of evidence and a growing outcry from civil rights and nonprofit activists in Alabama and Washington, D.C. Although no federation employees were ever indicted — in fact no charges were ever leveled against specific individuals — the group lost approximately half of its yearly budget as foundations and federal agencies held up or revoked funding during the inquiry.[15]

Federal Vote Fraud Investigations in the Western Black Belt, 1984–1985

Despite the Wilder and Bozeman trial, the reregistration battles, and the federation investigation, Black Belt African Americans continued their push for political power in 1982. And following the remarkable black victories in that election, local whites accelerated their attacks on black political organizers and voters. In the days following the election, white district attorneys Roy Johnson (D) and Nathan Watkins (D) initiated "vote fraud" investigations in each of the Black Belt counties where whites had lost power. These investigations revolved around allegations that local black political activists had committed vote fraud by coercing elderly and illiterate voters into voting for the slate of black candidates or altering these voters' absentee ballots without their permission. None of these investigations was successful. Black grand jurors, apparently convinced that both blacks and whites made extensive use of the absentee ballot and that whites had a long history of abusing the system, refused to return indictments.[16] Unable to beat back black political insurgency using local law enforcement, Black Belt whites turned to their newfound friends in Washington, D.C.

In 1984, following the failed grand jury investigation, District Attorney Johnson wrote to the assistant attorney general for civil rights, William Bradford Reynolds — by then a well-known opponent of aggressive voting rights enforcement — requesting DOJ intervention in the Black Belt vote fraud investigations.[17] Johnson had good reason to believe that Reynolds would assist him and the Black Belt whites he represented. In 1975, the Alabama legislature had passed legislation providing that the Greene County Racing Commission, which oversaw the Greenetrack Greyhound Racing Stadium, a dog-racing track in Greene County, consist of three members appointed by the legislative delegation that represented Greene County. In 1983, following the redistricting that would elevate Hank Sanders and Lucius Black into the state legislature from the southwest Black Belt, the owners of the Greenetrack asked lame-duck white representatives to pass legislation stripping the Greene County delegation to the state legislature of their racing commission appointment powers. The change was sent to the DOJ for preclearance; there career attorneys deemed it to be "retrogressive," that is, a dilution of black voting power, and suggested that Reynolds reject the request for a change. Reynolds ignored the career attorneys' opinion and approved the change, only to have his actions overturned by a federal judge.[18] Though he was predisposed to help, Reynolds told Johnson that he could not initiate an investigation in his capacity as assistant attorney general for civil rights. He suggested that Johnson contact the U.S. attorney for the Southern District of Alabama, Jefferson Sessions, instead. Johnson contacted Sessions and received a warm reception. A racial conservative who believed strongly in the ideological precepts of the Reagan revolution, Sessions saw the voting rights cases as a perfect opportunity to address what he and many of his fellow Alabama whites believed was an epidemic of black voter fraud.[19]

Although Carter DOJ attorneys had cited precedent to justify their refusal to intervene in state voter fraud investigations when asked by J. L. Chestnut in 1978, two recent developments in elections crime law made Sessions's involvement possible in 1984. First, in the early 1980s, federal courts issued a series of rulings that expanded the right of federal investigators to intervene in cases of election fraud at the state and local level. Second, during this same period, the DOJ's Election Crimes Branch had come to identify "new problem areas" in election law, namely, "voting by noncitizens and exploitation of the franchise of mentally infirm and socially dependent voters." In a September 1984 press release, Attorney General William French Smith declared voter fraud a department-wide priority and introduced several programs designed to increase the U.S. attorneys' attention to and ability to police the "new problem areas." Sessions used these developments to strengthen and expand Johnson's and Watkins's investigations.[20]

Working with Johnson, District Attorney Watkins, U.S. Attorney Frank Donaldson (Northern District), and U.S. Attorney John Bell (Middle District), Sessions orchestrated a regionwide joint state-federal vote fraud investigation in Greene, Lowndes, Perry, Sumter, and Wilcox counties, the very Black Belt counties where African Americans had secured majority control of county government in the previous six years. Although U.S. attorney Donaldson initiated investigations of alleged vote fraud in majority-white DeKalb and Winston counties, he abandoned those investigations almost as soon as they were begun.[21] By beginning the investigation in the way that he did, Sessions essentially took sides in an ongoing racial power struggle in the Black Belt. He had, in essence, transformed his office, indeed all three of the Alabama U.S. attorney's offices, into instruments for the defense of white-minority rule. The manner in which the investigations were conducted demonstrates that this was intentional. In August 1984, federal investigators worked with the local district attorneys and registrars, the very whites whom local blacks had repeatedly accused of fraud, to set up what amounted to a sting operation against the black political organizations in the five Black Belt counties. Local black organizations were placed under surveillance, and all the absentee ballots handed out to black voting rights organizers were surreptitiously numbered so that they could be traced to the organizers who handled them and the voters who cast them after the election.[22] Investigators only focused on the key black voting rights activists in the designated counties. All the targets were veterans of the civil rights movement who had devoted their lives to black political empowerment. In Perry County prosecutors targeted Albert Turner, his wife, Evelyn Turner, and Spencer Hogue, founding members of the Perry County Civic League and the Perry County citizenship schools respectively. Turner was also the state coordinator of the SCLC during the 1965 Selma campaign and was so close to Martin Luther King Jr. that he had led the mule train at his funeral. In Greene County, investigators targeted Spiver Gordon, a veteran of CORE, president of the Greene County Civic League, and the first African American elected to the Eutaw City Council (in the 1984 primary election). In Sumter, federal prosecutors targeted Wendell Paris, a veteran of SNCC and chairman of the county school board. Federal investigators in Lowndes County focused their energies on John Hulett, a founding member of the SNCC-inspired Lowndes County Freedom Organization and the sitting county sheriff. In Wilcox County, federal prosecutors targeted Rev. Thomas Threadgill, a prominent social justice preacher and community activist.[23]

While focusing their prosecutorial gaze on black political organizations and organizers, federal prosecutors turned a blind eye to the illegal activities of white political organizations. Following the 1984 primary election, black political organizations uncovered numerous election law violations by white political organizations and their black collaborators. As in previous elections, white political organizations were found to have cast absentee ballots on behalf of people who no longer lived in the county both with and without their permission. In one astonishing incident, Perry County circuit clerk Mary Auburtin, at the very same time that she was working with federal investigators to conduct a sting against the Perry County Civic League, knowingly handled absentee ballots from whites who had long since moved away from the county. Even when presented with this evidence during the subsequent trials of black voting rights organizers, the U.S. attorneys refused to investigate.[24] In short, federal prosecutors were targeting local black political organizations, not the crime of voter fraud.

Not only did federal investigators focus only on black voting rights activists, but they conducted the investigations in such a manner as to intimidate large numbers of black voters on the eve of the 1984 general election. Throughout the month of October, U.S. attorney Donaldson issued press releases and held public meetings in which he told residents that voter fraud violations would be prosecuted to the fullest extent of the law. At a late-October meeting in Greene County, Donaldson went so far as to tell residents that anyone who voted in the recently concluded September primary election or the upcoming November general election could be called before the grand jury for questioning. There was little question whom he was referring to. Just days later, FBI agents raided the Greene County government office building and seized the records of Greene County director of planning and development, Booker T. Cooke, a member of the Greene County Civic League.[25] Simultaneously, FBI agents fanned out across the Black Belt to interview between 1,000 and 1,500 voters, *all* of them African Americans, most elderly, who had voted absentee for the different black civic association slates. The agents arrived carrying these individuals' absentee ballots, itself a violation of DOJ guidelines for conducting election investigations. "Is this your ballot?" the voters were asked. "Is this how you voted? Did you make this change? Who picked up your ballot?"[26] Some of the agents took fingerprints, handwriting samples, and photographs of these witnesses. Over one hundred of these voters were also bused to Montgomery, Birmingham, or Mobile to testify before the three grand juries then collecting evidence in the investigations.

The FBI interrogations and their appearances before the grand juries were a traumatic experience for many of these African Americans. Less than twenty years before, most had been denied the vote by white authorities or through vigilante violence, and the FBI interrogations seemed eerily reminiscent of those times. A small number, like sixty-five-year-old Mamie Speight, refused to be intimidated. "Those FBI men showed me their badges and told me didn't I know it was wrong to vote absentee, but I knew I hadn't done anything wrong," she stated. "I've voted every year I've had the opportunity and I'm not going to give it up now." Not all of Speight's neighbors were as defiant. The vast majority were shaken by the experience. Testifying before a Mobile grand jury, Fannie May Williams, an elderly Perry County resident, was asked if her September 1984 ballot was the first one she had submitted absentee. "Uh-huh," she replied. "First and the last." Voting rights activist Wendell Paris found that the investigation had a similar effect on the African Americans in Sumter County. Speaking with reporters in June 1985, he stated, "A number of them have told me they will not vote anymore, period." The investigations depressed black voting so much in Greene County that a white-led "biracial coalition" secured six of the seven seats in the county government.[27]

In the early days of the investigation, the U.S. attorneys loudly announced that as many as forty individuals might be indicted. In the end, however, they brought only eight indictments in two counties. U.S. attorney Sessions had been unable to convince a Mobile grand jury to bring any indictments at all against black voting rights activists in Perry County. He nonetheless indicted Albert Turner, his wife, Evelyn Turner, and Spencer Hogue on a total of eighty-seven counts. Local activists would dub them the "Marion Three" after their hometown. Donaldson was able to secure indictments against Eutaw city councilman Spiver Gordon; James Colvin, mayor of Union; Frederick Daniels; Bessie Underwood; and Bobbie Neil Simpson, all of Greene County, on a total of 138 counts. Local activists would name this group the "Greene County Five."

Even before the U.S. attorneys announced the indictments, local activists had begun to organize for their defense. Central to these efforts were state senator Hank Sanders, whose district covered all the effected counties, and John Zippert, director of the Federation of Southern Cooperatives Rural Training and Research Center. Sanders and his wife, Rose, had moved to Selma fresh out of law school, hoping to contribute their talents to the ongoing freedom struggle in the Black Belt. With J. L. Chestnut, they had founded what became the largest black law firm in the state. That same law firm had handled the redistricting case that drew the majority-black state senate district that Sander's then represented. Using his extensive network, Sanders assembled an all-star legal team to represent the accused. Defense lawyers included Lani Guinier, James Liebman, and Deval Patrick of the NAACP-Legal Defense Fund; Morton Stavis of the Center for Constitutional Rights; Dennis Balske of the Southern Poverty Law Center; local legal heavyweights J. L. Chestnut and Robert Turner; Margaret Carey, a civil rights lawyer from Mississippi; and Howard Moore, who most recently had defended Zippert and four others from the Federation of Southern Cooperatives.[28] In order to pay for this legal talent, Sanders worked with Zippert to create the Black Belt Defense Fund. Zippert, a white man and veteran of the Louisiana CORE, first moved to Alabama in 1967 to work with the Southwest Alabama Farmers Co-op. As a target of the "Cotton Patch conspiracy," he possessed some expertise in defending the targets of DOJ investigations. Under the aegis of the Defense Fund, Zippert coordinated a national fund-raising effort that took Turner and Gordon to speaking engagements up and down the East and West coasts and raised close to twenty thousand dollars.[29] Last, Sanders coordinated a counterpropaganda campaign that brought national attention to the Black Belt and urged local blacks to keep participating in the electoral process. Central to this effort was the August 1985 "freedom caravan," consisting of voter registration drives and rallies at all the Black Belt county courthouses. Seeking to tie his efforts both to the civil rights movement and to a national black constituency, Sanders asked Maryland state senator and president of the National Black Caucus of State Legislators, Clarence Mitchell III (D-Baltimore) to lead the caravan. Mitchell, first son of the famed Baltimore civil rights family and a target of FBI and Baltimore Police Department surveillance in the late 1960s and early 1970s, enthusiastically answered the call.[30] The caravan was a phenomenal success. Following a rally at the Dallas County courthouse in Selma, several local and regional newspapers printed Mitchell's claim that "the Ku Klux Klan and the white Citizens' Council [could] close up shop, because the Justice Department [was] doing their work for them."[31] Just as important, the caravan succeeded in registering several hundred new black voters and reinforcing the will of those who were already on the rolls. Last, and perhaps most importantly, Sanders and Zippert succeeded in bringing the Black Belt vote fraud cases to the attention of the House Judiciary Committee. In the fall of 1985, the Subcommittee on Civil and Constitutional Rights held hearings on the then still-ongoing Black Belt investigations. Representative Don Edwards (D-Calif.), who had worked with Black Belt voting rights activists to pen the VRA and its subsequent reauthorizations, chaired the proceedings. The hearings gave Black Belt voting rights activists a national forum for exposing the activities of the Alabama U.S. attorneys.

On June 17, the trial of the three Perry County voting rights activists began in Selma. The defense opened the proceedings with a motion to dismiss the charges, claiming selective prosecution. Using the prosecution's own statistics, defense lawyers had established that blacks and whites used the absentee ballot at proportionally the same rate in the Black Belt. The Reagan DOJ, however, had pursued vote fraud charges only against black political organizations. Judge Emmett Cox, a Reagan appointee, denied the motion. He then went a step further and forbade the defense from mentioning race during the trial. Determined to enforce this stricture, Cox later ruled Howard Moore in contempt for asking the white registrar who had worked with federal investigators if two noncounty residents to whom she had mailed absentee ballots were white. (The two were, in fact, white.)[32]

Once the trial began, however, the advantage turned to the defense.

Prosecutors had built their case around the theory that the African American Black Belt political organization's voting assistance activities — that is, marking a ballot *with the voluntary consent* of the voter — constituted voting more than once by the organizers and was thus illegal. Organizers, on the other hand, had envisioned the process as one in which members of the community helped the elderly, the homebound, and migrant workers to express their collective will. Granted, from a legal standpoint, Black Belt African Americans absentee ballot programs posed a whole host of potential legal problems. By bringing absentee ballots to residents' homes, organizers denied other political factions access to these voters. Because many of the voters who submitted absentee ballots were elderly, illiterate, or infirm, organizers could coerce them in a multitude of ways such as mismarking the ballot or providing misleading information about candidates. There was thus a reasonable concern that black political organizers could be "exploit[ing] the franchise of mentally infirm and socially dependent voters." Some Black Belt African Americans themselves feared this possibility. Hasan Jeffries, in his study of Lowndes County, has noted that a black political faction that opposed Sheriff John Hulett in the 1984 election worried that Hulett and his allies were using the relationships they had with the county's elderly voters to peremptorily secure the votes of Lowndes County residents. "As soon as the circuit clerk posted the names of those requesting absentee ballots," Jeffries quotes one candidate as saying, "he [Hulett] and others began visiting them to make sure they voted their way."[33]

But the threat of fraud and actual fraud are two different things. FBI field reports demonstrate that the overwhelming majority of voters they interviewed did not report any deviation between their intent and the way in which their ballots were marked.[34] Of the two hundred African Americans the FBI interviewed in Perry County, for instance, only seventeen gave answers that suggested they may have been victims of fraud. When U.S. attorney Sessions brought them to trial, however, even the testimony of these seventeen witnesses fell apart. Defense lawyers claimed that many of the witnesses had been intimidated by the FBI agents who had come to their homes. As a result, they had dissembled, tailoring their answers to what they thought the agents wanted to hear. In the field, this dissembling appeared to confirm agents' belief that black political organizers had victimized these elderly African Americans. In court, however, these elderly African Americans' testimony appeared contradictory and confusing. It exasperated the prosecutors, moving them, in several instances, to badger their own witnesses.[35] Further undermining the prosecution's case, a majority of the witnesses expressed affection for and confidence in the defendants. One testified, "I been knowin' Albert [Turner] all my life. I know his daddy. I know his mama and that's his little brother sittin' there beside him. Albert's been pickin' my ballot for sixteen years."[36] Comments such as these, in fact, supported the defense's argument that black political organizers absentee ballot work was rooted in bonds of trust that mitigated the possibility of fraud. Only six of the seventeen witnesses for the prosecution, all members of a single family that had often feuded with the Turners, held firm to their initial allegations that the Turners and Hogue had engaged in fraud. The six, however, gave conflicting accounts, moving the jury to question their honesty. On July 6, after deliberating for only three hours, the jury returned verdicts of not guilty on all counts for the "Marion Three."

As the Perry County voting rights activists celebrated in Selma, attorneys for Spiver Gordon and Fredrick Daniels were preparing for jury selection in Tuscaloosa. Several weeks before, James Colvin and Bobbie Neil Simpson had been tried before racially mixed juries in Birmingham. In both cases, the black jurors, unconvinced by the prosecutor's presentation, held out for acquittals, thereby causing mistrials. Donaldson and his assistants were determined not to let that happen again. During the jury selection process for the Gordon and Daniels trial, prosecutors used their six preemptory strikes to eliminate the six African Americans from the forty-seven-member jury pool. Attorneys for the defense immediately filed a motion for a mistrial. Judge E. B. Haltom Jr., a Carter appointee, rejected the motion and scheduled opening statements for later in the week. Undeterred, defense attorneys filed an emergency request to stop the trial before the Eleventh Circuit Court of Appeals.[37] The justices, however, would take some time to review the request, leaving Gordon and Daniels to be tried before the all-white jury.

Despite their advantage, prosecutors were unable to convince the jury of Gordon's and Daniel's guilt. On October 11, after deliberating for eleven hours, the jury acquitted Daniels of all eleven counts. The following day, the jury acquitted Gordon of nine counts and announced that they were hopelessly deadlocked on the remaining twelve. Refusing to allow a mistrial, Haltom ordered the jurors back into chambers. As prosecutors anxiously awaited the jury's decision, they suffered embarrassing defeats in three of the other Greene County cases. On October 12, Bobbie Neil Simpson, whom Donaldson had retried following a mistrial the month before, was acquitted by a racially mixed jury. Soon afterward, Bessie J. Underwood and James Colvin pleaded guilty to one misdemeanor count each of improperly handling absentee ballots and received fines and probation. Considering that Underwood and Colvin had originally been indicted on several felony counts of vote fraud, the guilty pleas were not victories for Donaldson. On October 16, following five days of deliberation, the jury convicted Gordon of two counts of mail fraud and two counts of providing false information to an election official, but only after recommending that he be granted clemency.[38] That prosecutors were able to secure only one-tenth of their original indictments against Gordon, and none against his alleged coconspirators before majority-white and all-white juries is a testament to the utter weakness of their case. In July 1987, the Eleventh Circuit Court of Appeals found evidence of "selective prosecution" of black voters and voting rights activists in Greene County and declared that the U.S. attorney had violated Gordon's right to a trial by his peers by striking all the black jurors from the jury pool. The court noted that federal prosecutors had exhibited similar bias in the other Black Belt voter fraud cases.[39]

By the end of the voter fraud trials, most Black Belt African Americans believed that the investigations were a reaction to the rise of black political power in the region or an attempt to "chill" the black vote in advance of the 1986 senatorial contest in which arch-conservative Republican Jeremiah Denton was up for reelection. Denton had sponsored the appointment of Donaldson, Bell, and Sessions to the DOJ following his election in 1980. In retaliation, well over 90 percent of Alabama blacks threw their support to conservative Democrat Richard Shelby, sending Denton down to defeat. In that same year, several Black Belt voting rights activists traveled to Washington to testify before the Senate Judiciary Committee against Reagan's choice of U.S. attorney Sessions for the U.S. District Court for the Southern District of Alabama. As a result of their testimony, Sessions became the first Reagan judicial nominee to be rejected by the Senate.[40] Thus despite the initial decrease in black voting in the 1984 general election, the Black Belt vote fraud investigations had the effect of increasing black registration and voting and reinforcing the credibility of local black leadership.

Federal Official Corruption Investigations in Birmingham and Montgomery, 1988–1989

By the late 1980s, Thomas Edsall and Mary Edsall write, "race had become central to establishing partisan difference" in Alabama. Alabama whites had been voting against the *national* Democratic Party since 1948 — by either voting for the State's Rights Party (1948), the Republican Party (1964, 1972), or George Wallace's American Independent Party (1968) — but most had remained Democrats in state and local elections. In the 1980s and early 1990s, however, the rise of black voting and office-holding moved, first, middle-class and suburban whites and, later, working-class and rural whites, to abandon the *state* Democratic Party as well. Jefferson County, the state's most populous county and home to the city of Birmingham, presented the most stunning example of this trend. In the 1960s, all the seats in the Jefferson County delegation to the state legislature were held by white Democrats. By the late 1980s, the eighteen seats in the Jefferson County delegation were almost evenly split between black Democrats and white Republicans. Nine blacks and one white were Democrats.

The remaining eight whites were Republicans.[41] A similar division could be seen in Birmingham city government. As whites migrated to the suburbs and switched their party affiliation, black Democrats became a majority of the city electorate. Richard Arrington became the city's first black mayor in 1979 and was reelected in 1983, 1987, and 1991, each time with minimal white support. In each of these elections, city whites gave increasing percentages of their vote to the Republican challenger. Additionally, city blacks secured a majority of the nine seats on the Birmingham City Council and elected William Bell city council president in 1985.[42] In the midst of this racial-partisan shift and the racial tensions that it both reflected and produced, Republican state and federal authorities trained their investigative and prosecutorial guns on the black elected leadership of Jefferson County.

As in most major metropolitan areas, African Americans' successful push for political power in Jefferson County was in many ways a pyrrhic victory. Blacks gained control of municipal and county government at the very moment that Birmingham's industrial economy was being dismantled. Many of the steel plants that had made Birmingham the "Magic City" had closed or were operating at just a fraction of capacity. To make matters worse, the Reagan administration had made drastic cuts in federal assistance to cities. In Birmingham, these cuts removed approximately $11 million from the city's budget by 1985. Strapped for cash and with no new sources of revenue on the horizon, Mayor Arrington reduced city services, deferred public works projects, and increased taxes during his first term. In his second term, Arrington sought to shift Birmingham's economy from industry to tourism, gaming, and medical research by initiating a number of public-private development projects. Specifically, Arrington supported efforts to create Big Splash, a water park, and the Turf Club, a horse-racing track. It would be some time, however, before these projects bore fruit, and the city needed money immediately. To make up for the budget shortfalls, Arrington and his allies on the city council proposed a $65 million bond for school construction, city services, and a civil rights museum, the Birmingham Civil Rights Institute, slated to be built on the edge of Kelley Ingram Park, scene of the violent confrontations between civil rights protesters and police in the spring of 1963. The city council placed the bond before the electorate in the form of a referendum in 1986. The bond referendum stimulated the formation of a majority-white, antitax group called Tax Busters, led by attorney Robert McKee. In their campaign against the bond, Tax Busters claimed that "waste" at City Hall, not federal cuts in aid to cities and the declining industrial base, was the real reason for Birmingham's financial woes. Specifically, they attacked what they believed were, in Arrington biographer Jimmie Franklin's words, "city consulting fees that allegedly went to Arrington's friends, large amounts of money for city employee travel, and a one million dollar loan approved by the City

Council to bail out the Birmingham Stallions professional football team. A loan for the building of a water theme park also drew criticism," Franklin continues, "as did the construction of access roads to the new Birmingham racetrack [pushed through the legislature by Arrington allies state representative John Rogers (D) and state senator Earl Hilliard (D)]." With white turnout exceeding black turnout by fully 100 percent, the bond issue went down to defeat. Buoyed by Tax Busters' 1986 victory in the bond referendum, McKee challenged Arrington in the 1987 mayoral race. During the campaign, Franklin notes, McKee, "hammered away at waste in government. . . . Repeatedly, he turned to city loans to private concerns, to consulting fees the Arrington administration had paid out, and to travel by city politicians as prime examples of 'waste.'" This tactic was successful in that Arrington received only 10 percent of the white vote. Strong black turnout, however, more than made up for Arrington's lack of white support. He won the contest with 64 percent of the vote.[43]

The 1986–87 struggles of Tax Busters and McKee versus the black elected leadership of Jefferson County sparked a number of official corruption investigations by the office of U.S. attorney Donaldson. As early as 1984, Arrington had drawn the attention of federal investigators. That fall, Billy and Gwen Webb, the mayor's recently fired former bodyguards, alleged that Arrington had violated the Hatch Act by trading influence for money. Following a preliminary investigation, assistant U.S. attorney Herbert Henry III determined that there was insufficient evidence to proceed and closed the case. In August 1985, federal investigators conducted a separate preliminary investigation, this time of Arrington's alleged personal business dealings. Of particular interest to investigators was the mayor's part ownership of a marketing and consulting business called ABD Marketing Corporation, which the mayor had founded with his aide Willie Davis and Atlanta architect Tarlee Brown. After reviewing the results of the investigation, assistant U.S. attorney Henry again determined that there was insufficient evidence to proceed. In 1986–87 the U.S. attorney again opened an investigation of Arrington, this time in response to the multiple allegations of waste and fraud made by Tax Busters and McKee. Unlike with the previous two preliminary investigations, federal investigators opened full investigations of possible influence peddling by Arrington in connection with the city's efforts to build Big Splash Theme Park and the Turf Club, the refurbishing of Birmingham's historic Boutwell Auditorium, and the city's Minority Business Enterprise program. By spring 1987, agents had placed Arrington under heavy surveillance: taping his phone conversations, performing video and audio surveillance of him and his acquaintances, and interviewing the mayor about his activities. Their actions moved an increasingly suspicious Arrington to order his FBI dossier.[44] Because Arrington had worked on these projects with his black Democratic colleagues in the state legislature, they also became targets of

FBI surveillance. In August 1988, assistant U.S. attorney Henry again reviewed agents' findings and concluded that they had not produced evidence of wrongdoing sufficient to warrant an indictment. He ordered that the investigation be ended in October 1988.[45]

In the meantime, in early 1988, another clash between black elected officials and conservative whites escalated racial tensions and appeared to stimulate a repressive state response. On February 2, 1988, fourteen members of the Alabama Black Legislative Caucus (ABLC) were arrested for criminal trespass as they attempted to enter the old state capitol grounds in a symbolic attempt to remove the Confederate battle flag from atop the capitol dome. The protest was organized by Representative Thomas Reed (D-Tuskegee), chairman of the Alabama NAACP. Reed had vowed to climb the capitol dome and remove the flag himself if Governor Guy Hunt (R) had not issued an order to do so by February 2. Hunt had won the governorship in 1986 through what can only be called a tremendous stroke of luck. With few Republicans willing to take on the Democratic heavyweights then seeking to succeed Governor George Wallace, Hunt cruised to victory in the GOP primary. While he watched from the sidelines, the leading Democratic candidates — Attorney General Charles Craddick and Lieutenant Governor Bill Baxley — cannibalized each other in a vicious primary contest, subsequent legal battle over the results, and breakaway write in campaign by Graddick, who had lost the primary on a technicality. In the general election, Hunt received 56 percent of the vote, almost all of it from white Alabamans, while Graddick and Baxley split the Democratic coalition in two. Baxley received 96 percent of black Alabamans' votes.[46] Considering the 1986 election returns, it is not surprising that Hunt refused to remove the flag, claiming that no public support existed for such a move.[47] Within days of their arrest, Representatives James Buskey (D-Mobile), James Thomas (D-Selma), John Rogers, and state senator Earl Hilliard received audit notices from the Alabama Income Tax Division. Representative Jenkins Bryant Jr. (D-Newbern), who had not participated in the protest, also received an audit notice from the state. The audits covered five of the twenty-four black members of the Alabama legislature, or 21 percent of the membership. On February 25, the ABLC held a news conference at the state capitol. Representative Alvin Holmes (D-Montgomery) spoke for his colleagues when he said, "There is no way that five black legislators could be targeted by the Alabama Income Tax Division unless it's a definite effort on the part of the governor's office." Governor Hunt denied the black legislators' charges, attributing the audits to random selection. He then used the episode to attack the Democratic Party: "I would assume that, especially after the flap concerning the [former Democratic lieutenant governor] Bill Baxley returns that every person involved in politics in Alabama has their tax returns in order." Hunt's comparison, like his explanation, made no sense. Baxley had not been audited, nor were his returns out of order. Rather, a former clerk for the Alabama Department of Revenue had stolen Baxley's tax returns and given them to his 1986 Democratic primary opponent in an effort to embarrass the then lieutenant governor.[48]

Fast on the heels of the tax controversy, in June 1988, a grand jury under the guidance of the U.S. attorney for the Middle District, James Wilson, indicted Representative Reed for bribery and conspiracy. The indictment alleged that Reed was paid a bribe to use his position as cochairman of the Joint Prison Committee of the Alabama Legislature to secure the early parole of convicted murderer Anthony Chesser. At the time of his indictment, Reed was one of the most powerful black political figures in Alabama. First elected to the House in 1970, he was the dean of the ABLC and chairman of the House Prison Committee. In the months leading up to his September trial, Reed maintained his innocence, claiming that the charges were retribution for his campaign to remove the Confederate flag from atop the old state capitol dome. Although evidence presented at the trial strongly indicated Reed's guilt, many of his colleagues in the ABLC were wont to believe his version of events. Most were aware that similar charges had been leveled at Reed in the past. In 1976, he had been accused of bribery and, after two mistrials, tried again. In the third trial, Reed was convicted of "attempting . . . to bribe," and fined five hundred dollars. The conviction was later overturned on appeal. During the 1976 trial, Reed had established a defense fund and solicited the help of other black elected officials, making his case well known as an instance of political repression among black Alabama politicos.[49] The 1988 bribery case, however, was a different matter, and the jury of four blacks and eight whites found Reed guilty on two counts of bribery and conspiracy and not guilty on the three remaining charges. He was subsequently stripped of his seat in the house and sentenced to four years in prison.[50]

The Moussallem Affidavit

In light of the audit controversy and the Reed conviction, Alabama black elected officials had become increasingly suspicious of the U.S. attorney's motives. Were state and federal Republicans targeting black elected officials and political organizers as they had in the Black Belt in 1984–85? On the evening of April 25, 1989, Robert Moussallem, a forty-one-year-old Lebanese American who was a Jefferson County land developer, unexpectedly appeared at Mayor Arrington's home with an apparent answer. Moussallem, an acquaintance of Arrington's and a valuable supporter during his 1983 reelection campaign, had come, he told the mayor, to warn him of an FBI-IRS plot to "set him up." Since 1985, when he was apprehended for offering undercover IRS agents several hundred thousand dollars in bribes, Moussallem had worked intermittently as an informant for the IRS in the hopes of receiving limited immunity from prosecution.[51] In October 1988, IRS agent Marshall Mullins, FBI agent James Kiel, assistant U.S. attorney Bill Barrett, and at least one other unidentified federal official offered Moussallem full immunity from prosecution if he performed one more undercover operation. The operation, Moussallem told Arrington, was a sting aimed at several Birmingham black elected officials, the mayor foremost among them. The agents, he claimed, instructed him to purchase land in Birmingham that had recently been refused rezoning by the city council. He was then to approach Arrington, city council president Bell, city councilman Jeff Germany, state senator Hilliard, and Representative Rogers — all black Democrats — to "solicit their involvement and influence in getting the property rezoned" by offering each a "bribe." The agents stated that they could only offer Moussallem limited immunity before the operation so that the deal could not be used against the prosecution when the above-mentioned elected officials were brought to trial.[52]

On November 23, 1988, Moussallem received a cryptic letter from U.S. attorney Frank Donaldson promising "favorable consideration" for his cooperation in an "on-going criminal investigation."[53] Subsequently, he began to enact the plan outlined by his government handlers. He bought property near the Birmingham Airport that had previously been refused a commercial zoning permit. Moussallem then met with Representative Rogers and city councilman Bell and offered them bribes in exchange for their help in having the property rezoned. "Each declined the offer of money and appeared to be confused and irritated by my suggestion," Moussallem told the mayor.[54] Soon after the meeting with Bell, Moussallem claimed, Kiel and Mullins contacted him to tell him that his "role in the scheme was over, and that the deal for total immunity was dead." Fearing an impending indictment, Moussallem decided to go public with his story. He was sharing this information with the mayor, he said, because he planned to file a complaint against the agents in the very near future and did not want the resulting media coverage to catch him unaware.[55]

Moussallem's allegations sparked a four-year battle between the black Democratic elected leadership of Jefferson County, indeed of Alabama, and the Birmingham FBI, the IRS, and the Alabama U.S. attorneys. When Moussallem made his allegations to Arrington, the Alabama U.S. attorneys were investigating a majority of the high-ranking Democratic elected officials in Jefferson County. Seeking to protect themselves from what they believed was a racial-partisan attack on their ranks, Alabama black elected officials mounted a stunningly effective legal defense and counterpropaganda campaign. From the spring of 1989 to 1993, they fought the Alabama U.S. attorneys, the FBI, and the IRS to a legal and public relations stalemate. In the process, they contributed to the growing national outcry against the DOJ's disproportionate investigation of black Democrats under Reagan and Bush.

The morning after his encounter with Moussallem, Arrington related the matter to his special counsel, Donald Watkins. A former Montgomery city councilman who had spent most of his years in government opposing the policies of Montgomery mayor and Goldwater Republican Emory Folmar, Watkins had a keen understanding of the ways in which race was coming to define party politics in Alabama. As an attorney who had defended several black elected officials charged with official corruption in 1982, he believed that the Republican U.S. attorneys were using official corruption investigations to attack Alabama black elected officials.[56] He instructed the mayor to quietly document everything in preparation for what he expected would be politically motivated criminal charges. On April 27, Watkins had Arrington swear an affidavit describing his meeting with Moussallem. Only days later, on May 1, U.S. attorney Frank Donaldson indicted Moussallem for attempting to bribe an IRS agent, the same charges that prosecutors had used to convince him to work as a government informant. The following day, Watkins hand-delivered a letter to Donaldson requesting a DOJ inquiry into Moussallem's allegations. He also asked that Donaldson conduct an investigation of the "steady stream of . . . leaks regarding alleged criminal conduct by several black public officials" by grand juries impaneled in Montgomery and Birmingham. After "several years" of leaks with "no Grand Jury action," Watkins explained, "many in the black community [had come to] believe that these leaks are a deliberate effort . . . to place a cloud over the integrity and political future of the black public officials repeatedly mentioned in the leaks." Watkins was not convinced, however, that Donaldson was willing to police his own office. (Donaldson did, in fact, forward Watkins's complaint to the DOJ, OPR, on May 3, 1989. The OPR began an investigation of the complaint in July.) In an effort to force his hand, Watkins released the Arrington affidavit to the press. The Birmingham press, in turn, published a string of articles expounding on Moussallem's allegations.[57]

In the midst of the media frenzy created by the release of the Arrington affidavit, U.S. attorney James Wilson (Middle District) indicted state senator E. B. McClain (D-Brighton), Representative Bobbie McDowell (D-Bessemer), and Representative Lewis Spratt (D-Birmingham) — all black — for conspiring to swap stock options for their support of a proposed dog-racing track planned for the city of Bessemer, Jefferson County. The May 22 indictment also charged recently retired representative Hugh Boles (D-Hueytown), who is white, with offering the bribes. The charges centered around a 1987 bill to allow dog racing in Bessemer at the track formerly known as the Turf Club. The Turf Club had been completed in early 1987 with private funds. After a promising opening day, attendance dwindled and profits fell far below projections. By the end of the year, the owner was looking to sell. In an effort to increase track business, some Jefferson county legislators had fastened on the idea of dog racing, a sport they believed was more in tune with the working-class population of the county. Boles emerged as an early backer of the initiative. Seeking to ensure passage of his bill, Boles had worked the Jefferson County delegation, requesting support and offering bribes to lawmakers. Rather than offer money, Boles offered stock options in the proposed track, which were projected to net several thousand dollars per year. The FBI discovered the scheme when Representative Gary White (R-Homewood), who had been offered a bribe by Boles, reported his activities to local authorities. Agents then secured wiretaps on Boles's phones and enlisted White as an informant. On March 31 and April 1, 1988, agents met with Boles and confronted him with evidence of his activities that they had collected. He subsequently gave a statement claiming that McClain, McDowell, and Spratt had accepted his offers of stock options for their support of the bill. He went on to note that Bessemer mayor Ed Porter and Alabama House clerk John Pemberton, both white, had also been promised stock options. The indictment only mentioned Boles and the three black legislators.[58]

In reaction to the indictments, black elected officials went on the offensive. Speaking with reporters on May 27, Watkins stated, "The Arrington matter is just the latest incident that includes a string of indictments of black politicians. I know this is not a coincidence. It's part of a larger strategy to constrain and discredit black political leadership, particularly those who have been vocal on black issues." Having been pummeled in the press for most of May, federal officials sought to rebut Watkins's allegations. At a hastily arranged press conference, U.S. attorney Wilson stated, "We, in this office, do not consider race, nor the political affiliation of any party in our investigation. . . . To be quite candid, I didn't know the race or political affiliation of most of the people involved [in the Bessemer dog track indictment]."[59] William Hinshaw, special agent in charge of the Mobile and Montgomery offices of the FBI, reinforced Wilson's message of color-blind good-government reform days later at a press conference of his own. The FBI had sent African American agent Theodore Jackson to Mobile around the same time that the Moussallem affidavit was made public. Seeking to capitalize on his presence, Hinshaw had Jackson accompany him to the June 2 press conference. Speaking to reporters, Jackson stated, "The bottom line is, where we gather information on corruption, we weigh it and investigate it, black or white." He went on to note that to his knowledge, the FBI had never lost a public corruption case where the target had claimed entrapment.[60] In the coming weeks, the bureau would lose five such cases in Jefferson County alone. The following day, June 3, state senator Hank Sanders (D) raised the stakes with a startling accusation. Speaking from the state capitol, Sanders stated that he had "received information [from several confidential informants] indicating that more than half of the black elected officials in the state of Alabama [were] either under surveillance, investigation, or the targets of sting operations." By comparison, Sanders claimed, only 2 percent of white elected officials in the state were experiencing similar levels of scrutiny. In a 1991 article, Arrington would support Sanders's claim, writing, "Information about the list was corroborated by multiple confidential informants who have proven reliable and who do not know one another." Like Sanders, Arrington refused to name his informants, fearing that doing so would expose them to retaliation. Responding to Sanders, Donaldson and Hinshaw again repeated their denials.[61]

Moussallem's accusations, combined with the 1988 audit controversy, the Reed conviction, and the Bessemer dog track indictments, led many Alabama black elected officials to conclude that they were being targeted for repression by local Republicans, the Bush DOJ, the IRS, and the FBI. Federal officials continued to deny their accusations. Hoping to end the war of words with a state investigation, Arrington sent a formal request to Alabama attorney general Don Siegelman on May 30, requesting a special prosecutor's investigation of Moussallem's allegations. Siegelman rejected Arrington's request and instead assigned Assistant Attorney General Milt Belcher, chief of the Civil Rights Division, to look into the matter. Although Siegelman assured Arrington that Belcher would "interview witnesses, conduct a full and complete examination of all facts and evidence, and . . . submit . . . a report of his findings," neither Belcher nor Siegelman ever got back to him. No written record of Belcher's investigation can be found in Alabama state records. In the late 1980s, it was still politically perilous for a white elected official to seem too close to a black constituency, and Arrington suspected that Siegelman might bury the case.[62] As such, Arrington directed Watkins to continue investigating on his own. In the interim, he began to organize his fellow black elected officials for a collective defense.

The Alabama Black Elected and Appointed Officials Legal Defense Fund

As Arrington was preparing his letter to Attorney General Siegelman, he noticed an article in the Birmingham News covering ADC chairman Joe Reed's address to the group's annual convention. In the speech, Reed exhorted his organization to support the many black elected officials across the state then under investigation and indictment. Arrington was a cochairman of the ANSC, a statewide black political organization that had split off from the ADC in 1986 in protest of Reed's heavy-handed leadership style. There was no love lost between the two organizations in 1989. They consistently found themselves on different sides of intra–Democratic Party battles. Despite these differences, Arrington immediately penned a memo to the leaders of the ANSC [and cc'ed Joe Reed] imploring them to "all rally *publicly* and in a *united* effort to Joe's call." In the early stages of his investigation into Moussallem's allegations, Watkins had discovered Mary Sawyer's two reports on the harassment of black elected officials. He had also spoken to black elected officials in Atlanta, who alerted him to a sworn affidavit by former FBI informant Hirsch Friedman alleging a national FBI plot to entrap black elected officials.[63] The combined weight of this information led Arrington to believe that black elected officials across the country were the targets of "a carefully orchestrated plot to discredit and even destroy black political leadership." More important, he feared that Alabama was the eye of the storm. "I am totally convinced that the harassment, investigations, indictment and otherwise, is far more widespread in Alabama than even most black elected officials realize," Arrington stated. He went on to suggest that the state's black leadership "meet in Montgomery and enter into a joint pact on this issue and follow with a public announcement at a news conference of [their] activities."[64]

There was no need for Arrington to convince his colleagues. Nearly the entirety of Alabama's black political community felt as he did. And they demonstrated that belief by heeding his call. On June 7, 1989, representatives of the ANSC, ADC, ABLC, Alabama Conference of Black Mayors, Alabama Black Lawyers Association, National Black Caucus of State Legislators, NAACP, and SCLC met at Dexter Avenue Baptist Church in Montgomery to coordinate a collective defense. That afternoon, the group emerged from the church to announce the creation of the Alabama Black Elected and Appointed Officials Legal Defense Fund (ABEAO-LDF), "a statewide organization for the purpose of monitoring, investigating and, where deemed appropriate, providing funds for the defense of black elected officials." In a prepared statement, the group expressed concern over what they believed was "a biased pattern of investigations of black elected officials by federal agents." Citing the 1984–85 Black Belt vote fraud investigation; the recent indictment of Representatives McClain, McDowell, and Spratt; and the Moussallem allegations, the group declared, "In the investigation of black elected officials in Alabama the practices have often been unprofessional, unethical, selective, probably unlawful, and sometimes outright racist." The ABEAO-LDF, they asserted, would "protect black elected officials from this type of unethical and/or illegal conduct by federal agents and . . . work to bring a halt to racist tactics of targeting black elected officials in fishing expeditions on public corruption."[65]

Within days, the ABEAO-LDF dispatched a letter to Attorney General Richard Thornburgh, requesting a meeting concerning his U.S. attorneys' investigations of Alabama black leadership. Following Hank Sanders's example from the 1984–85 vote fraud trials, the group also sent letters to the House and Senate Judiciary Committees requesting oversight hearings concerning the

DOJ's activities in Alabama.[66] Thornburgh scheduled a meeting for June 29, only to refuse the originally agreed-upon twelve-member delegation on June 27 after speaking with his Alabama U.S. attorneys. He asked instead that the delegation be limited to Montgomery attorney Fred Gray, ADC chairman Joe Reed, and Earl Shinhoster. Though important to the coalition, not one of these individuals played a central role in the ABEAO-LDF. Rejecting these conditions as unacceptable, the ABEAO-LDF canceled the meeting.[67]

On the same day that members of the ABEAO-LDF declined to meet with Thornburgh, the *Birmingham Post-Herald* published another in a steady stream of leaks from the then-ongoing grand jury investigation of three state legislators alleged to have accepted bribes in return for their support of a bill requiring state power companies to buy coal mined in Alabama. The article identified Representatives Patricia Davis (D-Birmingham) and John Rogers (D-Birmingham), both African American, and the only white Democrat in the Jefferson County delegation to the state legislature, Representative Jim Wright (D-Adamsville), as the targets of the probe. The investigation had begun one year before when John Stewart, president of the United Mine Workers Local 1928, reported to local FBI agents that Representative Davis, chairwoman of the House Public Utilities and Transportation Committee, had requested twenty-five thousand dollars in exchange for her support of a bill requiring state power companies to buy coal mined in Alabama. In early October, all three were indicted by U.S. attorney Donaldson for extortion and conspiracy. The indictment alleged that Davis received over twenty thousand dollars in seven payments, and that Rogers and Wright each received single payments of five thousand dollars from Stewart. At the time the payments were allegedly made, Stewart was working undercover for the FBI.[68]

Over the next several months, the ABEAO-LDF kept the pressure on federal authorities by publishing two reports on the harassment of black elected officials in Alabama and Georgia and contributing funds to the defense efforts of the black legislators then awaiting trial in the Bessemer dog track and Alabama coal cases.[69] Watkins's strategy of keeping federal authorities' activities in the public spotlight would work to tremendous effect. The ABEAO-LDF campaign, combined with the simple weakness of the government's cases, led to a spate of acquittals in the fall of 1989.

The Jefferson County Cases Fall Apart

On August 2, Hugh Boles, who had been tried separately from the three black legislators with whom he was indicted, was convicted of extortion and conspiracy in connection with the Bessemer dog track investigation. He faced up to forty years in prison and several thousand dollars in fines. U.S. attorney Wilson's office immediately offered him leniency in return for his cooperation in prosecuting McClain, Spratt, and McDowell. The offer came as little surprise to Boles and his attorneys. Even before the trial, a federal official had been quoted in the press as saying that the primary objective of the prosecution was "convicting Boles and then making him an offer he can't refuse."[70]

Back in Montgomery, pretrial hearings in the bribery trials of McClain, Spratt, and McDowell revealed the selective nature of the investigations. During the hearings, which began in late October, Spratt's defense lawyers Carlos Williams and J. L. Chestnut filed motions alleging that Wilson had singled out black Democratic officeholders for indictment. Central to their allegations was the claim that the DOJ had "covered up" evidence of wrongdoing on the part of Governor Hunt (R) and Representative Bill Dickinson (R-Ala.), both white Republicans, while pursuing weak cases against black Democrats. Although Williams and Chestnut were unable to substantiate their allegations and Judge Truman Hobbs dismissed their motion to subpoena the two lawmakers, a close look at the allegations demonstrates that they indeed had merit. In the spring of 1985, the Agriculture Department's inspector general for the southeast region, Richard Allen, issued a report to his superiors in Washington containing what he deemed "significant evidence of substantive and continuing participation in prohibited political activities" by Guy Hunt, the executive director of the Alabama Agriculture and Conservation Service at the time. Specifically, Allen charged that Hunt had told his subordinates to "prepare on government premises, during official duty hours, voluminous political mailing lists, political correspondence, a political campaign budget, and lists of persons involved in Hunt's campaign for governor in 1978 and in a possible second such campaign in 1986." Noting that Hunt had tried to impede the investigation into his alleged illegal activities, Allen wrote that he was also guilty of obstruction of justice. Allen forwarded his report to the Agriculture Department in Washington with a recommendation that Hunt be removed from office immediately. In an attempt to head off an investigation, Hunt resigned on March 4, only days after Allen had dispatched his report, and declared his intention to run for governor. Determined that Hunt be prosecuted, Allen sent his report to U.S. attorney John Bell in Montgomery. Bell declined to initiate an inquiry. In November 1986, Hunt became the first Republican governor of Alabama since Reconstruction. The DOJ again declined to act in late 1988 when Hunt's 1986 Republican primary challenger, Doug Carter, filed a request for an investigation based on the Allen report with Bell's replacement, U.S. attorney James Wilson. Hunt went on to serve two terms in office. During both terms, he committed several legally questionable acts that Republican federal authorities declined to investigate.[71]

The DOJ had also failed to pursue the legally questionable behavior of Representative Dickinson. In October 1986, Dickinson entered into a joint venture with Alabama industrialist Ben Collier. In a written agreement, Collier promised to "contribute to the joint venture capital in the amount of $300,000," while Dickinson would "use his capabilities to cause the capital to be invested in as profitable a way as possible." Profits from the venture would be split "2/3 for Ben C. Collier and 1/3 for William L. Dickinson." The following year, Dickinson used his position as ranking Republican on the House Armed Services Committee to steer military contracts to Collier's several defense contracting businesses. The *New York Times* reported on Dickinson's activities in early October 1989, the very same time that the Bessemer dog track case was going to trial. In those articles, Dickinson admitted to writing to "most major defense contractors to say he [Collier] has a good product." U.S. attorney Wilson, a Dickinson-sponsored appointee, claims that upon seeing the press reports, he immediately contacted his superiors to ask that he be recused from any subsequent investigation. There was no need. His superiors did not investigate. Though Wilson steadfastly argued that there was "absolutely no race or politics" in the DOJ's decisions to start investigations, it was hard to imagine what other consideration could have guided the department's actions.[72]

Having lost its opening motions, the defense readied itself for the November 13 trial. Boles opened the proceedings as the prosecution's star witness. Under cross-examination, he testified that he had never received a verbal agreement to accept bribes from any of the three accused African American legislators. Boles simply "assumed" that they had accepted his offer. The only individual to whom he had actually sold stock was Representative White, who at the time was acting as an FBI informant.[73] Equally damaging to the prosecution, the FBI was unable to support Wilson's case. Although agents had taped hundreds of the defendants' phone conversations, they could not produce a single recording in which any of the indicted lawmakers agreed to accept a bribe. Only Porter was recorded as referring to his "monetary interest" in the bill.[74] After deliberating for six hours, the jury acquitted McClain and Spratt on November 16. The following day, they acquitted McDowell and Porter.[75]

The following month, the legislators charged in the Alabama coal case went to trial. During the proceedings, prosecutors proved that Patricia Davis had, in fact, solicited bribes from Stewart on several occasions and suggested that he pay smaller bribes to other members of the House Public Utilities and Transportation Committee. Stewart had given Rogers and Wright five-thousand-dollar payments. FBI wiretaps presented during the trial, however, demonstrate that Rogers and Wright understood these payments to be campaign contributions. Throughout his conversations with Stewart, Rogers refers to the five-thousand-dollar payment as a "campaign contribution." Indeed, when Stewart implied that the money was for Roger's vote on the Buy Alabama Coal bill by stating, "This is for your services tomorrow, I hope," Rogers immediately told him that the money would not influence his vote. The following day, Rogers abstained from voting on the Buy Alabama Coal bill. Confronted with this evidence under cross-examination, Stewart admitted that Rogers had never solicited a bribe. When Roger's lawyer Doug Stewart asked, "John Rogers never gave you any indication that bribes were the way to get things done in Montgomery, did he?" Stewart replied, "No, sir, he did not."[76] After two days of deliberation, the jury convicted Davis on four counts of extortion and acquitted Rogers and Wright. Frank Donaldson, having lost yet another official corruption investigation, was left to grumble, "The evidence was strong — more than ample evidence to convict all three defendants." Before leaving the courthouse, he vowed that his office would continue to investigate corruption in the Alabama legislature.[77]

The string of acquittals in the Jefferson County cases aside, the fall of 1989 brought a tremendous setback for the ABEAO-LDF. Since May 1989, Robert Moussallem had been cooperating with Watkins and Arrington to substantiate his allegations against federal agents. He had sworn an affidavit confirming the story he first told Arrington in April, turned over all written correspondence between himself and the office of the U.S. attorney, and had promised to provide Arrington with tapes he had allegedly made of his phone conversations with federal agents. This collaboration was interrupted in early September 1989 when a Birmingham jury found Moussallem guilty of conspiracy and offering a bribe to an undercover IRS agent. On the twenty-sixth of that month, only weeks before his sentencing, Moussallem attended a campaign planning meeting with GOP gubernatorial candidate Jim Watley and several local businessmen at the office of J. Hoyett Goggans, a convicted felon and former bail bondsman. During the meeting, Goggans accidentally, by the account of those present, shot Moussallem in the face from point-blank range while showing him a newly purchased shotgun. When police arrived on the scene, they found Moussallem lying on the floor in a pool of his own blood, his jaw missing, and parts of his face splattered on the wall and ceiling behind his lifeless body. On a nearby desk lay a copy of the July 3 issue of *Newsweek*, opened to "Backtracking in Birmingham," an article detailing Moussallem's accusations against Birmingham federal officials.[78]

The Moussallem killing, particularly the state of the crime scene and the subsequent actions of witnesses, further poisoned the political environment and moved a number of observers to suspect an FBI conspiracy. The day after the shooting, Arrington told reporters that he had heard a rumor that one of the men attending the meeting was an FBI operative. The implication of Arrington's statement appeared to be that the FBI assassinated a rogue informant after he revealed their entrapment scheme to the public. The rumor was apparently widespread, as Watley stated that he had heard "some things to that effect" when asked about Arrington's comments by the *Birmingham News*.[79] The Birmingham Police Department and Jefferson County district attorney David Barber gave some credence to this theory when they explored the possibility that Moussallem had been lured to the meeting to be killed. Goggan's lawyer, David Johnson, also raised concerns about an FBI cover-up when he claimed that agents were bullying his client and other eyewitnesses in their efforts to seize the tapes Moussallem had reportedly made of his government handlers, tapes that he allegedly had in his briefcase when he was shot. Moussallem's attorney, the noted Martin Luther King Jr. and John F. Kennedy assassination conspiracy theorist Mark Lane, also fanned the flames. Speaking to the *Montgomery Advertiser* after the shooting, Lane suggested that Moussallem was murdered by his government handlers, stating, "A lot of people didn't want Moussallem to talk anymore."[80] Although investigations by local and federal authorities ruled the shooting an accident and the alleged tapes never surfaced, black elected officials' remained deeply suspicious of federal investigators. Many, like Arrington, wanted to know "why it just happened that they had the *Newsweek* magazine article open to the part talking about the case involving [him] at the time that he [Moussallem] was killed."[81]

Arrington believed he received an answer in early 1990.

The Final Arrington Investigation

In January 1990, Jay Kelley, an indicted Palmerdale Country Club owner and FBI-IRS informant, told Donald Watkins that assistant U.S. attorney Barnett had offered him leniency when sentenced if he could provide information concerning illegal activity by Arrington. Kelley had been caught in the same 1985 IRS sting that ensnared Moussallem and had been working as an informant to secure immunity from prosecution. He had replied to Barnett that he had no such evidence, indeed was not even well acquainted with Arrington. Barnett, Kelley claims, then suggested that he provide "creative evidence" of the mayor's alleged misdeeds. Kelley refused and subsequently reported Barnett's alleged offer to city hall. Two days after Kelley informed Watkins of Barnett's alleged request, the U.S. attorney dropped all charges against him without explanation.[82] Kelley's allegations alerted Arrington to what would become the last and most controversial investigation of the mayor's office by the Birmingham U.S. attorney.

After two years of antiharassment organizing and research, Arrington was ready to aggressively confront the U.S. attorney. In February 1990, Watkins published "A Report from the City of Birmingham, Alabama to the United States Senate Judiciary Committee on the Harassment of African-American Birmingham City Officials by Offices of the United States Attorney, the Federal Bureau of Investigation, and the Internal Revenue Service (Criminal Division)," an eighty-eight-page complaint against the Alabama U.S. attorneys. Using Arrington's FBI file, the two Sawyer reports on harassment, the affidavits of former FBI informants Robert Moussallem and Hirsch Friedman, Agriculture Department inspector general for the southeast region Richard Allen's report on (Governor) Guy Hunt, correspondence between the city and the DOJ, a mountain of newspaper articles, and a longitudinal study of U.S. attorney prosecutions of black elected officials and civil rights activists in Alabama between 1981 and 1989, Watkins created perhaps the best-documented case study of DOJ "selective prosecution" of black leadership during the Reagan-Bush era. Critical to the report was Arrington's FBI file. Arrington had ordered his file in 1986 soon after he first began to suspect that federal agents were investigating him without cause. Two years later, he received 292 heavily redacted pages. The bureau withheld an additional 226 pages for "national security" reasons. The file began in January 1972, shortly after Arrington was elected to the Birmingham City Council on an anti–police brutality platform. Twelve years went by without another entry. In 1984, however, the file records the first of approximately eleven FBI-DOJ investigations and undercover operations that ran almost uninterrupted until the dossier was released. Time and again, the investigations were terminated for lack of evidence.[83] Before completing the report, Watkins added Kelley's allegations to his statement of findings.

Despite the breadth of the evidence presented in "A Report from the City of Birmingham," U.S. attorney Donaldson dismissed it as "substantially hogwash." The Senate Judiciary Committee, however, was not so flippant. Chairman Joe Biden (D-Del.) forwarded Watkins's report to the DOJ, OPR, and requested that the existing investigation of the Birmingham U.S. attorney be expanded to explore the new allegations. On March 9, Senator Hugh Heflin (D-Ala.) entered the report into the *Congressional Record*.[84]

While Watkins was making his case to the Senate Judiciary Committee and the OPR, Donaldson and Barnett were preparing their twelfth and last investigation of Arrington. In early 1990, local IRS investigators, working closely with Barnett, convened a grand jury to explore corruption in Birmingham's Minority Business Enterprise program. The investigation first became public in June 1990 when jurors issued the first of several subpoenas demanding lists of all vendors holding city contracts for the years 1985–90 and detailed financial records of several of those businesses. In response to the subpoenas, Watkins filed yet another "amendment" to "A Report from the City of Birmingham" with the Senate Judiciary Committee and the DOJ, OPR. Charging that "the IRS probe [was] simply a vehicle of convenience to give the U.S. Attorney's office one more shot at Arrington and other Birmingham African-American officials," Watkins demanded that the OPR investigate "the apparent vendetta Barnett [had] against Arrington."[85] Searching through the list of more than twenty-five thousand vendors, federal investigators fastened on Marjorie Peters, a consultant holding several thousand dollars worth of contracts in connection with a planned Civil Rights Institute. In July, the grand jury indicted Peters for bribery and conspiracy to defraud the city in connection with $220,000 in invoices she had filed for architectural planning of the Institute. The indictment did not name Peter's alleged coconspirators.[86]

Though the suit named Peters, the focus of the investigations quickly shifted to Arrington. During discovery, Peters's defense attorney filed a motion demanding that the prosecution reveal the names of the coconspirators. Barnett subsequently amended the indictment to name Arrington; Peters's friend and fellow consultant, Atlanta architect Tarlee Brown; and two other individuals. The following September, Barnett secured grand jury testimony from Brown implicating Arrington in the alleged fraud. Brown testified that he gave Arrington kickbacks totaling five thousand dollars in exchange for no-bid city contracts in October 1986 and February 1987. Arrington's attorney, David Cromwell Johnson, responded to these charges in the press the following day, stating that Arrington's daily logs showed that the mayor was out of the city when the kickbacks were allegedly delivered to him in his office.[87] In response to Johnson's claims, the grand jury subpoenaed Arrington's logbooks for the previous five years. Arrington refused to honor the subpoena, claiming that the U.S. attorney wanted his logbooks so that he could use them to "coach" Brown.[88] On January 17, 1992, Judge Edwin Nelson found Arrington in contempt for refusing to surrender his logs. Recognizing "the right of the people of Birmingham to have their mayor on duty," Nelson sentenced Arrington to prison from Thursday evening to Monday morning for eighteen months or until he agreed to abide by the subpoena. Arrington, seeing the sentence as an opportunity to shine a national spotlight on Donaldson's and Barnett's activities, determined to begin serving the time rather than surrender his logbooks. Speaking with reporters outside the federal courthouse after Nelson handed down his sentence, Arrington stated, "This may serve to drive home my point about abuse of power in the U.S. Attorney's office."[89]

Arrington's defense efforts forced the Bush administration to provide federal oversight of Donaldson's probe. On January 23, Arrington and seven hundred supporters, some draped in chains to symbolize "that [they were] brothers and sisters chained in oppression," marched from the Sixteenth Street Baptist Church to the federal courthouse to surrender to federal marshals.[90] The march and Arrington's surrender put tremendous pressure on the Bush administration to intervene. In the previous year, black elected officials' allegations of DOJ harassment had reached a fever pitch. Nearly the entirety of black political leadership, from Jesse Jackson to Representative John Conyers (D-Mich.) to NAACP executive director Benjamin Hooks, had accused the Bush DOJ of attacking black leadership. The Arrington episode not only added to that outcry, but like the 1985 "freedom caravan" through the Black Belt, imbued it with the powerful symbolism of the civil rights movement. A short twenty-seven years after Eugene "Bull" Conner had turned fire hoses on peaceful civil rights protesters in Kelley Ingram Park, the first black mayor of Birmingham was walking through that same park in chains on his way to jail — sent there by men his attorney, Donald Watkins, had called the "the modern day threat to civil and constitutional rights." Thus, by the time Arrington arrived at the Maxwell Federal Prison in Montgomery, the DOJ had already dispatched OPR lawyers from Washington to monitor Donaldson's probe.[91] Satisfied that the presence of OPR lawyers would keep Donaldson from misusing his appointment books, Arrington released them to investigators on January 24, 1992. Logbooks in hand, Donaldson declined to bring charges before leaving office later that spring.

Following Donaldson's resignation, President Bush appointed Jack Selden, an assistant U.S. attorney under Donaldson from 1982 to 1985 and then a lawyer in private practice, as the U.S. attorney for the Northern District of Alabama, opening the possibility for an end to the seven-year battle between his office and the black elected leadership of Jefferson County. Soon after Selden took office, Arrington contacted him to make an offer: the mayor would silence his criticism of the U.S. attorney's office and cooperate with the investigation if the U.S. attorney would end the investigation quickly, either by bringing an indictment or closing the case. Arrington apparently believed that Selden accepted his offer, because the city toned down its criticism of the investigation for much of the spring and early summer. In late July, however, things fell apart. That month, a Birmingham businessman approached the mayor and stated that the local office of the FBI had attempted to use him in a sting against Arrington in June and early July. Soon afterward, Selden extended the term of the grand jury investigating Arrington and issued several broad subpoenas for information from the city. Arrington and his allies responded in kind. On July 29, 1992, over two hundred Birmingham religious and community leaders signed a petition, addressed to U.S. attorney Selden and Attorney General William Barr, demanding an end to the Arrington investigation. The signers had expected that "with the transition to a new U.S. Attorney, and the end of the term of the grand jury, this intolerable situation would end." What they got instead was "harassment of the duly elected mayor of the city," actions that they interpreted as an attack on the "voting rights of the residents of Birmingham." Arrington held a press conference on August 6, 1992, at which he stated that he would resume antiharassment agitation. For yet another year, the black elected leadership of Birmingham and the U.S. attorney for the Northern District of Alabama hurled accusations of repression and corruption at each other in the press.[92]

On July 29 1993, Arrington's ordeal finally came to an end when U.S. attorney Selden signed a motion striking the mayor's name from the list of un-indicted coconspirators in the 1991 pretrial brief submitted by Barnett. The *Birmingham News* interpreted the agreement as a "peace treaty" between the mayor and the DOJ.[93] The motion, signed just after newly installed attorney general Janet Reno requested the resignations of all sitting U.S. attorneys, is perhaps better understood as Selden's attempt to clean up one of the longest and messiest selective prosecution campaigns of the DOJ under Reagan and Bush before the opposition assumed his office.[94]

In response to a 1989 *Newsweek* article detailing FBI informant Robert Moussallem's allegations against Birmingham federal investigators, U.S. attorney Frank Donaldson wrote an angry letter to the editor. In an effort to rebut Moussallem's allegations, Donaldson claimed that there were "relatively few" indictments of black elected officials in Alabama during the 1980s, and that "most were convicted and the majority of those convictions [were] still standing."[95] His claims were false. A 1992 report by the DOJ, OPR, found that between January 1, 1978, and May 22, 1990, the FBI conducted 189 investigations of city, county, state, and federal officials in Alabama that led to indictment. Of that number, 31, or 16.4 percent, were of African Americans. This was a relatively race-neutral rate of indictment (approximately 1.5 times the rate of whites), as African Americans constituted 7.6 percent of all Alabama elected officials in 1984, 10.8 percent in 1987, and 16.3 percent in 1990.[96] What is remarkable about the federal investigations of black elected officials in Alabama during the 1980s is not the percentage indicted but the outcomes of the cases. Of the 31 Alabama African Americans indicted for official corruption crimes between 1978 and 1990, the ABEAO-LDF identified 20 in "Report from the City of Birmingham." Of those 20, only 3 were found guilty and 2 more pleaded guilty to dramatically reduced charges because they could not afford the cost of a defense. This constitutes an indictment to conviction rate of 25 percent. Even if in the unlikely scenario that all the 11 unidentified indicted black elected officials were found guilty, that still only constitutes an indictment to conviction rate of 45 percent. The DOJ-wide average indictment to conviction rate in official corruption cases for this period was 83 percent.[97] Perhaps more important, considering the charges leveled at the U.S. attorneys, the above numbers do not include the multiple investigations of black elected officials that did not result in indictments, like those of Mayor Arrington, city councilman Germany, state senator Hilliard, and others.

How then to explain the nature of these investigations? Steve Suitts, executive director of the Southern Regional Council, offered a structural explanation to the *New York Times* in 1989. "In Alabama," Suitts stated, "the United States Attorneys are white conservatives tied to many of the white politicians turned out of office by blacks. As such, their sources of information and political ties tend to be with interests hostile to black politicians."[98] This was potentially the case with the 1984–85 Black Belt voter fraud investigations and the 1986–87 investigations of Mayor Arrington and his allies in the Jefferson County delegation to the state legislature. At their best, federal investigators took biased local whites at their word and showed remarkable insensitivity to the historical experiences of African Americans when conducting their probes. But the federal investigators should not be viewed as well-intentioned dupes of local whites. During the 1980s and early 1990s, there are clear instances when Alabama federal investigators took the initiative in investigating state blacks, and with little more evidence of wrongdoing than that offered by local whites. There is also strong evidence that they ignored well-documented allegations of fraud against white Republicans. What is therefore also likely is that the U.S. attorneys knowingly used the allegations of corruption made by conservative whites to commence cases that would benefit the Republican Party. Allegations of fraud or corruption, in this scenario, become a pretext for political warfare. Alabama black elected officials certainly embraced this latter interpretation, making it a cornerstone of their defense efforts. And through these defense efforts they fought federal authorities to a standstill.

There is a growing feeling among blacks that black elected officials are the target of a conspiracy by the white political establishment and the white dominated media. The perception is aggravated by the fact that almost all black elected officials are Democrats and the federal prosecutors that bring indictments are Republicans appointed by President Reagan.

—*Houston Chronicle,* August 2, 1987

After years on the political margins, an unsettling theory—that black elected officials have been harassed and unfairly prosecuted by the federal government—has been gaining ground in mainstream debate.

—*Boston Globe,* May 13, 1991

CHAPTER SIX

The Center for the Study of the Harassment of African Americans and the Decline of Antiharassment Organizing, 1987–1995

IN SEPTEMBER 1990, black elected officials and activists from across the country convened in Washington, D.C., for a "public hearing" on the harassment of black elected officials. The hearing capped four straight years of intense antiharassment activism that the influential Capitol Hill weekly *National Journal* called a "black counterattack." In response to the DOJ official corruption crackdown of the Reagan and Bush years, black elected officials had revived harassment ideology and commenced a flood of antiharassment organizing. In the late 1980s, they created defense and information-gathering organizations to document the pattern of investigations and filled the news with allegations of "selective prosecution." In his opening remarks to the hearing, CBC chairman Representative Mervyn Dymally (D-Calif.) argued that black officials had succeeded in mobilizing the entire black political community against harassment:

It is not just elected officials who sit here today firm in the conviction that African American elected and appointed officials have been and are being unduly harassed. Today those elected officials who have long had their own personal experiences to help them distinguish this pattern of prejudicial treatment are not alone. They are joined by church officials and church members, by members of civil rights organizations, and by African American citizens who now also see a pattern.[1]

In the weeks after the hearing, black elected officials attempted to institutional-ize the counterattack by creating the Center for the Study of the Harassment of African Americans (CSHAA)—an information gathering and advocacy organi-zation modeled on the Committee for the Study of Black Leadership. Thirteen years after Mary Sawyer had published *The Dilemma of Black Politics*, her de-fense strategy, it seemed, was finally taking shape.

Rather than signal a new era in antiharassment activism, however, the founding of the CSHAA marked its zenith and swift decline. From the outset, the CSHAA was beset by internal organizational problems that limited growth and undermined fundraising. But more important, the cresting of antiharass-ment activism coincided with the election of former Arkansas governor Bill Clinton (D) to the presidency. With a Democrat in the White House, DOJ in-vestigations of black Democratic elected officials declined precipitously. With the drop in high-profile investigations, the network of antiharassment activists and institutions that had led the black counterattack disintegrated. Deprived of the popular antiharassment mobilizations of the late 1980s and early 1990s, the CSHAA also declined. Bankrupt and months behind on its bills, the center closed its doors in 1995.

When the CSHAA ceased operations, several official corruption investiga-tions begun by the Bush DOJ were still making their way to the courts. The in-vestigations gave those targeted the impression that harassment was continuing despite the change in administrations. With few national black political figures discussing harassment after the close of the CSHAA, a void seemed to develop in antiharassment activism. In 1995, the Schiller Institute, an "international pro-paganda" organization affiliated with fascist intellectual and perennial presi-dential candidate Lyndon LaRouche, moved to exploit this situation. LaRouche hoped to use the issue of harassment as a way to gain an electoral base among African Americans and infiltrate the Democratic Party. The Schiller Institute's exploitation of harassment ideology moved even stalwart antiharassment activ-ists to abandon antiharassment organizing. Coupled with the continued drop in high-profile investigations of black elected officials after 1995, LaRouche's exploitation of harassment ideology doomed it to the realm of conspiracy theory.

The "Black Counterattack"

In the early 1980s, black elected officials made a number of scattered protests against the DOJ's disproportionate prosecution of black elected officials. In 1981–83, for instance, Tchula, Mississippi, Mayor Eddie Carthan and his supporters created the "National Campaign to Free Mayor Eddie Carthan and the Tchula 7 and Preserve Black Political Rights." The group, chaired by actor and civil rights activist Ossie Davis, drew support from hundreds of citizens, who formed support committees from Minnesota to Texas. The campaign received support from prominent civil rights activists, church organizations, and black elected officials. In 1983 Jesse Jackson claimed that the former mayor was "part of a national trend of black officials under siege," the United Methodist Church adopted a resolution condemning the "harassment and intimidation of black elected officials" in Tchula, and Representative George Crockett (D-Mich.) called for a House Judiciary Committee investigation of whether federal prosecutors were using the grand jury to "besmirch the good name of black leaders."[2] Though impressive, these protests were little noticed outside the black community. In 1987, however, this state of affairs changed markedly when a series of high-profile DOJ investigations of black elected officials made allegations of harassment front-page news across the county. Black elected officials' subsequent antiharassment activism grew to become a "black counterattack" that brought harassment to the fore of black political concerns and mainstream political debate.

Like previous antiharassment activism, the "black counterattack" of the late 1980s began with a series of federal investigations of black elected officials. In quick succession between April and August 1987, former Maryland state senator Clarence Mitchell III (D-Baltimore) and state senator Michael Mitchell, who had recently been elected to his brother's old seat, were indicted by the U.S. attorney in Baltimore for conspiracy to interfere with a congressional investigation; Representative Harold Ford (D-Tenn.) was indicted for bribery by the U.S. attorney in Memphis; Washington, D.C., U.S. attorney Joseph diGenova announced that he had just concluded a multiyear investigation of corruption in the administration of Mayor Marion Barry (D); the U.S. attorney in Atlanta investigated Mayor Andrew Young (D) for alleged obstruction of justice in the probe of Georgia state senator Julian Bond's (D-Atlanta) alleged drug use and indicted county commissioners Reginald Eaves (D-Fulton), Charles Williams (D-Fulton), and John Evans (D-DeKalb); and the House of Representatives Judiciary Committee began impeachment proceedings against Florida judge Alcee L. Hastings. All these black elected officials alleged that they were being harassed.[3]

These cases brought protests from nearly all quarters of the black political community. In late July 1987, Rev. Jesse Jackson expressed many African Americans' anxieties: "There is a sense in the black community that where the challenger once stood in the schoolhouse door and wore uniforms and sheets and hoods, now they are U.S. attorneys or attorneys general [who] use their office to drop rumors in the press [and] indict but never or seldom convict." Representative Mike Espy (D-Miss.) agreed, noting, "In some relevant areas there are prosecutors who have targeted black officials for selective prosecution." Ruth Harper, a New York state assemblywoman and member of the Democratic National Committee, argued that the recent spate of investigations was the product of a double standard, stating, "The whites have been doing the same things blacks have been doing for some time, but the white prosecutors haven't covered up for black officials." Responding to these officials' concerns, John Conyers announced that the House Judiciary Committee, Subcommittee on Criminal Justice, would hold hearings on harassment in late August.[4]

Attracted to conflict and scandal, the news media gave generous coverage to these black elected officials' allegations of harassment. Since 1987–88, when the Iran-Contra affair and Newt Gingrich's ethics charges against House Speaker Jim Wright demonstrated anew the tremendous public interest in political scandal, the news media had shifted increased resources and print space to the issue. For instance, the *Washington Post* created a "special projects staff" that focused on "congressional ethics" following the Wright scandal. This staff subsequently drove the ethics coverage of the Gray, Savage, Dymally, Wright, and Coelho investigations.[5] The increased public interest in political scandal during the 1980s, Ginsberg and Shefter argue, allowed "the national media to enhance their autonomy and carve out a prominent place for themselves in American government and politics." Thus, they continue, "the media came to have a stake in finding and revealing damaging information about prominent politicians."[6] This increased media attention to scandals had an unexpected corollary: the same impulse that drew reporters to allegations of official corruption also drew them to black elected officials' allegations of harassment. On November 15, 1987, for instance, the *Baltimore Sun*, which had provided extensive coverage of the Mitchell brothers' trial and conviction, devoted an entire page to an article by Mary Sawyer titled "Are Black Politicians Being Harassed?" The coverage even extended outside the media markets in which these investigations were taking place. In August, the *Houston Chronicle* published an overview of the numerous allegations of harassment emanating from black elected officials in Washington, D.C., Baltimore, Memphis, Philadelphia, and Atlanta.[7] By midsummer, black elected officials' allegations of harassment had become so widespread that the *National Journal* decided to catalog them in an article on the "black counterattack," an incisive exploration of black elected officials' strategy. "The black counterattack," the *National Journal* noted, "is being waged as much on television and in newspapers as in the courtroom, with the apparent goal of sensitizing public opinion so that rumors about investigations of black officials are put in a larger framework." And there is every indication, it continued, that the "news media coverage is helping."[8] Indeed, the counterattack was tremendously successful in redefining DOJ official corruption investigations of black elected officials as harassment. In late 1987, a *Washington Post* poll found that 28 percent of African Americans nationwide believed that most federal investigations of black elected officials were "attempts by whites to discredit or embarrass black leaders."[9]

The black counterattack was so successful, in fact, that it forced some black leaders who did not want to be associated with harassment ideology to speak out. In July 1987, Virginia lieutenant governor Douglass Wilder (D) told his state's black leaders not to "serve as a patsy for any public official who finds that they are in trouble with the legal authorities. . . . There are no black or white criminals . . . a guilty criminal is a guilty criminal." The statement drew a private rebuke from Representative Mervyn Dymally (D-Calif.), who reminded Wilder that both he and George Brown had "experienced harassment both by the media, and law enforcement agencies" when they were lieutenant governors. Wilder, who was aware of Brown's and Dymally's experiences, conceded in a return letter that he too "continue[d] to be scrutinized more than ordinary," but expressed his belief that "there [was] nothing that any elected official could do to preempt scrutiny."[10] More to the point, Wilder was preparing to run for governor in 1989. The explosion of antiharassment activism on Virginia's northern border threatened the postracial political identity that he had created during his successful run for lieutenant governor and one he would need in his impending run for the governorship. What made Wilder's speech noteworthy was not its content but its singularity. He was the only high-ranking black elected official to openly criticize harassment ideology in the late 1980s.

The "black counterattack" also took place in the streets and in the courts. Between 1987 and 1989, there were at least seven large antiharassment rallies and marches, and many revolved around suits by black elected officials alleging harassment. The first occurred in Fort Lauderdale, Florida, following the Eleventh Circuit Judicial Conference's release of a report recommending that Judge Alcee Hastings be impeached. Following his acquittal on charges of bribery and conspiracy in 1983, Hastings had returned to his position on the Eleventh Circuit Court. Within weeks of his return, two of his fellow federal judges, using a new and yet-unused 1980 law that allowed for the disciplining of judges by their peers and the transmission of impeachment recommendations to Congress, filed a complaint asking the Eleventh Circuit Court to investigate Hastings's defense effort. They believed that Hastings had lied under oath and fabricated evidence in order to secure acquittal. The Eleventh Circuit Judicial

Conference accepted the claim and on March 17, 1987, concluded that Hastings had perjured himself and fabricated evidence in an effort to conceal his involvement in the Romano bribery scheme. Earlier that year, Hastings had formed the African American Legal Defense Fund (AALDF) in anticipation of the Eleventh Circuit's ruling. Its first major action was an April 13, 1987, march on the federal courthouse in Fort Lauderdale. While clerks and judges stared quizzically out the windows, a crowd of approximately three hundred African Americans sang "We Shall Overcome" and chanted "Justice! Free Alcee!"[11]

Two weeks after the Fort Lauderdale march, on April 27, two thousand African Americans packed the CME Temple in Memphis, Tennessee, for a rally supporting Representative Harold Ford (D-Tenn.), who had been indicted for bribery three days before. In a combative speech, Ford characterized the indictment as a "personal vendetta" on the part of chief assistant U.S. attorney Dan Clancy against the Ford family and a "racist" attempt to reduce the political power of blacks in Memphis. A group of Memphis ministers agreed, likening the indictment to the DOJ probes of Adam Clayton Powell Jr. and Charles Diggs.[12] Two days after the rally, Judge James Jarvis of the U.S. District Court of Eastern Tennessee added fuel to the controversy by issuing a gag order barring all parties involved from talking about the case except to one another and court officials. The order, which was the first known gag order on a congressman in the history of the Republic, was handed down in response to the "extensive publicity" Ford's allegations of harassment had received in the local and national press. Ford's attorneys immediately protested, filing motions that the order be rescinded on the grounds that it violated the separation of powers clause of the Constitution and Ford's First and Sixth Amendment rights. Amid bipartisan congressional denunciation of the order expressed in an avalanche of amicus curiae briefs, Jarvis altered the order to allow Ford to discuss the case when he was performing his congressional duties. Soon afterward, Jarvis was forced to rescind the order altogether.[13]

The following June, seven hundred protesters took to the streets of Washington, D.C., demanding that U.S. attorney Joseph diGenova "stop the leaks." For three years, "unidentified sources close to the investigation" had been providing Washington-area reporters with a steady stream of information on the shifting focus of the grand jury investigating the administration of Washington, D.C., mayor Marion Barry (D). Barry had complained of these leaks in the past, even going so far as to demand DOJ and congressional investigations of "abusive governmental intrusion and government lawlessness" on the part of the U.S. attorney in August 1987.[14] The most recent round of leaks, which resulted in a late-June news report that a Barry associate had told the grand jury she bought and used drugs with the mayor, moved him to act on his own. On June 20, Barry filed a lawsuit in U.S. district court charging diGenova with employing "the longstanding and enormously successful tactic of utilizing . . .powerful law enforcement agencies to discredit black leadership." In a move that demonstrated the growing concern of black elected officials nationwide over the DOJ's activities, the National Black Leadership Roundtable, the National Black Caucus of State Legislators, the NBC-LEO, the NCBM, and the National Association of Black County Officials filed an amicus curiae brief in support of the Barry suit. Many of the black elected officials who signed the brief had "found themselves . . .the target of governmental investigations, of a similar nature, intricate and confidential details of which were mysteriously leaked to and reported by the press." Chief U.S. district court judge Aubrey E. Robinson Jr. dismissed Barry's suit later that month claiming that the examples on which the mayor based his claim did not demonstrate a violation of the secrecy of the grand jury.[15]

Fast on the heels of the Barry protest came a series of rallies organized by former Maryland state senators Clarence and Michael Mitchell. Following their indictment by federal prosecutors in 1987, the Mitchells had created the Clarence Mitchell Jr. Defense Fund—named for their father, the famed NAACP lobbyist. The defense fund was initially created to collect contributions for the Mitchell brothers' legal costs in the Wedtech trial, but the organization quickly took on a larger role. As the president of the National Black Caucus of State Legislators, Clarence Mitchell III had seen the national pattern of DOJ investigations that now threatened to end his and his brother's political careers. Indeed, Mitchell believed that his participation in the effort to defend the Alabama Black Belt voting rights activists in 1984–85 had precipitated the federal investigation that led to his indictment.[16] The defense fund's first major initiative was to host a "National Campaign for Justice," consisting of "freedom rallies" in several different cities. In the winter of 1988, the Mitchell brothers held rallies in Baltimore (for themselves) and Atlanta (for former Fulton County commissioner Reginald Eaves). They planned to hold a third rally in Washington, D.C. (for Mayor Barry), but were ordered to jail before it could take place. The rallies were impressive affairs, attracting nationally known black elected officials and large crowds numbering in the thousands. In Baltimore, former representative Parren Mitchell (D-Md.); the chairwoman of the National Political Congress of Black Women, C. Delores Tucker; and the president of the National Black Caucus of State Legislators, Representative David Richardson Jr. (D-Philadelphia), spoke to an overflow crowd of several thousand at Bethel AME Church. The goal of the campaign was to raise one million dollars for a national defense fund for black elected officials and increase popular awareness of harassment. Though the rallies did not achieve the former, they certainly achieved the latter. Each was well attended and received coverage from the local press. More importantly, the campaign created a national network of black elected officials, civil rights activists, and church leaders concerned with organizing against harassment.[17]

The largest and longest antiharassment mobilizations of the period, which involved thousands of African Americans in at least a dozen different states, took place in 1989 during the impeachment proceedings against Judge Alcee Hastings. The Eleventh Circuit had sent its impeachment recommendation to Congress only days before the April 1987 Fort Lauderdale protest. Its reception by the House Judiciary Committee, Subcommittee on Criminal Justice, chaired by Representative John Conyers (D-Mich.), spoke to the remarkable impact of the antiharassment activism of the previous two years.[18] At the start of his committee's hearings, Conyers stated that he was well aware of "racially motivated conduct throughout this country for many years" and was inclined to believe Hastings's claims of harassment. Several weeks later, however, after reviewing the evidence, Conyers stated, "[I] paid close attention to the charge of racism. . . . I looked for any scintilla of racism. I could not find any."[19] His committee voted 7 to 0 for impeachment. The full Judiciary Committee soon followed suit, voting 32 to 1 to approve the articles of impeachment. Only Representative Lawrence Smith (D-Fla.), a close friend of Hastings, voted no. Even Representative George Crockett (D-Mich.), who had raised the topic of harassment on the Judiciary Committee in 1983, voted for impeachment. Speaking with reporters, Crockett stated that he was initially concerned that Hastings may have been a victim of harassment, but added, "I am convinced an honest effort was made to put racism aside."[20] On August 3, 1988, following the Judiciary Committee's recommendation, the House voted to impeach Hasting by the margin of 413 to 3. Representatives Gus Savage (D-Ill.), Mervyn Dymally (D-Calif.), and Edward Roybal (D-Calif.), all of whom had been investigated by the DOJ in recent years (Dymally and Savage had claimed that they were harassed), voted no. The following year, the Senate followed suit, thereby ending Hastings's judicial career. The Senate vote, however, was far closer than that in the House. Approximately one in four Senators voted against impeachment. Additionally, the Senate refused to consider six of the seventeen articles of impeachment sent from the House and acquitted Hastings of three of the remaining eleven articles.[21]

Hastings's defense efforts made the difference between the House and the Senate votes. He had been claiming that he was the victim of racial targeting since he was first indicted in 1983. Prior to 1989, however, his defense efforts did not reach far beyond South Florida. Even during the House impeachment investigation, Hastings largely confined his organizing to this area. During the Senate trial, however, Hastings moved beyond his home base to engage in fund-raising, lobbying, and public protest in the home states of the twelve members of the Senate Impeachment Committee. On these visits, Hastings held fund-raisers, prayer vigils, rallies, and sold T-shirts that read "Not Guilty, but Not Free," his mantra during the impeachment. At all these stops, the AALDF distributed fly-ers listing the members of the Impeachment Committee and urging African Americans "to write their senators informing them that they support[ed] Judge Hastings."[22] These activities were remarkably successful, raising several hun-dred thousand dollars and producing a large number of letters protesting the impeachment.

While Hastings built a lobbying and fund-raising apparatus outside the nation's capital, his supporters generated public support in Washington, D.C. Critical to the D.C. mobilization was Kathy Hughes, owner of Washington, D.C., radio station WOL and host of her own talk-radio show. Hughes, who repeatedly hosted Hastings on her program, urged her predominantly black audience of over one hundred thousand to attend the committee hearings and trial. D.C. blacks heeded Hughes's call, packing the main hearing room of the Hart Senate Office Building for each day of the Senate Impeachment Trial Committee hear-ings. Hughes's efforts were supplemented by New York activists Al Sharpton and Alton Maddox and Minister Louis Farrakhan of the Nation of Islam (NOI), who held a rally for Hastings at Shiloh Baptist Church in Washington, D.C. Sharing the NOI's apocalyptic vision of America's racial future, Farrakhan told the crowd of approximately one thousand that "harassment" of Hastings and other black elected officials signaled "the end of the Caucasian civilization." Recognizing the political peril of appearing too close to Sharpton, Maddox, and Farrakhan, Hastings did not attend the rally but sent a thank-you telegram instead. When the full Senate voted on the articles of impeachment on October 18, Hughes again rallied the troops, handing out over six hundred Senate gallery passes to supporters, who showed up in force. At the conclusion of the Senate hearings, Hastings gave a defiant speech to several hundred supporters on the Capitol steps. The scene conjured memories of a similar address by Adam Clayton Powell Jr. following his exclusion from the House of Representatives twenty-two years before.[23]

The antiharassment activism of 1987–89 stimulated a new round of anti-harassment research, the first since the late 1970s. The first and most influential of these new reports was *The Harassment of Black Elected Officials: Ten Years Later*, by Mary Sawyer. Following the closing of the CSBL in 1979, Sawyer had moved to Washington, D.C., to pursue a master's degree in religion at Howard Divinity School. In 1980, Mervyn Dymally was elected to Congress. Between 1981 and 1982, Sawyer worked in Dymally's congressional office as a speech-writer and liaison for social change movements. Although she left Washington in 1982 to pursue a doctorate in religion at Duke University, Sawyer kept in close contact with Dymally, who remained a trusted friend and advisor. As the racially disproportionate impact of the Reagan administration's official cor-ruption crackdown became increasingly apparent in the early 1980s, Dymally urged Sawyer to update her 1977 report. Sawyer had anticipated Dymally's request. Since closing the CSBL she had received a multitude of requests for *The Dilemma of Black Politics* from black elected officials who found themselves the targets of DOJ investigations. She was unable to accommodate them, however, having long before exhausted her supply. Seeking a way to address the increase in official corruption investigations and the subsequent demand for information, Sawyer began collecting case studies for an updated report. She released her new study in September 1987 at the Congressional Black Caucus Foundation's Annual Legislative Conference. Former representative Shirley Chisholm (D-N.Y.) and Representative Harold Ford addressed a packed house for the three-hour session, which was hosted by Delegate Walter Fauntroy (D-D.C.). A DOJ representative, the *Washington Post* reported, was booed by the crowd when he claimed that race played no role in prosecutors' decisions to begin investigations.[24]

Sawyer conceived of *Ten Years Later* less as a new study than as an "updated, but condensed statement on the issue of harassment . . . accessible to a larger number of people." She was just as interested in giving readers access to *Dilemma* as to her new data. Thus nearly half of the seventy-seven case studies included in *Ten Years Later* were borrowed from *Dilemma*, and much of the report summarized her earlier findings. While this approach provided readers with a long view of harassment from 1967 to 1987, it also served to reproduce the methodological mistakes contained in *Dilemma*. Sawyer reprinted her conclusions wholesale, quoting large sections from *Dilemma*. Perhaps more importantly, by repeating her 1977 conclusions, Sawyer projected her analysis of the 1970s onto the changed landscape of the 1980s. In so doing, she distorted the meaning of her findings. This was most apparent in Sawyer's discussion of her thirty-six new case studies. Surveying this data, Sawyer observed that "recently, the leaking of information from grand jury investigations and the roles of U.S. Attorneys in initiating investigations and bringing charges [had] emerged as issues of particular concern [to black elected officials]." She nonetheless concluded, "The pattern of ten years ago is still operative. And the tactics—methods of harassment—for the most part remain unchanged."[25] In fact, the rapid increase in federal official corruption investigations was *the* government policy that raised allegations of harassment from black elected officials during the 1980s. When Sawyer wrote her 1977 report, black elected officials were disproportionately suffering from intelligence community surveillance and counterintelligence, IRS audits, and news media investigations. Only a few were the targets of official corruption investigations. Of the thirty-six new cases contained in *Ten Years Later*, twenty-four involved state or federal official corruption investigations. Half of the remaining case studies involved vigilante violence against black elected officials: cross burnings, shots fired, and threats.

(Here again, Sawyer mixed state scrutiny with the actions of private individuals in her analysis of harassment.)[26] By applying this outdated analysis to the late 1980s, Sawyer reinforced the incorrect postulate, first made in *Dilemma*, that harassment was an entity in and of itself to which different government policies contributed, rather than the cumulative effect of those policies. Smaller and therefore cheaper to reproduce, *Ten Years Later* would reach at least six times as many black elected officials as the original report, thereby ensuring that the insights and oversights of *Dilemma* would influence a new generation of antiharassment activists.[27]

The rising tide of indictments and investigations of black elected officials, combined with the subsequent growth of antiharassment activism, moved some members of the mainstream press to conduct their own research on harassment. In late 1987, the *Washington Post*, which for nearly a year had been running articles on the Barry investigation, the Hastings impeachment proceedings, and the Mitchell brothers' trial in nearby Baltimore, assigned reporter Gwen Ifill to look into black elected officials' charges. The following February, Ifill published her findings in "Black Officials: Probes and Prejudice; Is There a Double Standard for Bringing Indictments?" Ifill based her study on "465 public corruption probes over the last five years—limited to high ranking politicians above the level of school board." After several months of sifting through these cases, she found that "black elected officials [were], in fact, being prosecuted far more heavily than their representation in the population of elected officials." Specifically, Ifill discovered that black elected officials were five times more likely than their white counterparts to be investigated by the DOJ. The question that Ifill could not answer was why. DOJ representatives, for their part, maintained a posture of incredulity. "Race and religion and ethnic classification haven't the foggiest thing to do with how you are going to investigate corruption or organized crime or a drug ring," Rudolph Giuliani, U.S. attorney for the Southern District of New York, told Ifill. Giuliani did not, however, address the disparity. A number of political scientists interviewed for the article told Ifill that race played a role in the disproportionate number of prosecutions, but as Savannah State University professor Hanes Walton put it, "Some of it [federal investigation of black elected officials] is very real and very carefully orchestrated. Some of it grows directly out of racism and a desire to keep black political leaders at a certain level of participation. Other efforts are purely political and based purely on the ambition of local people. Some of it is based on improprieties of elected officials themselves. People have not sorted it all out." Mary Sawyer and the black elected officials whom Ifill interviewed repeated their allegations of overt racial targeting. Lacking any "hard evidence" to support black elected officials' allegations that the disparity she uncovered was the product of DOJ policy, Ifill declared the matter unresolved. As to the question of "whether the

Reagan Justice Department has unfairly targeted blacks for prosecution," Ifill stated, "the jury is still out."[28]

The antiharassment activism of 1987–89 also saw a revival of conspiracy theory among black elected officials. During his 1988 trial for alleged bribery and conspiracy, Fulton County commissioner Reginald Eaves, introduced into the record two sworn affidavits by Hirsch Friedman, a lawyer and former FBI "cooperating witness" (Friedman had worked voluntarily as an informant and advisor for the FBI between 1979 and 1982). In the affidavits, Friedman alleged that the FBI had an "unofficial policy" that agents termed *fruhmenschen*—a German word meaning primitive man. The purpose of the *fruhmenschen* policy, Friedman claimed, "was the routine investigation without probable cause of prominent elected and appointed black officials." Agents pursued this policy because they believed that African Americans were "intellectually inferior to white persons and hence prone to criminal activity." To illustrate his point, Friedman described his participation in an investigation run out of the Atlanta office of the FBI between 1979 and 1982 that targeted Fulton County commissioner Reginald Eaves in a series of sting operations. On multiple occasions, undercover FBI operatives offered Eaves bribes in return for his official actions, only to have the commissioner reject their entreaties. At the same time that the FBI was repeatedly attempting to sting Eaves, Friedman continued, agents ignored evidence of illegal conduct by white officials. "I understood that over a dozen indictable cases against white elected and appointed officials and others in the Northern District of Georgia were dropped and investigations discontinued altogether," Friedman stated, "while great effort was put forth in connection with the *Fruhmenschen* policy."[29]

Friedman's allegations were seized upon by black elected officials as proof that the FBI was targeting them for repression. The Mitchell brothers, and later Marion Barry, introduced the Friedman affidavits into their own trials in the form of motions for dismissal. In response to the appeals of several black members of Congress, including CBC chairman Mervyn Dymally, House Judiciary Committee chairman Peter Rodino requested an internal inquiry from FBI director William Sessions. The ABEAO-LDF incorporated the Friedman affidavits into its July 1989 and February 1990 reports on the DOJ's "selective prosecution" of black elected officials. In response to ABEAO-LDF lobbying, in July 1989, Senate Judiciary Committee chairman Joe Biden (D-Del.) requested a DOJ, OPR, investigation into the veracity of Friedman's claims.[30]

Though popular with antiharassment activists, Friedman's claims were wildly exaggerated. There was no question that Friedman worked for the FBI from 1979 to 1982, or that federal authorities in Atlanta had targeted Commissioner Eaves for multiple sting operations. Beyond this, however,

Friedman's allegations appear to be a dishonest attempt to punish the FBI for the loss of his legs. In 1982, Friedman's relationship with the FBI was abruptly terminated when a bomb planted underneath his car detonated, destroying his left leg and much of his right ankle. The bomb appears to have been planted by Atlanta organized crime figures who falsely believed that Friedman and the FBI were investigating them. Believing that the Atlanta FBI had known of the mob hit but failed to inform him, Friedman sued the bureau for $20 million in damages. On December 10, 1987, a judge rejected Friedman's allegations, arguing that the bureau's actions were only "casually related" to his injuries. Friedman swore the first *fruhmenschen* affidavit on December 1, after closing arguments. He swore the second affidavit on January 20, 1988, forty days after the ruling. Not only does the timing of Friedman's affidavit—nine years after the alleged policy was revealed to him and clustered around the ruling in his unsuccessful suit against the FBI—bring his allegations into question, but so too does their content. A 1992 OPR investigation concluded that Friedman, an amateur novelist, had borrowed the term *fruhmenschen* from science fiction writer John Barth's 1966 novel *Giles Goat Boy*. The story, which is a satire of American college-campus culture in the early 1960s, refers to different ethnic groups using fictional German-sounding names: Germans are referred to as "Siegfrieders," Jews as "Moishians," and dark-skinned students as "Frumentians." A paperback edition of *Giles Goat Boy* was issued by Anchor Books in August 1987, just four months before Friedman swore his first affidavit.[31] As with previous conspiracy theories, Friedman's claims would detract from antiharassment activists' legitimate evidence of disproportionate prosecution and open them to attack by their critics.

By 1989, the "black counterattack" had proved remarkably successful. Four detailed studies of harassment had been published in 1987, 1988, and 1989 (two), and the National Black Caucus of State Legislators had announced that it was working on a fifth.[32] Thousands of African Americans across the country had attended rallies, prayer vigils, and fund-raisers and had written letters on behalf of black elected officials under investigation. Most of the black elected, nationalist, and civil rights leadership in the nation had adopted some variant of harassment ideology. At least a third of African Americans believed that the DOJ was unlawfully targeting black elected officials for investigation. And despite the reassertion of conspiracy theory within their ranks, antiharassment activists had made breakthroughs with several influential members of the ever-skeptical mainstream news media. In 1990, the sentiments and beliefs antiharassment activists had created over the previous three years would save Washington, D.C., mayor Marion Barry (D) from a felony drug conviction. In the process, harassment ideology would be broadcast across the country and around the world.

Marion Barry: The "Black Counterattack" Hits Prime Time

The "black counterattack" of the late 1980s reached its apogee in 1990, following the January 18 arrest of Mayor Marion Barry in an FBI–Metropolitan Police Department sting at the Vista Hotel in Washington, D.C. Coming on the heels of three straight years of intense antiharassment agitation, much of it in the District of Columbia and nearby Baltimore, the ensuing trial became a flash point for antiharassment activism. But just as the Barry trial gave antiharassment activists national notoriety, it exposed the flaws of harassment ideology and undermined activists' credibility.

The belief among black Americans that Barry was the target of harassment was wide and deep. The morning following the sting, a crowd of African Americans assembled outside the U.S. District Courthouse and shouted, "Victim! Victim!" as Barry entered to be arraigned. Initially dismissed by reporters as a fringe, this group, the *Washington Post* soon found, represented the views of approximately one-half of D.C. blacks.[33] The effect of the "black counterattack" could also be seen in the way that black elected and civil rights leadership viewed the Barry arrest. Speaking with reporters outside the White House on January 22, NAACP director Benjamin Hooks stated: "We at the NAACP, across the past few years, have felt that there has been undue emphasis on harassing black elected officials. We had a meeting right here in this city a few weeks ago and Mayor [Richard] Arrington gave some graphic examples of what we considered to be undue harassment of black elected officials, and to that extent the Barry case might fit into it." Even those black leaders who condemned Barry's actions demonstrated an embrace of harassment ideology. Speaking to the *Guardian* newspaper just days after the arrest, Barry supporter Rev. Ernest Gibson stated, "The sad part of all this is that the mayor, with the knowledge and experience of all the attempts to undercut and discredit him, would fall for this particular entrapment."[34]

Because Barry was tried in D.C., which at the time had a 66 percent black population, African Americans' embrace of harassment ideology played a definitive role in the trial. Judge Thomas Jackson acknowledged as much during jury selection. Jackson mandated that prospective jurors be asked if they believed that the law was selectively enforced against blacks and not whites. Many of the blacks in the jury pool stated that they did. One stated, "It seems like some people are made to go through a little more than others. . . . I think race had a lot to do with it, as far as giving him [Barry] a hard time." Although that prospective juror was dismissed, others who held similar views made their way onto the jury.[35] During the trial, defense attorney R. Kenneth Mundy made a special appeal to them. In his opening statement, Mundy framed the Barry arrest as the culmination of a racial vendetta. "Seven years ago" Mundy began, "the government made a determination and a quest that it was going to get Mr. Barry, and the government was going to go to any length and any expense, expense that you will hear about, exorbitant expense, to make a case against Mr. Barry." In pretrial comments to the press, Mundy and Barry had repeatedly attempted to make the expense of the FBI sting an issue. They regularly speculated that the cost of the investigation had exceeded $40 million. Mundy also suggested that Barry was one among many black elected officials then being targeted by the DOJ. On July 27, he asserted that special agent Ronald Stern, the lead investigator in the Barry sting, moved "around the country as the head of an, in effect, assault force of FBI agents" who target black elected officials. Mundy cited Stern's participation in the Atlanta FBI's 1987 investigation of alleged cocaine use by state senator Julian Bond to support his allegation. Stern was, in fact, in the Atlanta office of the FBI in 1987, but he was not a lead agent in the Bond investigation. Also, contrary to Mundy's charge, the Bond investigation was not a sting. The FBI had been asked to join the investigation by the Atlanta police. Although Mundy's allegations were demonstrably false, they nonetheless placed the prosecution on the defensive. In a city where one black elected official after the other had been placed under investigation by the DOJ under Reagan and Bush, the burden of proof was on the prosecution to demonstrate its objectivity. Perhaps understanding this fact, assistant U.S. attorney Judith Retchin responded to Mundy's charge about Stern by stating: "What we would be prepared to prove is that there was absolutely no truth to the allegation that there is an FBI task force or any group of any sort within the FBI that has targeted black officials." Retchin's ability to prove or disprove her case aside, the jury had already heard Mundy's allegations, and the following day his claims were front-page news.[36]

While Mundy made his case in U.S. district court, Barry made his case in the court of public opinion. Since he had been arrested in January, Barry had executed a carefully crafted campaign to gain public sympathy. He checked himself into a drug-therapy program, attended church (often several churches each Sunday), spoke with reporters, dropped out of the coming mayor's race, and met with constituents, all for the purpose, Tom Sherwood and Harry Jaffe tell us, of "grooming an entire city of potential jurors."[37] His message was simple: he was an imperfect man, and federal prosecutors' investigation of his office was an unprincipled and undemocratic attack on the black mayor of a majority-black city. During the trial, Barry accelerated his efforts. At a July rally sponsored by NOI leader Minister Louis Farrakhan, Barry stated, "Let the people speak about what is happening in Washington, D.C. Not just here, but for other black elected officials all over the land who have misfortunately [sic] been harassed and arraigned by U.S. prosecutors."[38] And Judge Jackson played directly into Barry's hands. The day after the rally, when Farrakhan attempted to attend the trial as an invited guest of the mayor, he was barred by Judge Jackson on the grounds that the NOI leader would "intimidate" the jurors. Farrakhan learned of Jackson's decision outside the courthouse. Standing before the dozens of news crews that had gathered for the trial, he stated that Jackson's decision "demonstrate[d] the wickedness of the United States government and the lengths to which this government [would] go when it target[ed] a black leader to be discredited." Jackson was later forced to rescind his decision by a higher court.[39]

The defense's line of argument swayed several of the jurors. In a trial postmortem, the *Washington Post* noted that "the jurors frequently discussed matters the judge had told them to avoid. Some regularly discussed their disapproval of the government's methods in pursuing Barry, and what they thought were the government's bad motives for prosecuting him." None of the jurors disputed that Barry had an addiction to cocaine; that much was obvious. But several jurors believed that even had Barry not had an addiction, federal investigators would have conspired to entrap him. Sherwood and Jaffe write that "from the first hours of deliberation, the twelve jurors were deadlocked—some as frozen in their divergent views as were the people of Washington, D.C. There were two separate realities: One accepted and trusted the American system of justice; the other believed in a conspiracy against blacks."[40] Posttrial comments by Valerie Jackson-Warren, a leader of the group of jurors who consistently voted for acquittal, confirm this point. Speaking with the *Washington Post* following the trial, Jackson-Warren stated: "I believe they [federal investigators] were out to get Marion Barry. I believe that with all my heart." Unable to convince Jackson-Warren and several other black jurors to vote for conviction, the interacial group of jurors who favored conviction brokered a deal, trading one vote for acquittal for one vote for conviction. The jury deadlocked on the remaining twelve counts. The votes, Sherwood and Jaffe note, "had more to do with horsetrading than weighing of evidence."[41]

Just as Barry used the popular black belief in harassment to sway the jury, so did black elected officials use the increased public interest in harassment generated by the Barry trial to make their case to a greatly expanded audience. Public interest in the Barry arrest and trial exceeded that of any case since the House of Representatives denied Adam Clayton Powell Jr. his seat twenty-three years before. Throughout the spring and into the summer, the arrest and impending trial was front-page news not only in Washington but across the country.[42] When the trial was held in July, the Times Mirror Company found that 22 percent of Americans followed it "very closely." Another 30 percent followed the trial "fairly closely." Whether or not they followed the trial in the news, Times Mirror noted that 63 percent of Americans had seen the FBI surveillance tape of Barry smoking crack. Indeed, interest in the Barry arrest and trial was international, making the front page of newspapers around the globe.[43] Capitalizing on this flood of public interest, black elected officials spoke out against harassment in unprecedented numbers. In April, James Usry (D), Atlantic City mayor and president of the NCBM, denounced the "apparent attacks" against black elected officials epitomized by the Barry sting during his organization's annual conference. He was joined by several other black mayors who alleged that they too were targets of unwarranted government scrutiny.[44] During the House Judiciary Committee's May hearings on the DOJ's 1991 budget, Representative John Conyers (D-Mich.) accused Attorney General Dick Thornburgh of perpetuating an "ongoing pattern of selective prosecution of Black elected officials." Thornburgh angrily asserted that Conyers's accusation was "totally and absolutely false." Conyers, who had recently acted as counsel for the House in the impeachment proceedings against Judge Hastings, replied that he used to believe such claims; he did not anymore.[45] In June, Jesse Jackson joined the outcry at a prayer breakfast for Representative Harold Ford (D-Tenn.), whom federal prosecutors were then threatening to retry on charges of influence peddling and conspiracy following a mistrial two months before. Referring to the DOJ investigations of Representatives Ron Dellums (D-Calif.), Bill Gray (D-Pa.), Gus Savage (D-Ill.), and Ford, Jackson stated, "Not one of these people has been convicted, but they keep investigating. . . . There have been all these discrediting leaks and investigations, and not one conviction. . . . I wouldn't say it is a conspiracy," he continued, "but one can at least see a pattern here."[46] The following month, NAACP executive director Benjamin Hooks voiced his concerns. Although initially measured in his comments about the Barry trial, Hooks came to see it as a clear-cut case of repression. In his keynote address to the NAACP convention in Los Angeles, Hooks asserted, "Something is wrong with our system of justice when more than $40 million is spent and over 70 FBI agents assigned to trail and monitor one black elected official, to set up a sting operation to bring him down." (It was later revealed that the investigation cost somewhere in the area of $2 to 4 million plus agents' salaries. To this, Hooks replied, "Even if . . .the government spent only $4 million on this investigation, that figure seems excessive in the pursuit of recreational drug abuse, which is the essence of the government's case.")[47] Like other black leaders, Hooks saw the Barry case as symptomatic of a larger pattern of harassment. Across the country, he claimed, "overzealous, hostile—if not racist—district attorneys and U.S. Attorneys [were bringing] black elected officials to trial on the flimsiest of evidence."[48]

Although the Barry arrest and trial provided black elected officials with an expanded national platform for discussing harassment, it also compromised those same claims. Evidence presented during the trial, particularly the FBI surveillance tape of the mayor smoking crack, revealed Barry's tremendous personal failings.[49] While antiharassment activists fastened on the evidence of government overreaching, DOJ representatives and many in the news media focused on Barry's behavior. Historian Manning Marable noted in his syndicated column how Barry's behavior undermined his and other black activists' allegations of harassment. "Barry's central argument which attempted to justify his behavior was the thesis that a pattern of FBI and judicial harassment exists against African American civil rights leaders and elected officials," Marable wrote. "The argument is certainly true . . .[but] his behavior provides justification for racists and political reactionaries to undermine other African-American leaders."[50] At base, the Barry case was symptomatic of a basic problem facing antiharassment activists since the mid-1970s. Many of the marquee cases around which black elected officials organized featured eyebrow-raising if not damning evidence against the accused. While antiharassment activists focused on the actions of federal prosecutors, prosecutors worked to focus public attention on black elected officials' alleged misdeeds. When prosecutors were successful in so doing, antiharassment activists appeared to be protecting criminals from prosecution by "playing the race card." Carl Rowan, who first raised this concern in 1976, noted the problem such an impression may pose for black leadership in an editorial shortly after the Barry trial: "It would be outrageous to say that all black elected officials are crooks, but just as stupid to suggest that none of them is corrupt. We have to be extremely careful in deciding which ones we dare to defend publicly, especially when a grand jury finds reason to indict."[51] But as in the past, no antiharassment activists offered a mechanism for making such a distinction. Thus, although the "black counterattack" of 1987–90 spread harassment ideology to a majority of the African American population, some of the principal cases around which black elected officials organized undermined whatever legitimacy harassment ideology was gaining among white Americans, the mainstream news media, and perhaps even some African Americans.

The Center for the Study of the Harassment of African Americans

Despite the popularity of harassment ideology in black political circles in the late 1980s, black elected officials and civil rights leaders had failed to coordinate a collective defense. Throughout the decade, black elected officials and their supporters had created temporary organizations to coordinate defense efforts in response to certain incidents of harassment.[52] These organizations focused on the cases of their founding members and only secondarily, if at all, on a larger pattern of harassment, and all were dismantled once the precipitating crisis had passed. This state of affairs led Mary Sawyer to conclude in 1987 that "the overall response to the problem of harassment" had been "modest and haphazard."[53] In 1990, however, that would change. That year, former Maryland state senator Clarence Mitchell III created the CSHAA, an information clearinghouse and advocacy organization modeled on Sawyer's CSBL. Mitchell hoped to make the CSHAA a permanent organization focusing on the national pattern of harassment, not simply on the case of a single individual. He would succeed, but only for a time.

Mitchell had first attempted to create an organizational center for antiharassment activism in 1987 with the Clarence Mitchell Jr. Defense Fund's "National Campaign for Justice," only to have his efforts cut short in the spring of 1988 when he and his brother, Michael, were convicted and sent to prison. Clarence Mitchell III watched the growth of antiharassment activism in 1988–89 from a cell in the Lewisburg, Pennsylvania, federal penitentiary. A seasoned politician with a sense of entitlement and purpose derived from his family's six decades of civil rights activism, Mitchell did not remain idle while incarcerated. During his fifteen-month sentence, he worked with a white New York activist, Sandra Peters, to transform the Clarence Mitchell Jr. Defense Fund into the Clarence Mitchell Jr. Memorial Fund, a defense fund and information clearinghouse for black elected officials. Though little is known about Peters's background, it can be said that she first met Mitchell in the mid-1980s while doing contract work for the National Black Caucus of State Legislators. Over the years, they had become friends, and when the Mitchells were indicted, Peters volunteered at the Clarence Mitchell Jr. Defense Fund, helping to organize the "National Campaign for Justice." When the Mitchells were in prison, Peters secured credentials as a paralegal to defense attorney William Kunstler and used her visits to lay the groundwork for the new organization. At the time of Mitchell's release, Peters was working as a consultant for the National Council of Churches (NCC), a position that would soon become critical to the memorial fund's work.[54]

Mitchell emerged from prison in October 1989 to find a black community animated by antiharassment activism. Black leadership across the country was calling out for an organized defense against harassment. Seeking to capitalize on the black counterattack, Mitchell and Peters requested a meeting with the NCC within weeks of his release. Working through the NCC's associate general secretary Kenyon Burke and NCC racial justice director Tyrone Pitts, Mitchell and Peters were able to obtain a hearing before the NCC Racial Justice Working Group. Burke was the ideal contact. In 1978, as program director for the NAACP, he had worked with Mary Sawyer to ensure that the issue of harassment was included in the association's agenda. Through his efforts, the NAACP devoted more time and energy to antiharassment organizing than any other black political organization in the late 1970s. At the meeting, Mitchell delivered what working group member Joann Watson later called "earnest, tear-jerking testimony" describing his indictment, conviction, and incarceration.[55] His presentation moved the working group to adopt a resolution condemning the "effort[s] on the part of law enforcement agencies to discredit and remove African American elected officials from office." The resolution called for congressional investigations of the recent spate of DOJ investigations of black elected officials and urged public support for those black elected officials who came under investigation.[56] Additionally, the working group pledged to host a "public hearing" on harassment at its New York headquarters in May 1990. Commissioner Watson, who also served as the cochair of the National Interreligious Commission on Civil Rights (NICCR), offered to sponsor a similar hearing in Detroit in mid-September. Mitchell scored a third victory several days later when he secured a promise from Representative Mervyn Dymally (D-Calif.), then chairman of the CBC, to hold yet another hearing on harassment at the caucus's annual legislative conference in late September 1990.

The hearings were a watershed moment in antiharassment activism, uniting the entire spectrum of black political leadership around the issue of harassment. They included all the major antiharassment activists: Clarence Mitchell III, Mervyn Dymally, Mary Sawyer, Representative William Clay (D-Mo.), Richard Arrington, and state senator Andrew Jenkins (D-N.Y.)—who was then writing a report on harassment for the National Black Caucus of State Legislators—representatives from three of the seven national black caucuses (the CBC, National Black Caucus of State Legislators, and the NCBM); the country's leading civil rights organizations (the NAACP and the National Council of Negro Women); the country's leading black nationalist organization (the NOI); the social justice faith community (NCC Racial Justice Working Group, the NICCR, and the Commission for Racial Justice of the United Church of Christ); and the most active third world communist organization of the period (the National Alliance against Racist and Political Repression).[57]

The events were run as investigative hearings with black elected officials and researchers "testifying" to a panel of civil rights, political, and religious leaders. After the witnesses gave opening statements, the panel questioned them about their testimony. The proceedings were not adversarial, as nearly all the participants embraced harassment ideology. Indeed, at times the hearings resembled revivals in which witnesses and panelists alike exhorted the audience to take action against harassment. At the Washington, D.C., hearing, for instance, Louis Farrakhan preached what could only be called a sermon to shouts of "Amen!" and "Tell it!" before the standing-room-only crowd.[58]

There were dissenters, however. One was Russell Owens, director of the National Policy Institute at the Joint Center for Political and Economic Studies. Although he agreed that black elected officials were the targets of disproportionate state scrutiny, Owens took issue with the loose application of the term "harassment." Speaking at the New York hearing, Owens queried, "What is meant by harassment, selective prosecution, double standards for assessing performance and integrity, abuses of the grand jury process . . .violation of due process?" He did not receive a ready answer. Although most of the witnesses used harassment as shorthand for racially motivated federal investigations, others had a more elastic definition. At the New York hearing, Mervyn Dymally used the term to refer to criticism by a private group, the Rainbow Lobby, of his decision to hold talks with several controversial third world dictators. Former Black Panthers Dorubah Bin Wahad and Milwaukee city councilman Michael McGee (D) suggested that black elected officials were victims of an FBI counterintelligence program not unlike that directed at the Black Panther Party. Oak Park, Michigan, school board vice president Louise Mitchell (D) argued that white school board members' initial refusal to treat her as an equal was harassment. Rather than wrestle with Owens's questions and create a uniform definition of harassment, the black elected officials in attendance ignored his query. For them, and for the many African Americans who had adopted harassment ideology, the distinctions were immaterial. The question was not what is harassment, but what should be done about it. As in Sawyer's research thirteen years before, the "postulate," to use Owens's words, had "become the conclusion."[59]

The hearings amplified antiharassment activists' message, strengthened African Americans' embrace of harassment ideology, and energized a newly expanded network of activists determined to fight harassment. Each of the hearings received heavy print coverage in their respective media markets. They also generated TV coverage, with segments of the New York hearing appearing on the talk show *America's Black Forum*, and the Washington, D.C., hearing broadcast live on C-SPAN.[60] And African Americans responded positively to the expanded coverage of antiharassment activists claims. In June 1990, six months after the New York hearing, a sample group of African Americans in New York City were asked if they believed that the "government deliberately singles out and investigates black elected officials in order to discredit them in a way it doesn't do with white officials." Of those queried, 33 percent responded that the statement was "true," and another 45 percent stated that it "might possibly be true." Only 16 percent believed that the statement "almost certainly was not true."[61] The hearings also expanded and energized the antiharassment network generated by the individual defense efforts of the late 1980s. Whereas earlier antiharassment efforts were relatively parochial affairs bringing local black elected officials together to support a specific individual, the hearings drew black elected officials from across the nation, church leaders, communists, civil rights activists, and black nationalists into a single national network.

Perhaps most important, the hearings challenged this new coalition to take action. At each gathering, panelists and members of the audience demanded that a congressional investigation be undertaken, a defense fund be founded, and a "Center for the Study of Harassment" be created. Responding to these concerns, Representative John Conyers (D-Mich.), then chairman of the House Government Operations Committee, pledged to hold hearings on harassment sometime in 1991. Conyers planned to explore the tactics the DOJ used when investigating black elected officials, the number of investigations that had been undertaken, and the outcomes of those investigations. He then planned to compare those cases to the DOJ's treatment of white elected officials. Like Owens, the Detroit congressman wanted statistics, hard data that would answer conclusively the question of whether and why black elected officials were overrepresented among the DOJ's official corruption investigations. "What we're trying to do is take the emotional factor out of it as much as possible," Conyers stated to reporters following the Washington, D.C., hearing. More than seeking to generate a dispassionate study of harassment, Conyers was undoubtedly calling Attorney General Dick Thornburgh's bluff. Thornburgh had repeatedly refused to provide black elected officials with a racial breakdown of the DOJ's official corruption investigations. At the same time, he challenged black elected officials to provide statistics that proved their allegations of selective prosecution—the very statistics he refused to provide. Conyers's planned hearings would generate such numbers.[62]

While Conyers made plans for a hearing, Clarence Mitchell III and Sandra Peters worked to create a defense fund and information clearinghouse. For help in this endeavor, they turned to Mervyn Dymally. Dymally had known Mitchell for several years, well enough, in fact, to attend the Baltimore "Freedom Rally" in 1987. In early 1990, Dymally had enthusiastically supported Mitchell's public hearings idea, sending "dear colleague" letters to his fellow congressmen requesting their presence at the events, helping to secure speakers, and, of course, hosting the Washington, D.C., hearing.[63] Despite their collaboration, Mitchell and Dymally had never discussed forming a permanent antiharassment organization. This had been a longtime dream of Dymally's. At the Washington hearing, Dymally called on the gathering to establish a "formal institution" to study harassment and suggested that it be called the "Center for the Study of Harassment."[64] Within days of the September 27 event, Mitchell and Peters traveled to Capitol Hill to meet with Dymally and explore the feasibility of creating a national antiharassment organization. They hoped to generate support for the expansion of the Clarence Mitchell Jr. Memorial Fund. Dymally, on the other hand, reiterated his desire for an "information clearinghouse" and "depository" modeled on the CSBL. Representative Conyers also encouraged Mitchell and Peters to form an information clearinghouse.[65] Recognizing that they did not have the resources to operate a defense fund, the two adopted Dymally's idea.

Within a matter of weeks, Peters and Mitchell were seeking temporary office space and funding for the proposed "Center for the Study of the Harassment of African Americans." Mitchell took the role of acting chairman of the new organization, and Peters became acting director. Though the name was different, the new center used the phones and offices of the old Clarence Mitchell Jr. Memorial Fund. Mitchell and Peters had simply shifted the organization's focus from fund-raising and legal defense to data collection, analysis, and dissemination. The center, they hoped, would conduct work similar to the CSBL, though on a grander scale. Specifically, Peters hoped to use new computer technology to develop a "comprehensive database, . . .statistically analyze the significance of the data, and develop mechanisms to track . . .incident cases." The center would disseminate its findings through reports and educational symposia for black elected officials. Mitchell and Peters also hoped to institutionalize antiharassment advocacy by creating a "speakers' bureau" that individuals interested in harassment could use as a resource. Such a project would require substantial financial expenditures—substantial at least for a group with no resources. Peters drew up a grant proposal for a yearly operating budget of $390,000.[66]

Mitchell and Peters plunged into the work of the center. In June 1991, Peters convened a meeting of several lawyers engaged in antiharassment work "to evaluate possible litigation and concurrently help prepare evidentiary materials for" John Conyers's proposed House Committee on Government Operations hearings on harassment. This project was scuttled, however, when Conyers canceled the hearings following the outbreak of the Gulf War.[67] Undaunted, Peters spent the remainder of the year working to reprint Mary Sawyer's 1987 report on harassment. Working through Sawyer, Peters secured an agreement with the NAHRW to have Ten Years Later published in the fall 1991 issue of the association's organ, the Journal of Intergroup Relations. The issue, titled "Harassment of African American Elected Officials," included the full text of Ten Years Later, the 1989 NCC resolution calling for congressional investigations of harassment, summaries of the three 1990 "public hearings" on harassment, and the mission statement of the CSHAA. With the NCC covering the cost of production, Peters ordered five thousand copies of the journal and disseminated them to black elected officials.[68]

While Peters labored in Washington, Mitchell hit the lecture circuit. In 1990–91, he spoke before organizations as diverse as the National Baptist Convention, the Black American Political Association of California, and the American Civil Liberties Union. Additionally, he appeared on several television news programs and provided quotes for reporters writing articles on harassment. Perhaps the most noteworthy of Mitchell's media events was his appearance on CNN with Representative Harold Ford. Before a national television audience, the two accused fellow guests, former U.S. attorneys Rudolph Giuliani and Representative Bob Barr (R-Ga.), of being part of a DOJ that harassed black elected officials. The encounter was demonstrative of the wide public appeal of harassment ideology and the crisis of authority it had cause at the DOJ.[69]

The CSHAA's successes masked profound organizational and fund-raising problems that would severely limit its activities as early as mid-1991. First and foremost, the center did not raise more than 3 percent of its proposed operating budget. This was not for lack of trying. Mitchell courted nearly all the national black professional and political organizations. "I took time to go speak to all of their conferences to try to get them involved," Mitchell recalls, "even talked to all the fraternal organizations; tried to get them to develop an annual contribution which would have given us a base and would have also given us the credibility necessary to leverage funds from the various [white] church organizations and foundations that were sensitive to this issue." To his surprise, none of these organizations was willing to make a financial contribution to the center. "Black folks would say, 'You're doing a great job,' 'Keep up the good work,'" Mitchell remembers, "and no checks came."[70] While Mitchell canvassed black organizations, Peters worked to raise money among white church organizations and foundations. Like Sawyer before her, Peters sent off a stack of grant applications only to receive a stack of rejection letters several weeks later. Peters was, however, successful in obtaining in-kind support from several progressive church groups. The Methodist Church provided the CSHAA with office space in its building at 500 Maryland Avenue, directly across the street from the U.S. Capitol in Washington, D.C. Despite this generosity, the CSHAA could not meet its monthly bills. By September 1991, it had raised only about thirteen thousand dollars in grants and contributions, not even enough to cover office supplies and travel expenses.[71]

Mitchell blamed the center's failure to raise funds on African Americans' inability to grasp the import of harassment. He believed that black elected officials were inclined to dismiss harassment unless it happened to them personally. Mary Sawyer, the only other individual who had engaged in antiharassment fund-raising, had come to a similar conclusion. In *Ten Years Later*, Sawyer claimed that black elected officials had not implemented the recommendations set forth in *Dilemma* because "so many individuals are inclined to discount the problem—until it happens to him or her."[72] Mitchell further argued that African Americans' failure to support the CSHAA undermined its ability to raise funds among white organizations: "When they began to see that black folks wouldn't be supportive of an organization that was supposed to help black folks . . .why should the white church continue to be involved?"[73] Neither of these explanations comports to the facts. In the late 1980s, black elected officials had raised hundreds of thousands of dollars for their defense efforts. The social justice church community had paid for two of the three public hearings on harassment and was then providing the center with some of the best office space in

Washington, D.C., rent free. What appears to have hampered the CSHAA's fund-raising activities was its internal disarray and antiharassment activists' failure to make a clear distinction between harassment and law enforcement. A full three years after the September 1990 hearing, the CSHAA had not established itself as a registered organization or gained 501 (c)3 tax-exempt status. In September 1991, a CSHAA fund-raising letter characterized the center as "in formation." Two years later, a May 1993 report stated that the center was "being organized." Because it was not registered, contributions to the center had to be made payable to and sent to the NCC or the Mitchell Memorial Fund—a state of affairs that made giving confusing and likely dissuaded potential funders.[74] Just as importantly, many potential funders mistrusted Mitchell, an accomplished politician but also an ex-convict. As Kenyon Burke, a center supporter, noted in a 2004 interview, "Clarence had a cloud over his head. . . . People were suspicious of him." Suspicious of what exactly, Burke would not say.[75] It was clear, however, that Mitchell's felony conviction was a problem.

Though the decline of the CSHAA was, in part, a matter of internal organizational problems and an inability to raise funds, it was ultimately the product of a larger decline in antiharassment activism following the 1992 election. When former Arkansas governor Bill Clinton (D) defeated President Bush in the November 1992 election, ending twelve years of Republican rule, he also ended the official corruption crackdown. With the drop in DOJ investigations of black elected officials, the black counterattack of 1987–91 dissipated. In 1990–91, the CSHAA had acted as a coordinating institution for the counterattack. As such, it was more a product of antiharassment activism than a source. When black elected officials' concern with harassment waned in the years after Clinton entered the White House, the CSHAA lost even the meager support it had previously received. Unable to raise funds and lacking a proper infrastructure, the CSHAA dramatically curtailed its activities in late 1992. By 1994, news reports on harassment mentioned the center only in passing. In 1995, Mitchell and Peters abandon the project altogether.[76]

Exploiting the Void: The Schiller Institute

Although the Clinton transition team was in full control of the DOJ by the fall of 1993, many of the investigations begun by the Bush DOJ were inherited by the incoming U.S. attorneys. Specifically, the U.S. attorneys in Compton, California; Winston Salem, North Carolina; New Orleans, Louisiana; and Columbia, South Carolina, inherited cases against black elected officials built from FBI sting operations.[77] Faced with these cases, some of the black elected officials in these states suspected that the harassment of the Bush years was continuing despite the Clinton transition. With the CSHAA moribund and antiharassment activists like Mary Sawyer and Mervyn Dymally pursuing other endeavors, these black elected officials had no one to turn to for information or help in organizing a defense. Thus, in 1994–95, a void appeared to have developed in antiharassment organizing. Into this space stepped the Schiller Institute, a propaganda organization serving the interests of fascist intellectual Lyndon LaRouche.

LaRouche's interest in harassment was a product of his organizing strategy. LaRouche began his political career as the nominal leader of the labor caucuses of Students for a Democratic Society (SDS). When the caucuses were expelled from SDS in 1969, LaRouche renamed his roughly one thousand followers the National Caucus of Labor Committees (NCLC). In the early 1970s, Chip Berlett and Joel Bellman argue, LaRouche transformed the NCLC into a cult geared exclusively toward bringing him to power as president of the United States.[78] Modeling his crusade on the beginnings of the National Socialist (Nazi) movement during the Weimar Republic in Germany, LaRouche sought to build a political movement that could gain electoral support and, once in power, use the machinery of the state to crush his adversaries and revolutionize American society.[79] To accomplish this daunting task, LaRouche developed an elaborate patchwork of front groups to generate funds for the NCLC and spread his influence. LaRouche directed these organizations to undertake two specific functions. First, the propaganda and political organizations were directed to inject LaRouche's ideas into communities that were susceptible to conspiracy theory. LaRouche hoped to convince these groups that shadowy organizations and powerful individuals sought their destruction. The only way to avert disaster was to follow him in his crusade against these amorphous enemies. Second, these organizations were directed to establish vanguard roles on issues of concern to certain segments of the population. LaRouche believed that if he were able to establish himself as *the* authority on issues of concern to certain groups of Americans, he could also win these groups' support for his larger political program.[80] Both strategies—used repeatedly by LaRouche front groups from the mid-1970s into the new millennium—were aimed at gaining the support of individuals as voters, donors, and recruits.

Although several of these front groups became successful businesses, there never seemed to be enough money for LaRouche's expensive presidential campaigns. In order to fill this need, he and his followers turned to fraud. During the 1970s, LaRouche filed false matching funds applications with the FEC. The FEC uncovered his schemes and turned down his requests or forced him to repay funds he had already received. In both cases, LaRouche claimed that the FEC was engaging in "political harassment," designed to suppress his influence. In 1984, when LaRouche undertook his most ambitious run for the White House, NCLC fundraisers called thousands of individuals, mostly seniors, and asked them to make "loans" to a LaRouche front group in order to support various conservative causes or to fight drugs, AIDS, and other pressing social crises. In 1987, federal investigators uncovered 4,500 such loans totaling approximately $30 million, not a single one of which had been paid back in full, and few of which were being paid back at all.[81] By 1986, grand juries in several cities had indicted members of LaRouche's inner circle for fraud, and twelve states obtained cease and desist orders against NCLC fundraisers. In 1988, LaRouche himself was indicted and charged with multiple counts of mail fraud, income tax fraud, and conspiracy. That December he was convicted and sentenced to fifteen years in prison. During his trial, LaRouche claimed that the charges against him were a carefully orchestrated plot to "eliminate [him] from the political scene," by setting him up to be assassinated in prison.[82]

Before he was sentenced, LaRouche and his followers unsuccessfully attempted to use harassment ideology to discredit the DOJ and simultaneously win African Americans to their cause.[83] The NCLC first attempted to court African Americans using harassment ideology during the May 1990 hearings on harassment in New York, where a reporter for a LaRouche publication asked the black elected officials in attendance, "How does this assembly . . . expect to receive justice . . .[when] they remain silent on the U.S. government railroad and travesty of Lyndon LaRouche?" Benjamin Chavis, vice president of the NCC and an event cosponsor who was then at the microphone, dismissed the question stating, "Lyndon LaRouche is neither elected nor is he African American. No doubt there are other forms of harassment in this country but the reason we have called this press conference . . . is the . . . harassment of black elected officials."[84] At this moment black leadership dominated antiharassment organizing and was therefore able to rebuff the LaRouche organization's attempt to appropriate its cause. In the mid-1990s when LaRouche emerged from prison, however, these groups were no longer organizing around the issue.

In 1995, the Schiller Institute, a LaRouche front group, renewed its effort to appropriate harassment ideology when it held "Independent Hearings to Investigate Misconduct by the U.S. Department of Justice" in Tyson's Corner, Virginia. The hearings focused on what organizers referred to as "political harassment" by the "permanent bureaucracy of the U.S. Justice Department" and covered several cases that bore absolutely no relationship to one another. The first session focused on the "harassment of black elected officials—the FBI's Operation *Fruhmenschen*." The second session featured the case of John Demjanjuk—a Ukrainian émigré accused by Holocaust survivors of being Ivan the Terrible, the notorious Nazi ss guard from the Treblinka extermination camp—and his prosecution by the DOJ's Office of Special Investigations. The last panel featured LaRouche himself and described his 1988 conviction for fraud as "the largest single case involving the same corrupt DOJ apparatus that operated in the OSI and Operation *Fruhmenschen* cases." Thus the Schiller Institute structured the panels in such a way as to convey that all these groups had been victims of the same DOJ conspiracy. Because LaRouche's case was the "largest" of all those being aired, it was implied, other victims of the "permanent bureaucracy" could come to understand their predicament through him.[85]

The format for the hearings was familiar to many of the black elected officials in attendance, as the CSHAA had employed the same arrangement during its 1990 "public hearings." Several of the South Carolina black elected officials ensnared in Operation Lost Trust testified, as did Judge Ira Murphy of Tennessee, who related the DOJ prosecution of Congressman Harold Ford (D-Tenn.); former Compton city councilwoman Patricia Moore related the DOJ investigation of Compton elected officials; and Birmingham city councilman Roosevelt Bell discussed the DOJ-IRS investigations of Birmingham black elected officials. But it was here that the similarity ended. Having established a pattern of DOJ misconduct targeting black elected officials, the organizers turned the attendees' attention to the case of LaRouche. Nearly all of LaRouche's testimony was structured to present DOJ and FBI investigations of himself and his organization as the most "pervasive single campaign" in a larger pattern of "political targeting" by the "permanent bureaucracy" of the DOJ. LaRouche explained just what the permanent bureaucracy was and how it operated:

> We have a system of injustice whose center is within the Department of Justice, especially the Criminal Division of the U.S. Department of Justice. The problem lies not with one administration or another, though one administration or another may act more positively or negatively. You have permanent civil service employees . . .who are coordinators of a nest of institutions in the Criminal Division, which shows up repeatedly as leading or key associates of every atrocity which I've seen. . . .
>
> In my case, when the time came that somebody wanted me out of the way, they were able to rely upon that permanent injustice in the permanent bureaucracy of government, to do the job. As in the *Fruhmenschen* case, the Weaver case, the Waco case, the case of Waldhiem, the case of Demjanjuk, and other cases. Always there's that agency inside the Justice Department which works for contract, like a hitman, when somebody with the right credentials and passwords walks in and says, "we want to get this group of people," or "we want to get this person."[86]

LaRouche's idea of a permanent bureaucracy working for hire to eliminate political dissidents directly contradicted black elected officials' experience. They had faced disproportionate investigation by or at the behest of political appointees, not career lawyers and investigators. By erasing the political context for harassment from his discussion of "political targeting," LaRouche was able to claim that he and black elected officials shared the same political enemies and that those enemies still controlled—indeed had always controlled—the DOJ. He called on black elected officials in the room to join him in seeking to "remove from our system of government, a rotten permanent bureaucracy which acts like contract assassins."[87] The only way to do this, of course, was for black elected officials to join the LaRouche camp and work to elect him president.

The Schiller Institute dominated antiharassment organizing into the new millennium. It produced a video and companion transcript of the Tyson's Corner hearings that were distributed through its subsidiaries. This effort bore fruit when, later that year, the National Black Caucus of State Legislators passed a resolution, based on the Tyson's Corner hearings, calling on Congress to investigate alleged misconduct by the DOJ. Although it expressed "interest" in the resolution, the CBC did not hold hearings.[88] In 1998, the Schiller Institute planned a series of town hall meetings around the country on the issue of harassment. For these events, Harley Schlanger, who was then coordinating antiharassment propaganda for the institute, sought the help of prominent antiharassment activists. Schlanger phoned Mary Sawyer, who, being familiar with the NCLC's history, never returned his call.[89] Mervyn Dymally, however, chose to work with Schlanger. On March 5, 1998, Dymally traveled to Houston, Texas, scene of a recent FBI sting on local black and Hispanic elected officials, to participate in a Schiller Institute panel titled "Restoring Justice to the U.S. Department of Justice." Later that summer, Dymally granted Schlanger an interview that was subsequently printed in the LaRouche newspaper the *New Federalist*.[90] Dymally was well aware of the Schiller Institute's history when he collaborated with Schlanger in 1998. "It's a cult," he confided to the author. But he felt that he had no alternative. "They're the only ones now," he stated, "championing this cause and championing the cause of blacks who have been harassed. . . . They're the only ball game in town, and they're the only people who have taken this up."[91] The following year, Dymally's pragmatism turned into co-optation. In 1999, when information surfaced of an abortive FBI plan to conduct a sting against Washington, D.C., city councilman Marion Barry (D), Dymally was quoted in the *Final Call* as saying that the revelation offered a "new opportunity to look into the web of deceit and corruption buried within the permanent bureaucracy of the Department of Justice."[92] No longer was the former congressman using the Schiller Institute to disseminate his message; he was mouthing Schiller Institute propaganda.

The Schiller Institute's distortion of harassment ideology and co-optation of antiharassment activists demonstrated the crisis facing antiharassment activism in the late 1990s. Because DOJ investigations of black elected officials declined during the Clinton years, black political organizations ceased organizing around harassment. With no forum for discussing harassment among black elected officials, antiharassment activists had nowhere to turn but the Schiller

Institute. Rather than collaborate with LaRouche, many antiharassment activists abandoned the cause. Those who chose to work with the Schiller Institute found that their concerns were subverted to LaRouche's political agenda. By 2000, even LaRouche ceased antiharassment agitation, believing that harassment no longer held the potential to attract the black masses.

Within just under two decades, harassment ideology had gone from a marginal theory held by a small number of black elected officials to the dominant concern of a critical mass of African Americans. Now, at the dawn of the new millennium, harassment ideology was spent as a force in black politics. Lacking an evidentiary basis in contemporary politics and distorted by the LaRouche organization, it dissolved into the larger black mistrust of white-dominated government institutions.

Over the past three decades . . . politics outside of the electoral arena have become the norm, rather than the episodic deviation from the routine pattern of American politics.

— Benjamin Ginsberg and Martin Shefter, *Politics by Other Means*

Those who are racially marginalized are like the miner's canary: their distress is the first sign of a danger that threatens us all. It is easy enough to think that when we sacrifice this canary, the only harm is to communities of color. Yet others ignore problems that converge around racial minorities at their own peril, for these problems are symptoms warning us that we are all at risk.

— Lani Guinier and Gerald Torres, *The Miner's Canary: Enlisting Race, Resisting Power, Transforming Democracy*

CONCLUSION

Political Warfare Ascendant

FOLLOWING THE COLLAPSE of the CSHAA, the network of black elected officials, human rights workers, and civil rights activists who had organized around issues of harassment directed their attention to other pursuits. Clarence Mitchell III returned to Baltimore to settle his finances. The Wedtech trial had taken a financial toll on him and his family from which recovery proved difficult. In fact, Mitchell lost CSHAA's files in the late 1990s when he was unable to pay the fees to the Baltimore storage company where they were being held. Although in 1999 he expressed a desire to reopen the center sometime in the future, in actuality his participation in antiharassment activism had ended. Mervyn Dymally retired from the U.S. House of Representatives in 1992 and began directing several nonprofits in South Central Los Angeles. He spoke about harassment on panels organized by the Schiller Institute in 1998 and 2000 but never became actively involved with the organization. In 2002, the still-energetic seventy-six-year-old reentered California politics by running for and winning his old state assembly seat from Watts. He served three terms and retired in 2008. After leaving Washington, D.C., Mary Sawyer became a professor of religious studies at Iowa State University. She continued to receive requests for *The Dilemma of Black Politics* and *Ten Years Later* from interested black elected officials into the new millennium.[1]

Although activists like Mitchell, Dymally, and Sawyer ceased antiharassment organizing in the mid-1990s, their ideas continued to have an important influence on black political thought, and this despite the end of the DOJ's disproportionate and selective prosecution of black elected officials in 1993. Both the end of disproportionate prosecution and the effects of antiharassment activists' endeavors are well illustrated by the four federal investigations of members of the CBC between 1993 and 2000. Of the fifty-four African Americans to serve in Congress between 1993 and 2000, only four — Representatives Mel Reynolds (D-Ill.), Barbara Rose-Collins (D-Mich.), and Walter Tucker (D-Calif.), and Senator Carol Moseley Braun (D-Ill.) — faced federal investigations.[2] Tucker, Rose-Collins, and Reynolds claimed that they were victims of harassment. Moseley Braun did not. Shortly after being indicted for bribery in 1994, Tucker stated, "I think the case will show that I have been targeted and I am obviously an African American." Allegations of selective prosecution so surrounded the trial that prosecutors asked prospective jurors if they believed black elected officials were being targeted for a "takedown" by the federal government. These suspicions aside, an FBI videotape of Tucker stuffing envelopes of cash into his pockets moved the jurors to deliver a verdict of guilty.[3] Rose-Collins, who was investigated for possible misuse of clerk hire, nonprofit, and campaign funds in 1996, also made allegations of selective prosecution a cornerstone of her defense. Soon after news of the investigation broke, Rose-Collins queried, "I ask you, is this gender bias or is this racism?" With no evidence to indicate either, Rose-Collins's allegations fell on deaf ears. In the 1996 Democratic primary, her constituents elected Carolyn Cheeks Kilpatrick to replace her.[4] Reynolds, too, made allegations of selective prosecution a centerpiece of his defense strategy. In 1994, he was indicted for solicitation of child pornography, sex with a minor, and conspiracy to cover the whole thing up by the Public Integrity Unit of the Cook County State's Attorney's office. Speaking with reporters in August, he asked rhetorically, "If I were a white congressman . . . would this investigation have happened?" Reynolds's query was bizarre considering his political pedigree. He had been elected with the backing of the white-dominated Cook County Democratic machine, all of the city's white daily newspapers, and the overwhelming majority of the white voters in his 68 percent black district. His accuser was a black eighteen-year-old (she was sixteen at the time that she and Reynolds had sex) former campaign worker. He was convicted by a racially mixed jury and sentenced to five years in prison.[5] During the trial, the DOJ opened a criminal investigation of the former congressman's finances. In November 1996, as he sat in an Illinois state prison, Reynolds and his wife,

Marisol, were indicted on sixteen counts of fraud related to their handling of campaign funds. Although Reynolds did not repeat his claims of harassment in this trial, he did attempt to bring one prosecution witness's testimony into doubt by alleging that he was a racist. Adding a silent testament to Reynolds's allegations of racism, NOI leader Louis Farrakhan attended the trial on two occasions and was rumored to be paying for the former congressman's defense. Again, the jury was unconvinced. After deliberating for only four hours, they found Reynolds guilty on fifteen of sixteen counts in 1997. At the sentencing hearing, he confessed his guilt.[6]

Though these elected officials' allegations of harassment were questionable at best, they reflected a strong presumption of vulnerability held by members of the CBC. In 2001–2 the author interviewed eighteen sitting members of the CBC. All of them stated that harassment constituted an ongoing threat to their ranks. Many had firsthand experience with state repression. Representative Bennie Thompson (D-Miss.) had been a target of the white backlash during his time as a local and county official in Hinds County, Mississippi, in the 1960s and 1970s. Representative Earl Hilliard (D-Ala.) had been caught up in the official corruption crackdown of the late 1980s as a state senator in Alabama and believed that the *fruhmenschen* affidavit was real. Along with Representative Jim Clyburn (D-S.C.), who had served on the NAHRW board when Mary Sawyer published *The Dilemma of Black Politics*, they ordered their FBI files upon their arrival in Washington, D.C., in 1993. Others such as Representative John Conyers (D-Mich.) had been a witness to nearly all the major investigations of black elected officials during the previous forty years, including serving on the committees that disciplined Representative Powell and impeached Judge Hastings. On the opposite side of the seniority scale, freshman representative William Lacy Clay (D-Mo.) stated that he was, at the time of the interview, under investigation by the newly appointed Republican U.S. attorney in St. Louis at the behest of Senator Kit Bond (R-Mo.) for alleged voter fraud in the 2000 election. An FBI investigation later concluded that St. Louis Republicans who had worked with Bond to bring the charges against Clay were, in fact, the culprits in the fraud. Regardless of their personal experiences, all these black members of Congress agreed that the disproportionate state and news media scrutiny of black elected officials that had characterized post-civil-rights-era U.S. politics was an ever-present threat despite its recent decline. Representative Bobby Rush (D-Ill.), a former member of the Chicago Black Panther Party and a target of the FBI's COINTELPRO program during the late 1960s, voiced this sentiment when he stated, "Every African American member of Congress operates under the premise that it didn't happen today but tomorrow it could. Harassment could be — could hit you at any point in time. So we don't have a level of security. . . . We're not secure in our world."[7]

If this story were only about antiharassment activism, it would end here. But it is also an effort to place the experiences of antiharassment activists like Dymally, Sawyer, and Mitchell and the ideas that they produced in context. In so doing it has challenged the concept of "harassment" itself. Harassment is not, as many antiharassment activists have argued, a singular historical phenomenon directed specifically at black elected officials or black leadership. Rather, it is an ideology developed to understand the repression and disproportionate state scrutiny black elected officials experienced as they entered and rose through the ranks of U.S. electoral politics during the post–civil rights period. Harassment ideology, like any ideology, did not always provide a suitable framework for understanding black elected officials' relationship to the news media and the state. Many black elected officials discussed here embraced harassment ideology following an honest evaluation of the evidence and were, by and large, correct in assessing the nature of the surveillance, counterintelligence, audits, and investigations that dogged their ranks. But in some notable instances, adherents incorporated elements of conspiracy theory into their thinking or used harassment ideology to cover up their misdeeds. Despite these failings, antiharassment activists identified a troubling trend that has in recent years come to define modern American politics.

Although black members of Congress experienced a reprieve from the disproportionate prosecution of the Reagan and Bush years under Clinton, the political warfare that had stimulated many of those prosecutions did not abate. In the 1990s, the pattern of governance that characterized the period between 1968 and 1992 flipped. Democrats gained control of the White House, and Republicans secured control of the House of Representatives. Thus, in the 1990s, Democrats used the House Ethics Committee to seek revenge against Republican House leadership, putting pressure on Newt Gingrich (R-Ga.) to step down from his position as Speaker in 1998 and, in the process, joining an "ethics war" that crippled Congress's ability to police its own ranks for nearly a decade. Republicans, meanwhile, used congressional committees and independent counsels to attack the Clinton administration and impeach the president in 1998. As high-ranking white Democrats became subject to the political warfare that had been disproportionately directed at black elected officials in years past, they came to sound like antiharassment activists. Commenting on the multiple Republican-supported investigations directed at the president, First Lady Hillary Clinton alleged that a "vast right-wing conspiracy" had been "conspiring against [her] husband since the day he announced for president." Many of Newt Gingrich's supporters claimed that the Ethics Committee investigation of his office was "politically motivated."[8]

The political warfare of the Clinton years continued into the new century. In December 2000, following an exceedingly close election, contentious recount, and related court battles, Republican George W. Bush, son and name-sake of the former president George H. W. Bush, was declared president by a 5 to 4 Supreme Court decision. Republicans also secured slim majorities in both houses of Congress, creating the first unified Republican federal government in nearly half a century. Soon after assuming official power, the Bush White House began laying the groundwork for an expansive campaign of political warfare against state and local Democrats in swing states designed to increase the Republican Party's slim majorities. For this purpose, White House political advisor Karl Rove directed a broad effort to politicize nearly every facet of the executive branch. Rove took this approach to absurd levels, going so far as to brief U.S. ambassadors and foreign service political appointees on Republican electoral strategy. One agency where Rove had tremendous success was the DOJ. There, administration appointees created a political litmus test for civil service hires and authorized dozens of lawyers to discuss ongoing criminal cases with the White House. Simultaneously, Attorney General John Ashcroft revived the department's focus on official corruption and the sting as a law enforcement tool.[9] These actions had profound implications for Democratic elected officials. Although the overall number of federal prosecutions between 2001 and 2006 remained relatively constant with the period 1993 through 2000, the targets of those investigations shifted dramatically. A 2007 study by communications professors Donald Shields and John Cragan suggests that state-level Democrats were seven times more likely than their Republican counterparts to be targeted for official corruption investigations by the Bush DOJ. Subsequent reports by the House Judiciary Committee and the DOJ, OPR, suggest that this disparity was the product of conscious partisan targeting.[10]

State and local Democrats, however, were not the only elected officials damaged by the new official corruption crackdown. In the first two years of the second Bush administration, a number of high-ranking Republican members of Congress came under DOJ scrutiny for everything from bribery to soliciting sex with minors. Indeed, these scandals became so numerous that by themselves they threatened Republican control of the House of Representatives, as fifteen Republicans had resigned, were under indictment, or under investigation on the eve of the 2006 midterm election. Democrats exploited the scandals, campaigning against an alleged Republican "culture of corruption."[11] They won big, regaining the House for the first time since 1994. Once in office, House Democrats began oversight investigations that brought increased attention to existing scandals involving illegal or unethical conduct by members of the Bush administration. In 2008, these scandals helped Democrats pick up twenty-one seats in the House and eight in the Senate, retaking the upper chamber. At the top of the ticket, Illinois senator Barack Obama made history and brought the post–civil rights period to a symbolic close, beating the Republican nominee,

Senator John McCain (R-Ariz.) and becoming the first African American president of the United States.[12]

Since the election of 2008, political warfare has increased to a fever pitch. Republicans and members of the conservative movement have organized voter-suppression campaigns directed at black Democratic voters, created phony scandals via the selective editing of video to attack liberal organizations and Democratic-controlled government agencies in the press, and used the newly created Office of Congressional Ethics to attack Democratic members of the House of Representatives. (The OCE, which was created in 2008 in response to the corruption scandals of the previous Congress, accepts allegations of misconduct against members of Congress from any source, reviews the allegations, and when appropriate, forwards recommendations for further investigation to the House Ethics Committee.)[13] Democrats have offered only a tepid response, attempting to smear select right-wing figures and the Tea Party, a lily-white conservative movement that arose in the wake of the 2008 Wall Street bailout and the inauguration of Barack Obama. News media have either facilitated or succumbed to the spread of these attacks. Scandal sells, and even when news organizations recognize they are being used as conduits in a campaign of political warfare, they have reported the stories for fear of being scooped or criticized for not covering an issue that has captured the public interest. Additionally, conservative talk radio, Fox News, and, most recently, a host of conservative Web sites and blogs have emerged as active agents in the struggle, acting as an "echo chamber" for Republican elected officials and conservatives, creating and popularizing the scandals themselves, or putting pressure on more-objective media outfits to cover their stories of choice. Liberals have hit back by creating an impressive array of "accuracy in media" research organizations that have branded these new conservative media as biased, and a less successful group of liberal media organs.[14]

Today's political warfare has its roots in the white backlash against the civil rights and Black Power movements and the Nixon administration's efforts to exploit that backlash in pursuit of a political realignment. And just as black elected officials and voters were at the center of these transformations in the 1960s and 1970s, they remained so in the 1980s, emerging as some of the primary targets of Republican political warfare and the earliest and most persistent critics of the Reagan administration's use of the official corruption crackdown as a partisan political tool. In the past two decades, as political warfare has spread to become the new norm, African Americans have remained at the heart of these struggles. Throughout the Clinton and George W. Bush years, when black elected officials experienced rates of investigation roughly equal to those of their white counterparts, black voters were targeted for wave after wave of Republican voter suppression campaigns.[15] Since 2008 black elected officials have again come under the microscope. Of the forty-eight members of Congress investigated by the OCE and the House Ethics Committee between 2008 and 2010, fourteen, or 29 percent, were African American. Additionally, Senator Roland Burris (D-Ill.), the only African American member of the upper chamber, was investigated by the Senate Ethics Committee for allegedly offering Illinois governor Rod Blagojavich (D) a bribe in return for being named to the Senate seat previously occupied by President Obama. During this period, African Americans constituted roughly 8 percent of the 535 members of Congress. This disparity is no coincidence. Eight of these fifteen black members' cases were fed into the investigatory process by right-wing legal organizations with roots in the Reagan administration and long track records of attacking black, labor, and Democratic political leadership. Most recently, in 2011, Judicial Watch, a conservative government watchdog organization with a long history of filing suit against Democratic lawmakers, has filed sexual harassment charges against Representative Alcee Hastings (D-Fla.) on behalf of a Republican staffer on the Helsinki Commission, which Hastings chaired until 2010. The lawsuit has since sparked an OCE investigation.[16] Additionally, many of the organizations targeted in right-wing media smear campaigns during this period have been majority African American or are associated primarily with African Americans in the public mind, namely, ACORN, the NAACP, and the DOJ Civil Rights Division.[17]

By placing black elected officials' allegations of harassment in context, I hope I have demonstrated their significance to the larger body politic. Black elected officials operate in this narrative as a metaphorical "miner's canary," warning us of the toxicity of modern U.S. politics. These black elected officials, Lani Guinier and Gerald Torres tell us, should not be sacrificed to state repression or political warfare in the belief that "when we sacrifice this canary, the only harm is to communities of color." Quite the contrary. "Others ignore problems that converge around racial minorities at their own peril," they assert, "for these problems are symptoms warning us that we are all at risk." Today national politics, and increasingly state and local politics, are a blood sport in which the two parties and affiliated partisan organizations engage in what *Politico* recently called "permanent, total war."[18] And this spreading partisan warfare has made it increasingly difficult for Americans to determine if their elected officials are indeed corrupt or are simply the targets of politics by other means. As Carl Rowan first noted in 1976, political factions' use of the state to repress the opposition make it impossible to "determine which officials are victims of conspiracies to deprive them of power and which ones are crooks who deserve the contempt of the . . . community." This dilemma, first put to African Americans more than thirty-five years ago, now faces the entire U.S. electorate. Black elected officials' efforts to combat harassment, both their successes and their failures, may inform us as we struggle with this difficult question today.

APPENDIX

State Scrutiny of Black Congresspeople, 1929–2010

SEVEN AFRICAN AMERICANS served in Congress between 1965 and 1968. Of that number, one, Adam Clayton Powell Jr. experienced every measured form of state scrutiny except an IRS audit or surveillance.[1]

Sixteen African Americans served in Congress between 1969 and 1972. Of that number, fourteen, Ronald Dellums, Charles Diggs, Shirley Chisholm, William Clay, George Collins, John Conyers, Walter Fauntroy, Augustus Hawkins, Ralph Metcalfe, Parren Mitchell, Adam Clayton Powell Jr., Robert Nix, Charles Rangel, and Louis Stokes, experienced some form of municipal, state, or federal surveillance or counterintelligence; one, Charles Diggs, was the target of political surveillance by the IRS.[2]

In the years 1973 to 1976, eighteen African Americans served in Congress. Five, William Clay, Louis Stokes, Shirley Chisholm, Ralph Metcalf, and Andrew Young, faced a municipal, state, or federal criminal investigation; one, William Clay, faced federal criminal indictment; three, Charles Rangel, Augustus Hawkins, and William Clay, experienced IRS surveillance or audit; three, Andrew Young, Barbara Jordan, and Parren Mitchell, experienced municipal, state, or federal surveillance and/or counterintelligence.[3]

Between 1977 and 1980, twenty-two African Americans served in Congress.

Of these, two, Charles Diggs and Edward Brooke, were targeted in congressional ethics investigations; two, Diggs and Brooke, were subject to municipal, state, or federal criminal investigation; one, Diggs, was indicted and subsequently convicted; and one, Charles Rangel, was subject to municipal, state, or federal surveillance and/or counterintelligence.[4]

During the first Reagan administration, twenty-three African Americans served in Congress. Of that number, two, Ronald Dellums and Edolphus Towns, experienced a municipal, state, or federal criminal investigation. Dellums was also the subject of an ethics investigation.[5]

Between 1985 and 1988, twenty-five African Americans served in Congress. Of that number, one, Gus Savage, was the subject of an ethics investigation; five, Parren Mitchell, Walter Fauntroy, Gus Savage, Harold Ford, and Floyd Flake, were the targets of municipal, state, or federal criminal investigations; one, Harold Ford, was indicted.[6]

Between 1989 and 1992, thirty African Americans served in Congress. Of these, two, Gus Savage and Charles Hayes, were subject to ethics investigations; eight, Walter Fauntroy, Harold Ford, William Gray, Mervyn Dymally, Gus Savage, Charles Hayes, Mike Espy and Floyd Flake, were targeted in municipal, state, or federal criminal investigations; two, Harold Ford and Floyd Flake, were indicted; one, Mervyn Dymally, was subject to municipal, state, or federal surveillance and/or counterintelligence.[7]

Between 1993 and 1996, forty-eight African Americans served in Congress. Of that number, one, Barbara Rose-Collins, faced a congressional ethics investigation; four, Carol Moseley Braun, Mel Reynolds, Walter Tucker, and Barbara Rose-Collins, were targeted in municipal, state, or federal criminal investigations; two, Reynolds and Tucker, were indicted and convicted; and one, Moseley Braun, was the subject of an IRS investigation.[8]

During the years 1997 to 2000, forty-three African Americans served in Congress. Of that number, two, Corrine Brown and Earl Hilliard, were subject to congressional ethics investigations; two, Earl Hilliard and Carol Moseley Braun, were the targets of a municipal, state, or federal criminal investigation.[9]

During the first George W. Bush administration, forty-five African Americans served in Congress. Of that number, two, William Lacy Clay and Frank Balance, were subject to municipal, state, or federal criminal investigation; Balance was indicted and convicted.[10]

Between 2005 and 2008, forty-nine African Americans served in Congress. Of that number, one, William Jefferson, was investigated by federal authorities. Jefferson was indicted and convicted.[11]

In the two years following the election of Barack Obama, forty-two African Americans served in Congress. Of that number, fourteen, Donald Payne, Maxine Waters, Laura Richardson, Donna Christian-Christianson, Carolyn

Cheeks Kilpatrick, Charles Rangel, Bennie Thompson, Gregory Meeks, John Conyers, Keith Ellison, Edolphus Towns, Sanford Bishop, Jesse Jackson Jr., and Roland Burris, were investigated by the House Ethics committee, the Senate Ethics committee, and/or the newly created OCE (House); two, Roland Burris and Jesse Jackson Jr., were the subjects of municipal, state, or federal criminal investigations.[12]

The graph reflects publicly available information on state scrutiny of sitting African American members of Congress between 1929, the first year an African American was seated in Congress in the twentieth century, and 2010. It is organized into four-year increments that overlap with different administrations, excluding 1929–65, when too few African Americans served in Congress to make such a division practicable, and 2008–10.

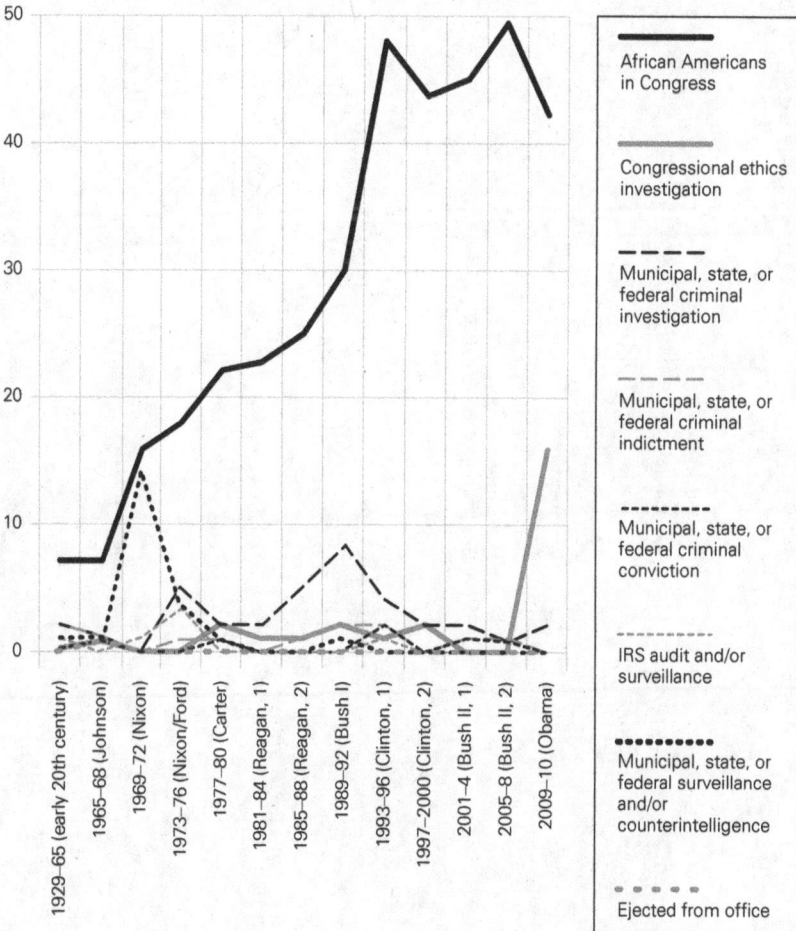

NOTES

INTRODUCTION. *"A Sense of History, Not Hysteria"*

1. Hooks, Ford, Flake, Arrington, Mitchell, Mueller, Donaldson, and Barr quoted from Cable News Network, *CNN Special Report,* June 19, 1991.

2. Manning Marable, *Race, Reform, and Rebellion: The Second Reconstruction in Black America, 1945–1990* (Jackson: University of Mississippi Press, 1991), 82. See also J. Morgan Kousser, *Colorblind Injustice: Minority Voting Rights and the Undoing of the Second Reconstruction* (Chapel Hill: University of North Carolina Press, 1999), 55.

3. Gerald David Jaynes and Robin Murphy Williams, *A Common Destiny: Blacks and American Society* (Washington, D.C.: National Academies Press, 1989), 238; David A. Bositis, *Black Elected Officials: A Statistical Summary, 2001* (Washington, D.C.: Joint Center for Political and Economic Studies, 2003), 5.

Using *Ebony* magazine's "List of 100 Most Influential Blacks by Institutional Affiliation," a nonscientific poll published annually between 1963 and 1991, political scientist Clarence Lusane outlined the impact of this transformation on the black leadership. Lusane notes that between 1963 and 1971, black elected officials rose from 9 percent to a list-leading 23 percent of the individuals named. In 1991, the year that the list was discontinued, elected officials had risen to 42 percent of the persons named. Although the mid-1990s resurgence of Black Nationalism and the co-optation of many black elected officials by the Democratic Party weakened their appeal among many African Americans, elected officials remained the dominant African American leadership group into the new millennium. Clarence Lusane, *African Americans at the Crossroads: The Restructuring of Black Leadership and the 1992 Elections* (Boston: South End Press, 1994), 24.

4. Benjamin Ginsberg and Martin Shefter, *Politics by Other Means: Politicians, Prosecutors and the Press from Watergate to Whitewater* (New York: W. W. Norton, 1999), 13–45.

5. Powell quoted from "15 Facts" reprinted in *Congressional Quarterly Almanac* (1967): 536–37.

6. Mary (Warner) Sawyer, *The Dilemma of Black Politics: A Report on the Harassment of Black Elected Officials* (Los Angeles: Report of the Committee on the Status of Minority Elected Officials, National Association of Human Rights Workers, 1977). In the late 1970s, Mary Sawyer went by her married name, Warner. She later reverted to her birth name, Sawyer. Although she published all her early articles and reports on harassment under the name Warner, for the sake of consistency I refer to her as Sawyer throughout the text. Mary Sawyer, *The Harassment of Black Elected Officials: Ten Years Later* (Washington, D.C.: Voter Education and Research Action, 1987).

7. See chapter 6.

8. Almost all the original research on harassment has come from black elected officials, their aides, or journalists. Those historians and political scientists who have used this original research to make claims about harassment are William Clay, *Just Permanent Interests: African Americans in Congress, 1870–1993* (New York: Amistad Press, 1992); James Jennings, *The Politics of Black Empowerment: The Transformation of Black Activism in Urban America* (Detroit: Wayne State University Press, 2001); Tyson King-Meadows and Thomas F. Schaller, *Devolution and Black State Legislators: Challenges and Choices in the Twenty-first Century* (Albany: State University of New York Press, 2006), quoted from 194; Clarence Lusane, *African Americans at the Crossroads: The Restructuring of Black Leadership and the 1992 Elections* (Boston: South End Press, 1994), 12–13; Clarence Lusane, *Pipe Dream Blues: Racism and the War on Drugs* (Boston: South End Press, 1991), 166–67; Manning Marable, "Foreword," in *The New Black Vote: Politics and Power in Four American Cities*, ed. Rod Bush, (San Francisco: Synthesis, 1984), 1–12; Marable, *Speaking Truth to Power: Essays on Race, Resistance, and Radicalism* (Boulder, Colo.: Westview Press, 1996), 27–33; Peter Phillips, *Censored, 1998: The News That Did Not Make the News* (New York: Seven Stories Press, 2003), 83–84; Bud Schultz and Ruth Schultz, *The Price of Dissent: Testimonies of Political Repression in America* (Berkeley: University of California Press, 2001), 250–64; Office of History and Preservation, Office of the Clerk, U.S. House of Representatives, *Black Americans in Congress, 1870–2007* (Washington, D.C.: U.S. Government Printing Office, 2008), quoted from 395.

For studies that treat allegations of harassment as "conspiracy theory," see Howard Gillette, *Between Justice and Beauty: Race, Planning, and the Failure of Urban Policy in Washington, D.C.* (Philadelphia: University of Pennsylvania Press, 2006), 201; Robert Smith and Richard Seltzer, *Contemporary Controversies and the American Racial Divide* (New York: Rowan and Littlefield, 2000), 89–90; Anita M. Waters, "Conspiracy Theories as Ethnosociologies: Explanation and Intention in African American Political Culture," *Journal of Black Studies* 28, no. 1 (September 1997): 112–25; Dinesh D'Souza, *The End of Racism: Principles for a Multiracial Society* (New York: Simon and Schuster, 1996), 489, quoted from 487.

9. Richard Hofstadter, *The Paranoid Style in American Politics and Other Essays* (New York: Vintage Books, 1967), 3–40.

10. Peter Knight, *Conspiracy Culture: From Kennedy to the X Files* (New York: Routledge, 2000), 1–22, quoted from 2.

11. Turner, *I Heard It through the Grapevine: Rumor in African American Culture* (Berkeley: University of California Press, 1994), 136. See also Knight, *Conspiracy Culture*, 143–67; and John Jackson, *Racial Paranoia: The Unintended Consequences of Political Correctness* (New York: Basic Books, 2008).

12. "Jackson Sees Pattern to Probes of Black Officials," *Los Angeles Times*, June 10, 1990.

13. Turner notes that "in the face of major institutional, social, and economic discrimination, African-Americans are most likely to fight back when presented with news that one identifiable, symbolically significant black individual's body has been ravaged by white racist aggression." *I Heard It through the Grapevine*, 136, quoted from 55–56.

14. Knight, *Conspiracy Culture*, 10–11, 149–53, 155–56.

15. See, for instance, Matt Bai, "Post-Race: Is Obama the End of Black Politics?" *New York Times Magazine*, August 6, 2008.

16. Ginsberg and Shefter, *Politics by Other Means*, 145.

17. Lani Guinier and Gerald Torres, *The Miner's Canary: Enlisting Race, Resisting Power, Transforming Democracy* (Cambridge, Mass.: Harvard University Press, 2002), 11.

CHAPTER ONE. *The White Backlash and the Roots of Harassment Ideology, 1965–1968*

1. Martin Luther King Jr., *A Testament of Hope: The Essential Writings and Speeches of Martin Luther King Jr.*, ed. James Melvin Washington, 555–57 (San Francisco: HarperSanFrancisco, 1991). For a concise discussion of the corresponding rise of the white backlash and Black Power, see Steven Lawson, *Civil Rights Crossroads: Nation, Community, and the Black Freedom Struggle* (Louisville: University of Kentucky Press, 2006), 105–6.

2. Taylor Branch notes that King was in the most intense stages of writing *Where Do We Go from Here?* in December 1966 through January 1967 when Julian Bond was seated in the Georgia legislature and Adam Clayton Powell was denied his seat in the U.S. House of Representatives. Taylor Branch, *At Canaan's Edge: America in the King Years, 1965–68* (New York: Simon and Schuster, 2006), 575–76.

3. King quoted from George R. Metcalf, *Up from Within: Today's New Black Leaders* (New York: McGraw Hill, 1971), 18.

4. Florence Murray, ed., *The Negro Handbook, 1946–47* (New York: Current Books, 1947), 308–10; Gerald David Jaynes and Robin Murphy Williams, *A Common Destiny: Blacks and American Society* (Washington, D.C.: National Academies Press, 1989), 238; Mervyn Dymally, preface, in *The Black Politician: His Struggle for Power*, ed. Mervyn Dymally, (Belmont, Calif.: Duxbury Press, 1977).

5. Steve Lawson, *Running for Freedom: Civil Rights and Politics in America since 1941* (New York: McGraw Hill, 1991), 131.

6. Harold Spaeth, *The Warren Court: Cases and Commentary* (San Francisco: Chandler, 1966), 86–113; "Court Reapportionment Decree Challenged," *Congressional Quarterly Almanac* (1965): 383–94.

7. Under the county-unit system, every county, regardless of population, had the same role in selecting statewide officers. Candidates for statewide office could therefore win by gaining a majority of the county-unit votes, despite loosing the popular vote. "Urban-Suburban-Rural Breakdown of All States and Districts," *Congressional Quarterly Almanac* (1964): 1175.

8. "Court Reapportionment Decree Challenged"; Leo Katcher, *Earl Warren: A Political Biography* (New York: McGraw Hill, 1967), 434. In 1960, 75 percent of the black population was urban. See John Preston Davis, ed., *The American Negro Reference Book* (Yonkers, N.Y.: Educational Heritage, 1966), 432–33.

9. *Toombs v. Fortson*, 205 F. Supp. 248 (N.D. Ga., 1962); *Toombs v. Fortson*, 241 F. Supp. 65 (N.D. Ga., 1965). The Supreme Court had already done away with the county-unit system in the case of *Gray v. Sanders*.

10. Reapportionment also gave greater representation to the majority-white suburban communities that ringed America's major cities, a development that would later reduce the political power of the cities and their black populations. See "Court Reapportionment Decree Challenged."

11. United States Commission on Civil Rights, *Political Participation* (Washington, D.C.: United States Commission on Civil Rights, 1968), 12.

12. Office of History and Preservation, Office of the Clerk, U.S. House of Representatives, *Black Americans in Congress, 1870–2007* (Washington D.C.: U.S. Government Printing Office, 2008), 452–55, 512–16; "Woodrow Wilson: Race, Community and Politics in Las Vegas, 1940s–1980s," University of Nevada Oral History Project, 1990, Nevada State Library and Archives, Carson City; Barbara Summers, *I Dream a World: Portraits of Black Women Who Changed America* (New York: Stewart, Tabori and Chang, 1999), 74–75; Chuck Stone, *Black Political Power in America* (New York: Delta Books, 1968), 12–13.

13. See Dan Carter, *The Politics of Rage: George Wallace, the Origins of the New Conservatism, and the Transformation of American Politics* (Baton Rouge: Louisiana State University Press, 1995), 195–225.

14. Ibid., 218. See also Robert Alan Goldberg, *Barry Goldwater* (New Haven, Conn.: Yale University Press, 1995), 196–97.

15. Taylor Branch, *Pillar of Fire: America in the King Years, 1963–65* (New York: Simon and Schuster, 1998), 403.

16. Goldberg, *Barry Goldwater*, 232–33.

17. The seven southern Democrats who lost in 1966 were Johnson supporters. See Andrew Busch, *Horses in Midstream: U.S. Midterm Elections and Their Consequences, 1894–1998* (Pittsburg: University of Pittsburg Press, 1999), 100–106.

18. James Patterson, *Grand Expectations: The United States, 1945–1974* (New York: Oxford University Press, 1996), 650; Branch, *At Canaan's Edge*, 548–50; Eastland quoted in Mary Dudziak, *Cold War Civil Rights: Race and the Image of American Democracy* (Princeton, N.J.: Princeton University Press, 2000), 242; Harvard Sitkoff, *The Struggle for Black Equality, 1954–1992* (New York: Hill and Wang, 1993), 211.

19. See John Neary, *Julian Bond, Black Rebel* (New York: William Morrow, 1971), 52–60; Roger Williams, *The Bonds* (New York: Athenaeum, 1972), 194–219.

20. Clayborne Carson, *In Struggle: SNCC and the Black Awakening of the 1960s* (Cambridge, Mass.: Harvard University Press, 1995), 166–68; Williams, *Bonds*, 216–17; Neary, *Julian Bond*, 75–82.

21. Neary, *Julian Bond*, 88–89.

22. SNCC press release, January 6, 1966, reprinted in Neary, *Julian Bond*, 90–91.

23. A lengthy transcript of the Spiva interview with Bond is reproduced in Neary, *Julian Bond*, 93–97.

24. "Rep. Bond Facing an Ouster Fight after Urging Draft Dodging," *Atlanta Constitution*, January 8, 1966; Bond quoted from Julian Bond, interview with Stanley Smith, January 22, 1968, RJB 133, pp. 67–68, Ralph Bunche Oral History of the Civil Rights Movement, Morland Springarn Collection, Howard University, Washington, D.C.

25. "Rep.-Elect Bond Facing an Ouster Fight after Urging Draft-Dodging," *Atlanta Constitution*, January 8, 1966; "Rights Leader Charges 'Murder' in Viet Nam," *Atlanta Journal*, January 7, 1966; Neary, *Julian Bond*, 103–8.

26. Sam Hopkins quoted in "House Petition to Delay Bond from Taking Seat as Assembly Convenes," *Atlanta Constitution*, January 10, 1966.

27. Williams, *Bonds*, 226.

28. Lane quoted from "Rep.-Elect Bond Facing an Ouster Fight." Recently, historians have begun to explore the ways in which segregationists used color-blind language to maintain systems of racial inequality, even segregation, before the post–civil rights period. Lane, Floyd, and Groover certainly fall into this category. See, for instance, Joseph Crespino, *In Search of Another Country: Mississippi and the Conservative Counterrevolution* (Princeton, N.J.: Princeton University Press, 2008).

29. Groover had also shown himself willing to use repression to blunt the growth of black political power. In 1960, Superior Court judge Oscar Long, encouraged by local white politicians fearful of the growing black vote, demanded a grand jury investigation of the "the Negro bloc vote" in Bibb County, which surrounded Macon. Groover acted as a witness for the prosecution, testifying that the Negro bloc vote, allegedly obtained through bribes by his opponent, had contributed to his 1956 and 1958 defeats. The grand jury investigation was later exposed, in the words of the racially moderate Bibb County sheriff James Wood as "a crude attempt at judicial intimidation of Negro voters and leaders," and no indictments ensued. Nonetheless, the investigation suppressed black voter turnout, allowing Groover to recapture his seat in 1962. He returned to the Georgia House determined to blunt the power of the African American vote. Within weeks of being sworn into office, Groover introduced and ushered through the legislature H.B. 117, a bill requiring that a candidate receive a majority of the popular vote in the primary and the general elections in order to win local or state office. Race neutral on its face, H.B. 117, blunted the power of organized minorities — in this case African Americans — to affect local and state elections. This new legislation aside, Macon's African American community again turned Groover out of office in 1964. See Morgan Kousser, *Colorblind Injustice: Minority Voting Rights and the Undoing of the Second Reconstruction* (Chapel Hill: University of North Carolina Press, 1999), 212–13, 215.

30. Howard Moore quoted in Neary, *Julian Bond*, 120–22.

31. Lane quoted in "Rep.-Elect Bond Facing an Ouster"; Bagby and Pafford quoted from Williams, *Bonds*, 229–30; Patterson expounded on Bagby's theory in "Here We Go on a Red Dog's Back," *Atlanta Constitution*, January 11, 1966; for other instances of segregationists blaming civil rights activists for their own repression, see Carter, *Politics of Rage*, 182–83, 223; Funk quoted in Metcalf, *Up from Within*, 165.

32. Starnes quoted from Williams, *Bonds*, 229. One of the two African American legislators who did not vote claimed that the automatic vote recorder did not register his selection. The other, Albert Thompson of Muskogee County, abstained. Representative Ben Brown (D-Atlanta), in a 1967 interview, argued that Thompson abstained because his county had a 4 to 1 white majority and he would not be reelected if he voted to seat Bond. Neary, *Julian Bond*, 122–24; Williams, *Bonds*, 230; Ben Brown interview with Robert Wright, RJB 27, p. 34, Ralph Bunche Oral History of the Civil Rights Movement, Morland Springarn Collection, Howard University, Washington, D.C.

33. Foreman quoted in "Bond Plans Court Fight if Necessary to Get Seat," *Atlanta Journal*, January 10, 1966; King quoted in "3 Man Court to Get Bond Case," *Atlanta Journal*, January 12, 1966; Pat Watters and Reese Cleghorn, *Climbing Jacobs's Ladder: The Arrival of Negroes in Southern Politics* (New York: Harcourt Brace and World, 1967), 319–20n14.

34. "3 Man Court to Get Bond Case," *Atlanta Journal*, January 12, 1966; "Troopers Repel Pickets Trying to Rush Capitol," *Atlanta Constitution*, January 15, 1966.

35. Though not covered by the Atlanta press, Bond's words were later reproduced in a full-page ad in the *New York Times* signed by twenty-four members of Congress (including five of the six sitting black members), a number of liberal celebrities, and the civil rights activists Martin Luther King Jr., Bayard Rustin, and A. Philip Randolph. See Citizens Committee for Julian Bond ad in the *New York Times*, January 20, 1966.

36. Williams, *Bonds*, 234.

37. Neary, *Julian Bond*, 146; Williams, *Bonds*, 233–34; Julian Bond, "Black Experiences in Politics," in *The Black Politician: His Struggle for Political Power*, ed. Mervyn Dymally, (Belmont, Calif.: Duxbury Press, 1971), 11–13.

38. *Julian Bond et al. v. James "Sloppy" Floyd et al.*, 87 U.S. (1966).

39. Bond quoted from Neary, *Julian Bond*, 140. Though some of the men who had worked to deny Bond his seat organized to give him the "silent treatment," he was seated without incident. Metcalf, *Up from Within*, 171–73.

40. Elmer J. Holland (D-Pa.), quoted in "Adam Clayton Powell Excluded from House; He Files Historic Lawsuit to Regain Seat," *Congressional Quarterly Almanac* (1968): 543.

41. Charles Hamilton, *Adam Clayton Powell Jr.: The Political Biography of an American Dilemma* (New York: Cooper Square Press, 2002), 41–69.

42. Ibid., 139–325.

43. Ibid., 249–57; Will Haygood, *King of the Cats: The Life and Times of Adam Clayton Powell Jr.* (New York: Houghton Mifflin, 1993), 143; "Adam Clayton Powell Excluded from House."

44. Jack Anderson, *Washington Exposé* (Washington, D.C.: Public Affairs Press, 1967), 60–61, 93–94.

45. Kenneth Clark, *Dark Ghetto: Dilemmas of Social Power* (Middletown, Conn.: Wesleyan University Press, 1965), 163.

46. "Builder Testifies Clayton Powell Borrowed $3,000," *New York Times*, September 28, 1954.

47. Hamilton, *Adam Clayton Powell Jr.*, 420.

48. During his first fifteen years in Congress, Powell had two shots at institutional power, both of which proved fleeting. In 1949–50, he served as chairman of the House Committee on Education and Labor, Special Subcommittee on the Fair Employment Practices Commission. This committee had little power beyond the subpoena, and the legislation it produced was quickly torpedoed by House conservatives. In January 1957, Powell's nine years of seniority placed him in line for a subcommittee chairmanship. In order to deny Powell such a position, Education and Labor Committee chairman Graham Barden (D-N.C.), a North Carolina conservative who did not mask his disdain for Powell, converted the five temporary subcommittees into permanent entities and reserved to the chairman the right to appoint subcommittee chairmen. Barden then denied Powell a subcommittee chairmanship. See Hamilton, *Adam Clayton Powell Jr.*, 278.

49. Democrats gained forty-nine seats in 1958, and Republicans picked up twenty-one seats. Many of these same members joined a liberal-sponsored push to enact ethics rules for members of Congress in 1963. The number of reform-minded freshman legislators would swell following the huge party gains and losses of 1964 and 1966. See Robert Remini, *The House: The History of the House of Representatives* (New York: HarperCollins, 2007), 383, 408–10, 413–15; "An Ethical Guide Sought for Congressional Behavior," *Congressional Quarterly Weekly*, June 7, 1967; Jonathan Schell, "Watergate," in *A History of Our Time: Readings in Postwar America*, ed. William Chafe and Harvard Sitkoff, (New York: Oxford University Press, 1983), 76.

50. Haygood, *King of the Cats*, 419; Hamilton, *Adam Clayton Powell Jr.*, 429–45.

51. Hamilton, *Adam Clayton Powell Jr.*, 411–15

52. "Key Developments in Dispute over Rep. Powell," *Congressional Quarterly Weekly*, March 1, 1963.

53. Ibid.

54. Ibid.

55. For the congressional response to these articles, see "Ethical Guide Sought for Congressional Behavior," *Congressional Quarterly Weekly*, June 7, 1963. The articles were later expanded into a 1967 book titled *Washington Exposé*.

56. Congressman Thomas B. Curtis (R-Mo.) quoted in Hamilton, *Adam Clayton Powell Jr.*, 418.

57. Notably, only Education and Labor Committee member Rep. James Roosevelt (D-Calif.) rose to defend Powell. Yet even this defense was half-hearted. Roosevelt identified Republicans' criticisms of Powell as an attempt to discredit the Johnson legislative agenda then being channeled through the Education and Labor Committee. "Key Developments in Dispute over Rep. Powell," *Congressional Quarterly Weekly*, March 1, 1963.

58. Ibid.; "House Cuts Powell, Patman Committee Funds," *Congressional Quarterly Weekly*, March 8, 1963.

59. "Controversies Surround Rep. Adam Clayton Powell," *Congressional Quarterly Almanac* (1967): 519. From this moment until March 1968, Powell would be in exile from his own congressional district, trading his time between Washington and his home in Bimini.

60. Hamilton, *Adam Clayton Powell Jr.*, 28; Adam Clayton Powell Jr., *Adam by Adam: The Autobiography of Adam Clayton Powell Jr.* (New York: Kensington, 1971), 208.

61. Andrew Jacobs, *The Powell Affair, Freedom minus One* (Indianapolis: Bobbs-Merrill, 1973), 64.

62. Report of the Committee on House Administration, Special Subcommittee on Contracts, H. Rep. 2349, 89th Cong., 2d sess., 1967. In a move that reinforced Powell's double-standard allegations, the committee concluded that Powell's misdeeds uncovered systematic flaws in congressional "accounting controls" and recommended that they be strengthened for all House committees.

63. "15 Facts," reprinted in *Congressional Quarterly Almanac* (1967), 536–37.

64. "McCormack Takes a Neutral Stand on Powell's Case," *New York Times*, January 6, 1967.

65. "Democrats Vote to Oust Powell as House Committee Chairman; He May Be Kept from Seat Today," *New York Times*, January 10, 1967.

66. Under House rules any member-elect may object to the swearing in of another member-elect. Such an objection forces the member-elect against whom it is registered to stand aside as the other members-elect are sworn in. The member in question may be sworn in or ejected later by way of a special resolution.

67. "House Roll-Call on the Powell Debate," *New York Times*, January 11, 1967; "Vote Is 364 to 64," *New York Times*, January 11, 1967; "Adam Clayton Powell Excluded from House; He Files Historic Lawsuit to Regain Seat," *Congressional Quarterly Almanac* (1968): 538.

68. House Resolution I, reprinted in Jacobs, *Powell Affair*, 237–38.

69. *Julian Bond et al. v. James "Sloppy" Floyd et al.*, 87 U.S. The House had excluded several members in its history. These cases of exclusion, however, were less legal guideposts than examples of majoritarian impositions on minority rights in the service of popular prejudice. Most were eventually overturned by the Supreme Court. See *Powell v. McCormack*, 395 U.S. 486 (1969).

70. *The Finding Conclusions, and Recommendations of the Select Committee, and the Additional Views of Congressman Conyers*, reprinted in Jacobs, *Powell Affair*, 249–56.

71. Celler, Conyers, Holland, and Teague quoted in *Congressional Quarterly Almanac* (1968), 533, 543. For further discussion of mail on the Powell issue, see also Jacobs, *Powell Affair*, 24, 36; Haygood, *King of the Cats*, 349.

72. "Powell Removal Favored," *Washington Post*, February 6, 1967.

73. The protesters had come to Washington via chartered bus from Harlem, Bedford-Stuyvesant, Philadelphia, and Baltimore. "Powell Backers Besiege Capitol," *New York Times*, January 11, 1967.

74. Hamilton, *Adam Clayton Powell*, 454.

75. Haygood, *King of the Cats*, 360.

76. Harry Jaffe and Tom Sherwood, *Dream City: Race, Power, and the Decline of Washington, D.C.* (New York: Simon and Schuster, 1994), 49.

77. Metcalf, *Up from Within*, 17–22

78. Jacobs, *Powell Affair*, 210, 214, 224.

79. Ibid., 215, 233–34.

80. Jacobs and Moore quoted in Jacobs, *Powell Affair*, 162, 173–74, 228–30.

81. Hamilton, *Adam Clayton Powell Jr.*, 464–68.

82. See *Powell v. McCormack*, 395 U.S.; and Haygood, *King of the Cats*, 387, 390.

83. Powell, *Adam by Adam*, 240; "Powell Prober May Face Same Music," *Washington Post*, September 30, 1970.

84. "Earnest Southerner, Lester Garfield Maddox," *New York Times*, September 30, 1966.

85. "Upheaval in the South: Maddox Victory Confirms Toughening of Resistance in Area to Negro Gains," *New York Times*, September 30, 1966; "Arnall Beaten by Segregationist in Georgia's Governor Primary," *New York Times*, September 29, 1966.

86. "Former Georgia Gov. Lester Maddox Dies," *Washington Post*, June 25, 2003.

87. "Conservative Coalition Shaped Major 1968 Bills," *Congressional Quarterly Almanac* (1969): 819–23; Steven Hayward, *The Age of Reagan: The Fall of the Old Liberal Order, 1964–1980* (New York: Random House, 2009), 127; Kevin Phillips, *The Emerging Republican Majority* (New Rochelle, N.J.: Arlington House, 1969), 36.

88. Phillips, *Emerging Republican Majority*, 462–64.

89. Goldberg, *Barry Goldwater*, 256.

CHAPTER TWO. *Black Elected Officials, White Resistance, and the Surveillance State, 1965–1974*

1. Huey Newton, *War against the Panthers: A Study of Repression in America* (New York: Harlem River Press, 1996), 8.

2. Manning Marable, *Race, Reform, and Rebellion: The Second Reconstruction in Black America, 1945–1990* (Jackson: University Press of Mississippi, 1991), 111–12; William Chafe, *The Unfinished Journey: America since World War II* (New York: Oxford University Press, 1995), 413.

3. For just a few of these scholarly studies and memoirs that deal with police and intelligence community repression of the Panthers, see Ward Churchill and Jim Vander Wall, *Agents of Repression: The FBI's Secret War against the Black Panther Party and the American Indian Movement* (Boston: South End Press, 1988); Churchill and Vander Wall, *The Cointelpro Papers: Documents from the FBI's Secret Wars* (Boston: South End Press, 1990); Charles Jones, ed., *The Black Panther Party Reconsidered* (Baltimore: Black Classic Press, 1998), 363–90 and 417–42; Huey Newton, *War against the Panthers: A Study of Repression in America* (New York: Harlem River Press, 1996); Kenneth O'Reilly, *Racial Matters: The FBI's Secret File on Black America, 1960–1972* (New York: Free Press, 1989); O'Reilly and David Gallen, eds., *Black Americans: The FBI Files* (New York: Carroll and Graf, 1994); Bobby Seale, *Seize the Time: The Story of the Black Panther Party and Huey P.*

Newton (Baltimore: Black Classic Press, 1991); Assata Shakur, *Assata: An Autobiography* (Westport, Conn.: L. Hill, 1987); Curtis J. Austin, *Up against the Wall: Violence in the Making and Unmaking of the Black Panther Party* (Little Rock: University of Arkansas Press, 2006).

4. The evidence of state repression of black elected officials presented in this chapter is, to a certain degree, anecdotal. In 1972, the Supreme Court ruled in the case of *Laird v. Tatum* that individuals adversely affected by state surveillance or counterintelligence could sue for damages if they could prove that their injuries were intentionally caused by authorities and that state surveillance or counterintelligence was conducted in violation of the targets' constitutional rights. The crucial piece of evidence in such cases would necessarily be intelligence dossiers and files. In response to *Laird v. Tatum*, many federal, state, and local police and intelligence outfits destroyed their intelligence files in order to shield themselves from suits by their targets. In so doing, they destroyed the historical record of much of the state crackdown on the liberal-Left of this period. This has made specific information on the police and intelligence community targeting of black elected officials difficult to find or incomplete. For a description of *Laird v. Tatum* and its effects, see Frank Donner, *Protectors of Privilege: Red Squads and Police Repression in Urban America* (Los Angeles: University of California Press, 1990), 347–48.

5. Steven Lawson, *Running for Freedom: Civil Rights and Black Power in America since 1941* (New York: McGraw Hill 1991), xi; Marable, *Race, Reform, and Rebellion*, 108. See also Tom Sugrue, *Sweet Land of Liberty: The Forgotten Struggle for Civil Rights in the North* (New York: Random House, 2008), 500–501, for a more recent iteration of this point.

6. See Marable, *Race, Reform, and Rebellion*, 119–20; Mary Sawyer, *The Dilemma of Black Politics: A Report on the Harassment of Black Elected Officials*, (Los Angeles: Report of the Committee on the Status of Minority Elected Officials, National Association of Human Rights Workers, 1977), 141.

7. Representative William Clay (D-Mo.), quoted in William Clay, *Just Permanent Interests: Black Americans in Congress, 1870–1991* (New York: Amistad Press, 1992), 126; Komozi Woodard, *A Nation within a Nation: Amiri Baraka (Leroi Jones) and Black Power Politics* (Chapel Hill: University of North Carolina Press, 1999), 159–218; "Black Officials Meet in D.C., Sen. Brooke Speaker," *Pittsburg Courier*, December 13, 1975.

8. Manning Marable, *Black American Politics: From the Washington Marches to Jesse Jackson* (New York: Verso, 1985), 172.

9. Robert Smith, *We Have No Leaders: African Americans in the Post–Civil Rights Era* (Albany: State University of New York Press, 1996), 6–8, 19–20. Recently, political scientist Cedric Johnson has provided a more nuanced view, noting that in the early 1970s, at least, the FBI made an "explicit differentiation" between "legitimate" and "extremist" black political leaders, often targeting the former for surveillance and the latter for counterintelligence. Cedric Johnson, *Revolutionaries to Race Leaders: Black Power and the Making of African American Politics* (Minneapolis: University of Minnesota Press, 2007), 100–101. Additionally, historian Devin Fergus has explored the ways in which the Nixon administration actively funded more-moderate Black Power activists willing to support the administration, even going so far as to pump millions of dollars into their develop-

ment projects at the very same time it was conducting an active campaign of repression against more-radical black activists and those who opposed the administration. Devin Fergus, *Liberalism, Black Power, and the Making of American Politics, 1965–1980* (Athens: University of Georgia Press, 2009).

10. Chuck Stone, *Black Political Power in America* (New York: Delta, 1970), 249.

11. Lawson, *Running for Freedom*, 136; Dan Carter, *The Politics of Rage: George Wallace, the Origins of the New Conservatism, and the Transformation of American Politics* (Baton Rouge: Louisiana State University Press, 1995), 287; Frances Fox Piven, Lorraine Minnite, and Margaret Groarke, *Keep Down the Black Vote: Race and the Demobilization of American Voters* (New York: New Press, 2009), 51–66; George Derek Musgrove, "Parren Mitchell," in *African American National Biography*, ed. Henry Louis Gates and Evelyn Brooks-Higginbotham, vol. 5 (New York: Oxford University Press, 2008).

12. Hancock whites did not always resort to repression. In cases where county blacks acted deferentially, they were met with co-optation or incorporation. This was the case for the African American county commissioner James Smith, who had also been elected in the 1966 election, and who also worked for the state. Smith regularly deferred to his white colleagues, even on matters that harmed his black constituents. Smith would also be forced to find alternative employment, but by county blacks. For discussions of the racial power struggle in Hancock County, see Lawrence Hanks, *The Struggle for Black Political Empowerment in Three Georgia Counties* (Knoxville: University of Tennessee Press, 1987); John Rozier, *Black Boss: Political Revolution in a Georgia County* (Athens: University of Georgia Press, 1982). Rozier's book, while the most detailed account of black political power in Hancock County, is troubled by two specific narrative frameworks. First, Rozier makes the case that black political power in Hancock was the product of John McCown, the "black boss" referenced in his title. The black community appears in this framework as a group of pliable followers. This view was prevalent in white reporters' articles on Hancock County, but it does not conform to the facts. Several local blacks ran for and were elected to office before McCown settled in Hancock. They created the political organization he later came to dominate. Second, Rozier, himself a Hancock County native, seeks to speak for the white minority of Hancock County. In so doing, he adopts many local whites' interpretations of events and their impressions of black leaders. As such, the only "reasonable" or "responsible" black leaders to emerge from Rozier's narrative are those who acquiesce to continued white control and reject an assertive, independent black politics.

13. Minion Morrison, *Black Political Mobilization: Leadership, Power, and Mass Behavior* (Albany: State University of New York Press, 1987), 84–93.

14. Bennie Thompson, interview with the author, Washington, D.C., November 14, 2001.

15. Amerson quoted in Sawyer, *Dilemma of Black Politics*, 119; Danielson, *After Freedom Summer: The Voting Rights Act and the Creation of Black Politics in Mississippi, 1965–1986* (Gainesville: University of Florida Press, 2011), 74–75, 90, 136; Lester Salamon, "Leadership and Modernization," *Journal of Politics* 35 (1973): 639. I am grateful to Christopher Danielson for bringing this important article to my attention.

16. Carl Stokes, *Promises of Power: A Political Autobiography* (New York: Simon and Schuster, 1973), 229.

17. Ibid., 154–64.

18. "U.S. Finds No Misdeed by Stokes," *Cleveland Press*, April 29, 1971.

19. Stokes, *Promises of Power*, 160–64, 229–31, 235–36, 244–47.

20. For discussions of local authorities' use of fraud allegations to undercut black efforts to gain political and economic self-determination, see, for example, J. Todd Moye, *Let the People Decide: Black Freedom and White Resistance Movements in Sunflower County, Mississippi, 1945–1986* (Chapel Hill: University of North Carolina Press, 2004); Emilye Crosby, *A Little Taste of Freedom: The Black Freedom Struggle in Claiborne County, Mississippi* (Chapel Hill: University of North Carolina Press, 2005); Kent Germany, "Poverty Wars in the Louisiana Delta," in *The War on Poverty: A New Grassroots History, 1964–1980*, ed. Annelise Orleck and Lisa Hazirjian (Athens: University of Georgia Press, 2011); Hasan Jeffries, *Bloody Lowndes: Civil Rights and Black Power in Alabama's Black Belt* (New York: New York University Press, 2009).

21. Just as these cases were about to go to trial in 1978, all but one of the defendants worked out plea agreements with the prosecution. The defendants claimed to have done so to avoid the legal costs of a prolonged court battle. The prosecution appears to have accepted the pleas both because John McCown, former county commissioner and director of the ECCO, who investigators believed had committed the majority of the fraud, had died in a plane crash, and because on the eve of the trial one of the primary prosecution witnesses changed critical parts of his testimony. Prosecutors scored their only conviction against former county commissioner Johnny Warren, who was found guilty of perjury. See Rozier, *Black Boss*.

22. Marable, *Race, Reform, and Rebellion*, 93; Terry H. Anderson, *The Movement and the Sixties* (New York: Oxford University Press, 1995), 333–37; Robert Justin Goldstein, *Political Repression in Modern America from 1870 to 1976* (Urbana: University of Illinois Press, 2001), 429–32.

23. O'Reilly, *Racial Matters*, 9–47, quoted from 12; Theodore Kornweibel, *Seeing Reds: Federal Campaigns against Black Militancy, 1919–1925* (Bloomington: Indiana University Press, 1998).

24. For the text of Hoover's memo requesting background information on Powell, see O'Reilly and Gallen, *Black Americans*, 265. For a discussion of Powell's announcement that he would seek the Twenty-second Congressional District seat from Harlem, see Charles Hamilton, *Adam Clayton Powell Jr.: The Political Biography of an American Dilemma* (New York: Cooper Square Press, 2002), 145–46. For a discussion of DOJ studies of congressional districts where blacks were emerging as a majority, and in particular DOJ reports on Harlem and Powell, see Will Haygood, *King of the Cats: The Life and times of Adam Clayton Powell Jr.* (New York: Houghton Mifflin, 1993), 91.

25. O'Reilly, *Racial Matters*, 126, 131, 132, 334.

26. Sawyer, *Dilemma of Black Politics*, 137.

27. Dellums quoted in Sawyer, *Dilemma of Black Politics*, 126. Dellums makes his allegations of FBI and phone company warrantless wiretapping in "Ron Dellums Alleges FBI Wiretapping," KQED, April 23, 1974, housed in the Digital Information Virtual Archive

at San Francisco State University. Dellums's suspicions cannot be confirmed because he refuses to order his FBI dossier.

28. Frank J. Donner, *The Age of Surveillance: The Aims and Methods of America's Political Intelligence System* (New York: Vintage Books, 1981), 152.

29. Bud Schultz and Ruth Schultz, *The Price of Dissent: Testimonies to Political Repression in America* (Berkeley: University of California Press, 2001), 252.

30. See Goldstein, *Political Repression in Modern America*, 449–60; Donner, *Age of Surveillance*, 477–86; Tom Sherwood and Harry Jaffe, *Dream City: Race, Power, and the Decline of Washington, D.C.* (New York: Simon and Schuster, 1994), 93; Sawyer, *Dilemma of Black Politics*, 125, 136–37, 130, 139–40.

31. Goldstein, *Political Repression in Modern America*, 504; Donner, *Protectors of Privilege*, 65–90, quoted from 67.

32. Donald Black and Albert Reiss, "Patterns of Behavior in Police and Citizen Transactions," in *Studies in Crime and Law Enforcement in Major Metropolitan Areas: A Report to the President's Commission on Law Enforcement and Administration of Justice*, Field Surveys III, vol. 2 (Washington, D.C.: U.S. Government Printing Office, 1967), 243.

33. Donner, *Protectors of Privilege*, 290–91.

34. Marable, *Black American Politics*, 185.

35. Donner, *Protectors of Privilege*, 67.

36. Ibid., 296; Goldstein, *Political Repression in Modern America*, 506; "Mayor Got Spy Reports," *Baltimore Sun*, January 15, 1975.

37. "Mayor Got Spy Reports"; "Top Cop Faces Enemies, Friends" *Baltimore Afro American*, June 10, 1978.

38. Yasuhiro Katagiri, *The Mississippi State Sovereignty Commission: Civil Rights and States Rights* (Jackson: University Press of Mississippi, 2001), 152, 217, 224–26. For all Mississippi cases, see Mississippi State Sovereignty Commission Records, Mississippi Department of Archives and History, at http://mdah.state.ms.us, accessed March 24, 2009. For the Alabama Peace Commission cases, see Sawyer, *Dilemma of Black Politics*, 119, 137, 153; Goldstein, *Political Repression in Modern America*, 506.

39. David Burnham, *A Law unto Itself: Power, Politics, and the IRS* (New York: Random House, 1989), 226–90; Donner, *Age of Surveillance*, 321–52; John Andrew, *Power to Destroy: The Political Uses of the IRS from Kennedy to Nixon* (Chicago: Ivan R. Dee, 2002), 138–65.

40. Schultz and Schultz, *Price of Dissent*, 255–56; Donner, *Age of Surveillance*, 252–53; O'Reilly, *Racial Matters*, 263. The Johnson White House regularly submitted the names of political opponents and supporters alike to the FBI for "background checks." O'Reilly is clear that the president's use of the FBI to uncover "derogatory information" about individuals was not aimed at blacks exclusively.

41. Donner, *Age of Surveillance*, 328.

42. Donner, *Age of Surveillance*, 336; Andrew, *Power to Destroy*, 290, 275; United States Senate, *Select Committee to Study Governmental Operations with Respect to Intelligence Activities*, vol. 3 (Washington: U.S. Government Printing Office, 1976), 10.

43. Donner, *Age of Surveillance*, 339–41; Andrew, *Power to Destroy*, 297–313.

44. Sawyer, *Dilemma of Black Politics*, 96–97.

45. Jason Berry, "The IRS Bullies the New South," *Nation*, March 6, 1976.

46. In 1968, Clemon founded the law firm of Adams and Clemon in Birmingham, Alabama. He and his partner, Oscar Adams Esq., specialized in job discrimination and school desegregation cases. The audits continued after Clemon's 1975 election to the Alabama Senate. Adams, a frequent legal representative for Martin Luther King Jr. and Fred Shuttlesworth in the early 1960s, was also audited repeatedly in the years after 1964. Berry, "IRS Bullies the New South"; Sawyer, *Dilemma of Black Politics*, 138, 140.

47. Johnson's defense, however, cost somewhere in the area of thirty-five thousand dollars, registering a net loss of twenty-nine thousand dollars.

48. See Sawyer, *Dilemma of Black Politics*, 130, 135–36, 139–40, 154, 162; Berry, "IRS Bullies the New South"; Carl Rowan, "Is There a Conspiracy against Black Leaders?" *Ebony*, January 1976.

The IRS's investigation of Johnson may have been a product of Operation Bird Dog. Operation Bird Dog was an Atlanta regional office investigation of people who attended the Mohammed Ali-Jerry Quarry fight in Atlanta. Agents selected targets based on the make and model of their cars and their dress. See United States Senate, *Report of the Select Committee to Study Government Operations with Respect to Intelligence Activities*, 87–89, 90–95; James Jennings, *The Politics of Black Empowerment: The Transformation of Black Activism in Urban America* (Detroit: Wayne State University Press, 2001), 131n38.

49. Berry, "IRS Bullies the New South."

50. Rangel first saw the allegations in an article in the Mississippi *Delta Democrat Times*. General Accounting Office, *Allegations That IRS Harassed Mississippi Civil Rights Activists Unsupported*, GGD-78-32 (January 27, 1978). See also Burnham, *Law unto Itself*, 268–69, for a summary of the report.

51. O'Reilly and then Nixon quoted in Kenneth O'Reilly, *Nixon's Piano: Presidents and Racial Politics from Washington to Clinton* (New York: Free Press, 1995), 280–81.

52. Jules Witchover, *White Knight: The Rise of Spiro Agnew* (New York: Random House, 1972), 359.

53. O'Reilly, *Nixon's Piano*, 322.

54. Goldstein, *Political Repression in Modern America*, 501–2; Andrew, *Power to Destroy*, 218.

55. "23 Blacks on White House 'Screw' List," *Baltimore Afro American*, July 7, 1973; Memo from Charles Colson to John Dean III, September 9, 1971, reprinted in "Watergate: Most Damaging Charges Yet by Dean," in *Watergate: Chronology of Crisis* (Washington, D.C.: Congressional Quarterly, 1974), 1:153.

56. Goldstein, *Political Repression in Modern America*, 484.

57. Bruce Schulman, *The Seventies: The Great Shift in American Culture, Society, and Politics* (New York: Free Press, 2001), 45; Goldstein, *Political Repression in Modern America*, 502; James Rosen, *The Strong Man: John Mitchell and the Secrets of Watergate* (New York: Doubleday, 2008), 286.

58. Carter, *Politics of Rage*, 449.

59. Postelection polls showed that four in every five southern Wallace voters and three in every five northern Wallace voters listed Nixon as their second choice. Dan Carter, *From George Wallace to Newt Gingrich: Race in the Conservative Counterrevolution, 1963–*

1994 (Baton Rouge: Louisiana State University Press, 1996), 35; Carter, *Politics of Rage*, 415–48.

60. James Patterson, *Grand Expectations: The United States, 1945–1974* (New York: Oxford University Press, 1996), 764–65.

61. The congresspeople who were placed on Nixon's enemies list were Ronald Dellums, Charles Diggs, Shirley Chisholm, William Clay, George Collins, John Conyers, Augustus Hawkins, Ralph Metcalfe, Parren Mitchell, Robert Nix, Charles Rangel, and Louis Stokes. See "23 Blacks on White House 'Screw' List." The congresspeople targeted for state and municipal intelligence unit surveillance were Shirley Chisholm, John Conyers, Barbara Jordan, Parren Mitchell, and Charlie Rangel. See note 35 above. Those targeted for federal surveillance were John Conyers, Charles Diggs, Walter Fauntroy, Augustus Hawkins, Barbara Jordan, Adam Clayton Powell Jr., and Andrew Young. For Young, see O'Reilly, *Nixon's Piano*, 347–48. The congresspeople who were investigated by the DOJ are William Clay, Ralph Metcalfe, Adam Clayton Powell Jr., and Charles Rangel. For Clay and Metcalfe, see Rowan, "Is There a Conspiracy?" and note 27 above; for Rangel, see Mary Sawyer, *The Harassment of Black Elected Officials: Ten Years Later* (Washington, D.C.: Voter Education and Research Action, 1987), 128.

62. See Robert H. Mast, ed., *Detroit Lives* (Philadelphia: Temple University Press, 1994), 169–70; for Dymally, see note 39 above; John Lewis with Michael D'Orso, *Walking with the Wind: A Memoir of the Movement* (New York: Houghton Mifflin Harcourt, 1999), 278–80; O'Reilly, *Racial Matters*, 303–4; for Thompson, see notes 13 and 37 above; Marable, *Black American Politics*, 224.

63. Chisholm quoted in Rowan, "Is There a Conspiracy?"

64. Marable, *Race, Reform, and Rebellion*, 131.

65. Goldstein, *Political Repression in Modern America*, 462.

66. "Last Two Guilty in Watergate Plot," *Washington Post*, January 31, 1973; Schulman, *Seventies*, 47.

67. Kathryn Olmstead, *Challenging the Secret Government: The Post-Watergate Investigation of the CIA and FBI* (Chapel Hill: University of North Carolina Press, 1996), 16.

68. "FBI Spied on Mrs. King, Abernathy and Others, Top Columnist Testifies," *Jet*, July 13, 1972, 20–22; "Caucus Holds 'Lawlessness' Hearings," *Jet*, July 20, 1972, 8–9; O'Reilly, *Racial Matters*, 348.

69. Olmstead, *Challenging the Secret Government*, 11–12, 36–37, 59–60; Andrew, *Power to Destroy*, 303; Donner, *Protectors of Privilege*, 345–57.

70. Frank Donner, *Age of Surveillance*, 452; Donner, *Protectors of Privilege*, 345–57; Maryland General Assembly, *Report to the Senate of Maryland by the Senate Investigating Committee Established Pursuant to Senate Resolutions 1 and 151 of the 1975 Maryland General Assembly* (December 31, 1975), 8–9.

71. Sean Wilentz, *The Age of Reagan: A History, 1974–2008* (New York: HarperCollins, 2008), 34; Carter quoted from William Shade and Ballard Campbell, eds., *American Presidential Campaigns and Elections*, vol. 3 (Armonk, N.Y.: Sharpe Reference, 2003), 932–33.

CHAPTER THREE. *Discovering "Harassment" in the Post-Watergate Period, 1975–1980*

1. Mary Sawyer, *The Dilemma of Black Politics: A Report on the Harassment of Black Elected Officials* (Los Angeles: Report of the Committee on the Status of Minority Elected Officials, National Association of Human Rights Workers, 1977), 10–11; handwritten notes of Mary Sawyer for the October 11, 1977, press conference, copy in possession of the author.

2. Handwritten notes of Mary Sawyer, George Brown, and Mervyn Dymally for the October 11, 1977, press conference, copies in possession of the author; Mervyn Dymally, interview with the author, Compton, California, January 8, 2001; "Black Officials in the Crossfire," *Black Enterprise*, December 1977.

3. Founded in 1947 as the National Association of Intergroup Relations Officials, the NAHRW functioned as a professional organization for human-relations specialists, producing training materials and providing networking opportunities for members. In 1975, the NAHRW — which had changed its name in 1970 — boasted a membership of about four hundred individuals and no paid staff. Hilary Poole, ed., *Human Rights: The Essential Reference* (Phoenix: Oryx Press, 1999), 171.

4. George Brown, Address to the Annual Conference of the National Association of Human Rights Workers, October 15, 1975, copy in possession of the author.

5. "Brown's Branding Linked to College Fraternity Initiation Rite," *Rocky Mountain News*, September 10, 1975; "Brown Explains Alabama Speech in 'Democrat,'" *Rocky Mountain News*, September 21, 1975. California lieutenant governor Mervyn Dymally (D), who attended the conference, described the effect of the speech on the gathering: "When George Brown gave this dramatic speech . . . I mean, you could drop a pin. . . . He became the instant hero." Dymally, interview.

6. Brown and Lamm quoted in "Governor to Brown: Set Story Straight," *Denver Post*, September 8, 1975; George Brown, interview with the author, Washington, D.C., August 2, 2002. See also "Brown's Branding Linked to College Fraternity Initiation Rite."

7. "State Probing $4,090 Travel Expense Billed by Brown," *Denver Post*, September 10, 1975; "Brown's Traveling Charged to State," *Rocky Mountain News*, September 10, 1975; Brown quoted in "DA Probe of Brown Sought," *Denver Post*, September 11, 1975.

8. Kathryn Olmstead, *Challenging the Secret Government: The Post-Watergate Investigation of the CIA and FBI* (Chapel Hill: University of North Carolina Press, 1996), 17.

9. Benjamin Ginsberg and Martin Shefter, *Politics by Other Means: Politicians, Prosecutors, and the Press from Watergate to Whitewater*, 3rd ed. (New York: W. W. Norton, 2002), 31–34. In his 1991 investigation of the role of the media in post-Watergate U.S. politics, Larry Sabato makes a similar point. See Larry Sabato, *Feeding Frenzy: How Attack Journalism Has Transformed American Politics* (New York: Free Press, 1991), 5–6.

10. Ginsberg and Shefter, *Politics by Other Means*, 26–39; Robert Remini, *The House: The History of the House of Representatives* (New York: HarperCollins, 2007), 420–56.

11. After Lamm ordered Tooley to investigate, Republicans called for a special counsel, claiming Tooley, a Democratic Party stalwart, was not impartial. Lamm ignored them, and Tooley convened a grand jury on September 11. "Brown Previously Failed to Mention Funds Owed to State," *Rocky Mountain News*, September 13, 1975; "State Probing $4,090 Travel Expense Billed by Brown"; "DA Probe of Brown Sought"; "Brown Promises to Repay State $4,090," *Rocky Mountain News*, September 11, 1975; "DA Gets Brown Case for Grand Jury Probe," *Rocky Mountain News*, September 12, 1975.

For a sampling of the media coverage of the Brown scandal, see "Dem Leaders Not Discussing Brown Actions," *Rocky Mountain News*, September 11, 1975; "DA Gets Brown Case for Grand Jury Probe"; "Nonpartisan Prosecutor Proposed," *Denver Post*, September 14, 1975; "GOP Chief Wants Tooley out of Brown Case," *Rocky Mountain News*, September 14, 1975.

12. "Coverage of Brown Criticized," *Denver Post*, September 14, 1975; "6 Blacks Attack Media on Brown Case," *Rocky Mountain News*, September 14, 1975; "'Rush to Judgment' of Brown Unfair — CU Regent Johnson," *Rocky Mountain News*, September 15, 1975; "Brown Receives Offer of NAACP Legal Aid," *Denver Post*, September 20, 1975; "NAACP Pledges Its Support to Brown," *Rocky Mountain News*, September 20, 1975.

13. White reporters had been banned from the meeting in question. In retaliation, Brown and later Sawyer claim, they had placed a sinister spin on the events inside. Sawyer, *Dilemma of Black Politics*, 56; Brown, interview.

14. Brown, interview.

15. C. Delores Tucker quoted in "Mrs. Tucker's Sweet Charity," *Philadelphia Inquirer*, February 20, 1975; "Mrs. Tucker's Fees: $22,000," *Philadelphia Inquirer*, February 22, 1975; "Mrs. Tucker Used Aides in Campaigns," *Philadelphia Inquirer*, February 24, 1975; "Shapp Asks Ethics Board to Rule on Tucker Case," *Philadelphia Inquirer*, February 28, 1975; "Ethics Board Ruled Well on Delores Tucker Case," *Philadelphia Inquirer*, May 3, 1975; "Tucker, Kane Confirmed by Pa. Senate," *Philadelphia Inquirer*, July 2, 1975. The Board of Ethics concluded that Tucker had only accepted honoraria from out-of-state NAACP branches and had not shown the Pennsylvania NAACP any special favor. Though technically legal, Tuckers actions were politically inadvisable as they created the appearance of impropriety. As such, her reaction to the investigation can be characterized as hyperbolic.

16. Sawyer, *Dilemma of Black Politics*, 143–44. The Lake County Democratic machine was indeed corrupt, and the Nixon DOJ had every reason to investigate its activities. Hatcher had run against the machine as a clean-government candidate and cracked down on vice in Gary once in office. Considering this, Brown had reason to question the U.S. attorney's actions. The U.S. attorney was, in essence, investigating the one government entity in Lake County determined to fight machine corruption. See James B. Lane, *City of the Century: A History of Gary, Indiana* (Bloomington: University of Indiana Press, 1978), 270–305; "Gary Probe Continues," *Chicago Tribune*, August 26, 1976.

Brown was not the only elected official to suspect that the DOJ investigation of the Hatcher administration was not in good faith. President Jimmy Carter believed so as well. See "Carter Says He Knew of Inquiry When He Offered Hatcher a Job," *New York Times*, December 3, 1978.

17. Dymally quoted in "Dymally Links Accusations to a 'Wave of Repression,'" *Los Angeles Times*, August 24, 1975. See also "Dymally Denies Charges, Indicates He'll Reply Later," *Los Angeles Times*, July 4, 1975; "Minority Aid Funds Misused by Dymally," *Los Angeles Times*, July 3, 1975; "Dymally Shows Cancelled Checks That Repaid Salary," *Los Angeles Times*, July 5, 1975; Sawyer, *Dilemma of Black Politics*, 76–78.

18. Oddly, during his September 18 speech, Brown does not include himself among the list of black elected officials who he claims were being "harassed," adding, "I am not accusing anyone of anything." By the end of the month, however, Brown had reversed course. See "NAACP Pledges Its Support to Brown."

19. "Denver Blacks Support Brown," *Chicago Defender*, September 27, 1975.

20. Brown, Address to the Annual Conference of the National Association of Human Rights Workers.

21. Mary Sawyer, interview with the author, Washington, D.C., October 3, 2000. Colorado State has since changed its name to the University of Northern Colorado at Greeley.

22. Ibid.

23. National Association of Human Rights Workers, "Minutes of the Board Meeting," October 16, 1975; Bill Jessup, letter to Mary Sawyer, October 29, 1975; Mary Sawyer, letter to Bill Jessup, November 19, 1975, all copies in possession of the author.

24. Following Brown's 1975 address to the NAHRW, Sawyer read Martin Luther King Jr.'s *Where Do We Go from Here: Chaos or Community?* She adopted King's argument that black voting and office-holding were the natural outgrowth of the civil rights movement. Taking King's thinking one step further, Sawyer came to believe that black elected officials were the vanguard of the New Left. See Sawyer, *Dilemma of Black Politics*, 8–9; Sawyer, interview, October 3, 2000.

25. Sawyer, letter to Bill Jessup, November 19, 1975. A more detailed description of the clearinghouse proposal is contained in Mary Sawyer, memo to NAHRW membership, January 12, 1976, copy in possession of the author.

26. Eddie Williams, letter to Mary Sawyer, November 14, 1975, copy in possession of the author; Sawyer, letter to Bill Jessup, November 21, 1975, copy in possession of the author; Eddie Williams, "Black Political Dynamics," *New York Amsterdam News*, December 3, 1975; "Black Officials Meet in D.C., Sen. Brooke Speaker," *Pittsburg Courier*, December 13, 1975.

27. Mary Sawyer, bulletin to NAHRW membership, January 12, 1976; Mary Sawyer, letter to Congressman Andrew Young, January 20, 1976, both copies in possession of the author. In 1991, the moderator of the panel, Maryland state senator Clarence Mitchell III, would cofound the Center for the Study of the Harassment of African Americans (CSHAA), an information clearinghouse and advocacy organization modeled on the CSMEO. See chapter 6.

28. Investigators noted that the ISD used similar tactics against Mitchell's brother, Baltimore city councilman Michael Mitchell (D), and his uncle, Congressman Parren Mitchell (D-Md.). Maryland General Assembly, Senate Investigating Committee Established Pursuant to Senate Resolutions 1 and 151 of the Maryland General Assembly,

Report to the Senate of Maryland, December 31, 1975. See also Sawyer, *Dilemma of Black Politics*, 136; "Mayor Got Spy Reports," *Baltimore Sun*, January 15, 1975.

29. See chapter 2.

30. Mary Sawyer, letter to Representative Andrew Young (D-Ga.).

31. Mary Sawyer, memo to NAHRW chapter chairpersons and clearinghouse participants, April 29, 1976; Mary Sawyer, CSMEO Quarterly Report to the NAHRW Board of Directors, October 5, 1976, both copies in possession of the author.

32. See Noliwe Rooks, *White Money/Black Power: The Surprising History of African American Studies and the Crisis of Race in Higher Education* (Boston: Beacon Press, 2006), 83–92; Mary Sawyer, "List of Grants Applied for and Received by the CSMEO," 1976, copy in possession of the author.

33. Batick Wine and Spirits Company was formed in 1969 as part of a "black capitalist" attempt to create a niche for African Americans in the California wine industry. Dymally was a cofounder and a member of the board of directors. Within a year, it became apparent that Batick would not be able to compete with more-established white-owned wine dealers. In an effort to turn a profit for investors, Batick was merged with Comprehensive Health Care Systems, a health care company seeking a "corporate shell," in February 1971. At this point, Dymally resigned from the board of directors and donated his $650 in company stock to charity, sighting a conflict of interest because of his position on the Senate Health and Welfare Committee. The *Los Angeles Times* demanded a Legislative Ethics Committee investigation, which was commenced only days after the publication of the articles. Following a three-month investigation, the California attorney general issued an opinion that Dymally had no conflict of interest and that the *Times* charges had no merit. See Sawyer, *Dilemma of Black Politics*, 70.

34. See "Campaign Fund Donations? Dymally Is Linked to Controversial Pharmacist," *Sacramento Bee*, September 10, 1976; "The View from Where I Sit," *Sacramento Bee*, November 3, 1976. For a summary of this story as Dymally told it to Sawyer, see Sawyer, *Dilemma of Black Politics*, 66–94.

35. Mary Sawyer, letter to NAHRW chapter chairpersons, July 1, 1976, copy in possession of the author.

36. The Joint Center for Political Studies provided the mailing list and paid for postage. Sawyer followed up the questionnaire with a series of interviews that summer. She paid for the trip, which she conducted via bus, with grants from the United Parcel Service and the Women's Division of the United Methodist Church. See Mary Sawyer, Annual Report, Committee on the Status of Minority Elected Officials, October 24, 1976; Mervyn Dymally, form letter to black elected officials requesting their participation in the CSMEO study, August 20, 1976, both copies in possession of the author.

37. Carl Rowan, *Breaking Barriers: A Memoir* (Boston: Little Brown, 1990), 288–307.

38. Carl Rowan, "Is There a Conspiracy against Black Leaders?" *Ebony*, January 1976.

39. Ibid.

40. Ibid.

41. Ibid.

42. "Letters to the Editor," *Ebony*, March 1976; "Letters to the Editor," *Ebony*, April 1976.

43. Robert Allen Goldberg, *Enemies Within: The Culture of Conspiracy in Modern America* (New Haven, Conn.: Yale University Press, 2001), 254–55.

44. Belief in government conspiracies saw a steady rise during this period. Popular skepticism of the Warren Commission Report (1964), which concluded that Lee Harvey Oswald had acted alone when he assassinated President John F. Kennedy, rose from an average of 50 percent of the population in the early 1970s to 80 percent by the early 1980s. James Patterson, *Restless Giant: The United States from Watergate to Bush v. Gore* (New York: Oxford University Press, 2005), 72–73.

45. Lana Stein, *St. Louis Politics: The Triumph of Tradition* (St. Louis: Missouri History Museum, 2002), 130–33; "Law and Order Upheld!" *St. Louis Globe Democrat*, October 25, 1963. See also Clarence Lang, *Grassroots at the Gateway: Class Politics and Black Freedom Struggle in St. Louis, 1936–75* (Ann Arbor: University of Michigan Press, 2009) for a discussion of the black freedom struggle in St Louis.

46. See "The Unrepresentative Mr. Clay," *St. Louis Globe Democrat*, July 12, 1974; "Clay's 'Staff Assistant' Also Defended Drug Traffic Kingpin," *St. Louis Globe Democrat*, July 24, 1974; "Gates, Supporter Report Threats," *St. Louis Globe Democrat*, July 26, 1974; "Shape Up or Ship Out, CORE Tells Clay," *St. Louis Globe Democrat*, August 1, 1974; "Feet of Clay" [illustration], *St. Louis Globe Democrat*, August 2, 1974; "Gates for Congress," *St. Louis Globe Democrat*, August 2, 1974; "Hoodlum Support for Clay," *St. Louis Globe Democrat*, August 5, 1974.

47. See Sawyer, *Dilemma of Black Politics*, 44; Rowan, "Is There a Conspiracy against Black Leaders?"

48. Representative William Clay (D-Mo.), "dear colleague" letter, undated, copy in possession of the author.

49. See "The Unrepresentative Mr. Clay"; "Clay's 'Staff Assistant' Also Defended Drug Traffic Kingpin"; "After Evading Reporters, Clay Denounces the Globe," *St. Louis Globe Democrat*, December 11, 1974; "City Policeman's Job with Clay Is under Investigation," *St. Louis Globe Democrat*, December 14–15, 1974; "Board to Discuss Discipline of Unauthorized Aide to Clay," *St. Louis Globe Democrat*, January 28, 1975; "FBI Turns Eye on Clay," *St. Louis Globe Democrat*, March 13, 1974; "U.S. Broadens Clay Inquiry; Clay Incensed," *St. Louis Globe Democrat*, April 24, 1975; "Possible Fraud in Clay Payroll Is under Investigation by U.S.," *St. Louis Globe Democrat*, July 18, 1975. For a concise treatment of this episode see Sawyer, *Dilemma of Black Politics*, 47–48.

50. "Clay Allegedly Present during Drug Dealing," *St. Louis Globe Democrat*, December 10, 1974; "Conley Case Goes to Jury," *St. Louis Post-Dispatch*, December 11, 1974; "U.S. Supports Use of Clay's Name in Trial," *St. Louis Globe Democrat*, January 29, 1975; "Clay Denies Allegations in Trial Brief," *St. Louis Globe Democrat*, January 30, 1975; "Secrecy Surrounds Clay Inquiry," *St. Louis Globe Democrat*, January 31, 1975.

51. Clay quoted from "Conspiracy between *Globe Democrat* and U.S. Attorney to Destroy Congressman Clay," press release from the office of William Clay to all black newspapers, undated, copy in possession of the author. The FBI investigation of Clay is detailed in "No Evidence of Drug Ties in Clay Inquiry," *St. Louis Post-Dispatch*, March

14, 1975. Eighty-four members of Congress signed a letter demanding that the attorney general resolve the matter by either pressing charges or exonerating Clay. The letter led to a meeting between Attorney General Levi, Representative Clay, Representative Louis Stokes, Representative Barbara Jordan, and House majority leader Thomas "Tip" O'Neill at which the congressional delegation requested an inquiry into the source of the allegations against Clay. It was only in the face of this pressure that Levi moved on the case and investigated the source of the accusations. Although Clay received a letter exonerating him, he was not informed of the results of the investigation into the source of the allegations against him. See Sawyer, *Dilemma of Black Politics*, 44–46; Rowan, "Is There a Conspiracy against Black Leaders?"

52. "Rep. Clay Cleared in Inquiry," *St. Louis Post-Dispatch*, August 11, 1975.

53. "How a Congressman Billed Government for Phony Travel," *Wall Street Journal*, March 23, 1976; "Clay Cites Errors for Double Claims on Travel Expenses," *Wall Street Journal*, March 24, 1976; "False Travel Expenses Net Some Congressmen Thousands of Dollars," *Wall Street Journal*, April 30, 1976; "Law Student Sues a Congressman," *Washington Post*, June 5, 1976; Clay quoted from "Conspiracy against Blacks?" *St. Louis Post-Dispatch*, May 24, 1976; Burke quoted from Sawyer, *Dilemma of Black Politics*, 53; "Rep. Clay Pays $1754 to Settle Dispute on Travel Expenses," *St. Louis Post-Dispatch*, October 28, 1976.

54. See "Firm Ordered to Produce Clay Records," *St. Louis Globe Democrat*, September 24, 1975; Internal Revenue Service, summons to Riggs National Bank in Washington D.C. requesting the tax records of William and Carol Clay, December 5, 1975, copy in possession of the author; "IRS Renews Efforts to Get Clay's Records," *St. Louis Post-Dispatch*, March 16, 1977; "Justice Department Agrees to End Tax Probe of Rep. Clay," *Washington Star*, July 12, 1977.

55. Sawyer, *Dilemma of Black Politics*, x, xii.

56. Ibid., 54–94, 128, 129.

57. Ibid., 124. As stated in chapter 2, this number was actually higher.

58. Ibid., 29–174.

59. Press release of the Committee on the Study of Minority Elected Officials, NAHRW, October 11, 1977, copy in possession of the author. I quote the press release here because it is the most concise statement of the tactics of harassment compiled by Sawyer.

60. Sawyer, *Dilemma of Black Politics*, 6–7.

61. Ibid., 10–11.

62. Ibid., 4–5.

63. Ibid., 132, 149, 161, 165.

64. Like Rowan before her, Sawyer was willing to concede that "there are undoubtedly some Black officials who are corrupt." "Where such corruption does exist," she writes "no excuse is offered." She went on, however, to reveal that her methodology made no room for evidence of that corruption, arguing that because of this country's history of racism "Black officials cannot legitimately be charged with the same irresponsibility, as can white officials. Yet they are being attacked." Sawyer, *Dilemma of Black Politics*, 32.

65. Ibid., 14, emphasis in original.

66. Mary Sawyer, "The List of Fallen Black Leaders," *Sepia*, February 1978.

67. Ibid., 256.

68. The People's Temple founder and pastor, Rev. Jim Jones, was a political ally of Lieutenant Governor Dymally. Though Jones and the People's Temple would become infamous for the 1978 mass suicide at their compound in Guyana, in 1977 they were still understood as a positive force in San Francisco politics, and most of the city's leading liberal politicians maintained close ties to the church. See Manning Marable, *Race, Reform, and Rebellion: The Second Reconstruction in Black American, 1945–1990* (Jackson: University of Mississippi Press, 1991), 161–63.

69. "Black Officials in the Crossfire," *Black Enterprise*, December 1977; "Blacks Say Whites Cause Harassment and Racism," *New York Times*, October 12, 1977; "Dymally Sees News Media 'Conspiracy,'" *Los Angeles Times*, October 12, 1977. The *Atlanta Journal* and the *Atlanta Constitution*, more regional than national dailies, also published an article that mentioned *Dilemma* in their combined Sunday edition. Unlike the articles above, the *Journal and Constitution* article focused on the activities of a local group that cited the report as justification for their activities. See "Black Study Echoes Claims of Bias in the News," *Atlanta Journal and Constitution*, November 27, 1977. Sawyer also describes the response of the white press in Mary Sawyer, Quarterly Report of the Committee on the Status of Minority Elected Officials, October 14, 1977; and Sawyer, Quarterly Report of the Committee on Black Leadership, February 25, 1978, both copies in possession of the author.

70. "New Witch Hunt," *Paso Robles (Calif.) Press*, October 19, 1977; "Non-existent Conspiracy," *Oceanside (Calif.) Blade Tribune*, October 18, 1977; "Prove It Doesn't Exist," *Riverside (Calif.) Daily Express*, October 14, 1977.

71. Sawyer, Quarterly Report, February 25, 1978; "Suggests Media Conspire to Discredit Black Officials," *Jet*, November 3, 1977; Sawyer, "List of Fallen Black Leaders"; "Black Officials in the Crossfire," *Black Enterprise*, December 1977.

72. "Black Study Echoes Claims of Bias in the News," *Atlanta Journal and Constitution*, November 27, 1977; "NBC/LEO Expresses Concern for Black Leaders," *Focus*, June–July 1978. Starks first heard of harassment in December 1977 at a panel discussion titled "The Media and Black Elected Officials" held at the NBC-LEO annual conference in San Francisco, California. Sawyer had been invited to sit on the panel by then-NBC-LEO president Maynard Jackson (D-Atlanta), who is featured in *Dilemma*.

73. "Black Mayors to Check FBI Harassment Charge," *Sacramento Bee*, August 28, 1978.

74. Cooper had been indicted on June 7 by a federal grand jury for allegedly receiving several thousand dollars in kickbacks from a firm contracted to perform water-drainage services for his city. At the time of the meeting, he was awaiting trial. Cooper was later acquitted but declined to run for reelection, citing the investigation. Mary Sawyer, "Harassment of Black Elected Officials," *Journal of Intergroup Relations* 18, no. 3 (1991): 4, 29, 23n1.

75. "Southern Report," *Minority News Digest*, September 4, 1978.

76. Kenyon Burke, "Black Officials under Fire," *Observer Newspapers*, June 8–14, 1978; Roy Wilkins, "Political Harassment," *Indianapolis Star*, July 10, 1978; Benjamin Hooks "Political Harassment," *Sacramento Bee*, August 24–30, 1978.

77. Mary Sawyer, letter to Pamela Douglass, July 16, 1979, copy in possession of the author; "NAACP Gears Up to Battle 1970s-Style 'Reverse' Bus Boycott," *Jet*, July 19, 1979.

78. Mary Sawyer, Quarterly Report, February 25, 1978.

79. Mark Grossman, *Political Corruption in America: An Encyclopedia of Scandals, Power, and Greed* (Santa Barbara, Calif.: ABC-CLIO, 2003), 99–100.

80. "Censure of Rep. Diggs," *Congressional Quarterly Almanac* (1979): 561–66.

81. Ibid.

82. "Diggs' Removal from Hill Posts Is Pushed by Pa. Congressman," *Washington Post*, April 12, 1978; "Censure of Rep. Diggs," *Congressional Quarterly Almanac* (1979): 561–66; "Ethics and Criminal Prosecutions," *Congressional Quarterly Almanac*, 4th ed. (1991): 778.

83. "Senator Edward Brooke," *Congressional Quarterly Almanac* (1978): 858. The following spring, in its March 1979 report, the Senate Ethics Committee concluded that the discrepancies citied in news reports could have been the result of sloppy bookkeeping and determined them too minor to warrant punishment. "Brooke Ethics Decision," *Congressional Quarterly Almanac* (1979): 593.

84. "Political Harassment," *Indianapolis Star*, July 10, 1978.

85. "Harassing Black Politicians," *Gary (Ind.) Informer*, August 24, 1978.

86. Herschelle Sullivan Challenor, "Is Charles Diggs a Victim of Selective Justice?" *Encore American and World News*, April 2, 1979. For a description of the Hastings indictment, see "Indictments — a Grand Congressional Tradition since 1798," *Los Angeles Times*, June 8, 1994.

87. "The Charles Diggs Case," *Africa*, no. 82 (June 1978): 87–90.

88. "Indictments — a Grand Congressional Tradition since 1798."

89. Biden quoted in Edward Brooke, *Bridging the Divide: My Life* (New Brunswick, N.J.: Rutgers University Press, 2007), 255.

90. Mary Sawyer, letter to Charles Diggs, July 9, 1978; Sawyer, letter to Edward Brooke, July 9, 1978, both copies in possession of the author.

91. Sawyer had changed the name in late 1977 to reflect the committee's focus on black elected officials. Sawyer, Quarterly Report, October 14, 1977.

92. Mary Sawyer, interview with the author, Washington, D.C., March 3, 2000; Mary Sawyer, *The Harassment of African American Elected Officials: Ten Years Later* (Washington, D.C.: Voter Education Research Action, Inc., 1987), 8–9.

93. Mervyn Dymally, letter to George Brown, July 3, 1978, copy in possession of the author.

94. In 1980, after four years of being investigated for unspecified illegal activities in office, Dymally was cleared of any wrongdoing by a grand jury, and the FBI dropped the investigation. See letter from United States Attorney, Central District of California, Andrea Sheridan Ordin to Attorney for Mervyn Dymally, Edward L. Masry, Esq., January 10, 1980, copy in possession of the author. Soon after the FBI dropped the investigation, the *Los Angeles Times* printed a minuscule article on p. 28 acknowledging that one of its reporters had set in motion the events that led to Dymally's 1978 electoral defeat. See "Query Led to False Report on Dymally," *Los Angeles Times*, October 15, 1980.

95. "Curb's Charge Stems from Prober's Memo," *Los Angeles Times*, November 2, 1978;

"Michael Franchetti, 64; Financial Advisor to Former Gov. Deukmejian," *Los Angeles Times*, February 22, 2007.

96. "Michael Franchetti, 64"; "Dymally Assails Younger on FBI Remarks," *Los Angeles Times*, October 13, 1978.

97. Curb and Younger quoted from "Curb Asserts Belief Dymally Is Guilty," *Los Angeles Times*, October 31, 1978.

98. "Dymally's Attorneys Seek Slander Probe," *Los Angeles Times*, November 2, 1978.

99. Dymally states that the FBI called these clients to gather information for its investigation. The calls had the effect, he argues, of frightening the clients away. Dymally quoted in Bud Schultz and Ruth Schultz, *The Price of Dissent: Testimonies to Political Repression in America* (Berkeley: University of California Press, 2001), 262.

100. Neither Brown nor Dymally directed public funds to the CSMEO or the CSBL. Rather, each lent the prestige of his office to Sawyer's efforts, and Dymally provided Sawyer with employment in his office from 1976 to 1978. Because Sawyer was the most active member of the CSMEO and the CSBL and often donated a fraction of her earnings to its operating budget, any provision made for her employment essentially subsidized the committee.

101. Mary Sawyer, letter to Larry Groth, August 3, 1979, copy in possession of the author.

102. See Mary Sawyer, letter to Benjamin Hooks, May 16, 1978; Mary Sawyer, letter to Joseph E. Lowery, December 19, 1978; Mary Sawyer, letter to Barbara Williams, December 4, 1978, all copies in possession of the author.

103. Mary Sawyer, Annual Report of the Committee on the Status of Black Leadership, October 12, 1979, copy in possession of the author.

104. Mary Sawyer, handwritten notes, NAHRW meeting of the board of directors, October 16, 1979, copy in possession of the author.

CHAPTER FOUR. *Prosecution as Political Warfare in the Reagan and Bush Years, 1981–1992*

1. Between 1970 and 1972, Leuci had worked undercover as a government informant for the Knapp Commission, a investigatory body established by Mayor John Lindsay to address NYPD corruption. Leuci, however, had held out on his government handlers, concealing his own crimes, protecting many of his accomplices, and in the process, threatening many of the prosecutions in which he had acted as a witness. Giuliani convinced Leuci to come clean and implicate a significant number of his former colleagues in corruption. Although a majority of the cases had already been tried by the time Giuliani inherited Leuci, *Prince of the City* gave him credit for all the corruption prosecutions that arose from the Leuci undercover operation, a credit that the ambitious young prosecutor gladly accepted. Wayne Barrett, *Rudy: An Investigative Biography of Rudolph Giuliani* (New York: Basic Books, 2000), 77–83.

2. Ronald Brownstein and Nina Easton, *Reagan's Ruling Class: Portraits of the President's Top 100 Officials* (Washington, D.C.: Presidential Accountability Group, 1982), 376.

3. Typically the deputy attorney general sets policy for the DOJ Criminal Division, which handles official corruption investigations. In 1981, however, Attorney General William French Smith gave this assignment to Associate Attorney General Giuliani because he had experience as a prosecutor, while Deputy Attorney General Edward Schmults, a corporate lawyer, did not. Ibid.

4. Beth A. Rosenson, *The Shadowlands of Conduct: Ethics and State Politics* (Washington, D.C., Georgetown University Press, 2005), 57–114.

5. Thomas Edsall and Mary Edsall, *Chain Reaction: The Impact of Race, Rights, and Taxes on American Politics* (New York: W. W. Norton, 1992), 185. Giuliani biographer Wayne Barrett highlights a number of instances in which Giuliani's political allegiances and ambition determined the manner in which he pursued allegations of official corruption. Barrett, *Rudy*, 107–10, 124, 137–38, 213–15.

6. I borrow this insight from Ginsberg and Schefter. See Benjamin Ginsberg and Martin Schefter, *Politics by Other Means: Politicians, Prosecutors, and the Press from Watergate to Whitewater*, 3rd ed. (New York: W. W. Norton, 2002), 103.

7. "Ethics and Criminal Prosecutions," *Congressional Quarterly Almanac* (1991): 785–809; Ginsberg and Shefter, *Politics by Other Means*, 24–28; James Crockett, *Operation Pretense: The FBI's Sting on County Corruption in Mississippi* (Jackson: University Press of Mississippi, 2003), 8–9; Mary Fischer, "The Witch Hunt," *GQ Magazine*, December 1993; and David Burnham, *Above the Law: Secret Deals, Political Fixes, and Other Misadventures of the U.S. Department of Justice* (New York: Scribner, 1996), 335. The independent counsel portion of the ethics-in-government law, which was subject to renewal every five years, was allowed to lapse in 1999. Congress and the attorney general, however, can still appoint special counsels on an interim basis. "U.S. Prosecution of State and Local Officials for Political Corruption: Is the Bureaucracy out of Control in a High-Stakes Operation involving the Constitutional System?" *Publius* 17, no. 3 (Summer 1987): 195–230, here 199.

8. Ginsberg and Schefter, *Politics by Other Means*, 14, 21, 36–37, 49–80.

9. The DOJ does not keep statistics noting the race or party affiliation of individuals subject to investigation or prosecution. Outside studies reveal a partisan disparity. Arnold J. Heidenheimer, Michael Johnston, and Victor T. Levine, *Political Corruption: A Handbook* (New Brunswick, N.J.: Transaction Books, 1990), 583–84; Kenneth Meier and Thomas Holbrook, "I Seen My Opportunities and I Took 'Em," *Journal of Politics* 54, no. 1 (February 1992): 149–51; "Indictments — a Grand Congressional Tradition since 1798," *Los Angeles Times*, June 8, 1994.

10. United States Senate, Committee on the Judiciary, *Final Report of the Select Committee to Study Undercover Activities and Components of the Department of Justice to the U.S. Senate*, 97th Cong., 2nd sess., rep. 97-682; "Drug Probes on Capitol Hill End Quietly; Investigation Cost $2 Million, Involved 1,400 Allegations, Resulted in 6 Prosecutions," *Washington Post*, January 15, 1984; "House Plans 2 Reports on Post Office Scandal," *New York Times*, July 22, 1992; "As Casualty List Grows, G.O.P. Shows Doubts about House Bank Scandal," *New York Times*, April 16, 1992; "Congress' Bad Apples Problem: A Blight That's Nothing New," *Congressional Quarterly Weekly*, June 4, 1994, 1451.

11. "Scandals Cast New Light on Statehouse Ethics," *Washington Post*, February 24, 1991; "AzScam Isn't the Only Sting Going Down," *Arizona Daily Star*, March 12, 1991; "Why Mitch McConnell Should Know Better," *Washington Monthly*, October 1, 1997; "S.C. Sting Snares Dozens," *Atlanta Constitution*, April 15, 1992.

12. "Seven Lawmakers in Arizona Indicted in Corruption Inquiry," *New York Times*, February 6, 1991; "Home from the War and You Can Barely See Alan Stephens' AZCAM Scars," *Phoenix New Times*, April 17, 1991.

13. See "Chicago Corruption Probe Yields Indictment of 7 Men; 2 Aldermen among Those Named in Bribery Charges," *Washington Post*, November 22, 1986; "The Spy Who Came in Cold to D.C. Contracting," *Washington Post*, June 14, 1987; "U.S. Prosecution of State and Local Officials for Political Corruption System."

14. The number of impeachments registered during the Reagan and Bush years is a startling increase over previous periods in U.S. history. In the 194 years before Reagan took office, only ten federal judges had been impeached. Mark Curriden, "Selective Prosecution: Are Black Elected Officials Targets?" *ABA Journal* 78 (February 1992): 54–60. Burnham states that six federal judges were indicted by federal prosecutors between 1981 and 1992. The author can account for only five. Burnham, *Above the Law*, 328.

15. "FBI Sting Nets 44 in New York," *Washington Post*, August 11, 1987; U.S. Lists Corruption Suspects, *New York Times*, August 12, 1987; Crockett, *Operation Pretense*, xi.

16. Ronald Walters, *White Nationalism, Black Interests: Conservative Public Policy and the Black Community* (Detroit: Wayne State University Press, 2003), 22–37; James Patterson, *Restless Giant: The United States from Watergate to Bush v. Gore* (New York: Oxford University Press, 2005), 108–51; Manning Marable, *Race, Reform, Rebellion: The Second Reconstruction in Black America, 1945–1990* (Jackson: University of Mississippi Press, 1991), 175–76, 188–93, Jackson quoted from 178; Edsall and Edsall, *Chain Reaction*, 102–3.

17. Garry Wills, *Reagan's America: Innocents at Home* (New York: Penguin Books, 1987), 332–43; Edsall and Edsall, *Chain Reaction*, 138.

18. Joseph Crespino, *In Search of Another Country: Mississippi and the Conservative Counterrevolution* (Princeton, N.J.: Princeton University Press, 2007), 1; Kiron Skinner, Serhiy Kudelia, Bruce Bueno de Mesquita, and Condoleeza Rice, *The Strategy of Campaigning: Lessons from Ronald Reagan and Boris Yeltsin* (Ann Arbor: University of Michigan Press, 2007), 102, 132–34. For the text of the speech in which Reagan proclaims his support for "states' rights," and a description of the event, see "Ronald Reagan Speaks at Fair Sunday," *Philadelphia (Miss.) Neshoba Democrat*, August 7, 1980. One of Reagan's favorite parables during the campaign was the story of a "welfare queen" in Chicago who was drawing between $50,000 and $150,000 in tax-free income — historian Kenneth O'Reilly notes that the figure was inflated with each telling — from welfare and other federal programs. The (Democratic) liberal state, Reagan argued, was funding this woman's carefree lifestyle while hard-working (white) Americans footed the bill. In actuality, the woman in question, Linda Taylor, had been convicted in 1977 for fraudulently collecting $8,000 in public aid. This mattered little. Reagan continued to repeat the story well into his first term not for its accuracy but because it communicated what he believed to be an

essential truth about the New Deal state. See Kenneth O'Reilly, *Nixon's Piano: Presidents and Racial Politics from Washington to Clinton* (New York: Free Press, 1995), 360–78.

19. "Reagan Buries Carter in Landslide," *Congressional Quarterly Weekly*, November 8, 1980; William G. Shade and Ballard C. Campbell, eds., *American Presidential Campaigns and Elections* (Armonk, N.Y.: Sharpe Reference, 2003), 3:951. Although exit polls show that the majority of Democrats and independents who voted for the former California governor did so in protest of the Carter administration's failed economic and foreign policies, those same polls show that a substantial number voted *for* Reagan's racial policies. Edsall and Edsall, *Chain Reaction*, 164.

20. Shade and Campbell, *American Presidential Campaigns and Elections*, 3:950–51.

21. Brock and Meese quoted in "Reagan Buoyed by National Swing to Right; Position Bolstered by G.O.P.," *New York Times*, November 6, 1980.

22. Raymond Wolters, *Right Turn: William Bradford Reynolds, the Reagan Administration, and Black Civil Rights* (New Brunswick, N.J.: Transaction Books, 1996), 7; Marable, *Race, Reform, and Rebellion*, 197–200; William Chafe, *The Unfinished Journey: America since World War II* (New York: Oxford University Press 2007), 453. See also Walters, *White Nationalism, Black Interests*.

23. Manning Marable, *Black American Politics: From the Washington Marches to Jesse Jackson* (New York: Verso, 1985), 294; Marable, *Race, Reform, and Rebellion*, 185–220. Fauntroy and the NBLR were also pivotal in electing Michael Espy (D-Miss.), Floyd Flake (D-N.Y.), and John Lewis (D-Ga.) to the House. Espy and Lewis were the first African Americans to represent their respective states in Congress since Reconstruction. African American candidates Faye Williams (Louisiana) and Bobby Scott (Virginia) made strong showings, losing by only the narrowest of margins. "Celebrating Black Margins of Victory," *Washington Post*, November 6, 1986.

24. Fischer, "Witch Hunt." In the late 1980s and 1990s a combined total of over six hundred black and Latino FBI agents won separate class-action lawsuits alleging discrimination in hiring and promotion. In both cases the bureau was forced to overhaul its training and promotion programs. Many white agents reacted to the settlements by filing a bevy of "reverse discrimination" claims to the EEOC — 50 percent of all claims in 1992 and 1993. None of the claims were found to be true. George Derek Musgrove, "The Desegregation of the United States Intelligence Community, 1993–2002," in *REACH* (Washington, D.C.: Congressional Black Caucus Foundation, 2004), 9–15.

25. "Black Officials: Probes and Prejudice; Is There a Double Standard for Bringing Indictments?" *Washington Post*, February 28, 1988.

26. The black members of Congress investigated by the DOJ between 1981 and 1992 are Ronald Dellums, Parren Mitchell, Walter Fauntroy, Harold Ford, Gus Savage, Edolphus Towns, Floyd Flake, William Gray III, Mervyn Dymally, and Charles Hayes. Only Ford and Flake were indicted. See "Drug Use by Dellums Alleged to Grand Jury," *Washington Post*, March 16, 1983; "Parren Is Furious over Bribe Reports," *Baltimore Afro American*, February 7, 1987; "Decision Is Postponed in Probe of Fauntroy," *Washington Post*, March 15, 1989; "Ford Indicted on Fraud Counts," *Memphis Commercial Appeal*, April 25, 1987; Wayne Barrett, "Ed Towns, Watchdog? Has Congress Forgotten Ed's Past?" *Village Voice*, December 9, 2008; "Rep. Flake Indicted on Charges of Siphoning Off Church Funds,"

Congressional Quarterly Weekly, August 4, 1990; "The Attack on Rep. Gray," *Washington Post*, June 5, 1989; "Dymally Sought Bribe, Informant Says," *Los Angeles Times*, Metro, October, 12, 1995; "House Members Who Wrote Overdrafts Are Listed," *Los Angeles Times*, April 17, 1992.

The FBI also placed several black members of Congress under surveillance for their criticism of the Reagan administration's foreign policy aims on Central America. Those members were Ron Dellums, John Conyers, George Crockett, Mervyn Dymally, and Mickey Leland. See Ross Gelbspan, *Break-ins, Death Threats and the FBI: The Covert War against the Central America Movement* (Boston: South End Press, 1991), 150.

27. See Public Integrity Section, *Report to Congress on the Activities and Operations of the Public Integrity Section*, 1981–1992, available at http://www.justice.gov/criminal/pin/; "Indictments — a Grand Congressional Tradition."

28. See Curriden, "Selective Prosecution." The three federal judges impeached during this period were Harry E. Claiborne, U.S. District Court for the District of Nevada (1986); Alcee L. Hastings, U.S. District Court for the Southern District of Florida (1989); and Walter L. Nixon, U.S. District Court for the Southern District of Mississippi (1989). Robert Collins, U.S. District Court for the Eastern District of Louisiana, resigned on July 28, 1993, as impeachment proceedings were under way in the House of Representatives. See "Collins Resigns Federal Judgeship; Resignation Letter Is Given to Clinton," *New Orleans Times Picayune*, August 7, 1993.

29. Rep. George Crockett, letter to Rep. Peter Rodino, July 19, 1983; Rep. Mervyn Dymally, letter to Rep. Peter Rodino, July 21, 1983, both copies in possession of the author.

30. Gibson and Harris, who had made peace with both the mob and the Italian American political machine that had previously dominated Newark, probably gave Botempo the job as a form of political patronage. For a short discussion of Gibson's and Harris's relationship with the mob and Newark's Italian American political machine, see Komozi Woodard, *A Nation within a Nation: Amiri Baraka (Leroi Jones) and Black Power Politics* (Chapel Hill: University of North Carolina Press, 1999), 230–54. For details of the trial, see "Gibson Acquitted of a Conspiracy in 'No Show' Case," *New York Times*, October 22, 1982; Mary Sawyer, *The Harassment of Black Elected Officials: Ten Years Later* (Washington, D.C.: Voter Education and Research Action, 1987), 31.

31. Mary Volcansek, who has conducted the most detailed study of the investigation, argues that "the case was, by the prosecution's own admission, a circumstantial one; no direct evidence of Hastings culpability was ever produced." See Mary Volcansek, *Judicial Impeachment: None Called for Justice* (Urbana: University of Illinois Press, 1993), 68–95.

32. Representative Alcee L. Hastings, interview with the author, Washington, D.C., March 12, 2002.

33. Agents arrested Borders in the hopes of flipping him and using him as an informant to gather information on Hastings. Rather than agree to a deal with investigators, Borders stopped talking. Indeed, he refused to discuss the case even after he was convicted and sentenced to jail in 1982. See "FBI Arrest Bungled '81 Hastings Case, Ex-prosecutor Says," *Miami Herald*, August 1, 1989.

34. "Drug Use by Dellums Alleged to Grand Jury," *Washington Post*, March 16, 1983;

"Dellums Allegations Detailed; Hill Aide Given Drug Term," *Washington Post*, April 16, 1983; "Drug Probes on Capitol Hill End Quietly; Investigation Cost $2 Million, Involved 1,400 Allegations, Resulted in 6 Prosecutions," *Washington Post*, January 15, 1984.

35. "Cross Examination," *Detroit Metro Times*, March 3–17, 1988.

36. "Young Says Effort for Black-White Unity Is Eroding," *Detroit Free Press*, March 7, 1983; "Jurors Fail to Agree at Bribery Trial of Detroit City Aide" *New York Times*, December 14, 1983.

37. John Kincaid, "Beyond the Voting Rights Act: White Responses to Black Political Power in Tchula, Mississippi," *Publius: The Journal of Federalism*, 16 (Fall 1986): 155–72; Minion Morrison, *Black Political Mobilization: Leadership, Power, and Mass Behavior* (Albany: State University of New York Press, 1987), 141–61; affidavit of Mayor Eddie Carthan, Holmes County, Mississippi, September 24, 1982, copy in possession of the author. All subsequent information on the Carthan cases, unless otherwise indicated, is drawn from these three sources.

38. In 1978, Alderman Odell Hampton, an employee of B. T. Taylor, resigned from the board stating that he could not "cope with the pressure" of public office. Taylor revealed the type of pressure Hampton was under to the *Los Angeles Times*: "I told Odell to get off that board because I didn't like the funny things going on in the town." Hampton was replaced by Jacyn Gibson, an African American more comfortable with client politics, who immediately formed an alliance with the black alderman and Carthan critic Roosevelt Granderson, and the only remaining white member of the board, local plantation owner John Edgar Hayes. Gibson expressed his and Granderson's governing philosophy in a 1982 comment to the *Los Angeles Times*: "I imagine any black person who needs a favor from a white, all he's got to do is ask." At the time, Gibson worked for Billy Johnson, who, during the same interview, and in his employee's presence, referred to Carthan as a "nigger." "Town's New Promise Faded to Violence," *Los Angeles Times*, October 6, 1982.

39. The lockout was a product of the ongoing struggle between the board majority and Carthan over mayoral appointment powers. Carthan had fired Ford some months before. The board argued that Carthan did not have the authority to hire and fire city officials without board approval. They not only posted Ford outside city hall but sued to have him reinstated with back pay—acting on the very issue that was then a subject of their suit. The Mississippi Supreme Court ruled against the board majority in 1980. "Revenge of the Good Ole Boys," *In These Times*, January 20–26, 1982.

40. National Campaign to Free Mayor Eddie Carthan and the Tchula 7 and Preserve Black Political Rights, "Fact Sheet and Chronology of Events in the Legal Lynching of Eddie Carthan and the Tchula 7," 1982, copy in possession of the author.

41. During the trial the defense introduced Mary Sawyer as an expert witness on the "harassment of black elected officials." Prosecutors attacked her testimony, noting, in the words of the *Jackson (Miss.) Clarion-Ledger*, that "she based her opinions on questionnaires and interviews with elected black officials and did not question members of the alleged conspiracy." "Carthan Attorneys Quiz Armed Robber," *Jackson (Miss.) Clarion Ledger*, October 8, 1982.

42. Bolden was correct to argue that the fraud scheme he undertook was common in Mississippi. Known as a "busted invoice," the scheme was most commonly used by

county supervisors when purchasing road repair equipment and services. The supervisors would order a certain amount of equipment from a friendly contractor, the contractor would deliver only a percentage of the order, and the remainder of the money would be kicked back to the supervisor. Crockett, *Operation Pretense*, 11.

43. "Town's New Promise Faded to Violence," *Los Angeles Times*, October 6, 1982.

44. Peter W. Rodino, letter to Mary Sawyer, October 27, 1983, copy in possession of the author.

45. The figures cited above include only monies spent by the FBI on "special costs of the operations," e.g., informant payments, bribes, lease and rental expenses. The vast majority of the expenses for these operations — specifically agents' salaries — are not included. Subcommittee on Civil and Constitutional Rights of the Committee on the Judiciary, House of Representatives, *FBI Undercover Operations: A Report of the Subcommittee on Civil and Constitutional Rights of the Committee of the Judiciary, House of Representatives Together with Dissenting Views* (Washington, D.C.: United States Government Printing Office, 1984), 12–13. David Burnham of the Transactional Records Access Clearinghouse estimates that by 1991 the FBI was conducting "several thousand" sting operations per year. David Burnham, "The FBI: A Special Report," *Nation*, August 11, 1997.

46. In March 1982, the Senate formed the Select Committee to Study Undercover Activities, which focused on Abscam specifically. Its report was issued in December 1982. "Operation Abscam: The FBI Stings Congress," *Time*, February 18, 1980.

47. Phillip Heyman, assistant attorney general, Criminal Division, and Paul Mitchell, associate deputy attorney general, quoted from Subcommittee on Civil and Constitutional Rights, *FBI Undercover Operations*, 36–39. Attorney General Benjamin Civiletti later codified these "safeguards" as "The Attorney General's Guidelines for FBI Undercover Operations" on January 5, 1981.

48. *FBI Undercover Operations*, 51–70, 41, 10–11.

49. Ibid., 101–19.

50. "Senator Mitchell Said to Be Target of Federal Probe," *Baltimore Sun*, March 2, 1986; "Md. Sen. Mitchell under U.S. Probe," *Washington Post*, April 18, 1986; "Mitchell Probe Expands to Fee Paid Law Firm," *Baltimore Sun*, October 28, 1986; "Mitchell Criticizes Media over Probe, Defends 2 Nephews," *Baltimore Sun*, February 5, 1987; "Parren Mitchell Denies He's a Target," *Baltimore Evening Sun*, February 3, 1987; "Parren Is Furious over Bribe Reports," *Baltimore Afro American*, February 7, 1987. For a detailed discussion of the Wedtech case, see James Traub, *Too Good to Be True: The Outlandish Story of Wedtech* (New York: Doubleday, 1990).

51. There is some logic to this line of reasoning. The Mitchell brothers had to have known that Wedtech was hiring them because of their relationship to their uncle, Representative Parren Mitchell (D-Md.), then chairman of the House Committee on Small Business. Unbeknownst to the brothers, Parren Mitchell was conducting an investigation into whether Wedtech was indeed a minority firm (it was not) at the time that they were hired. Wedtech hoped that the Mitchell brothers would intervene with their uncle to have the investigation stopped. There is no evidence that they did, however, nor is there any clear evidence that they led Wedtech to believe that they would do so. In all likelihood, the Mitchell brothers were angling to make easy money from their associa-

tion with a powerful elected official, an unsavory, but widespread and generally legal undertaking.

52. "Mitchell Brothers Convicted of Taking Wedtech Money: Jury Acquits Baltimoreans of Conspiracy," *Washington Post*, November 7, 1987.

53. "Meese Financial Partner Hired in 1985 as Wedtech Consultant," *Washington Post*, April 17, 1987; "Meese Asks Special Prosecutor to Examine Ties to Wedtech," *Congressional Quarterly Weekly*, May 16, 1987.

54. "Md. Ex-Sen. Mitchell Alleges Meese Conflict in Wedtech Case," *Washington Post*, June 25, 1987; "Mitchell's Lawyers Cite 'Blatant Misconduct' in Federal Probe," *Baltimore Evening Sun*, June 25, 1987; "Kunstler Calls the Jailing of Mitchell 'Outrageous,'" *Baltimore Evening Sun*, April 20, 1988.

55. The report claims that Meese (1) filed a false tax return in 1985 when he failed to declare $20,706 in capital gains from the sale of stock; (2) had a conflict of interest because he owned stock in Bell Telephone Company in 1985–86 at the same time that he was assisting officials of the regional Bell Telephone companies in seeking to revise a court antitrust order so they could expand their services; (3) improperly influenced White House officials in an effort to help Wedtech secure 8(a) status in 1982; and other, minor infractions. In conclusion, McKay argues that he did not have sufficient evidence to prosecute. "The McKay Report: Excerpts from the Independent Prosecutor's Report on Edwin Meese 3d," *New York Times*, July 19, 1988; "The McKay Report: An Ambiguous Conclusion to a 14 Month Investigation," *New York Times*, July 19, 1988.

56. "Ford Indicted on Fraud Counts," *Memphis Commercial Appeal*, April 25, 1987; "Trouble Traced to Butcher Plea," *Memphis Commercial Appeal*, April 25, 1987; "Controversy over Ford's Trial Could Have Repercussions," *Congressional Quarterly Weekly*, February 27, 1993.

57. Since his appointment in 1983, Joseph diGenova, the U.S. attorney for the District of Columbia, had energetically investigated allegations of drug use by Barry and corruption in D.C. municipal government. There was certainly reason for diGenova to follow up on these leads. Barry was well known in the city as a drug user, and a small number of his appointees were convicted for engaging in graft (though corruption in the first two Barry administrations does not appear to have been any more widespread than in other major cities). "The Federal Investigation: Highlights," *Washington Post*, September 13, 1987; Tom Sherwood and Harry Jaffe, *Dream City: Race, Power, and the Decline of Washington, D.C.* (New York: Simon and Schuster, 1994), 160–99.

58. "2 Officials in Atlanta Indicted in Extortion," *New York Times*, October 19, 1987; "Blacks' Indictments Raise Double-Standard Issue," *Atlanta Journal and Constitution*, October 31, 1987.

59. "Beneath Bond Saga: An Old City Hall Story," *Atlanta Constitution*, June 19, 1987; "What's Next?" *Washington Post Magazine*, June 21, 1987; Young quoted in "Hearing for Five Officers in Bond Probe to Open," *Atlanta Journal and Constitution*, November 30, 1987; "'Bond Affair' a Year Later: Much Has Happened, Little Has Changed," *Atlanta Journal and Constitution*, March 19, 1988.

60. "Blacks' Indictments Raise Double-Standard Issue," *Atlanta Journal and Constitution*, October 31, 1987; "Eaves Persecuted Marchers Claim," *Atlanta Journal and*

Constitution, February 14, 1988. Despite these expressions of support, Williams pled guilty and Eaves was found guilty in May 1988. See "County Aide in Atlanta Guilty of Extortion in Zoning Plot," *New York Times*, May 3, 1988; "Ga. Official Sentenced Today," *USA Today*, June 27, 1988.

61. Department of Justice, Office of the Attorney General, Title 28 — Judicial Administration, order no. 1297-88, part O.

62. Richard Keil, "Candidate in Chicago Was Paid in Washington," Associated Press, November 29, 1988; Keil, "Fauntroy Denies Violating House Rules in Hiring Colleague's Son," Associated Press, December 1, 1988; Keil, "Illinois Candidate Says D.C. Job Was Stuffing Envelopes," Associated Press, December 12, 1988; Keil, "Officials Say They Didn't See Congressman's Son," Associated Press, December 2, 1988. These articles were picked up by the *Washington Post* and the *Washington Times*. Keil continued to write articles on this topic and send them over the AP wire in 1989. See, for instance, Keil, "Ethics Chairman Demands Explanation of Possible Payroll Padding," Associated Press, January 13, 1989.

63. Ross accompanied several members of Delegate Fauntroy's staff to the offices of the Public Integrity Section of the DOJ on March 10, 1989, to be interviewed by the FBI under guidelines agreed upon the previous day by the attorney general. In this letter, Ross notes that FBI agents refused to interview members of Fauntroy's staff unless Ross agreed not to discuss those aspects of the interview that concerned the privileges and prerogatives of the House of Representatives with the leadership of the House. These stipulations violated a verbal agreement between Ross and Attorney General Thornburgh made on March 9, 1989, in preparation for the interview. Also, as Ross tersely noted at the end of his letter, these stipulations were unprecedented: "In the twelve years that I have been representing the House . . . never have I been asked . . . to agree to a total gag order prohibiting me from giving even a generic description of the matter to the elected leadership of the House." General Council to the Clerk, U.S. House of Representatives Steven Ross, letter to Assistant Attorney General Edward Dennis, March 11, 1989, copy in possession of the author. Fauntroy's defense attorney Abbe Lowell asserts that no member of the attorney general's office had contacted him concerning the failed March 10, 1989, interview despite his having left several phone messages at the office. Abbe Lowell, letter to Attorney General Richard Thornburg, March 13, 1989, copy in possession of the author. A formal response from the attorney general's office was not received until March 17, 1989. See Chief of the Public Integrity Section, Criminal Division of the Justice Department, Gerald McDowell, letter to Steven Ross, March 17, 1989, copy in possession of the author.

64. Richard Keil, "Fauntroy Probe," Associated Press, March 15, 1989. Versions of this story appeared in both major Washington, D.C., dailies: "Decision Is Postponed in Probe of Fauntroy," *Washington Post*, March 15, 1989; "Fauntroy Probe by FBI to Be Extended," *Washington Times*, March 15, 1989.

65. "Thornburgh Lifts Order on Council," *Washington Post*, April 13, 1989.

66. In the 1988 election, Republicans lost three seats in the House and one in the Senate. Shade and Campbell, *American Presidential Campaigns and Elections*, 3:983–87; "GOP Honing Wedges for Next Campaign," *Washington Post*, February 26, 1989.

67. In 1980, Republicans picked up 12 seats in the Senate (and control of the chamber), 33 seats in the House, 4 governorships, and 189 state legislative seats. See Skinner et al., *Strategy of Campaigning*, 106–7; Shade and Campbell, *American Presidential Campaigns and Elections*, 3:950–51.

68. In one famous fund-raising pitch, Coelho told business leaders that Democrats were "going to be a majority for a very long time, so it [did] not make good business sense to give to Republicans." Coelho quoted in William Connelly and John Pitney, *Congress' Permanent Minority: Republicans in the U.S. House* (Boston: Rowan and Littlefield, 1994), 136.

69. John Barry, *The Ambition and the Power* (New York: Viking Penguin, 1989), 365. In the late 1980s, Gingrich and several of his colleagues tried to cobble information from these speeches together into a study of Democratic corruption titled "The House of Ill Repute." It was never published. See Connelly and Pitney, *Congress' Permanent Minority*, 27–29. Though allegations of political corruption weighed disproportionately on Democrats, Ethics Committee investigations of congressmen were evenly split along party lines for sexual offenses. Between 1980 and 1991, six Democrats and five Republicans were investigated for sexual misconduct. See "Ethics and Criminal Prosecutions," *Congressional Quarterly Almanac* (1991): 800–809.

70. Barry, *Ambition and the Power*, 366–67; House Subcommittee on Civil Service, "Index of Clippings of Alleged Ethics Violations by Reagan Administration Appointees," September 15, 1987, copy in possession of the author.

71. Barry, *Ambition and the Power*, 215, 369.

72. "GOP Honing Wedges for Next Campaign."

73. George Thomas Kurian, ed., *The Encyclopedia of the Republican Party* (Armonk, N.Y.: Sharpe Reference, 1997), 758–59; "Bush Moving to Solidify Ties to Republican Right," *New York Times*, April 28, 1988.

74. The attendees at the February 1989 meeting in Washington D.C. were Representatives Newt Gingrich (R-Ga.), Jon Kyl (R-Ariz.), Vin Weber (R-Minn.), and Steven Gunderson (R-Wis.); consultants Eddie Mahe and Charles Black; White House domestic policy aide James Pinkerton; Bush speechwriter Peggy Noonan; pollsters Linda Divall and Fred Steeper; Heritage Foundation executive director Burton Pines; demographic specialist John Morgan; staff members of the RNC, RNCC, and the National Republican Senatorial Committee; and black conservatives Robert Woodson and Keith Butler. See "GOP Honing Wedges for Next Campaign."

75. *CBS Evening News*, May 30, 1989. The *Los Angeles Times* had reported on May 19, 1989, that the IRS had begun an investigation into Wright's finances. The story was incorrect. The IRS had not started such investigation. See Barry, *Ambition and the Power*, 745.

76. "Bradley, Coelho Targets of Criminal Probe," *Los Angeles Times*, May 25, 1989; "It's Time for Me to Move On, for My Party to Move On," *Washington Post*, May 28, 1989. See also Barry, *Ambition and the Power*, 742–44, 752.

77. "Gingrich Capitalized on Wright Inquiry," *St. Louis Dispatch*, June 15, 1989. Even these new charges were questionable. Wright biographer John Barry, who has conducted the most comprehensive investigation of the Wright controversy, rebuts them point by point. He argues that the committee pursued this flimsy evidence because the Republican

committee members sought revenge on Wright for the heavy-handed way he had treated them in the 100th Congress; outside investigator Richard Phelan misled the committee with his adversarial (as opposed to his proper role as an impartial investigator) conduct of the investigation; committee members, both Democrat and Republican, feared that they would be seen as whitewashing the investigation by the press; and committee chairman Representative Julian Dixon (D-Calif.), who could have saved Wright by narrowing the scope of the investigation or refusing to release the committee report, ceded control of the proceeding to the ranking Republican John Myers (R-Ind.) and Phelan. See Barry, *Ambition and the Power*, 667–763.

78. "Fauntroy Records Subpoenaed in Hiring Probe," *Washington Post*, June 2, 1989.

79. Gingrich was using news reports based on leaks from several ongoing DOJ official corruption investigations to arrive at this number. See "G.O.P. Keeping Up Ethics Pressure on the Democrats," *New York Times*, May 29, 1989; "Gingrich Seeks to Seize 'Reform' Label," *New York Times*, June 3, 1989; "War Drums in the House; Republicans Vow to Press Attack on Ethics while Digging in for Democratic Reprisals," *New York Times*, May 28, 1989; Barry, *Ambition and the Power*, 744.

80. Rep. William Gray, press release, May 30, 1989, copy in possession of the author. The CBS broadcast also brought an angry response from Gray staffer Leslie Baskerville. Following the CBS broadcast, "informed official sources" told the *Washington Post* that the FBI investigation involved a "no-show" employee on Gray's staff and identified Baskerville as said staffer. On June 1, she held a press conference at which she sternly refuted claims that she was a "no-show" worker. "No show?" she asked indignantly. "Ask the guards on night duty in House Annex I and Rayburn. No show? Ask my colleagues who left me at my desk and went home at 6 p.m. No show? Ask the members of Congress for whom I have worked." She went on to charge that the DOJ was using the allegations against her to discredit her employer and dared the department to ask her about her work habits. It never did. Leslie Baskerville, "Statement of Leslie Baskerville," June 1, 1989, copy in possession of the author; "Fauntroy Reportedly Paid Aide to Promote NBLR's Interests," *Washington Times*, October 27, 1988; "The Attack on Rep. Gray," *Washington Post*, June 5, 1989.

81. "Probe of Gray's Office Causes Uproar," *Washington Post*, June 1, 1989; "The Resignation of Speaker Wright; U.S. Orders Probe of Stories about Gray," *Boston Globe*, June 1, 1989; "Fauntroy Asks Thornburgh to Stanch Leaks on Probe," *Washington Post*, June 3, 1989; "Inquiry Set on Leaks Disclosures Called Politically Inspired," *St. Louis Dispatch*, June 2, 1989.

82. "Thornburgh Asks Disclosure Inquiry," *New York Times*, June 1, 1989.

83. Richard Thornburgh, *Where the Evidence Leads: An Autobiography* (Pittsburgh: University of Pittsburgh Press, 2003), 280–84.

84. "Thornburgh Took Polygraph Test in Leak Inquiry," *New York Times*, May 26, 1990.

85. "Thornburgh Reassigns 2 Top Aides; Mounting Criticism Cited in Shakeup," *Washington Post*, May 15, 1990.

86. "Thornburgh Urged Not to Punish In-House Leakers," *Washington Post*, May 17, 1990.

87. "Former Thornburgh Deputy Faults Handling of Leak Probe," *Washington Post*, May 21, 1990.

88. "Thornburgh Denies Squelching Inquiry at Justice," *New York Times*, May 24, 1990.

89. Although it is impossible to determine when Barry began using cocaine, a 1982 D.C. police investigation revealed that he had used the drug as early as 1981. Jaffe and Sherwood, *Dream City*, 137–38; "Police Handling of Allegations Stirs Dispute," *Washington Post*, March 13, 1983. For more on the Barry case, see chapter 6.

90. Six of the eight House members investigated for nonsexual offenses between 1989 and 1991 were Democrats, with most of the initial complaints against them coming from Republicans. "Ethics and Criminal Prosecutions," *Congressional Quarterly Almanac* (1991): 800–809. In the fall of 1991, when House Speaker Foley announced that the House bank would be closed due to a history of sloppy bookkeeping and members' overdrawing their accounts, a group of Republican backbenchers led by Gingrich demanded that the names of all members who had overdrawn their accounts be published. Bowing to Republican pressure, the House Ethics Committee published a list of "worst offenders." Of the twenty-two members on the list, five were African American. "As Casualty List Grows, G.O.P. Shows Doubts about House Bank Scandal, *New York Times*, April 16, 1992; Office of History and Preservation, Office of the Clerk, U.S. House of Representatives, *Black Americans in Congress, 1870–2007* (Washington, D.C.: U.S. Government Printing Office, 2008), 395–96. For the text of the Republican Party platform, see Kurian, *Encyclopedia of the Republican Party*, 808–9. For a description of Tennessee Republicans' efforts to use the ethics issue to take the state legislature, see "Tennessee Republicans See an Election Weapon in State's Bingo Scandal," *New York Times*, January 28, 1990.

91. See "Winston Salem Verdicts Teach Lessons: 3 Defendants Found Guilty on Most Charges," *People's Advocate* 3, no. 3 (June–July 1992): 1, 3–5; "Rep. Tucker Is Indicted; Denies Bribery Charges," *Los Angeles Times*, August 4, 1994; "Dymally Sought Bribe, Informant Says," *Los Angeles Times*, Metro, October 12, 1995; "U.S. Prosecutors Move to Block Racism Defense in Moore's Trial," *Los Angeles Times*, Metro, July 12, 1996.

92. Testimony of Herbert Fielding, in Schiller Institute, *Independent Hearings to Investigate Misconduct by the U.S. Department of Justice* (Washington, D.C.: Schiller Institute, 1995), 12.

93. Interestingly enough, Mitchell had refused the money because he believed that the DOJ was trying to set him up. In 1982, while Mitchell was a state representative, U.S. attorney Henry McMaster had indicted him for food-stamp fraud. The ensuing trial ended in a hung jury. From that time forward, Mitchell claims, he "walked on eggshells." See Testimony of Theo Mitchell, in Schiller Institute, *Independent Hearings*, 3–11.

94. "Cobb Finds Some good in His Lost Trust Role," *Charleston Post and Courier*, August 23, 1999; "Cobb to Get Bonus as Informant," *Rock Hill (S.C.) Herald*, January 16, 1992; Fant quoted in "Investigation of Vote Buying Shakes S. Carolina Capitol," *New York Times*, July 22, 1990.

95. "Operation Broken Trust," *Rock Hill (S.C.) Herald*, March 11, 1997; "Justice' Inspector General to Review Lost Trust," *Rock Hill (S.C.) Herald*, September 24, 1997; Testimony of Theo Mitchell, in Schiller Institute, *Independent Hearings*, 4–11.

96. "Rep. Flake Indicted on Charges of Siphoning Off Church Funds," *Congressional Quarterly Weekly*, August 4, 1990.

97. "Embezzlement and Tax Charges against Rep. Flake Dropped," *Congressional Quarterly Weekly*, April 6, 1991.

98. "U.S. Dismisses Charges Faced by Rep. Flake," *New York Times*, April 4, 1991; "Two Jurors Visit Church to Hear Flake's Sermon," *New York Times*, April 8, 1991.

99. Reno's activities were not unusual. Incoming administrations typically replace all or most of the sitting U.S. attorneys. What made it exceptional was the scale of the firing and the speed with which it was done. Typically incoming administrations replace U.S. attorneys gradually and keep those U.S. attorneys who have gained the support of members of their own party in the state in question. "Washington Area to Lose 2 High-Profile Prosecutors," *Washington Post*, March 24, 1993.

100. In 1995, Deputy Attorney General Jamie Gorelick told the Senate Judiciary Committee that Attorney General Reno was aware of black elected officials' allegations of harassment when she entered office. Her comments do not suggest that Reno took any specific steps to address those officials' concerns. United States Senate, Committee on the Judiciary, *Federal Law Enforcement and the Good Ol' Boys Roundup*, July 21, 1995, 86–91, folder 005 Roundup (ATF etc.) [3], box 009, Kagan Counsel, William J. Clinton Library, Little Rock, Arkansas.

101. The three sitting black members of Congress investigated by the DOJ during the Clinton years were Representatives Mel Reynolds (D-Ill.), Barbara Rose-Collins (D-Mich.), and Walter Tucker (D-Calif.). For discussions of the Tucker investigations, see "Trial Opens in Tucker Bribery Case," *Los Angeles Times*, October 4, 1995; "Rep. Tucker Found Guilty of Bribery and Tax Evasion," *Los Angeles Times*, December 9, 1995; "Tucker Gets Prison Term for Extortion," *Los Angeles Times*, April 18, 1996. For discussions of the Rose-Collins investigations, see "Collins' Aides Performed Personal, Campaign Duties," *The Hill*, August 16, 1995; "Rep. Collins Uses Tax Money for Stamps," *Detroit News*, May 27, 1995; "Collins Seen as Lax Lawmaker" *Detroit Free Press*, August 19, 1995. Rose-Collins was defeated and later replaced in Congress by Carolyn Cheeks Kilpatrick (D-Mich.). For discussions of the Reynolds investigations, see "Reynolds Indicted," *Chicago Sun-Times*, August 19, 1994; "Reynolds Guilty on All Counts," *Washington Post*, August 23, 1995; "Reynolds Sentenced to 5 Years for Sex Offenses, Obstruction," *Washington Post*, September 29, 1995. One other sitting member of the CBC experienced a federal investigation. Senator Carol Moseley Braun (D-Ill.) was investigated by the FEC. Also, one former member, Walter Fauntroy, was investigated by the DOJ. See the conclusion of this volume for details.

CHAPTER FIVE. *The "Selective Prosecution" of Black Elected Officials in Alabama, 1981–1992*

1. The NAACP had called the gathering as a follow-up to its August 26, 1989, "Silent March," where nearly one hundred thousand participants marched past the Supreme Court to protest several recent high court decisions that had eroded civil rights protections. The conference was designed to discuss remedial legislation for addressing those

decisions and serve as a forum for formulating effective strategies for achieving congressional action. In the intervening month, however, the scope of the conference grew to include issues of political empowerment, economic empowerment, and the problems of the underclass. Arrington was invited to speak as part of the political empowerment session. See Memorandum from Executive Director Benjamin Hooks to Invitees to Conference on the Present Crisis, October 16, 1989, 344, folder 13, box 8, NAACP Papers, Library of Congress, Washington, D.C.

2. Richard Arrington, "The Federal Government and the Harassment of Black Elected Officials," speech delivered to the NAACP Conference on the Present Crisis, October 30, 1989, file 1935, Richard Arrington Jr. Investigation Files, Department of Archives and Manuscripts, Birmingham Public Library.

3. The DOJ's 1983 reversal was less a product of a change of heart by the same attorneys than infighting between career attorneys and political appointees. Under Reagan, political appointees regularly reversed or overruled the decisions of career attorneys as they attempted to steer the DOJ away from the liberal consensus of the Carter years and toward the "color-blind justice" of the Reagan administration. See Ronald Wolters, *Right Turn: William Bradford Reynolds, the Reagan Administration, and Black Civil Rights* (New Brunswick, N.J.: Transaction, 1996), 278–79.

4. Jimmie Lewis Franklin, *Back to Birmingham: Richard Arrington Jr. and His Times* (Tuscaloosa: University of Alabama Press, 1989), 321–23.

5. United States Commission on Civil Rights, *The Voting Rights Act: Unfulfilled Goals* (Washington, D.C.: Government Printing Office, 1981), 22–35.

6. See J. L. Chestnut Jr. and Julia Cass, *Black in Selma: The Uncommon Life of J. L. Chestnut Jr.* (New York: Farrar, Straus, and Giroux, 1990), 322; United States Commission on Civil Rights, *Voting Rights Act*, 35–36.

7. Lani Guinier, *Lift Every Voice: Turning a Civil Rights Setback into a New Vision for Social Justice* (New York: Simon and Schuster, 1998), 186. For similar discussions of white absentee ballot fraud in the Alabama Black Belt, see also Bud and Ruth Schultz, *The Price of Dissent: Testimonies of Political Repression in America* (Berkeley: University of California Press, 2001), 208; "Black Lawmakers Say Probes Inconsistent," *Selma Times Journal*, May 26, 1985; Chestnut and Cass, *Black in Selma*, 381; Allen Tullos, "Crackdown in the Black Belt," *Southern Changes* 7, no. 1 (1985): 1–5; Tullos, "Crackdown in the Black Belt: Not So Simple Justice," *Southern Changes* 7, no. 2 (1985): 2–11.

8. The DOJ attorneys may also have refused to help Black Belt voting rights activists because they did not want to split Alabama's biracial Democratic coalition — a coalition that President Carter would need in his 1980 reelection bid — by taking sides in an interracial, intraparty struggle.

9. Chestnut and Cass, *Black in Selma*, 322. Perry County voting rights activist Albert Turner recalls being given similar advice by DOJ attorneys in the 1970s. Guinier, *Lift Every Voice*, 187.

10. Chestnut and Cass, *Black in Selma*, 322.

11. Allen Tullos, "Crackdown in the Black Belt: Not So Simple Justice," 9.

12. Chestnut and Cass, *Black in Selma*, 311; Guinier, *Lift Every Voice*, 188; "Wilder, Bozeman Go Free," *Montgomery Advertiser*, November 10, 1982.

13. "2 Alabama Rights Workers Are Jailed for Voting Fraud," *New York Times*, January 12, 1982; "4,000 March for Vote-Fraud Duo's Freedom," *Washington Post*, February 19, 1982; "Wilder, Bozeman Go Free," *Montgomery Advertiser*, November 10, 1982.

14. Thomas Bethell, *Sumter County Blues: The Ordeal of the Federation of Southern Cooperatives* (Washington, D.C.: Committee in Support of Community Based Organizations, 1982), 17–18; Testimony of State Senator Hank Sanders before the House Subcommittee on Civil and Constitutional Rights, Subcommittee on Civil and Constitutional Rights of the Committee on the Judiciary, House of Representatives, *Civil Rights Implications of Federal Vote Fraud Prosecutions*, September 26, 1985, (Washington, D.C.: U.S. Government Printing Office, 1986), 18; "Justice Department to Check Wilcox Voter Plan," *Montgomery Advertiser*, September 23, 1981.

15. Bethell, *Sumter County Blues*. Unless otherwise noted, all information on the 1978–80 investigation was gleaned from this source. For information on the outcome of the investigation, see "Filling Cooperative Coffers," *Washington Post*, March 5, 1981.

16. House Subcommittee on Civil and Constitutional Rights, *Civil Rights Implications*, September 26, 1985, 26.

17. By 1983, Reynolds had already made his hostility to aggressive VRA enforcement, and his openness to the concerns of southern whites, well known. Particularly noteworthy were Reynolds's efforts to undermine several voting rights cases in 1981, and his efforts to thwart congressional liberals' attempts to strengthen the VRA in 1981–82. Norman Amaker, *Civil Rights and the Reagan Administration* (Washington, D.C.: Urban Institute Press, 1988); Joel Selig, "The Reagan Justice Department and Civil Rights: What Went Wrong?" *University of Illinois Law Review* 785 (1985); United States Congress, Senate Committee on the Judiciary, *Nomination of William Bradford Reynolds to Be Associate Attorney General for the United States*, 99th Cong. (Washington, D.C.: GPO, 1985).

18. Wolters, *Right Turn*, 79–80. As early as 1983, Reynolds had a notable record of approving voting changes in covered jurisdictions that clearly violated the VRA and then having those decisions overturned by federal judges. See Senate Committee on the Judiciary, *Nomination of William Bradford Reynolds*, 1985, 372–445; David Burnham, *Above the Law: Secret Deals, Political Fixes, and Other Misadventures of the U.S. Department of Justice* (New York: Scribner, 1996), 265–66.

19. Randall Williams, "Crackdown in the Black Belt: On to Greene County," *Southern Changes* 7, no. 3 (1985): 2–5.

20. For a short description of both of these changes, see the DOJ guidelines for U.S. attorney involvement in election crimes investigations: Craig Donsanto, *Federal Prosecution of Election Offenses*, 4th ed. (Washington, D.C.: Department of Justice, Criminal Division, Public Integrity Section, 1984), vii–viii, 7, 17. I am indebted to David Burnham for his discovery of this little-noticed press release. See Burnham, *Above the Law*, 257–58. Smith's directive was likely a direct response to the multiple left-liberal voter registration campaigns of 1983–84 that were designed to bring two million new black and poor voters to the polls in the 1984 election. For a description of the 1983–84 voter registration drives and both major parties' responses, see Frances Fox Piven, Lorraine Minnite, and Margaret Groarke, *Keeping Down the Black Vote: Race and the Demobilization of American Voters* (New York: New Press, 2009), 102–9.

21. As early as October 1984, local papers make no mention of DOJ investigations in white-dominated counties. "Election Violators to Be Prosecuted," *Greene County (Ala.) Democrat*, October 10, 1984; "FBI Agents Raid County Office Building," *Greene County (Ala.) Democrat*, October 17, 1984; "U.S. Attorney Donaldson to Speak Here on Thursday," *Greene County (Ala.) Democrat*, October 24, 1984.

22. In Greene County, local whites and a small number of blacks created a "biracial coalition" during the 1984 election and selected "responsible" black candidates to run for office against the black incumbents who were backed by the Greene County Civic League. Thus what had traditionally been a white versus black power struggle morphed into a struggle between the ruling (black) coalition and an insurgent (white-dominated) coalition. Ronald Wolters, *Right Turn*, 81–83.

23. House Subcommittee on Civil and Constitutional Rights, *Voting Rights Implications of Federal Vote Fraud Prosecutions*, September 26, 1985, 17–18.

24. See Williams, "Crackdown in the Black Belt: On to Greene County"; Guinier, *Lift Every Voice*, 207.

25. "Election Violators to Be Prosecuted," *Greene County (Ala.) Democrat*, October 10, 1984; "FBI Agents Raid County Office Building," *Greene County (Ala.) Democrat*, October 17, 1984; "U.S. Attorney Addresses Vote Fraud Issue in County," *Greene County (Ala.) Democrat*, October 31, 1984.

26. Guinier, *Lift Every Voice*, 189. J. L. Chestnut, a lawyer for the defense in the Perry County vote fraud trials, paraphrased the questions posed to black voters by FBI agents in Chestnut and Cass, *Black in Selma*, 379.

27. Mamie Speight and Wendell Paris quoted in "Blacks Charge Bias in Voter Fraud Indictments," *Atlanta Journal and Constitution*, June 16, 1985; Fannie Mae Williams, quoted in Guinier, *Lift Every Voice*, 193. In his description of the 1984 general election in Greene County, Wolters ignores this intimidation and argues that the results of the 1984 general elections are a show of popular black support for a change of government. Wolters, *Right Turn*, 79–90.

28. Chestnut and Cass, *Black in Selma*, 380–81.

29. John Zippert, interview with the author, Eutaw, Alabama, August 10, 2001; Hank Sanders, interview with the author, Selma Alabama, August 14, 2001; Chestnut and Cass, *Black in Selma*, 380–81.

30. For discussions of FBI, Baltimore Police Department, and DOJ investigations of Clarence Mitchell III, see chapters 2 and 4.

31. "Voter Fraud Case Motion," *Washington Post*, June 4, 1985; "Black Lawmakers Say Probes Inconsistent," *Selma Times Journal*, May 26, 1985.

32. Chestnut and Cass, *Black in Selma*, 381; House Subcommittee on Civil and Constitutional Rights, *Civil Rights Implications of Federal Voting Fraud Prosecutions*, September 26, 1985, 59.

33. Hasan Jeffries, *Bloody Lowndes: Civil Rights and Black Power in Alabama's Black Belt* (New York: New York University Press, 2009), 239.

34. Guinier, *Lift Every Voice*, 196.

35. For one such remarkable exchange, see Guinier, *Lift Every Voice*, 211–12.

36. See Chestnut and Cass, *Black in Selma*, 383.

37. "Vote Fraud Jury Is Protested," *New York Times*, September 26, 1985; "All-White Jury Picked to Hear Alabama Vote Fraud Trial," *Washington Post*, September 26, 1985; "U.S. Appeals Court to Review Selection of Vote Fraud Jury," *New York Times*, September 27, 1985.

38. "Black Activist Guilty in Alabama Voting Case," *New York Times*, October 17, 1985; "Justice Department Dealt Setbacks in Prosecuting Black Activists," *Washington Post*, July 4, 1987.

39. "Justice Department Dealt Setbacks in Prosecuting Black Activists"; *United States v. Gordon*, 817 F.2d 1538, 1540 (11th Cir. 1987) and 836 F.2d 1312 (1988).

40. "Celebrating Black Margins of Victory," *Washington Post*, November 6, 1986; United States Senate, Committee of the Judiciary, *Hearings on the Nomination of Jefferson B. Sessions III to Be U.S. District Judge for the Southern District of Alabama*, 99th Cong., 2nd sess., 1987.

41. Thomas Edsall and Mary Edsall, *Chain Reaction: The Impact of Race, Rights, and Taxes on American Politics* (New York: W. W. Norton, 1992), 126. This shift was slightly more nuanced that Edsall and Edsall suggest. As in other parts of the South, class and geography determined when certain groups of white Alabamans left the state Democratic Party. See Alexander Lamis, *Southern Politics in the 1990s* (Baton Rouge: Louisiana State University Press, 1999), 221–48.

42. Franklin, *Back to Birmingham*, 329–31.

43. Ibid., 307–11, 325–28.

44. Arrington states in his autobiography that he first heard rumors that the FBI was investigating corruption in his administration "about 1985." He ordered the file in 1986 as these rumors increased in frequency. Richard Arrington, *There's Hope for the World: A Memoir of Birmingham, Alabama's First African American Mayor* (Tuscaloosa: University of Alabama Press, 2008), 116.

45. FBI dossier of Richard Arrington, in Richard Arrington Jr. Investigation Files, file 1935, Department of Archives and Manuscripts, Birmingham Public Library.

46. Alexander Lamis, *The Two-Party South* (New York: Oxford University Press, 1990), 266–72.

47. In the weeks leading up to the start of the legislative session, Hunt's office received an avalanche of calls from white Alabamans demanding that the flag not be taken down. "House Lets Flag Remain," *Birmingham Post-Herald*, February 3, 1988.

48. See "Black Lawmakers Say Hunt Ordered Audits," *Birmingham Post-Herald*, February 26, 1987; ABLC President James Buskey, letter to Attorney General Richard Thornburgh, June 16, 1989, copy in possession of the author; "Ex-Clerk Convicted in Alabama Election Case," *New York Times*, June 6, 1987.

49. Mary Sawyer, *The Dilemma of Black Politics: A Report on the Harassment of Black Elected Officials* (Los Angeles: National Association of Human Rights Workers, 1977), 138–39; Sawyer, *The Harassment of African American Elected Officials: Ten Years Later* (Washington, D.C.: Voter Education Research Action, 1987), 38.

50. "Legislator in Alabama Is Accused of Extortion," *New York Times*, May 28, 1988; "NAACP Official Is Indicted in Alabama," *New York Times*, June 18, 1988. Not long after Reed was sent to prison, Chesser was released on parole. He received the early release

in return for cooperation in the Reed case. See "Convicted Killer Who Was Key in Reed Conviction Is Released," *Birmingham News*, October 10, 1989.

51. Moussallem had run a complex bribery scheme in which he offered IRS agents large bribes in order to have them reduce the penalties assessed to wealthy individuals from the northern plains. Those wealthy individuals would then pay Moussallem for his help. He was captured in an elaborate IRS-FBI sting and offered lenience in return for his service as an informant. "Anatomy of a Sting," *Birmingham News*, October 29, 1989.

52. Affidavit of Robert Moussallem, June 5, 1989, in "File on Harassment of Richard Arrington Jr., Mayor of the City of Birmingham, Alabama and Other Black Elected Officials by the Offices of the Federal Bureau of Investigation, Internal Revenue Service, United States Attorney, 1989," Richard Arrington Jr. Investigation Files, file 1935, Department of Archives and Manuscripts, Birmingham Public Library. An investigation by the DOJ, OPR, confirmed that Moussallem worked as an informant for the FBI from October 25, 1988 to April 1989. George J. Terwilliger III, memorandum to Michael Shaheen Jr. regarding U.S. Attorney Frank Donaldson, January 8, 1992, p. 7, n. 4, in Richard Arrington Jr. Investigation Files, file 1935, Department of Archives and Manuscripts, Birmingham Public Library.

53. U.S. Attorney Frank Donaldson, letter to Robert Moussallem, November 23, 1988, in "File on Harassment of Richard Arrington Jr."

54. Affidavit of Robert Moussallem.

55. Affidavit of Richard Arrington Jr., April 27, 1989, in "File on Harassment of Richard Arrington Jr."

56. Watkins had served as counsel for the three black Bullock County commissioners in the 1982 official corruption case brought by the federal prosecutors. He did not claim that the prosecution was racial repression at the time. The Moussallem revelations, however, appear to have convinced him that the 1982 case was the first in an unbroken string of DOJ repression. *United States of America v. Alonza Ellis, Fred Crawford, and Benjamin Jordan*, 82-7271 (11th Cir., July 11, 1983).

57. Donald Watkins, letter to Frank Donaldson, May 2, 1989, in "File on Harassment of Richard Arrington Jr."; Frank Donaldson, letter to Donald Watkins, May 5, 1989, in "File on Harassment of Richard Arrington Jr."; Terwilliger memorandum to Shaheen.

For media coverage of the Arrington affidavit, see "Arrington Says U.S. Agents behind Plot to Frame Him," *Birmingham News*, May 19, 1989; "Zoning Case Used to Bait Arrington Attorney Charges," *Birmingham News*, May 20, 1989; "Arrington Wasn't Only Target, Lawyer Says," *Birmingham Post-Herald*, May 22, 1989; "Mayor Says Feds May Have Tried to Frame Him," *Birmingham Times*, May 23, 1989; "Moussallem Was Offered Deal by Donaldson," *Birmingham Post-Herald*, May 24, 1989; "Arrington Not First Black leader under Microscope," *Birmingham News*, June 3, 1989.

58. "Boles Claims FBI Used Sons as Threat," *Birmingham News*, May 24, 1989; "Prosecutors Seek Boles' Help in Three Cases," *Birmingham News*, August 11, 1989.

59. Watkins and Wilson quoted in "Black Leaders: Arrests Are New Form of Racism," *Montgomery Advertiser*, May 28, 1989.

60. "FBI Agents Vow to Continue Public Corruption Probes," *Montgomery Advertiser*, June 3, 1989.

61. "Sanders: Blacks Targets of Sting,", *Birmingham News Post-Herald*, June 3, 1989; "Black Senator Says Majority of Black Officials Being Probed," *Montgomery Advertiser*, June 3, 1989; Richard Arrington, "Dancing with the FBI: Two Decades of Federal Harassment," *Covert Action Information Bulletin*, no. 36 (Spring 1991): 9–11. While it is impossible to determine how many of the 694 Alabama black elected officials sitting in June 1989 were under investigation, it can be said with certainty that certain classes of elected officials did, in fact, experience the level of scrutiny cited by Sanders. For instance, as will be seen later, approximately half of the 24 black members of the Alabama Legislature were being investigated by federal authorities in 1989.

62. Richard Arrington, letter to Don Siegelman, May 31, 1989; Don Siegelman, letter to Richard Arrington, June 6, 1989, both in "File on Harassment of Richard Arrington Jr."

In an effort to smear Siegelman as a pawn of black Birmingham politicians, *The Advocate*, a right-wing Alabama newspaper, claimed to have uncovered evidence of a secret deal between Arrington and Siegelman to whitewash the investigation in exchange for black political support. Specifically, it claimed: "*The Advocate* has received information from normally reliable sources that Alabama Attorney General Don Siegelman and Birmingham Mayor Richard Arrington have made a political deal whereby Siegelman agreed to appoint a 'special prosecutor' selected by Arrington to whitewash the financial dealings between federally indicted Robert Moussallem and Mayor Arrington, former Arrington aide Willie Davis, State Senator Earl Hilliard, State Representative John Rogers and Birmingham City Councilmen Jeff Germany and William Bell. In exchange, according to the information received by *The Advocate*, Siegelman has been promised the political support, endorsement and votes of the New South Coalition and the Jefferson County Citizen's Coalition in the 1990 Alabama Gubernatorial election." "Siegelman — Arrington Deal: Appoint Special Prosecutor in Exchange for Votes in Gubernatorial Election," *Advocate*, June 4, 1989. *The Advocate* never produced any evidence to back up its claims.

Ironically, in 2006, former governor Siegelman was convicted and sent to jail in what many observers believe was a politically motivated criminal prosecution by two Republican U.S. attorneys working in concert with political operatives in the George W. Bush White House. "The Strange Case of an Imprisoned Alabama Governor," *New York Times*, September 10, 2007.

63. For a discussion of the Freidman affidavit, see chapter 6.

64. Richard Arrington, handwritten memo to Hank Sanders, Michael Figures, Earl Hilliard, and J. L. Chestnut, May 30, 1989, in "File on Harassment of Richard Arrington Jr."

65. Press release, Alabama Black Elected and Appointed Officials Legal Defense Fund, June 7, 1989, copy in possession of the author.

66. Richard Arrington Jr. and Joseph Reed, letter to Attorney General Richard Thornburgh, June 12, 1989, copy in possession of the author.

67. "Black Leaders Hit Wall in D.C.," *Birmingham Post-Herald*, June 30, 1989.

68. "FBI Aims at Three Officials," *Birmingham Post-Herald*, July 27, 1989; "3 Legislators Charged with Extortion," *Birmingham Post-Herald*, October 13, 1989.

69. Alabama Black Elected and Appointed Officials Legal Defense Fund, *The FBI Investigation of Black Elected Officials: Atlanta and Birmingham* (July 1989); Alabama Black Elected and Appointed Officials Legal Defense Fund, *The FBI Investigation of Black Elected Officials* (December 1989), both in file 1935, Richard Arrington Jr. Investigation Files, Department of Archives and Manuscripts, Birmingham Public Library.

70. "Prosecutors Seek Boles' Help in 3 Cases."

71. Allen report quoted from Burnham, *Above the Law*, 260; Donald Watkins, "A Report from the City of Birmingham, Alabama to the United States Senate Judiciary Committee on the Harassment of African American Birmingham City Officials by Offices of the United States Attorney, the Federal Bureau of Investigation, and the Internal Revenue Service (Criminal Division)," February 21, 1990, 42–47, in Richard Arrington Jr. Investigation Files, file 1935, Department of Archives and Manuscripts, Birmingham Public Library. In April 1993, Hunt was convicted of directing two hundred thousand dollars in inaugural and campaign funds to personal use and was stripped of the governorship. Although all the governor's alleged crimes occurred between 1985 and 1992, when the Reagan and Bush DOJs were investigating black and Democratic Alabama elected officials at an extremely high rate, the charges were not brought until Democratic state attorney general Jimmy Evans assumed office in 1993. In 1997, Hunt was granted "a pardon based on innocence" by the Alabama Board of Pardons and Paroles, raising claims by state Republicans that he had been the victim of a political prosecution by a Democratic attorney general. Two of the three board members who issued the pardon, however, were Hunt appointees presenting a clear conflict of interest. "Ex-Gov. Hunt of Alabama Cleared by Pardon Board," *New York Times*, June 12, 1997.

72. Watkins, "Report from the City of Birmingham." Wilson testified that he had called the DOJ to recuse himself from any investigation resulting from the early October press reports on the financial relationship between Collier and Dickinson during the October 26, 1987, pretrial hearing for the Bessemer dog track case. "Spratt's Selective Prosecution Claims Unfounded, Judge Says," *Birmingham Post-Herald*, October 27, 1987. Wilson quoted from "U.S. Attorney Says Case Is Colorblind," *Birmingham Post-Herald*, October 21, 1989.

73. "No Bribes Accepted Boles Says," *Birmingham Post-Herald*, November 15, 1989; "Jury Set to Get Case of Porter, Three Legislators," *Birmingham News*, November 16, 1989.

74. "Federal Extortion Conspiracy Trial Gets Underway," *Birmingham News*, November 14, 1989; "Jury Set to Get Case of Porter, Three Legislators"; Porter quoted in "No Bribes Accepted Boles Says." The prosecutors' inability to make their case was not necessarily evidence of the defendants' innocence. In a 2002 interview, Earl Hilliard alleged that McDowell had, in fact, accepted the stock options deal and had urged him to accept it as well. Earl Hilliard, interview with the author, Washington, D.C., February 14, 2002.

75. "2 Acquitted in Track Trial," *Birmingham Post-Herald*," November 17, 1989; ""Jury Acquits Porter, McDowell in Bribe Case," *Birmingham News/Birmingham Post-Herald*, November 18, 1989.

76. "FBI Accuracy under Attack in Bribe Trial," *Birmingham News*, December 12, 1989.

77. "Jury Convicts Rep. Pat Davis, Clears Rogers and Wright," *Birmingham News*, December 21, 1989.

78. Arrington, *There's Hope for the World*, 143–44.

79. Arrington's statement brought an uncharacteristically direct rebuttal from Allen Whitacker, special agent in charge of the Birmingham office of the FBI. Speaking to reporters, Whitacker stated, "Not only were none of the people present FBI employees, but none of them were acting in a capacity as an informant or a source of the FBI, and none had ever acted in that capacity." "Moussallem's Briefcase May Hold Clues," *Birmingham News*, September 29, 1989.

80. "Backtracking in Birmingham," *Newsweek*, July 1989; "Moussallem's Briefcase May Hold Clues"; "Watley Claims He Left Table after Fatal Shot," *Birmingham News*, September 30, 1989; "Lawyer: Feds Seek Moussallem Tapes," *Birmingham News*, October 5, 1989; "Watley Passed Lie Detector Test about Moussallem's Death," *Birmingham News*, October 12, 1989; "Grand Jury Subpoenas Partner of Goggans," *Birmingham News*, October 23, 1989; "Watley Agrees to Testify in Moussallem Shooting," *Birmingham News*, October 27, 1989; "Developer's Shooting Called Accident," *Montgomery Advertiser*, September 28, 1989.

There is some dispute about whether Moussallem had the tapes with him on September 26. Chief Deputy District Attorney Roger Brown, who was leading the local investigation of the shooting, stated that he did not recall investigators finding any tapes in Moussallem's briefcase. Indeed, there is a question of whether the tapes even existed. Richard Arrington and Moussallem's attorney, Doug Jones, claimed to have copies of the tapes, but they never produced them for investigators or the media. "Watley Passed Lie-Detector Test about Moussallem's Death"; "Watley Agrees to Testify in Moussallem Shooting"; Whittaker quoted in "Moussallem Briefcase May Hold Clues."

81. "Alabama," *USA Today*, February 23, 1990. For a short description of black elected officials' suspicion of foul play, see ABEAO-LDF, "FBI Investigation of Black Elected Officials" (December 1989), 7–8; Arrington quoted from "Has Tapes of Moussallem Mayor Says," *Birmingham News*, October 31, 1989.

82. Arrington claims that federal prosecutors dropped the charges against Kelley because "his attorneys filed an affidavit in his January 1990 criminal proceeding stating that he immediately reported to his lawyers in January 1985 an apparent bribery solicitation by someone he believed to be a corrupt IRS official. The attempted bribe was reported by Kelley's attorneys to federal prosecutors, who agreed not to indict him if he cooperated in the prosecution of other cases. Despite assisting federal prosecutors over a considerable time, Kelley was eventually indicted anyway. His attorneys then became witnesses against the government." Arrington, "Dancing with the FBI." See also "U.S. Will Drop IRS Bribery Charges," *Birmingham News*, January 20, 1990. Watkins reported Kelley's claims to the OPR on January 24, 1990. Donald Watkins, letter to Senator Joseph Biden and Assistant Counsel, DOJ, OPR, David Bobzien, September 21, 1990, in Richard Arrington Jr. Investigation Files, file 1935, Department of Archives and Manuscripts, Birmingham Public Library.

83. Watkins, "Report from the City of Birmingham"; Birmingham SAC Cecil Moses,

letter to Mayor Richard Arrington in response to Arrington's October 29, 1986, FOIA request, November 12, 1986, in Richard Arrington Jr. Investigation Files, file 1935, Department of Archives and Manuscripts, Birmingham Public Library; FBI dossier of Richard Arrington.

84. Watkins, "Report from the City of Birmingham"; "Donaldson Disputes Arrington's Claims about Harassment," *Birmingham News*, February 22, 1990; *Congressional Record*, Senate, 101st Congress, 2nd sess., vol. 136, no. 24., pp. 2533–46.

85. Watkins, letter to Biden and Bobzien.

86. Ibid. Arrington describes the indictment in *There's Hope for the World*, 121.

87. "Birmingham Mayor Cited for Contempt" *New York Times*, January 18, 1992. In his autobiography, Arrington notes that on the first date named by Barnett and Brown, he was leading a citizens' delegation to Israel that included Birmingham-area reporters. On the date of the second alleged payoff, Arrington claims that he was at the Democratic National Committee headquarters in Washington, D.C., attending a fund-raiser for his reelection campaign. Arrington, *There's Hope for the World*, 155.

88. "Birmingham Mayor Faces Jail in Corruption Probe," *Atlanta Constitution*, January 17, 1992.

89. "Birmingham Mayor Cited for Contempt."

90. "With 700 Supporters Rallying Round, Birmingham Mayor Goes to Prison," *New York Times*, January 24, 1992. Quote from president of the Birmingham chapter of the SCLC, Rev. Abraham Woods, in "Birmingham Mayor Going to Jail Today; Supreme Court Justice Denies Appeal of Contempt Sentence," *Atlanta Constitution*, January 23, 1992.

91. "Integrity Unit to Enter City Hall Probe," *Atlanta Constitution*, January 28, 1992.

92. "New U.S. Attorney Approves Recent Entrapment Scheme Aimed at Mayor," Press release of the Office of the Mayor, Birmingham, Alabama, August 6, 1992, Richard Arrington Jr. Investigation Files, file 1935, Department of Archives and Manuscripts, Birmingham Public Library.

93. "Justice Department, Mayor Make Peace," *Birmingham News*, July 30, 1993.

94. Ibid.; "Washington Area to Lose 2 High-Profile Prosecutors," *Washington Post*, March 24, 1993.

95. Donaldson quoted in Watkins, "Report from the City of Birmingham."

96. Joint Center for Political and Economic Studies, *Black Elected Officials: A National Roster* (Washington, D.C.: Joint Center for Political and Economic Studies, 1984), 14; Joint Center for Political and Economic Studies, *Black Elected Officials: A National Roster* (Washington, D.C.: Joint Center for Political and Economic Studies, 1990), 11.

97. The OPR's findings are contained in Memorandum from Department of Justice, Office of Professional Responsibility counsel Michael Shaheen Jr. to Acting Deputy Attorney General George Terwilliger III, January 8, 1992, in Richard Arrington Jr. Investigation Files, file 1935, Department of Archives and Manuscripts, Birmingham Public Library; the ABEAO-LDF findings are contained in Watkins, "Report from the City of Birmingham."

98. "Black Officials Charge U.S. Harassment," *New York Times*, June 26, 1989.

CHAPTER SIX. *The Center for the Study of the Harassment of African Americans and the Decline of Antiharassment Organizing, 1987–1995*

1. Mervyn Dymally quoted in "Summary of Hearing in Washington, D.C., September 27, 1990," *Journal of Intergroup Relations* 18, no. 3 (Fall 1991): 42–66.

2. In November 1981, black Mississippi state senator Henry Kirksey (D) wrote to supporters alleging that the Carthan cases were part of a "rerunning [of] the post-Reconstruction drama" and urging them to send donations to the national campaign. "The Ordeal of Eddie James Carthan and the Fight for Democratic Rights," *Freedomways* 23, no. 1 (1983): 10–13; "Resolution on Issues Arising from the Eddie James Carthan Case," in Minutes of the General Board of Church and Society, March 23–26, 1983, appendix 12, United Methodist Church Archives-GCAH, Madison, N.J.

3. For a detailed discussion of these cases, see chapter 4.

4. "Black Leaders Paint Justice Department as New KKK," *Houston Chronicle*, August 2, 1987. Conyers failed to hold the proposed hearings for reasons unknown.

5. "'The Plan' Comes to Congress?" *Roll Call*, February 26, 1990.

6. Benjamin Ginsberg and Martin Shefter, *Politics by Other Means: Politicians, Prosecutors, and the Press from Watergate to Whitewater*, 3rd ed. (New York: W. W. Norton, 2002), 36. See also Nicol Rae, *Conservative Reformers: The Republican Freshman and the Lessons of the 104th Congress* (New York: M. E. Sharpe, 1998), 21.

7. "Black leaders Paint Justice Department as New KKK." See also "U.S. Probes Assailed as Racist," *Washington Post*, August 9, 1987

8. "Black Heat," *National Journal* 19, no. 35 (August 29, 1987): 2188–90.

9. All those polled were African American. Pollsters noted that 50 percent of respondents had no opinion on whether the investigations were being brought to embarrass blacks, and 12 percent believed that they were based on sound evidence. "Probes and Prejudice," *Washington Post*, February 28, 1988.

10. "Wilder to Blacks: Don't Be Patsies," *Washington Post*, July 17,1987; Mervyn Dymally, letter to Douglass Wilder, July 23, 1987, copy in possession of the author; Douglass Wilder, letter to Mervyn Dymally, August 3, 1987, copy in possession of the author.

11. "Marchers Back Hastings in Impeachment fight," *South Florida Sun-Sentinel*, April 14, 1987. By the time the marchers descended on downtown Fort Lauderdale, however, the Eleventh Circuit report was already before the House of Representatives. As early as 1983, many South Florida blacks were receptive to Hastings's claims of harassment, citing federal investigations of several other high-ranking area African American elected and appointed officials as evidence that the Hastings investigation was part of a pattern. "Arrest of Black Police Chief Stirs Blacks' Fears in Florida," *New York Times*, August 17, 1983.

12. "'Fight Is On,' Ford Tells Supporters," *Memphis Commercial Appeal*, April 28, 1987.

13. "Congressman Plans to Defy Gag Order," *Washington Post*, May 10, 1987; "House Leaders Protest 'Gag Order' on Ford," *Congressional Quarterly Weekly*, May 9, 1987; "Ford's Attorneys File Motion to Halt Gag Order," *Memphis Commercial Appeal*, May 5, 1987.

14. "District Building Rally Backs Barry; Crowd Protests Tactics in Probe," *Washington Post*, June 26, 1987; "Washington Mayor Assails Disclosure in Inquiry," *Washington Post*, August 30, 1984; "Barry Aide Criticizes News Leaks," *Washington Post*, September 1, 1984; "Mayor of Washington Seeks Investigation of Prosecutor," *Washington Post*, August 26, 1986; "Cocaine Use by Washington Mayor Alleged," *Washington Post*, June 19, 1987; "Washington's Mayor Assails U.S. Attorney on Drug Report," *Washington Post*, June 20, 1987; "The Federal Investigation: Highlights," *Washington Post*, September 13, 1987.

15. "6 National Black Groups Assail Probe of District," *Washington Post*, July 8, 1987; "Suit Against U.S. Attorney by Mayor Barry Dismissed," *Washington Post*, July 25, 1987.

16. Clarence Mitchell III, interview with the author, Baltimore, November 16, 1999. In the interview, Mitchell stated, "As a result of my efforts in Alabama, we know that [then Alabama U.S. attorney for the Southern District Jefferson] Sessions called the U.S. attorney here [Baltimore] and . . . asked [him] to put the heat under me." Mitchell based this claim on a memo he says his defense team found during the Wedtech trial. He did not produce the memo for the author, nor was it entered into evidence during the Wedtech trial.

17. Tape recording of Baltimore "freedom rally," in possession of the author; "Eaves Persecuted, Marchers Claim," *Atlanta Journal and Constitution*, February 14, 1988; Clarence Mitchell III, phone interview with the author, January 11, 2005.

18. Conyers accepted the assignment after two senior Judiciary Committee Subcommittee chairs, Barney Frank (D-Mass.) and Robert Kastenmeier (D-Wis.), declined the position for fear that the case was too volatile. Mary L. Volcanseck, *Judicial Impeachment: None Called for Justice* (Urbana: University of Illinois Press, 1993), 104.

19. The Hastings case was agonizing for Conyers. He wrestled with his sincere belief that the DOJ under Reagan and Bush was selectively prosecuting black elected officials and with the facts of the case. "Panel Calls for Impeachment, but Hastings Vows to Fight On," *Congressional Quarterly Weekly*, July 8, 1988; "Conyers Hears Echoes of Civil Rights Struggle," *Congressional Quarterly Weekly*, July 8, 1988.

20. "Judiciary Committee Votes to Impeach Hastings," *Congressional Quarterly Weekly*, July 30, 1988.

21. "By Wide Margin, House Impeaches Hastings," *Congressional Quarterly Weekly*, August 6, 1988; "Hastings Removed from Bench after Conviction by the Senate," *Congressional Quarterly Weekly*, October 21, 1989. The House sent seventeen articles of impeachment to the Senate for consideration. The Senate decided to consider only eleven of those articles as is its prerogative. "Impeachment a Needed Change?" *Congressional Quarterly Weekly*, October 21, 1989.

22. African American Legal Defense Fund, "Update of Federal Judge Alcee Hastings Impeachment Trial," July 27, 1989; African American Legal Defense Fund, "Update of Federal Judge Alcee Hastings Impeachment Trial," August 4, 1989; African American Legal Defense Fund, "Update of Federal Judge Alcee Hastings Impeachment Trial," October 8, 1989, all copies in possession of the author.

23. "D.C. Talk Show Host Backs Hastings' Cause," *Miami Herald*, March 11, 1989; "Black Leaders Back Hastings, Pledge Protests," *Fort Lauderdale News*, July 13, 1989; African American Legal Defense Fund, "Update of Federal Judge Alcee Hastings

Impeachment trial," July 27, 1989; "Farrakhan Speaks at Rally; Hastings Sends His Regrets," *South Florida Sun Sentinel*, August 2, 1989; "Farrakhan Rallies for Judge Hastings; Gathering at NW Church Also Hears Tawana Brawley's Adviser," *Washington Post*, August 2, 1989; African American Legal Defense Fund, "Update of Federal Judge Alcee Hastings Impeachment Trial," August 4, 1989; "Hastings: Judgment Is for God, Not Senate," *Miami Herald*, October 19, 1989.

24. Mary Sawyer, interview with the author, Washington, D.C., October 3, 2000; Mervyn Dymally, interview with the author, Los Angeles, California, January 8, 2001. Dymally again helped Sawyer to publish her findings by directing the VERA Center to absorb the cost of printing. The VERA Center relocated to Washington, D.C., following Dymally's election to Congress in 1980. Dymally's colleague, Delegate Walter Fauntroy (D-Washington, D.C.), doubtless animated by the ongoing DOJ investigation of Washington, D.C., city government, provided an attention-grabbing venue for Sawyer to release the report by hosting a "brain trust," or public forum, on harassment at the Congressional Black Caucus Foundation's Annual Legislative Conference. For a short description of the brain trust, see "Probes and Prejudice," *Washington Post*, February 28, 1988; "Blacks' Education, Political Welfare, Major Subjects of D.C. Caucus Weekend," *Jet*, October 19, 1987.

25. Using her established connections with black elected officials and political activists, Sawyer collected thirty-six new case studies of harassment for the new study. Mary Sawyer, *The Harassment of Black Elected Officials: Ten Years Later* (Washington, D.C.: Voter Education and Research Action, 1987), 13, 3.

26. Sawyer does present a detailed discussion of the "the present context" in which harassment was taking place in *Ten Years Later*. In this section, she explores the historical developments that "[gave] rise to those actions which constitute harassment." She rightly portrays harassment as the product of three historical developments in post-civil-rights-era U.S. politics: "the increase in the number of Black elected officials, . . . the conservative backlash against the protest movements of the 1960s, and the attendant emergence of the political right, . . . [and] the aftermath of the misadventures of President Richard Nixon known as 'Watergate.'" Sawyer goes on to identify the Reagan DOJ and the increasingly racist mood of certain segments of the white population as the motors of harassment in the 1980s. Yet, as in *Dilemma*, Sawyer fails to define harassment; treats harassment as an ahistorical relationship between blacks and whites; and conflates the actions of the state, the news media, and private individuals in her case studies. Sawyer, *Ten Years Later*, 13, 14, 21–25, 40–49.

27. I base my estimate of *Ten Years Later*'s readership on the printings of the two reports. Sawyer printed eight hundred copies of *Dilemma* and, through word of mouth, exhausted her supply within three years. In fall 1991, the *Journal for Intergroup Relations* reprinted Sawyers's 1987 study. The fall 1991 issue was one of the most popular in the journal's history. Approximately five thousand copies were distributed. This number is in addition to the several hundred copies of *Ten Years Later* printed and distributed by the VERA Center between 1987 and 1991.

28. "Black Officials: Probes and Prejudice; Is There a Double Standard for Bringing Indictments?" *Washington Post*, February 28, 1988. Several black opinion columnists

also wrote on harassment in 1988. In January 1988, *Philadelphia Inquirer* associate editor Acel Moore published an op-ed titled "Do Black Officials Get Treated Fairly?" In partial answer to her own question, she stated, "I agree that black politicians who attain high public office and particularly for the first time are held to a higher or different standard than whites who had preceded them in office." Just one week later, *Washington Post* columnist Dorothy Gilliam published an op-ed titled "The FBI and Black Leaders," which detailed the affidavit submitted by FBI informant Hirsch Friedman in the case of Fulton County commissioner Reginald Eaves. Though Friedman's allegations against the FBI "may or may not be true," Gilliam argued, "They are deeply serious and deserve a full investigation, not a back of the hand dismissal as the Justice Department has done so far." "Do Black Officials Get Treated Fairly?"; "The FBI and Black Leaders," *Washington Post*, January 18, 1988.

29. In 1979, Friedman reported to local agents that a city zoning inspector had solicited a bribe from him in return for fixing a zoning case for one of his clients. The agents who recorded his complaint were impressed by Friedman and asked him to work undercover for the bureau. Friedman agreed and worked for the bureau from 1979 to 1982. See "The FBI and Black Leaders"; Affidavit of Hirsch Friedman, December 17, 1989, and Affidavit of Hirsch Friedman, January 20, 1988, in Alabama Elected and Appointed Officials Legal Defense Fund, *The FBI Investigation of Black Elected Officials* (Montgomery: Alabama Elected and Appointed Officials Legal Defense Fund, December 1989), in Richard Arrington Jr. Investigation Files, file 1935, Department of Archives and Manuscripts, Birmingham Public Library.

30. "Judge Dismisses Jury in Clarence Mitchell Case," *Washington Post*, January 13, 1988; "Lawyers for Barry Seek to Quash Jail Term," *New York Amsterdam News*, January 26, 1991; Representative Don Edwards (D-Calif.), letter to Mary Sawyer, April 5, 1988, copy in possession of the author; Donald Watkins, "A Report from the City of Birmingham, Alabama to the United States Senate Judiciary Committee on the Harassment of African American Birmingham City Officials by Offices of the United States Attorney, the Federal Bureau of Investigation, and the Internal Revenue Service (Criminal Division)," February 21, 1990, 35, in Richard Arrington Jr. Investigation Files, file 1935, Department of Archives and Manuscripts, Birmingham Public Library.

On April 14, 1988, Sessions responded to Rodino, stating that Friedman's claims had no merit. Memorandum from Department of Justice Office of Professional responsibility counsel Michael Shaheen Jr. to Acting Deputy Attorney General George Terwilliger III, January 8, 1992, in Richard Arrington Jr. Investigation Files, file 1935, Department of Archives and Manuscripts, Birmingham Public Library.

31. Memorandum from Shaheen to Terwilliger; John Barth, *Giles Goat Boy* (New York: Anchor Books, 1987). Freidman would publish his first novel, which revolves around a murder conspiracy involving Georgia politicians, in 2006. Hirsch Friedman, *Murder under the Golden Dome: The Planned Assassination of Governor George Busbee by the Columbian Cartel* (Atlanta: AMG Network, 2006).

32. The report, which was being prepared by a committee under the leadership of state senator Alfred Jenkins (D-N.Y.), was never completed. "Stalking the Black Leaders," *National Affairs*, October 1989, 18–19.

33. A late January 1990 *Washington Post* poll found that 50 percent of African American respondents believed that federal investigators had targeted Barry because he was African American. See Harry Jaffe and Tom Sherwood, *Dream City: Race, Power, and the Decline of Washington, D.C.* (New York: Simon and Schuster, 1994), 274.

34. Hooks made this statement while standing on the White House lawn following a meeting with President George H. W. Bush concerning a recent rash of mail bombings of NAACP offices in the South. "Informal Question and Answer Session with Benjamin Hooks, Chairman, NAACP, and William F. Gibson, Chairman of the National Board, NAACP," Federal Information Systems Corp., January 22, 1990. Gibson quoted in "Blacks Dubious after Barry Bust," *Guardian* (London), January 31, 1990. Most D.C. blacks shared Gibson's nuanced view of Barry and the federal investigators. As Clarence Lusane notes, "Immediately following the arrest . . . a substantial number of Blacks were angry with the Mayor. This anger persisted and was manifested again when Barry ran for city council (following his trial, in the 1990 election) against the desires of about 70 percent of the electorate and subsequently received only about 20 percent of the vote in that election." Many African Americans saw Barry's behavior and the behavior of federal agents as two distinct issues. The FBI and the DOJ may have had a history of selective prosecution of black elected officials, but the mayor had a history of substance abuse and corruption. Lusane, *Pipe Dream Blues: Racism and the War on Drugs* (Boston: South End Press, 1991), 188. See also "Marion Barry's Toughest Campaign: A Bid for Respect as Well as Office," *New York Times*, November 3, 1990.

35. Unnamed female juror quoted in "Blacks Cite Selective Prosecution," *South Florida Sun-Sentinel*, June 10, 1990. The jury is described in detail in "Chasm Divided Jurors in Barry Drug Trial; Differing Outlooks Led to Deadlock," *Washington Post*, August 23, 1990.

36. "Prosecution Denies That FBI Targeted Blacks," *Washington Post*, July 28, 1990.

37. Jaffe and Sherwood, *Dream City*, 276.

38. "Marion Barry's Battle for Public Opinion Engrosses Many," *St. Louis Post-Dispatch*, July 6, 1990.

39. Jaffe and Sherwood, *Dream City*, 288.

40. Ibid., 292.

41. "Chasm Divided Jurors in Barry Drug Trial."

42. On January 19, 1990, all the major U.S. dailies ran front-page articles on the Barry arrest. "Sources Say Mayor Used Crack in Downtown D.C. Hotel Room," *Washington Post*, January 19, 1990; "Washington Mayor Seized in Drug Sting," *Atlanta Constitution*, January 19, 1990; "U.S. Agents Arrest Mayor of Capital on Drug Charges," *New York Times*, January 19, 1990; "Mayor of D.C. Arrested on Drug Charges," *Los Angeles Times*, January 19, 1990; "D.C. Mayor Arrested in Drug Bust," *Chicago Tribune*, January 19, 1990; "D.C. Mayor Arrested on Drug Charges," *Boston Globe*, January 19, 1990; "D.C. Mayor Held on Drug Charges," *USA Today*, January 19, 1990. These same papers followed up with heavy coverage of the evolving scandal and the trial later that summer.

43. For the Times Mirror poll, see "From Texas to Tokyo, the Trial's Hot; Barry Drama Rivets Readers across Country, around the World," *Washington Post*, July 30, 1990. For a sampling of newspaper coverage of the Barry trial abroad, see "Bogotá Newspapers

Carry News of Arrest on Their Front Pages," *Washington Post*, January 20, 1990; "Hotel Drug 'Sting' Nets Washington's Mayor," *Toronto Star*, January 19, 1990; "U.S. Mayor Arrested in Crack 'Sting,'" *Independent* (London), January 20 1990; "Washington Mayor on Drug Charges; United States," *Sydney Morning Herald*, January 20, 1990; "ETATS-UNIS: Déjà plusieurs fois inquiété Le maire de Washington a été arrêté alors qu'il achetait de la drogue," *Le Monde*, January 20, 1990.

44. "Stallings Denounces Barry Drug Arrest; Minister, Mayor's Peers Allege 'Harassment,'" *Washington Post*, April 8, 1990.

45. Conyers quoted from "Harassment: Black Leadership under Attack," *New Orleans Tribune*, June 1990; Thornburgh quoted from "Conyers Charges Thornburgh Harasses Black Elected Officials," *Los Angeles Times*, May 17, 1990.

46. "Jackson Sees 'Pattern' to Probes of Black Officials," *Los Angeles Times*, June 10, 1990.

47. Lusane, *Pipe Dream Blues*, 186.

48. "Hooks Alleges U.S. Harassment of Black Officials," *Washington Post*, July 16, 1990.

49. For detailed discussions of the corruption of the Barry administrations and the mayor's drug use, see Lusane, *Pipe Dream Blues*; Jaffe and Sherwood, *Dream City*.

50. "The Tragedy of Marion Barry," *Michigan Citizen*, September 29, 1990.

51. Carl Rowan, "'Racism' and Reality," *Louisville (Ky.) Courier-Journal*, February 18, 1990.

52. Eddie Carthan created the National Campaign to Free Mayor Eddie Carthan and the Tchula 7 and Preserve Black Political Rights in 1981; black voting rights activists in southwest Alabama created the Black Belt Defense Fund in 1984; in 1987, Alcee Hastings created the AALDF, and the Mitchell brothers created the Clarence Mitchell Jr. Defense Fund; and in 1989 Alabama black elected officials created the ABEAO-LDF.

53. Alcee Hastings and the Mitchell brothers attempted to transform their defense funds into permanent organizations. Soon after the impeachment trial, Hastings's Washington supporters transformed the AALDF into the African American Legal Defense Political Action Committee — a fund-raising and lobbying organization for African Americans based in Washington, D.C. Although the organization appears to have existed in 1990, there is no record of its activities. "African American Legal Defense Political Action Committee" pamphlet, copy in possession of the author. The Mitchell brothers were able to transform the Mitchell Defense Fund into the CSHAA in 1990.

54. Clarence Mitchell III, interview with the author, Baltimore, October 17, 1999.

55. Watson quoted from Transcript of the New York Hearing on Harassment, New York, New York, May 4, 1990, p. 25, copy in possession of the author.

56. "Harassment of African American Elected Officials," Resolution of the National Council of the Churches of Christ in the U.S.A., adopted by the Governing Board, November 16, 1989, in *Journal of Intergroup Relations* 18, no. 3 (Fall 1991): 33–34. The resolution was based, in large measure, on Mary Sawyer's two studies on harassment.

57. *Journal of Intergroup Relations* 18, no. 3, (Fall 1991).

58. "The Harassment of African-American Officials," C-SPAN, September 27, 1990, ID: 14238.

59. Transcript of the New York Hearing on Harassment, 8–15, 17–19, 46–48, 51–53, 55–57. Owens argued that antiharassment activists must reject "anecdotes and strongly held suspicions" for the "monumental undertaking" of conducting a comparative analysis of federal prosecutions of black and white elected officials that controlled for all the possible variables. Having said that, Owens conceded, "There is no existing data set which would allow us to do the kind of rigorous research we would need to demonstrate such a pattern."

60. See, for instance, "Black Politicians Charge Federal Conspiracy," *USA Today*, September 28–30, 1990; "Black Caucus Takes Aim at Probes of Officials," *Washington Post*, September 29, 1990; "FBI Hopes to Erase Poor Image on Racism," *New York Times*, October 18, 1990. For TV coverage of the hearings, see Transcript of the New York Hearing on Harassment; "Harassment of African-American Officials."

61. "Talk of Government Being Out to Get Blacks Falls on More Attentive Ears," *New York Times*, October 29, 1990. These numbers are a product of a fifty-question WCBS-TV News–*New York Times* poll on race relations delivered to 1,047 adults throughout the city, including 408 blacks and 484 whites, conducted June 17–20, 1990. WCBS-TV News–*New York Times* Race Relations Poll, June 1990, New York, N.Y., Inter-university Consortium for Political and Social Research, Ann Arbor, Mich.

62. "Black Caucus Takes Aim at Probes of Officials," *Washington Post*, September 29, 1990.

63. Mervyn Dymally, "dear colleague" letter concerning the May 1990 New York hearing, April 20, 1990, copy in possession of the author.

64. Dymally quoted from "Summary of Hearing in Washington, D.C.," 42–45.

65. Sandra Peters, letter to Mervyn Dymally, October 20, 1990, copy in possession of the author.

66. Sandra Peters, "The Center for the Study of the Harassment of African Americans," report to potential funders, winter 1991, copy in possession of the author.

67. Vernice Miller and Sandra Peters, letter to Mary Sawyer, May 21, 1991; Sandra Peters, letter to Mary Sawyer, January 18, 1991, both copies in possession of the author.

68. *Journal of Intergroup Relations* 18, no. 3 (Fall 1991); Fred Cloud [editor in chief, *Journal of Intergroup Relations*], letter to Frank Waterhouse [printer], October 3, 1991, copy in possession of the author.

69. Sandra Peters, "The Center for the Study of the Harassment of African Americans: The History Background Work & Initiatives," unpublished report of the CSHAA, June 1991, copy in possession of the author; Cable News Network, *CNN Special Report*, June 19, 1991.

70. Mitchell, interview, November 16, 1999.

71. Sandra Peters, letter to Mary Sawyer, September 19, 1991, copy in possession of the author.

72. Sawyer, *Ten Years Later*, 3.

73. Mitchell, interview, November 16, 1999.

74. Sandra Peters, "Proposal to Institutionalize the Center for the Study of the Harassment of African American elected Officials," September 1991, copy in possession of the author; CSHAA, "The Center for the Study of the Harassment of African

Americans: Background Report," May 14, 1993, in the Richard Arrington, Jr. Files, file 1935, Department of Archives and Manuscripts, Birmingham Public Library.

75. Kenyon Burke, interview with the author, Maplewood, N.J., December 27, 2004.

76. Mitchell, interview, November 16, 1999.

77. In Winston Salem, North Carolina, black alderman Patrick Hairison, lobbyist Rodney Sumler, and community activist Rev. Lee Faye Mack were appealing a May 1992 conviction for bribery and conspiracy in the letting of city contracts. "Winston Salem Verdicts Teach Lessons: 3 Defendants Found Guilty on Most Charges," *People's Advocate* 3, no. 3 (June–July 1992): 1, 3–5. In Compton, California, the FBI had just concluded a sting against newly elected representative Walter Tucker (D-Calif.) and city councilwoman Patricia Moore (D). The two would later be indicted for bribery and conspiracy in 1994. "Rep. Tucker Is Indicted; Denies Bribery Charges," *Los Angeles Times*, August 4, 1994; "Dymally Sought Bribe, Informant Says," *Los Angeles Times*, Metro, October, 12, 1995; "U.S. Prosecutors Move to Block Racism Defense in Moore's Trial," *Los Angeles Times*, Metro, July 12, 1996. Additionally, federal district judge Robert Collins of New Orleans was appealing his conviction for bribery and conspiracy to the Supreme Court. "Federal Judge Is Focus of Bribe Inquiry," *New York Times*, September 27, 1990; "Impeachment Proceeding OK'd," *New Orleans Times-Picayune*, June 24, 1993. For a discussion of the South Carolina investigation, see chapter 4.

78. Chip Berllett and Joel Bellman, *Lyndon LaRouche: Fascism Wrapped in the American Flag* (Boston: Political Research Associates, 1989).

79. For a discussion of LaRouche's vision for a fascist takeover of the U.S. government and world domination, see Lyndon LaRouche, *The Case of Walter Lippmann* (New York: Campaigner Publications, 1977); Lyndon LaRouche, *The Power of Reason* (New York: Benjamin Franklin, 1979). A concise summation of LaRouche's ideology can be found in David King, *Lyndon LaRouche and the New American Fascism* (New York: Doubleday, 1989), 51–53.

80. King, *Lyndon LaRouche*, xiii.

81. Simultaneously, thousands of individuals who had paid for LaRouche literature or donated to the campaign with a credit card began finding unauthorized purchases on their accounts credited to one of the many LaRouche front groups. Ibid., 304–6, 311–13.

82. "LaRouche Sentenced to 15 Years in Prison; Political Extremist Proclaims Innocence," *Washington Post*, January 28, 1989.

83. Harassment ideology reached its peak of influence among African Americans at the same time that LaRouche was on trial, and Manning Marable notes that "it was during the federal government's successful prosecution of LaRouche that the organization accelerated its efforts to cultivate friends and allies among black Americans." Manning Marable, *Black Leadership: Four Great American Leaders and the Struggle for Civil Rights* (New York: Penguin Books, 1999), 180.

84. Transcript of the New York Hearing on Harassment. For a short description of Chavis's criticisms of LaRouche, see Marable, *Black Leadership*, 179–80, 182. Ironically, Marable notes, Chavis would eventually become national spokesman for the NOI and one of the primary organizers of the Million Man March at the very moment that the NOI formed a close relationship with LaRouche and his organization.

85. Founded in 1984 by LaRouche's German wife, Helga Zepp LaRouche, the Schiller Institute operated as the "international propaganda" arm of the NCLC. Its sole purpose was to disseminate LaRouche's ideas in the United States and abroad. The hearings, an institute press release read, were a response to the refusal of the "House Judiciary Committee probe of the incident at Waco, Texas to actually hear evidence of rampant corruption inside the permanent bureaucracy at the U.S. Department of Justice." The organizers were referring to the botched ATF-FBI raid on the Branch Davidian compound in Waco, Texas, which resulted in the death of eighty of the sect's members. The Schiller Institute, the release stated, would expose the "massive cover-up of the flagrant DOJ corruption the Congress had refused to investigate." There, of course, had been no cover up. The House Judiciary Committee had convened to examine the Waco incident only. It was LaRouche who had called for a larger hearing on "rampant corruption" in the "permanent bureaucracy." This type of misrepresentation would characterize the hearings. *Independent Hearings to Investigate Misconduct by the U.S. Department of Justice* (Washington, D.C.: Schiller Institute, 1995).

86. Ibid., 41.

87. Ibid., 42.

88. "Black Politicians Seek Protection against Harassment," *Philadelphia Tribune*, December 26, 1995.

89. Sawyer, interview.

90. "From 'Operation Fruhmenschen' to the McDade-Murtha Act," *New Federalist*, August 3, 1998.

91. Dymally, interview.

92. "Court Documents Reveal a 1998 FBI Plot against Mayor Barry," *Final Call*, December 7, 1999. It is noteworthy that the *Final Call* ran this quote from Dymally. Since at least 1996, the NOI had been working with LaRouche on a variety of projects. See Marable, *Black Leadership*, 165.

The Schiller Institute was also successful in co-opting former South Carolina state senator Theo Mitchell (D), then one of the most recognizable black faces in South Carolina politics. Following the 1995 Tyson's Corner hearings, at which Mitchell was a witness, the senator began collaborating with the Schiller Institute and soon joined its board of directors. In 1998, he traveled to Baltimore to be the featured speaker at a "Stop the Lynchings" town hall meeting. Prior to arriving in Baltimore, Theo Mitchell phoned his old friend and colleague Clarence Mitchell III and invited him to the meeting. During his remarks, Theo pointed to Clarence in the crowd and asked him to address the audience. Clarence, who, in an interview with the author referred to LaRouche as a "fascist," reluctantly obliged, "out of respect for [his] former colleague," he explained. When Clarence stood at the podium to address the crowd, a photographer from the *New Federalist* snapped his picture. The paper would later run the photo in its article on Mervyn Dymally with a misleading caption that implied Mitchell was a scheduled speaker. Thus, by 1998, LaRouche had been successful in co-opting the image of two of the three primary antiharassment activists and developing surrogates among black elected officials. "From 'Operation Fruhmenschen' to the McDade-Murtha Act"; Mitchell, phone interview, January 11, 2005.

The co-optation of antiharassment activists by LaRouche mirrored a larger pattern of increasing black adoption of white right-wing conspiracy theory in the mid-1990s. See Peter Knight, *Conspiracy Culture: From Kennedy to the X Files* (New York: Routledge, 2000), 164.

CONCLUSION. *Political Warfare Ascendant*

1. Clarence Mitchell III, phone interview with the author, January 11, 2005; Mervyn Dymally, interview with the author, Los Angeles, California, January 8, 2001; Mary Sawyer, interview with the author, Washington, D.C., October 3, 2000.

2. A fifth investigation during this period involved former Washington, D.C., Delegate Walter Fauntroy. In 1995 Fauntroy pleaded guilty for understating his income on his 1988 and 1989 financial disclosure statements. The investigation was begun during the House banking scandal of 1992. "Former Delegate Fauntroy Is Charged, Agrees to Plead Guilty," Department of Justice press release, March 22, 1995, copy in possession of the author. I do not count this investigation in my tally for the Clinton years because it was begun after Fauntroy left office.

3. Tucker and prosecution lawyers quoted from "Congressman Heads to Trial in California," *New York Times*, September 25, 1995; "Rep. Tucker Is Indicted; Denies Bribery Charges," *Los Angeles Times*, August 12, 1994; "Trial Opens in Tucker Bribery Case," *Los Angeles Times*, October 4, 1995; "Rep. Tucker Found Guilty of Bribery and Tax Evasion," *Los Angeles Times*, December 9, 1995; "Tucker Gets Prison Term for Extortion," *Los Angeles Times*, April 18, 1996.

4. Rose-Collins quoted from "Oh, Stop Your Whining," *Weekly Standard*, January 15, 1996; "Collins' Aides Performed Personal, Campaign Duties," *The Hill*, August 16, 1995; "Rep. Collins Uses Tax Money for Stamps," *Detroit News*, May 27, 1995; "Collins Seen as Lax Lawmaker," *Detroit Free Press*, August 19, 1995. Rose-Collins was defeated in the 1996 Democratic primary and later replaced in Congress by Carolyn Cheeks Kilpatrick (D-Mich.).

5. Reynolds quoted from "Reynolds' Conduct, Not Race, Is Probed," *Chicago Sun-Times*, August 16, 1994; "Reynolds Indicted," *Chicago Sun-Times*, August 19, 1994; "Reynolds Guilty on All Counts," *Washington Post*, August 23, 1995; "Reynolds Sentenced to 5 Years for Sex Offenses, Obstruction," *Washington Post*, September 29, 1995.

6. "Legal Woes Not Over; Federal Probe Ongoing," *Chicago Sun-Times*, August 23, 1995; "Reynolds' Lawyer Hit on Racial Query," *Chicago Sun-Times*, March 28, 1997; "Farrakhan Visit Stirs Reynolds Courtroom," *Chicago Tribune*, April 12, 1997; "Jury Finds Former Rep. Reynolds Guilty of Fraud," *Washington Post*, April 17, 1997; "Reynolds Admits Guilt during Sentencing," *Chicago Sun-Times*, July 16, 1997.

7. Sanford Bishop, interview with the author, Washington, D.C., December 18, 2001; Corrine Brown, interview with the author, Washington, D.C., July 12, 2002; William Lacy Clay, interview with the author, Washington, D.C., October 17, 2001; Eva Clayton, interview with the author, Washington, D.C., May 8, 2002; James Clyburn, interview with the author, Washington, D.C., March 10, 2002; John Conyers, interview with the author, Washington, D.C., March 5, 2002; Elijah Cummings, interview

with the author, Washington, D.C., December 19, 2001; Alcee Hastings, interview with the author, Washington, D.C., March 12, 2002, May 9, 2002, and June 21, 2002; Earl Hilliard, interview with the author, Washington, D.C., February 14, 2002; Gregory Meeks, interview with the author, Washington, D.C., May 23, 2002; Carrie Meek, interview with the author, Washington, D.C., November 29, 2001.; Donald Payne, interview with the author, Washington, D.C., November 14, 2001; Bobby Rush, interview with the author, Washington, D.C., November 14, 2001; Bobby Scott, interview with the author, Washington, D.C., June 19, 2002; Edolphus Towns, interview with the author, Washington, D.C., May 23, 2002; Bennie Thompson, interview with the author, Washington, D.C., November 14, 2001; Diane Watson, interview with the author, Washington, D.C., April 12, 2002. For a discussion of the 2000 St. Louis vote fraud investigation, see Lorraine C. Minnite, "An Analysis of Voter Fraud in the United States," *Demos* (2005): 14–17.

8. Robert Remini, *The House: The History of the House of Representatives* (New York: Harper Collins, 2007), 457–95; Hillary Clinton quoted from *Today Show*, January 27, 1998. On the Right, Clinton's allegations were dismissed in much the same way that black elected officials allegations of harassment had been in years past. Among liberals, however, the idea gained a not-insignificant degree of support. Paul Krugman explored Clinton's alleged "vast right wing conspiracy" in *The Great Unraveling: Losing Our Way in the New Century* (New York: W. W. Norton, 2004), 217, 269–70. The nonpartisan media investigated the allegations and came to conclusions similar to Krugman. Shortly after Clinton made her allegation, for instance, CNN did a short report on Richard Mellon Scaife. The network reported that Scaife had used millions of dollars to fund anti-Clinton propaganda through his own newspaper and other conservative news organizations, foundations, and think-tanks. "Who Is Richard Mellon Scaife?: He's Very Rich and Very Partisan, but Is He Behind an Anti-Clinton Conspiracy?" CNN, April 27, 1998. Gingrich's claims received the same divided partisan response.

9. "Diplomats Received Political Briefing: Bush Aides Listed Election Targets," *Washington Post*, July 24, 2007; "Jefferson Raids May Signal Return of the Sting," *New Orleans Times-Picayune*, August 21, 2005; "Justice Dept.'s Focus Has Shifted: Terror, Immigration Are Current Priorities," *Washington Post*, October 17, 2007.

10. Public Integrity Section, Criminal Division, Department of Justice, *Report to Congress on the Activities of the Public Integrity Section for 2007* (Washington, D.C.: Government Printing Office, 2008). By searching newspapers for public reports of DOJ investigations of elected officials, Shields and Cragan found that 79.47 percent of reported cases between 2001 and 2006 were of Democrats and 17.87 percent were of Republicans. Donald Shields and John Cragan, "Political Profiling of Elected Democratic Officials: When Rhetorical Vision Participation Runs Amok," *ePluribus Media*, February 18, 2007. Shields and Cragan's methodology was controversial, and in 2009 political scientist Sanford Gordon sought to test their findings using a different methodology. He found that during the sample years 2004 to 2006, Democratic elected officials were six times more likely than Republicans to be prosecuted by the DOJ. Gordon also notes that the DOJ disproportionately investigated Democrats under President Bill Clinton, though the disparity was less severe than under George W. Bush. See Sanford Gordon,

"Assessing Partisan Bias in Federal Public Corruption Prosecutions," *American Political Science Review* 103, no. 4 (November 2009): 542. For reports that suggest that this partisan disparity was a product of conscious political targeting, see Office of Professional Responsibility, United States Department of Justice, *An Investigation into the Removal of Nine U.S. Attorneys in 2006*, (Washington, D.C.: Government Printing Office, September 2008); Majority Staff, House Judiciary Committee, *Allegations of Selective Prosecution in Our Federal Criminal Justice System* (Washington, D.C.: Government Printing Office, 2008). See also "Target of Political Prosecution by Bush-Era Justice Department Fights Back," *Huffington Post*, October 22, 2009; "Firings Had Genesis in White House: Ex-Counsel Miers First Suggested Dismissing Prosecutors 2 Years Ago Documents Show," *Washington Post*, March 13, 2007.

11. "Corruption Issue Comes to Fore," *Washington Post*, July 20, 2006; "Scandals Alone Could Cost Republicans Their House Majority," *Washington Post*, November 2, 2006; "Republican Scandals Helped Pave the Way for Democratic Gains," *Washington Post*, November 8, 2006. Although Democrats used the corruption issue to trounce Republicans in the 2006 midterm elections, it does not appear that any of the investigations were begun by Democrats seeking to gain partisan advantage or revenge, i.e., as political warfare. Most of the scandals were self-inflicted, and only House Speaker Tom Delay (R-Tex.) made repeated claims that his indictment by Travis County, Texas, district attorney Ronnie Earle for alleged money laundering was politically motivated. (Regardless of Earle's motivation, Delay was found guilty in 2011.) For its part, the FBI explained the spike in investigations as a product of increased attention to official corruption. See "FBI Focus Yields Spike in Corruption Cases," *Washington Post*, December 7, 2006.

12. "White House Feels Waxman's Oversight Gaze," *Washington Post*, October 25, 2007; "The Year of Oversight," *Mother Jones*, December 24, 2007; "Scandals Dog Incumbents in Both Parties," *USA Today*, October 28, 2008.

13. "Dozens in Congress under Ethics Inquiry," *Washington Post*, October 30, 2009; "Office of Congressional Ethics Focuses on Auto Amendment Offered by Rep. Watt," *The Hill*, June 15, 2010; "House Panel Won't Investigate Six Lawmakers' Use of Travel Stipends," *Washington Post*, January 3, 2011; "The Risk of Voter Suppression," *National Journal*, October 18, 2010; "When Race Is the Issue, Misleading Coverage Sets Off an Uproar," *New York Times*, July 26, 2010.

14. David Brock, *The Republican Noise Machine: Right-Wing Media and How it Corrupts Democracy* (New York: Crown Publishers, 2004); "33 Internal FOX Editorial Memos Reviewed by MMFA Reveal FOX News Channel's Inner Workings," Media Matters for America, July 14, 2004; "Cable Channel Nods to Ratings and Leans Left," *New York Times*, November 6, 2007; "Liberal Talk-Radio Station Air America Files for Bankruptcy, Will Go off the Air," *Washington Post*, January 22, 2010; "Liberal Radio, Even without Air America," *New York Times*, January 24, 2010; Eric Boehlert, *Bloggers on the Bus: How the Internet Changed Politics and the Press* (New York: Free Press, 2009); "Right Seeks an 'Edge' in Oppo Wars," *Politico*, April 3, 2011.

15. Chandler Davidson, Tanya Dunlap, Gale Kenny, and Benjamin Wise, *Republican Ballot Security Programs: Vote Protection or Minority Vote Suppression — or Both?*

(Washington D.C.: Center for Voting Rights and Protection, 2004); Lorraine C. Minnite, *The Myth of Voter Fraud* (Ithaca, N.Y.: Cornell University Press, 2010).

16. In 2009, the National Legal and Policy Center (NLPC), a self-described "conservative watch-dog organization," filed claims with the OCE against Representatives Donald Payne (D-N.J.), Maxine Waters (D-Calif.), Laura Richardson (D-Calif.), Donna Christian-Christianson (D-V.I.), Carolyn Cheeks Kilpatrick (D-Mich.), Charles Rangel (D-N.Y.), and Bennie Thompson (D-Miss.). In 2010, the NLPC bypassed the OCE to directly petition the Ethics Committee to investigate Representative Gregory Meeks (D-N.Y.) for alleged bribery. The NLPC had been founded in 1991 by movement conservatives Peter Flaherty and Ken Boehm, both veteran leaders of Citizens for Reagan. In the intervening years, the NLPC had focused nearly all its energies on petitioning state and federal agencies to investigate liberal Democrats and labor and civil rights organizations; a wildly disproportionate number of the organizations and elected officials they targeted were African American. Additionally, in 2009, the Landmark Legal Foundation, an antilabor, conservative legal group led by Reagan administration veteran Mark Levin, asked the OCE to investigate chairman of the House Judiciary Committee John Conyers (D-Mich.). "Dozens in Congress under Ethics Inquiry," *Washington Post*, October 30, 2009; "Racial Disparity: All Active Ethics Probes Focus on Black Lawmakers," *Politico*, November 3, 2009; "New Twist in Rangel Ethics Inquiry," *Politico*, June 25, 2009; National Legal and Policy Center, letter to Representative Zoe Lofgren, Chair of Committee on Standards of Officials Conduct, March 19, 2010, copy in possession of the author; "Conservative Group Calls for Probe of Conyers," *Washington Post*, July 17, 2009; "Conservative Group Files Suits against Rep. Hastings," *Politico*, March 7, 2011.

17. "A Conservative Dismisses Right-Wing Black Panther 'Fantasies,'" *Politico*, July 17, 2010; "The $1,300 Mission to Fell ACORN," *Washington Post*, September 8, 2009; "FDA Official Receives Apologies from White House, Vilsack," *Washington Post*, July 22, 2010.

18. "DC's Leading Export: Partisan Warfare," *Politico*, March 31, 2011.

APPENDIX. *State Scrutiny of Black Congresspeople, 1929–2010*

1. See Charles Hamilton, *Adam Clayton Powell Jr.: The Political Biography of an American Dilemma* (New York: Cooper Square Press, 2002); Kenneth O'Reilly and David Gallen, eds., *Black Americans: The FBI Files* (New York: Carroll and Grant, 1994).

2. See "23 Blacks on White House 'Screw' List," *Baltimore Afro American*, July 7, 1973; Hamilton, *Adam Clayton Powell Jr.*; Frank Donner, *The Age of Surveillance: The Aims and Methods of America's Political Intelligence System* (New York: Vintage Books, 1981), 336; Donner, *Protectors of Privilege: Red Squads and Police Repression in Urban America*, (Los Angeles: University of California Press, 1990), 296; Robert Goldstein, *Political Repression in Modern America from 1870 to 1976* (Urbana: University of Illinois Press, 2001), 506; "Mayor Got Spy Reports," *Baltimore Sun*, January 15, 1975; John Andrew, *Power to Destroy: The Political Uses of the IRS from Kennedy to Nixon* (New York: Rowan and Littlefield, 2002), 290, 275.

3. See Kenneth O'Reilly, *Nixon's Piano: Presidents and Racial Politics from Washington to Clinton* (New York: Free Press, 1995), 347–48; Donner, *Age of Surveillance*, 339–41;

Andrew, *Power to Destroy*, 297–313; Louis Stokes, interview with the author, March 26, 2002; Mary Sawyer, *The Harassment of Black Elected Officials: Ten Years Later* (Washington, D.C.: Voter Education and Research Action, 1987), 25; Carl Rowan, "Is There a Conspiracy against Black Leaders," *Ebony*, January 1976; "23 Blacks on White House 'Screw' List."

4. See "Senator Edward Brooke," *Congressional Quarterly Almanac* (1978): 858; "Brooke Ethics Decision," *Congressional Quarterly Almanac* (1979): 593; Sawyer, *Ten Years Later*, 29; Edward Brooke, *Bridging the Divide, My Life* (New Brunswick, N.J.: Rutgers University Press, 2007); Carolyn P. Dubose, *The Untold Story of Charles Diggs: The Public figure, the Private Man* (Arlington, Va.: Barton Publishing House, 1998); Mark Grossman, *Political Corruption in America: An Encyclopedia of Scandals, Power, and Greed* (Santa Barbara, Calif.: ABC-CLIO, 2003), 99–100; "Censure of Rep. Diggs," *Congressional Quarterly Almanac* (1979): 561–66; "Rangel Seeks F.B.I. Denial of Memo Accusing Him," *New York Times*, May 22, 1985.

5. See "Drug Probes on Capitol Hill End Quietly; Investigation Cost $2 million, Involved 1,400 Allegations, Resulted in 6 Prosecutions," *Washington Post*, January 15, 1984; "Wayne Barrett: Ed Towns, Watchdog? Has Congress Forgotten Ed's Past?" *Village Voice*, December 9, 2008; Edolphus Towns, interview with the author, Washington, D.C., May 23, 2002.

6. See "Parren Is Furious over Bribe Reports," *Baltimore Afro American*, February 7, 1987; "U.S. Probes Fauntroy's Hiring of Illinois Rep. Savage's Son," *Washington Post*, January 13, 1989; "Fauntroy Won't Be Prosecuted," *Washington Post*, April 25, 1989; "Ford Acquitted on Charges of Fraud, Conspiracy," *Congressional Quarterly Weekly*, April 10, 1993; Mary Fischer, "The Witch Hunt," *GQ*, December 1993; "Embezzlement and Tax Charges Against Rep. Flake Dropped," *Congressional Quarterly Weekly*, April 6, 1991.

7. See "Decision Is Postponed in Probe of Fauntroy," *Washington Post*, March 15, 1989; "Fauntroy Probe by FBI to Be Extended," *Washington Times*, March 15, 1989; "Controversy over Ford's Trial Could Have Repercussions," *Congressional Quarterly Weekly*, February 27, 1993; Fischer, "Witch Hunt"; "Thornburgh Took Polygraph Test in Leak Inquiry," *New York Times*, May 26, 1990; "Dymally Sought Bribe, Informant Says," *Los Angeles Times*, Metro, October, 12, 1995; "Anti-Defamation League Settles Spying Lawsuit," *Los Angeles Times*, September 28, 1999; "Panel to Probe Savage, 2 Others," *Chicago Tribune*, August 5, 1989; "Ethics Panel Concludes Savage Violated House Code of Conduct," *Chicago Tribune*, February 3, 1990; "House Members Who Wrote Overdrafts Are Listed," *Los Angeles Times*, April 17, 1992; "Espy Cruises through Hearing, Vows to Cut Bureaucracy," *Congressional Quarterly Weekly*, January 16, 1993.

8. See "Rep. Tucker Found Guilty of Bribery and Tax Evasion," *Los Angeles Times*, December 9, 1995; "Collins' Aides Performed Personal, Campaign Duties," *The Hill*, August 16, 1995; "Reynolds Guilty on All Counts," *Washington Post*, August 23, 1995; "Reynolds Admits Guilt during Sentencing," *Chicago Sun-Times*, July 16, 1997; "State to Probe Moseley Braun Tie to Contract," *Chicago Tribune*, March 23, 1994; "U.S. Audit Clears Moseley Braun," *Chicago Tribune*, May 8, 1996; "Moseley Braun Aides Say IRS Data Illegally Leaked," *Chicago Tribune*, July 14, 1998.

9. See "Treasury Clears Hilliard of Libya Trip," *National Journal's Congress Daily*,

October 1, 1997; "Ethics Panel Dismisses Complaint against Hilliard," *National Journal's Congress Daily*, November 10, 1997; "Ethics Probe Targets Hilliard," *National Journal's Congress Daily*, September 24, 1999; "Probe of Florida's Brown Opens," *Congressional Quarterly Weekly*, June 12, 1999; "No Ethics Violation Found in Brown Probe," *Congressional Quarterly Weekly*, September 23, 2000; "Investigation Targets Former Moseley Braun Aide," *Chicago Tribune*, February 21, 1997; "Moseley Braun Campaign Paid for Trip to Hawaii, Panel Says," *Chicago Tribune*, July 17, 1998.

10. See Lorraine C. Minnite, "An Analysis of Voter Fraud in the United States" (New York: Demos, 2005): 14–17; "Balance Indictment," *Carolina Journal*, September 13, 2004; "N.C.'s Balance Pleads Guilty to Conspiracy," *Washington Post*, November 10, 2004.

11. See "Lawmaker Indicted on Corruption Charges," *Washington Post*, June 5, 2007; "Jefferson Convicted in Bribery Scheme," *Washington Post*, August 6, 2009; "Ex-Rep. Jefferson (D-La.) Gets 13 Years in Freezer Cash Case," *Washington Post*, November 14, 2009.

12. See "Dozens in Congress under Ethics Inquiry," *Washington Post*, October 30, 2009; "Racial Disparity: All Active Ethics Probes Focus on Black Lawmakers," *Politico*, November 3, 2009; "New Twist in Rangel Ethics Inquiry," *Politico*, June 25, 2009; National Legal and Policy Center, letter to Representative Zoe Lofgren, Chair of Committee on Standards of Officials Conduct, March 19, 2010, copy in possession of the author; "Conservative Group Calls for Probe of Conyers," *Washington Post*, July 17, 2009.

INDEX

Italicized page numbers locate tables and illustrations. Pages 144p1–44p6 refer to the photo gallery following page 144.

and exclusion of, 11, 14, 16, 20–27, 85, 144p1; government surveillance and investigation of, 57, 62; on second Reconstruction, 6, 26, 44; support of, for Adam Clayton Powell Jr., 38

Bond, Kit, 211

Boon, Ina, 76

Borders, William, 120

Boston Globe, 179

Botempo, Michael, 119, 248n30

Bozeman, Maggie, 149

Bradley, Thomas, 61, 138

Branch, Taylor, 223n2

Branch Davidian raid (Waco, Tex., 1993), 274n85

Braver, Rita, 136–37

Breaux, John, 117

Bremer, Arthur, 66

Brock, Bill, 116

Brooke, Edward, 93, 101–3, 218, 243n83

Brooks, Cornelius, 123

Brooks, J. R., 151

Brown, Ben, 62

Brown, Corrine, 218

Brown, George, 6, 71–79, 81, 85–88, 93, 103–4, 144p3

Brown, Jerry, 82

Brown, Tarlee, 161, 175

Bryant, Jenkins, 149, 162

Buckley, John, 137

Burke, Kenyon, 99, 197, 203

Burke, Yvonne Braithwaite, 91

Burnham, David, 250n45, 258n20; *Above the Law*, 108, 245n7

Burris, Roland, 215, 219

Bush, George H. W., 5, 109, 133–34, 175–77, 246n14, 270n34

Bush, George W., 213

busing, 4, 114–15

Buskey, James, 162

busted invoice fraud scheme (Miss.), 249n42

Butler, Martyn, 74–76

Buy Alabama Coal Bill, 169, 171–72

California Commission on Economic Development, 83

Callaway, Howard "Bo," 42

"Campaign Fund Donations?" (*Sacramento Bee*), 83, 239n34

Canty, Henrietta, 62

Capehart, Homer, 29–30

Capitol Hill "drug ring" investigation, 121

Carey, Margaret, 155

Carlton, Frank, 124

Carter, Doug, 170

Carter, Jimmy, 54, 70, 237n16, 247n19

Carthan, Eddie, 122–25, 144p6, 181, 271n52

CBC (Congressional Black Caucus), 48–49, 106, 188, 198

Celler, Emmanuel, 36–39

Center for Constitutional Rights, 155

Challenor, Herschelle, 102

Chavis, Benjamin, 205, 273n85

Chenault, William, 85

Chesser, Anthony, 163

Chestnut, J. L., 155, 170; *Black in Selma* (with Cass), 148, 257n6

Chicano movement, 54

Chinn, Franklyn, 130

Chisholm, Shirley, 58, 65, 67–68, 85, 188, 217, 235n61

Christian-Christianson, Donna, 218, 278n16

CHSAA (Center for the Study of Harassment of African Americans), 180, 198, 201–3

Church Committee (Senate Select Committee to Study Governmental Operations with Respect to Intelligence Activities), 61, 75

Churchill, Ward, 229n3

CIA (Central Intelligence Agency), 47, 69

Citizens' Councils and sovereignty or peace commissions, 19, 46–47, 59, 115

Civil Rights Commission, 116

Civil Rights Division, DOJ, 215

Claiborne, Harry E., 248n28

Clancy, Dan, 184

Daley, Richard, 19
Daniels, Frederick, 155, 158
Danielson, Christopher, 52, 231n15
Dark Ghetto (K. Clark), 29, 227n45
Davis, Charles, 87
Davis, Earl, 89, *144p4*
Davis, Ossie, 181
Davis, Patricia, 169, 171
Davis, Willie, 161
Deacons for Defense, 52
Dean, Douglass, 62
Dean, John, 65
Delay, Tom, 277n11
Dellums, Ronald, 56, 65, 121, 217–18,
    232n27, 235n61, 247n26
Demjanjuk, John, 205–6
Democratic Party: and black political
    participation, 3–4, 43, 47–48, 77; and
    corruption investigations, 112–14,
    128, 253n69
Democratic Select Committee, 48
Democratic Study Group, 35
Denton, Jeremiah, 159
Denver Post, 73–75
DePriest, Oscar, 28
Detroit Free Press, 121–22
Detroit Metro Times, 122
Detroit News, 121–22
Dickinson, Bill, 41, 170–71
diGenova, Joseph, 184, 251n57
Diggs, Charles: and Adam Clayton Powell
    Jr., 41; corruption conviction of,
    100–103, 134, *144p5*; government sur-
    veillance of, 60, 65, 217–18, 235n61
Dilemma of Black Politics, The (Sawyer),
    71–72, 93–100, *144p4*, 188–89, 210,
    222n6
Dixon, Julian, 253–54n77
Dobson, Hattie, 29
DOJ (Department of Justice): and civil
    rights, 115, 257n3, 257n8; and local
    and state elections, 148; and of-
    ficial corruption, 5, 108–14; order
    1297-88, 132; *Report to Congress on*

*the Activities and Operations of the
    Public Integrity Section*, 113, 248n27
Donaldson, Frank: and Alabama Black
    Belt investigations, 153–55, 158–59;
    and Alabama coal bill bribery case,
    169, 172; and Birmingham investiga-
    tions, 2, 161, 164–65, 167, 174–77
Donaldson, Ivanhoe, 20
Donner, Frank, 58, 60–61
Douglass, Paul, 19
Dredge, William, 120–21
Drexel Burnham Lambert Inc., 137
D'Souza, Dinesh, 7, 222n8
Dukakis, Michael, 133
Dymally, Mervyn, 82–84, 93, *144p3*,
    223n4; and Adam Clayton Powell
    Jr., 38; on Alcee Hastings impeach-
    ment, 186; antiharassment activ-
    ism of, 84–85, 119, 179–80, 183, 198,
    200–203; *The Black Politician*, 83,
    223n4; and *fruhmenschen* affidavits,
    190; on George Brown, 104, 236n5;
    and Mary Sawyer, 71–72, 187–88;
    and media, 82–83, 87, 243n94; on
    Reconstruction parallel, 26, 78; and
    Schiller Institute, 207, 209; surveil-
    lance and investigation of, 59–60,
    67, 104, 142, 218, 243n94, 247n26,
    268n24

Earle, Ronnie, 277n11
East Central Committee for Opportunity
    (ECCO, Hancock County, Ga.), 54
Eastland, James, 19
Eaves, Reginald, 131–32, 181, 185, 190
Ebony, 84, 87
Edsall, Thomas and Mary, 109, 115, 159
Edsall, Tom, 133
Edwards, Don, 156
Eisenhower, Dwight, 28
elections: in 1960, 18; in 1964, 18–19; in
    1966, 19, 41–42, 50; in 1968, 42–43;
    in 1980, 116, 253n67; in 1988, 133,
    252n66

"How a Congressman Billed Government for Phony Travel" (*Wall Street Journal*), 91, 241n53
Huff, Corrine, 31–32
Hughes, Kathy, 187
Hulett, John, 153, 157
Humphrey, Hubert, 43
Hunt, Guy, 162, 170–71, 263n71
Huot, Paul, 120

Ifill, Gwen, 118, 189–90; "Black Officials," 189, 247n25
IGRS (Intelligence Gathering Retrieval Service), 60–61, 69
I Heard It through the Grapevine (Turner), 1, 233n11
impeachments of federal judges, 111, 246n14, 267n21
independent and special counsels, 245n7
"Independent Hearings to Investigate Misconduct by the U.S. Department of Justice" (Tyson Corners, Va., 1995), 205
Ingram, Robert, 51
Interstate Sovereignty Association, 59
IRS (Internal Revenue Service): audits and investigations by, 54, 61, 67, 78, 90, 92; surveillance by, 47, 59–63, 69, 88, 234n46
"IRS Bullies the New South, The" (Berry), 61, 234n45
ISD (Inspectional Services Division, Baltimore), 70, 81, 95
"Is There a Conspiracy against Black Leaders?" (Rowan), 84, 234n48

Jackson, Ira, 62
Jackson, Jesse, 1, 8, 115–16, 175, 181–82, 195
Jackson, Jesse, Jr., 219
Jackson, Maynard, 78
Jackson, Theodore, 166–67
Jackson, Thomas, 192–94
Jackson-Warren, Valerie, 194

Jacobs, Andy, 13, 39–40, 228n61
Jaffe, Harry, 193–94
James, Esther, 31, 34
James, Fob, 149
Jarvis, James, 184
Jefferson, William, 218
Jeffries, Hasan, 157
Jenkins, Andrew, 198
Jennings, James, 222n8
Jet, 98
Jim Crow segregation, 15
Johnson, Billy, 249n38
Johnson, Carol Ann, 91
Johnson, Cedric, 230n9
Johnson, David, 173
Johnson, David Cromwell, 175
Johnson, Jim, 19
Johnson, Josie, 74
Johnson, Leroy, 62, 85
Johnson, Lyndon, 17–19, 30, 59–60, 233n40
Johnson, Presley, 149
Johnson, Roy, 151–53
Joint Center for Political Studies, 78, 80, 92, 239n36
Joliff, James, 52
Jones, Charles, 229n3
Jones, Jim, 242n68
Jordan, Barbara, 58, 217, 235n61, 240–41n51
Joseph, Charles, 93
Judicial Councils Reform and Judicial Disabilities Act (1980), 111
Julian Bond et al. v. James "Sloppy" Floyd et al. (1966), 26–27, 37
Junkin, Clatus, 149

Kastenmeier, Robert, 267n18
Keil, Richard, 133
Kelley, Clarence, 84–85
Kelley, Jay, 173, 264n82
Kelley Ingram Park (Birmingham), 160
Kennedy, John F., 18, 30, 32, 240n44
Kessler, Ronald, 69

www.ingramcontent.com/pod-product-compliance
Lightning Source LLC
Chambersburg PA
CBHW010113270326
41926CB00024B/4507